A Kodansha Comics Trade Paperback Original
Perfect World 6 copyright © 2017 Rie Aruga
English translation copyright © 2021 Rie Aruga

Published in the United States by Kodansha Comics, an imprint of Kodansha USA Publishing, LLC, New York.

Publication rights for this English edition arranged through Kodansha Ltd., Tokyo.

First published in Japan in 2017 by Kodansha Ltd., Tokyo as *Perfect World*, volume 6.

ISBN 978-1-64651-106-8

Original cover design by Tomohiro Kusume and Maiko Mori (arcoinc)

Printed in the United States of America.

www.kodanshacomics.com

9 8 7 6 5 4 3 2 1
Translation: Erin Procter
Lettering: Thea Willis
Additional lettering: Sara Linsley
Editing: Nathaniel Gallant, Jesika Brooks
Kodansha Comics edition cover design by Phil Balsman

Publisher: Kiichiro Sugawara

Director of publishing services: Ben Applegate
Associate director of operations: Stephen Pakula
Publishing services managing editors: Alanna Ruse, Madison Salters
Assistant production managers: Emi Lotto, Angela Zurlo

The beloved characters from *Cardcaptor Sakura* return in a brand new, reimagined fantasy adventure!

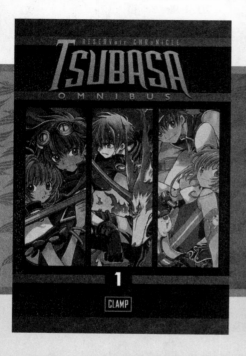

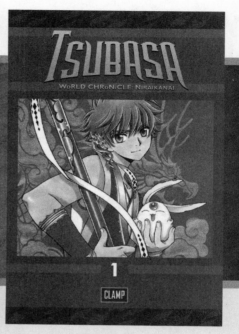

"[*Tsubasa*] takes readers on a fantastic ride that only gets more exhilarating with each successive chapter." —Anime News Network

In the Kingdom of Clow, an archaeological dig unleashes an incredible power, causing Princess Sakura to lose her memories. To save her, her childhood friend Syaoran must follow the orders of the Dimension Witch and travel alongside Kurogane, an unrivaled warrior; Fai, a powerful magician; and Mokona, a curiously strange creature, to retrieve Sakura's dispersed memories!

Tsubasa Omnibus © CLAMP © CLAMP·ShigatsuTsuitachi CO.,LTD./Kodansha Ltd.   Tsubasa: WoRLD CHRoNiCLE © CLAMP·ShigatsuTsuitachi CO.,LTD./Kodansha Ltd.

The art-deco cyberpunk classic from the creators of *xxxHOLiC* and *Cardcaptor Sakura*!

"Starred Review.
This experimental sci-fi work from CLAMP reads like a romantic version of *AKIRA*."
—Publishers Weekly

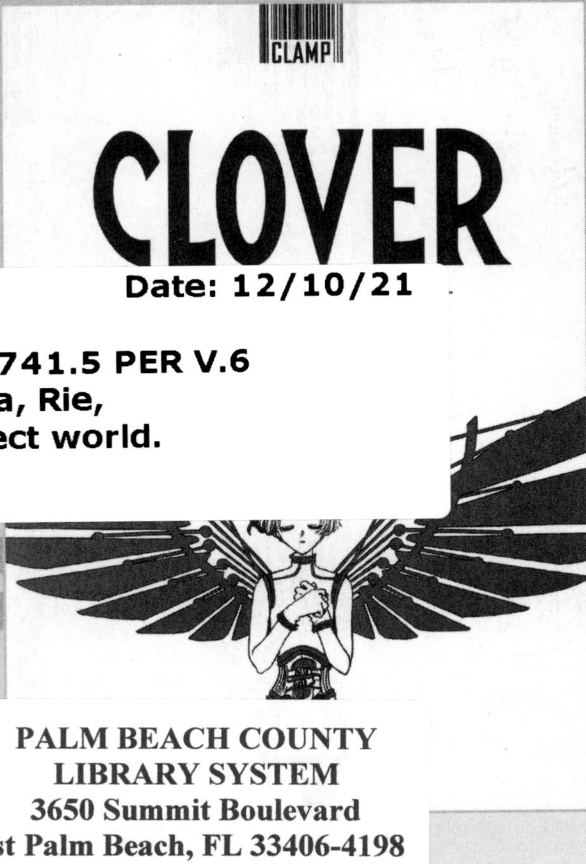

CLAMP
CLOVER

Su was born into a bleak future, where the government keeps tight control over children with magical powers—codenamed "Clovers." With Su being the only "four-leaf" Clover in the world, she has been kept isolated nearly her whole life. Can ex-military agent Kazuhiko deliver her to the happiness she seeks? Experience the complete series in this hardcover edition, which also includes over twenty pages of ravishing color art!

KC KODANSHA COMICS

One of CLAMP's biggest hits returns in this definitive, premium, hardcover 20th anniversary collector's edition!

Poor college student Hideki is down on his luck. All he wants is a good job, a girlfriend, and his very own "persocom"—the latest and greatest in humanoid computer technology. Hideki's luck changes one night when he finds Chi—a persocom thrown out in a pile of trash. But Hideki soon discovers that there's much more to his cute new persocom than meets the eye.

MAGIC KNIGHT RAYEARTH
25TH ANNIVERSARY EDITION
CLAMP

A BELOVED CLASSIC MAKES ITS STUNNING RETURN IN THIS GORGEOUS, LIMITED EDITION BOX SET!

This tale of three Tokyo teenagers who cross through a magical portal and become the champions of another world is a modern manga classic. The box set includes three volumes of manga covering the entire first series of *Magic Knight Rayearth*, plus the series's super-rare full-color art book companion, all printed at a larger size than ever before on premium paper, featuring a newly-revised translation and lettering, and exquisite foil-stamped covers.

A strictly limited edition, this will be gone in a flash!

◄ KAMOME ►
SHIRAHAMA

Witch Hat Atelier

A magical manga
adventure for
fans of Disney
and Studio
Ghibli!

Witch Hat Atelier © Kamome Shirahama/Kodansha Ltd.

**The magical adventure that took
Japan by storm is finally here,
from acclaimed DC and Marvel
cover artist Kamome Shirahama!**

In a world where everyone takes wonders like magic spells
and dragons for granted, Coco is a girl with a simple dream:
She wants to be a witch. But everybody knows magicians
are born, not made, and Coco was not born with a gift for
magic. Resigned to her un-magical life, Coco is about to
give up on her dream to become a witch...until the day
she meets Qifrey, a mysterious, traveling magician. After
secretly seeing Qifrey perform magic in a way she's never
seen before, Coco soon learns what everybody "knows"
might not be the truth, and discovers that her magical
dream may not be as far away as it may seem...

PERFECT WORLD

6 Rie Aruga

Research Help /
Kazuo Abe (Abe Kensetsu Inc.)

contents

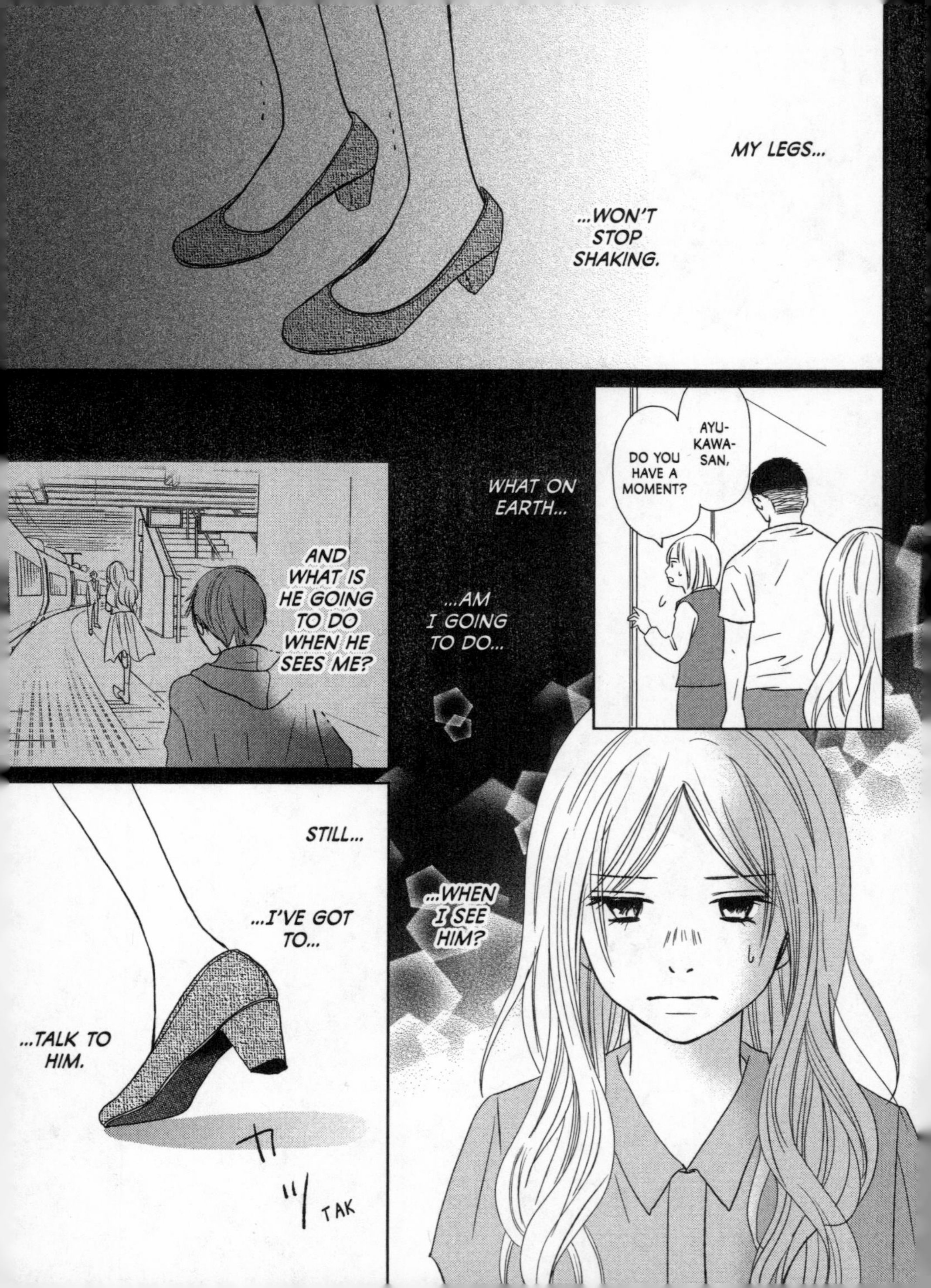
MY LEGS...
...WON'T STOP SHAKING.
AYUKAWA-SAN, DO YOU HAVE A MOMENT?
WHAT ON EARTH...
...AM I GOING TO DO...
AND WHAT IS HE GOING TO DO WHEN HE SEES ME?
...WHEN I SEE HIM?
STILL...
...I'VE GOT TO...
...TALK TO HIM.
TAK

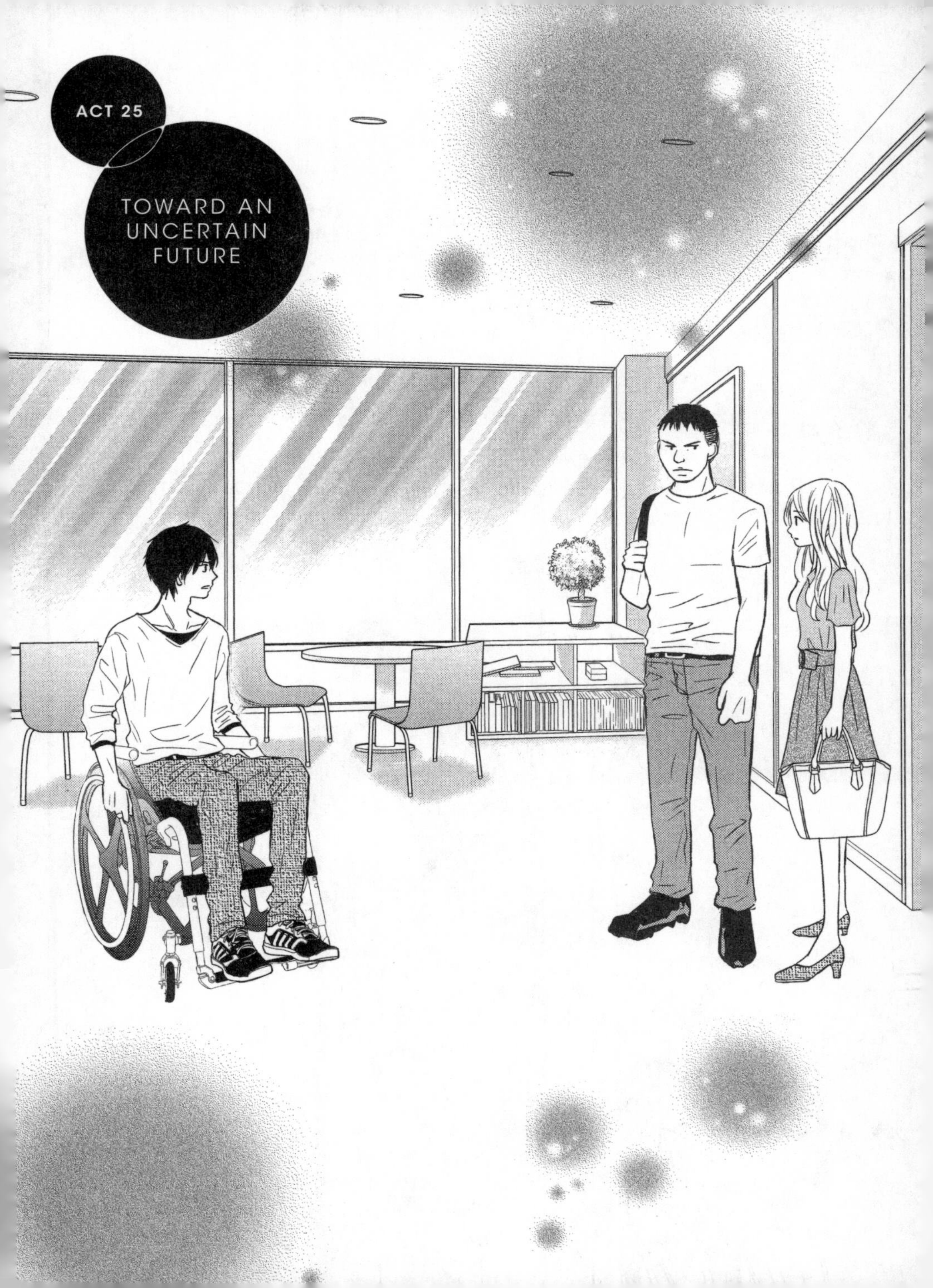
ACT 25
TOWARD AN UNCERTAIN FUTURE

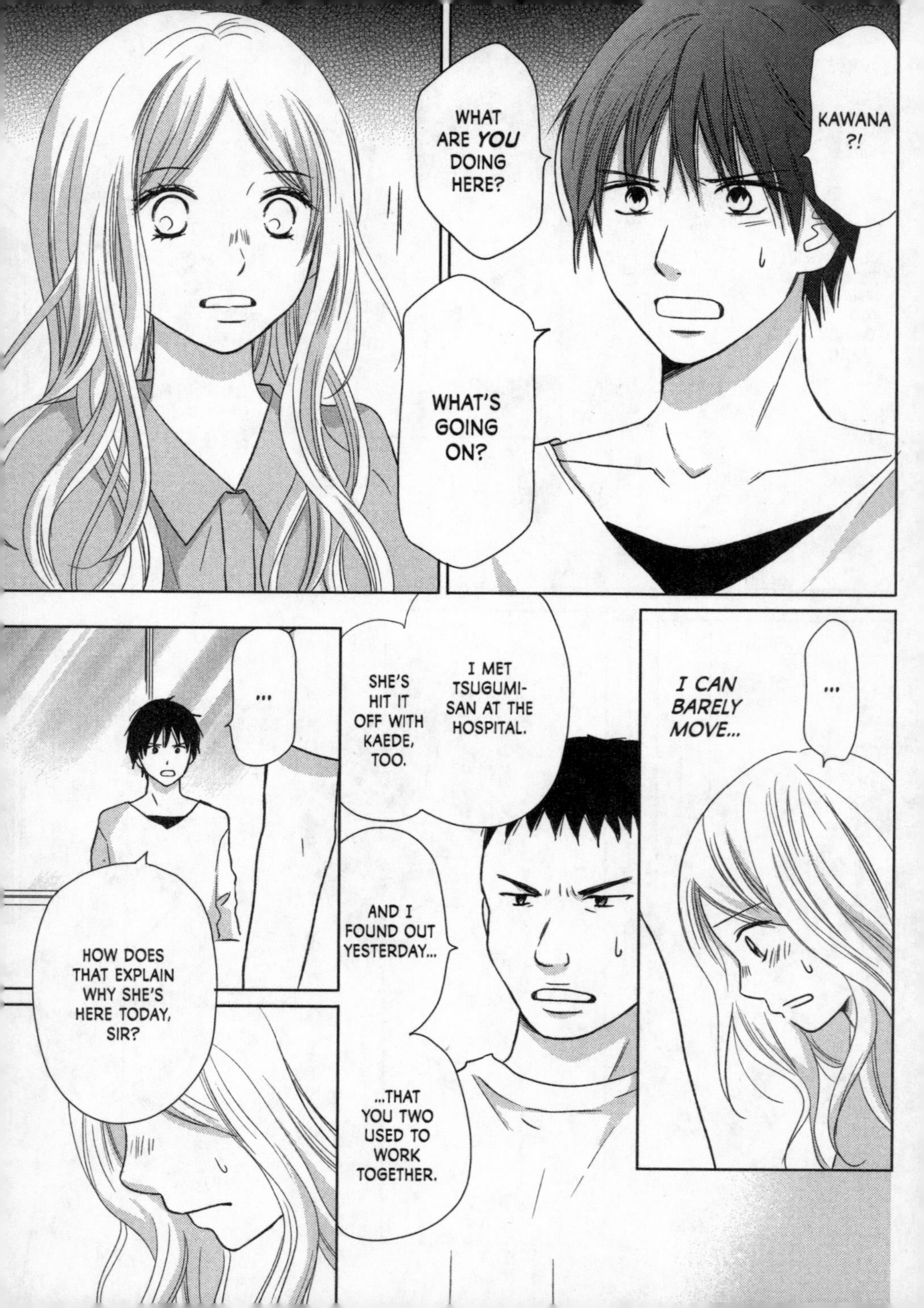
KAWANA ?!
WHAT ARE *YOU* DOING HERE?
WHAT'S GOING ON?
...
I CAN BARELY MOVE...
I MET TSUGUMI-SAN AT THE HOSPITAL.
SHE'S HIT IT OFF WITH KAEDE, TOO.
AND I FOUND OUT YESTERDAY...
...THAT YOU TWO USED TO WORK TOGETHER.
...
HOW DOES THAT EXPLAIN WHY SHE'S HERE TODAY, SIR?

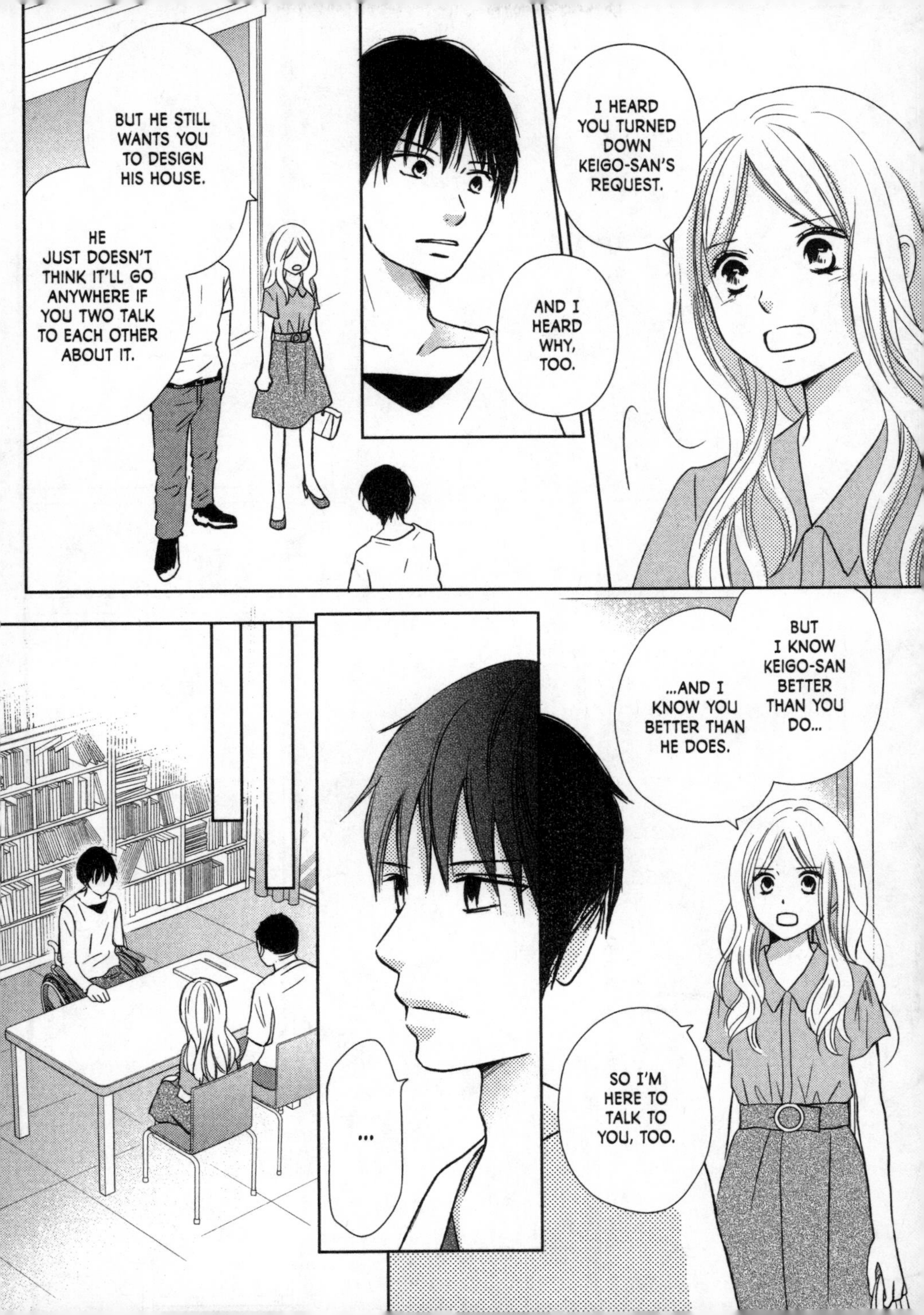
I HEARD YOU TURNED DOWN KEIGO-SAN'S REQUEST.
AND I HEARD WHY, TOO.
BUT HE STILL WANTS YOU TO DESIGN HIS HOUSE.
HE JUST DOESN'T THINK IT'LL GO ANYWHERE IF YOU TWO TALK TO EACH OTHER ABOUT IT.
BUT I KNOW KEIGO-SAN BETTER THAN YOU DO...
...AND I KNOW YOU BETTER THAN HE DOES.
SO I'M HERE TO TALK TO YOU, TOO.
...

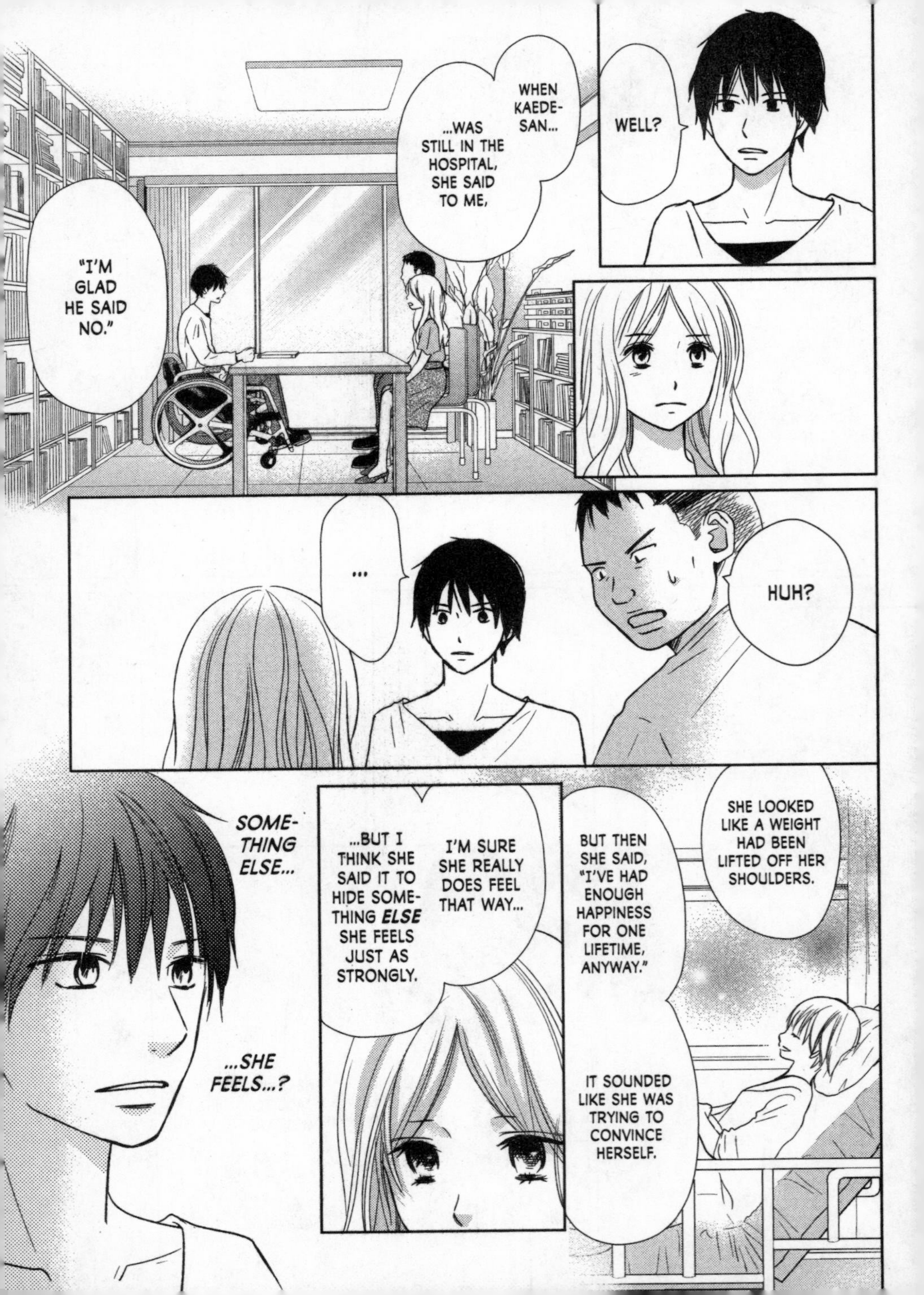
WELL?
WHEN KAEDE-SAN...
...WAS STILL IN THE HOSPITAL, SHE SAID TO ME,
"I'M GLAD HE SAID NO."
HUH?
...
SHE LOOKED LIKE A WEIGHT HAD BEEN LIFTED OFF HER SHOULDERS.
BUT THEN SHE SAID, "I'VE HAD ENOUGH HAPPINESS FOR ONE LIFETIME, ANYWAY."
IT SOUNDED LIKE SHE WAS TRYING TO CONVINCE HERSELF.
I'M SURE SHE REALLY DOES FEEL THAT WAY...
...BUT I THINK SHE SAID IT TO HIDE SOME-THING *ELSE* SHE FEELS JUST AS STRONGLY.
SOME-THING ELSE...
...SHE FEELS...?

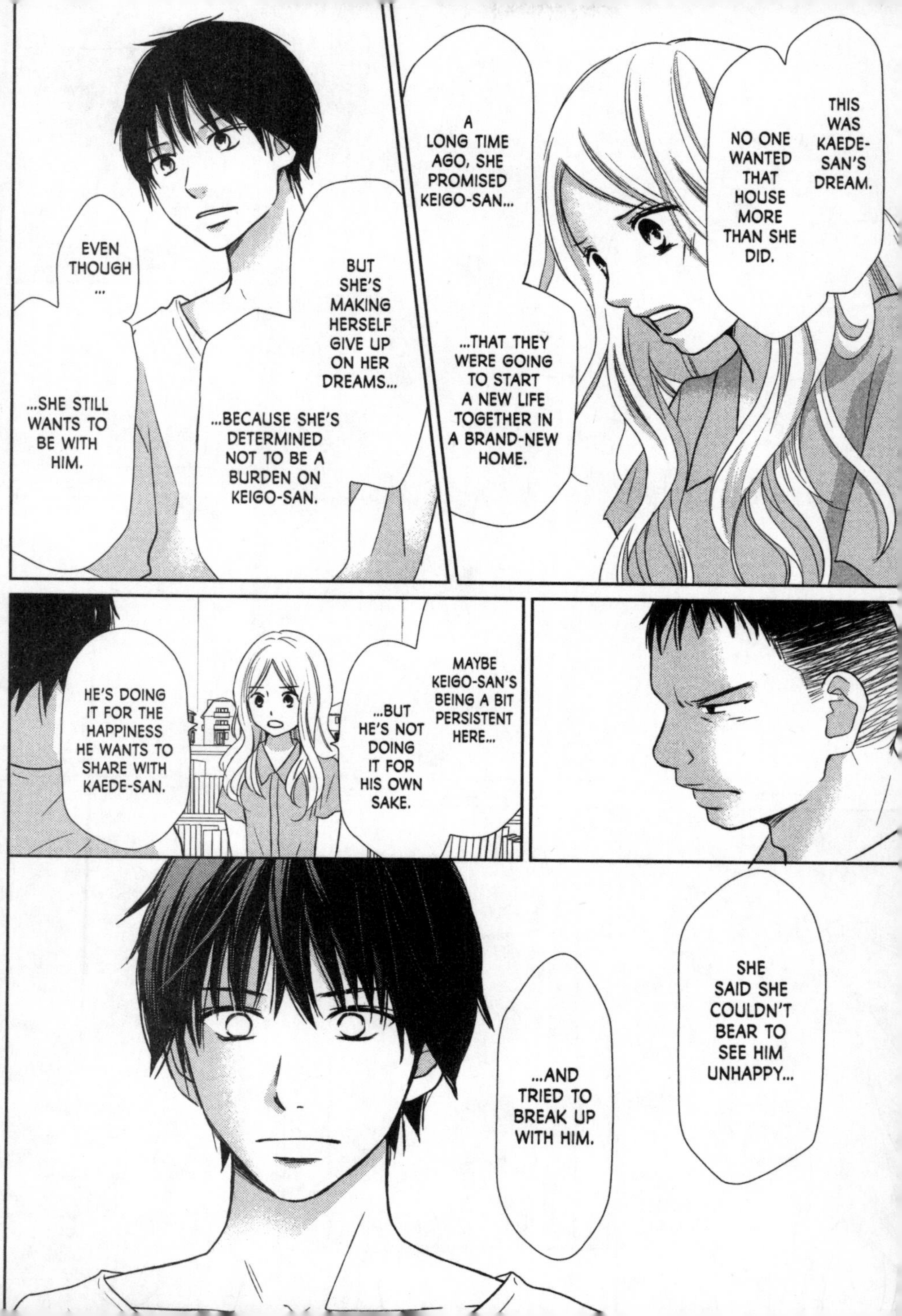
THIS WAS KAEDE-SAN'S DREAM.
NO ONE WANTED THAT HOUSE MORE THAN SHE DID.
A LONG TIME AGO, SHE PROMISED KEIGO-SAN...
...THAT THEY WERE GOING TO START A NEW LIFE TOGETHER IN A BRAND-NEW HOME.
BUT SHE'S MAKING HERSELF GIVE UP ON HER DREAMS...
...BECAUSE SHE'S DETERMINED NOT TO BE A BURDEN ON KEIGO-SAN.
EVEN THOUGH ...
...SHE STILL WANTS TO BE WITH HIM.
MAYBE KEIGO-SAN'S BEING A BIT PERSISTENT HERE...
...BUT HE'S NOT DOING IT FOR HIS OWN SAKE.
HE'S DOING IT FOR THE HAPPINESS HE WANTS TO SHARE WITH KAEDE-SAN.
SHE SAID SHE COULDN'T BEAR TO SEE HIM UNHAPPY...
...AND TRIED TO BREAK UP WITH HIM.

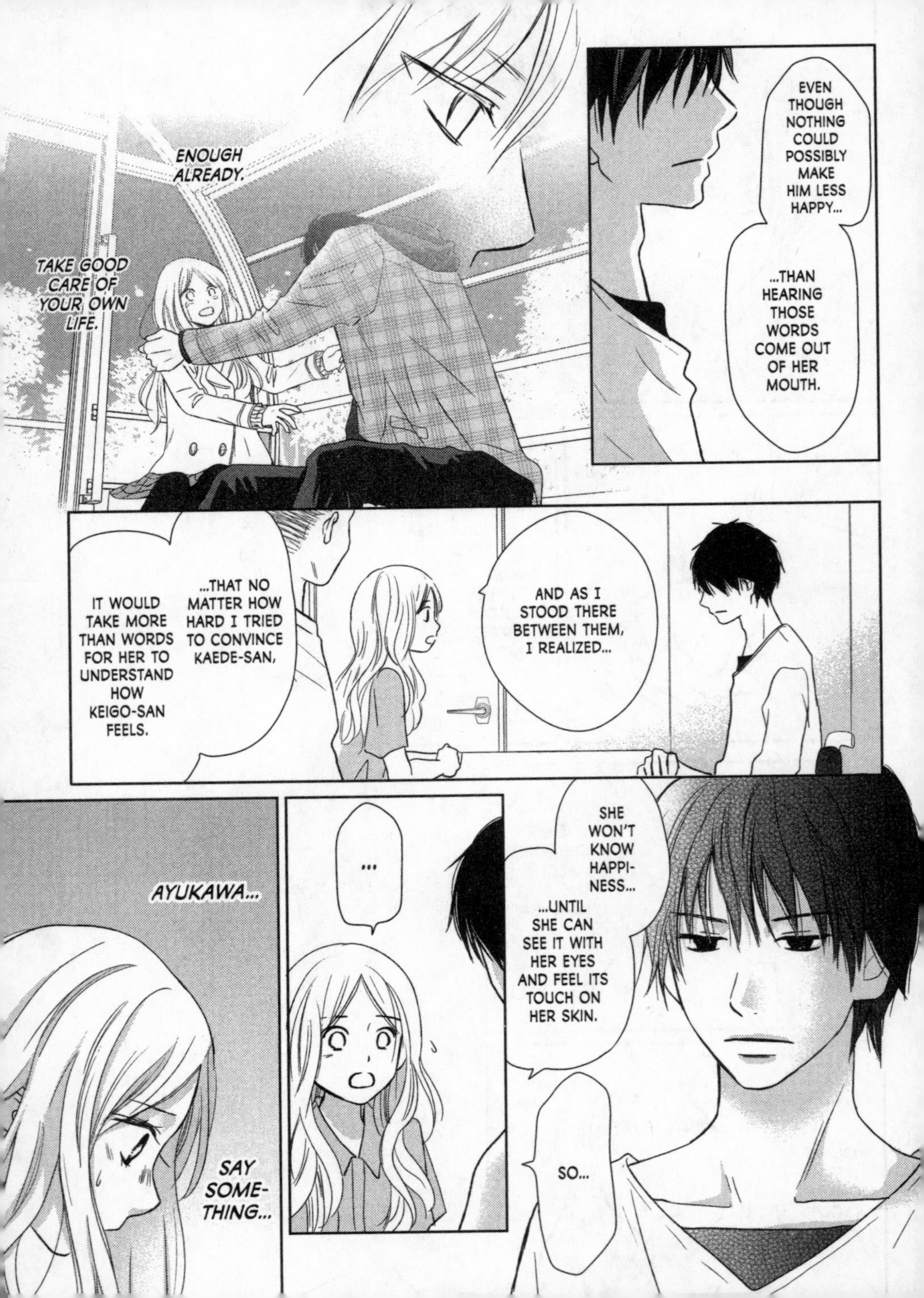
EVEN THOUGH NOTHING COULD POSSIBLY MAKE HIM LESS HAPPY...
...THAN HEARING THOSE WORDS COME OUT OF HER MOUTH.
ENOUGH ALREADY.
TAKE GOOD CARE OF YOUR OWN LIFE.
AND AS I STOOD THERE BETWEEN THEM, I REALIZED...
...THAT NO MATTER HOW HARD I TRIED TO CONVINCE KAEDE-SAN,
IT WOULD TAKE MORE THAN WORDS FOR HER TO UNDERSTAND HOW KEIGO-SAN FEELS.
SHE WON'T KNOW HAPPI-NESS...
...UNTIL SHE CAN SEE IT WITH HER EYES AND FEEL ITS TOUCH ON HER SKIN.
SO...
...
AYUKAWA...
SAY SOME-THING...

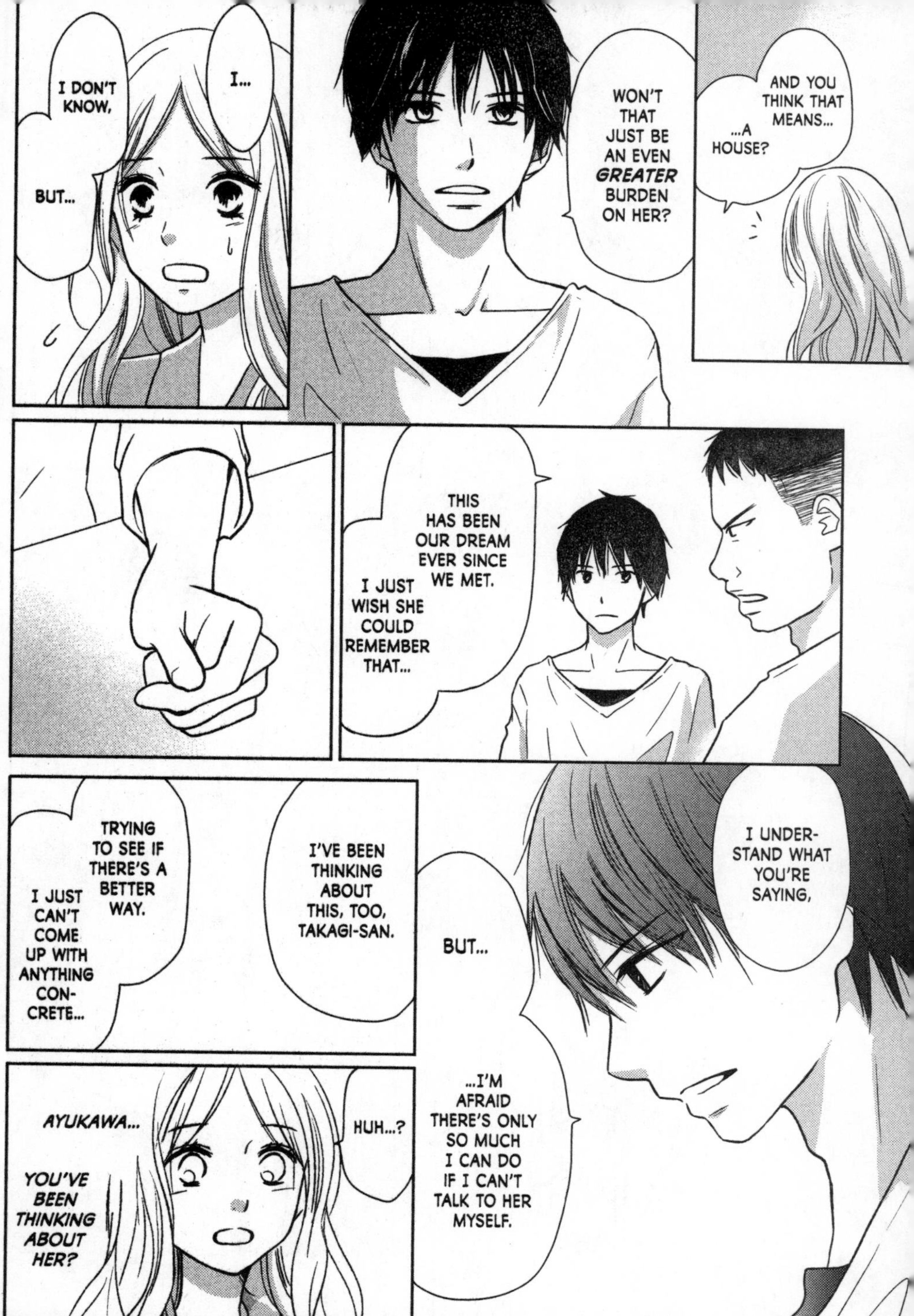
AND YOU THINK THAT MEANS... ...A HOUSE?
WON'T THAT JUST BE AN EVEN GREATER BURDEN ON HER?
I...
I DON'T KNOW,
BUT...
THIS HAS BEEN OUR DREAM EVER SINCE WE MET.
I JUST WISH SHE COULD REMEMBER THAT...
I UNDER-STAND WHAT YOU'RE SAYING,
BUT...
...I'M AFRAID THERE'S ONLY SO MUCH I CAN DO IF I CAN'T TALK TO HER MYSELF.
I'VE BEEN THINKING ABOUT THIS, TOO, TAKAGI-SAN.
TRYING TO SEE IF THERE'S A BETTER WAY.
I JUST CAN'T COME UP WITH ANYTHING CON-CRETE...
HUH...?
AYUKAWA...
YOU'VE BEEN THINKING ABOUT HER?

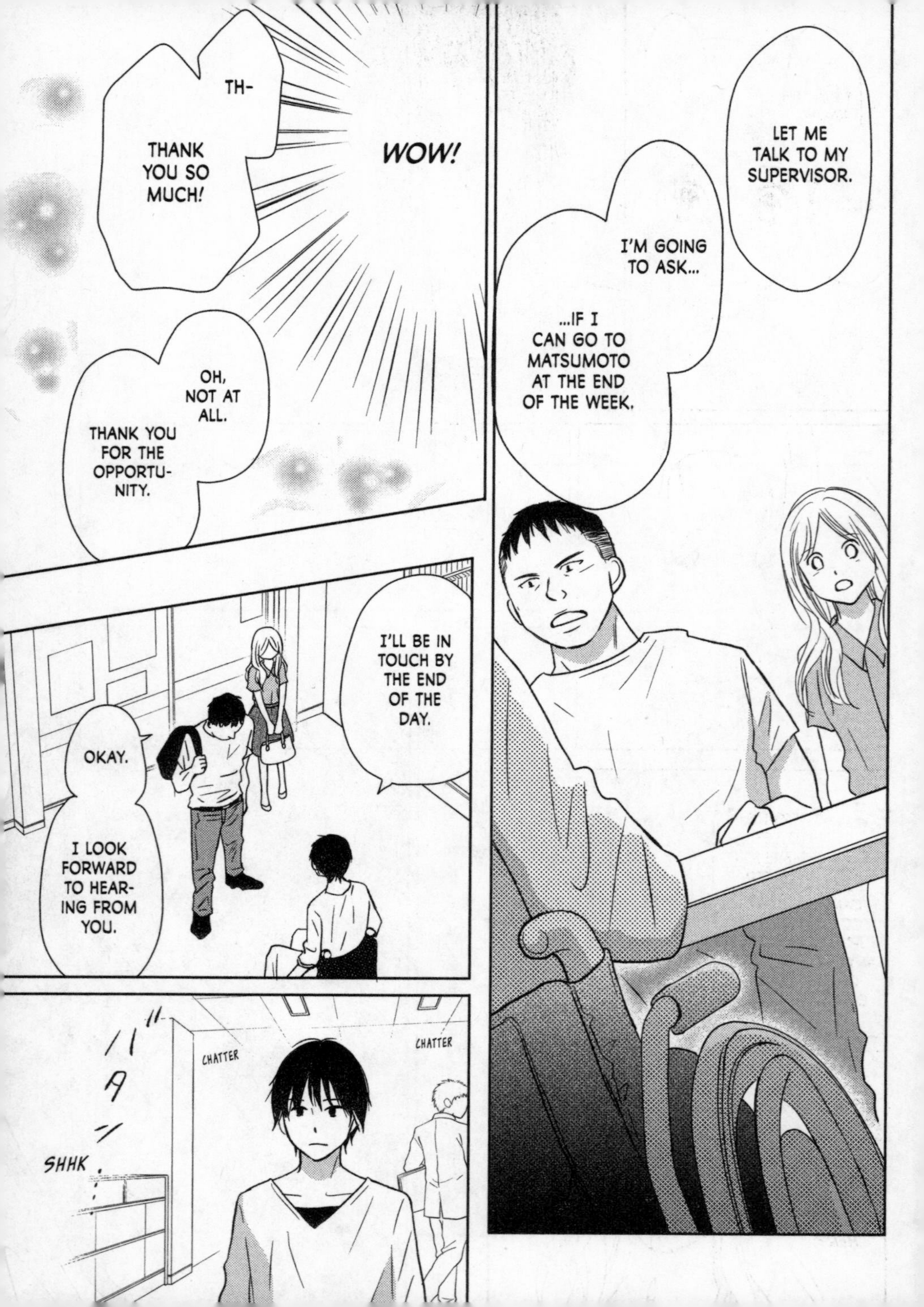
LET ME TALK TO MY SUPERVISOR.
I'M GOING TO ASK...
...IF I CAN GO TO MATSUMOTO AT THE END OF THE WEEK.
WOW!
TH-
THANK YOU SO MUCH!
OH, NOT AT ALL.
THANK YOU FOR THE OPPORTU-NITY.
I'LL BE IN TOUCH BY THE END OF THE DAY.
OKAY.
I LOOK FORWARD TO HEAR-ING FROM YOU.
CHATTER
CHATTER
SHHK

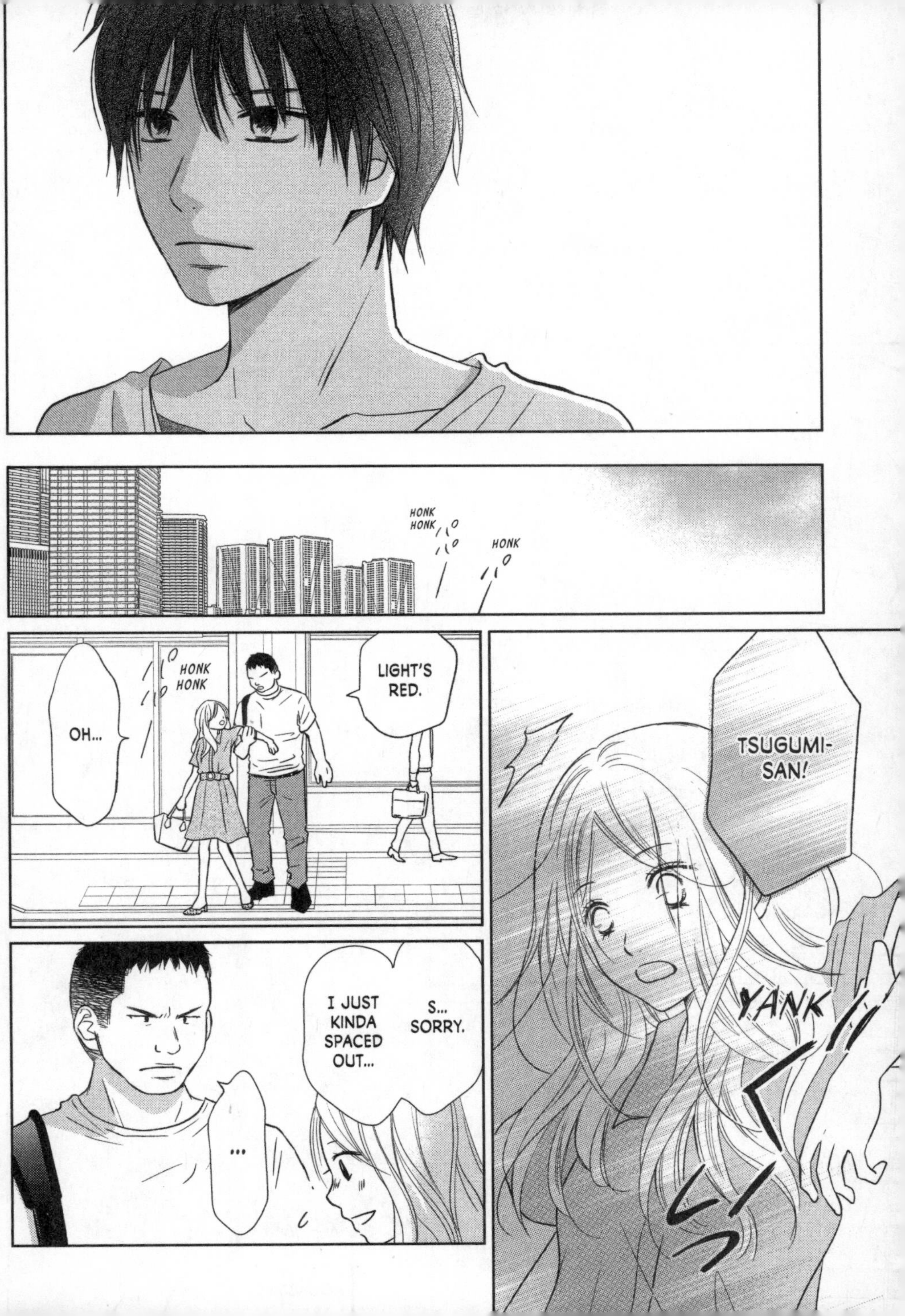
HONK HONK
HONK
TSUGUMI-SAN!
YANK
LIGHT'S RED.
HONK HONK
OH...
S... SORRY.
I JUST KINDA SPACED OUT...
...

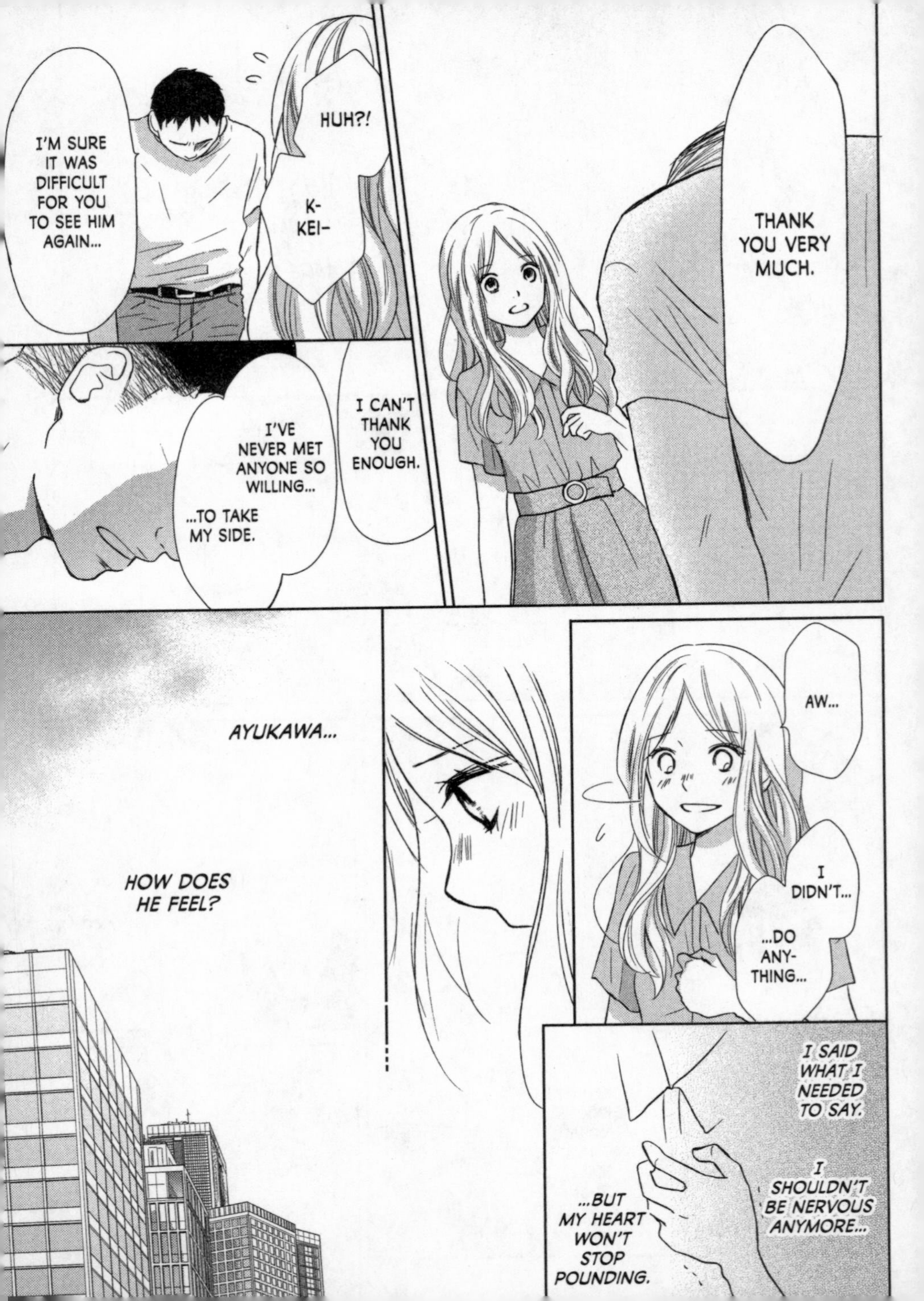
THANK YOU VERY MUCH.
HUH?!
K-KEI-
I'M SURE IT WAS DIFFICULT FOR YOU TO SEE HIM AGAIN...
I CAN'T THANK YOU ENOUGH.
I'VE NEVER MET ANYONE SO WILLING...
...TO TAKE MY SIDE.
AW...
I DIDN'T...
...DO ANY-THING...
I SAID WHAT I NEEDED TO SAY.
I SHOULDN'T BE NERVOUS ANYMORE...
...BUT MY HEART WON'T STOP POUNDING.
AYUKAWA...
HOW DOES HE FEEL?

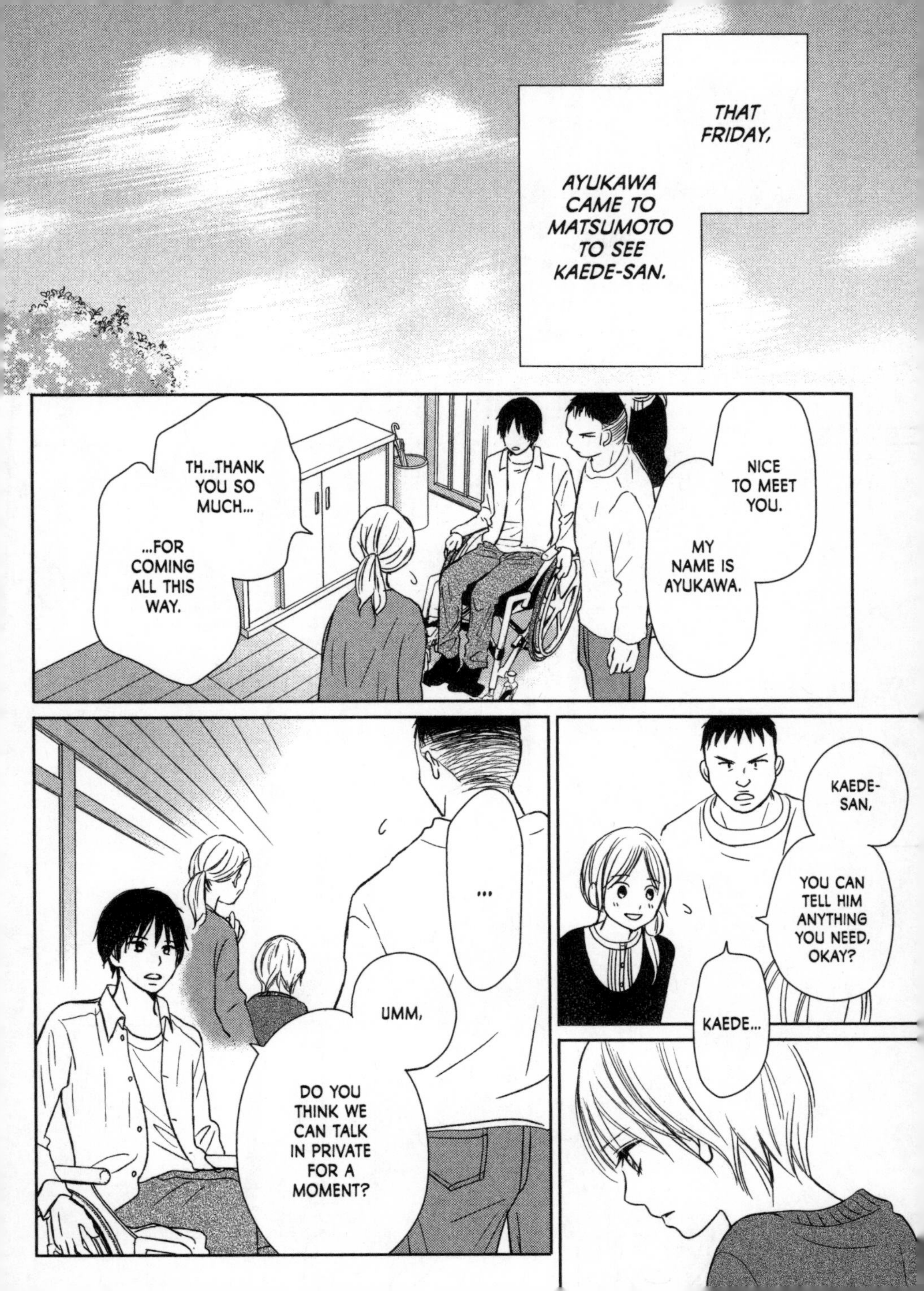
THAT FRIDAY,
AYUKAWA CAME TO MATSUMOTO TO SEE KAEDE-SAN.
NICE TO MEET YOU.
MY NAME IS AYUKAWA.
TH...THANK YOU SO MUCH...
...FOR COMING ALL THIS WAY.
KAEDE-SAN,
YOU CAN TELL HIM ANYTHING YOU NEED, OKAY?
KAEDE...
...
UMM,
DO YOU THINK WE CAN TALK IN PRIVATE FOR A MOMENT?

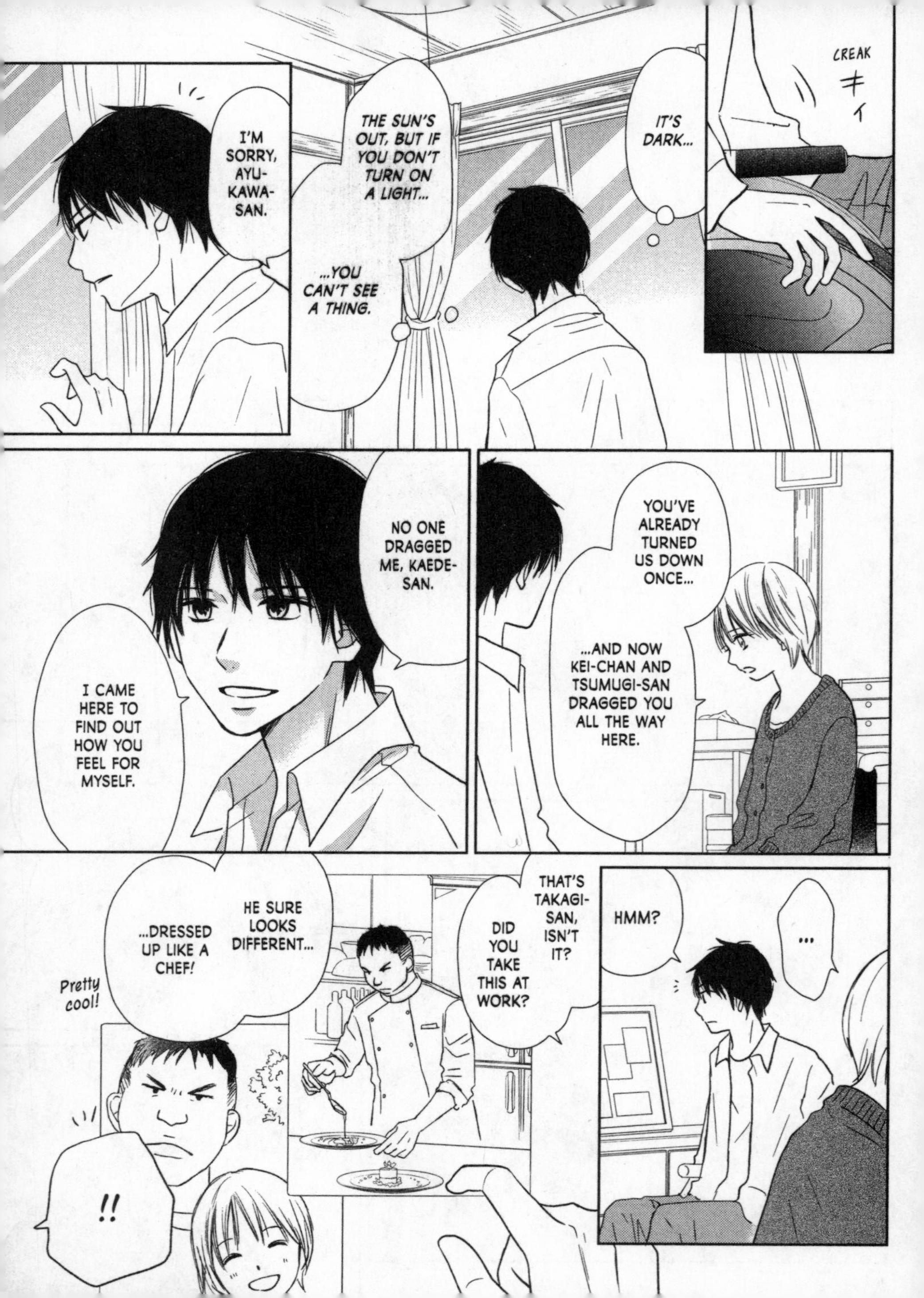
CREAK
キィ
IT'S DARK...
THE SUN'S OUT, BUT IF YOU DON'T TURN ON A LIGHT...
...YOU CAN'T SEE A THING.
I'M SORRY, AYU-KAWA-SAN.
YOU'VE ALREADY TURNED US DOWN ONCE...
...AND NOW KEI-CHAN AND TSUMUGI-SAN DRAGGED YOU ALL THE WAY HERE.
NO ONE DRAGGED ME, KAEDE-SAN.
I CAME HERE TO FIND OUT HOW YOU FEEL FOR MYSELF.
...
HMM?
THAT'S TAKAGI-SAN, ISN'T IT?
DID YOU TAKE THIS AT WORK?
HE SURE LOOKS DIFFERENT...
...DRESSED UP LIKE A CHEF!
Pretty cool!
!!

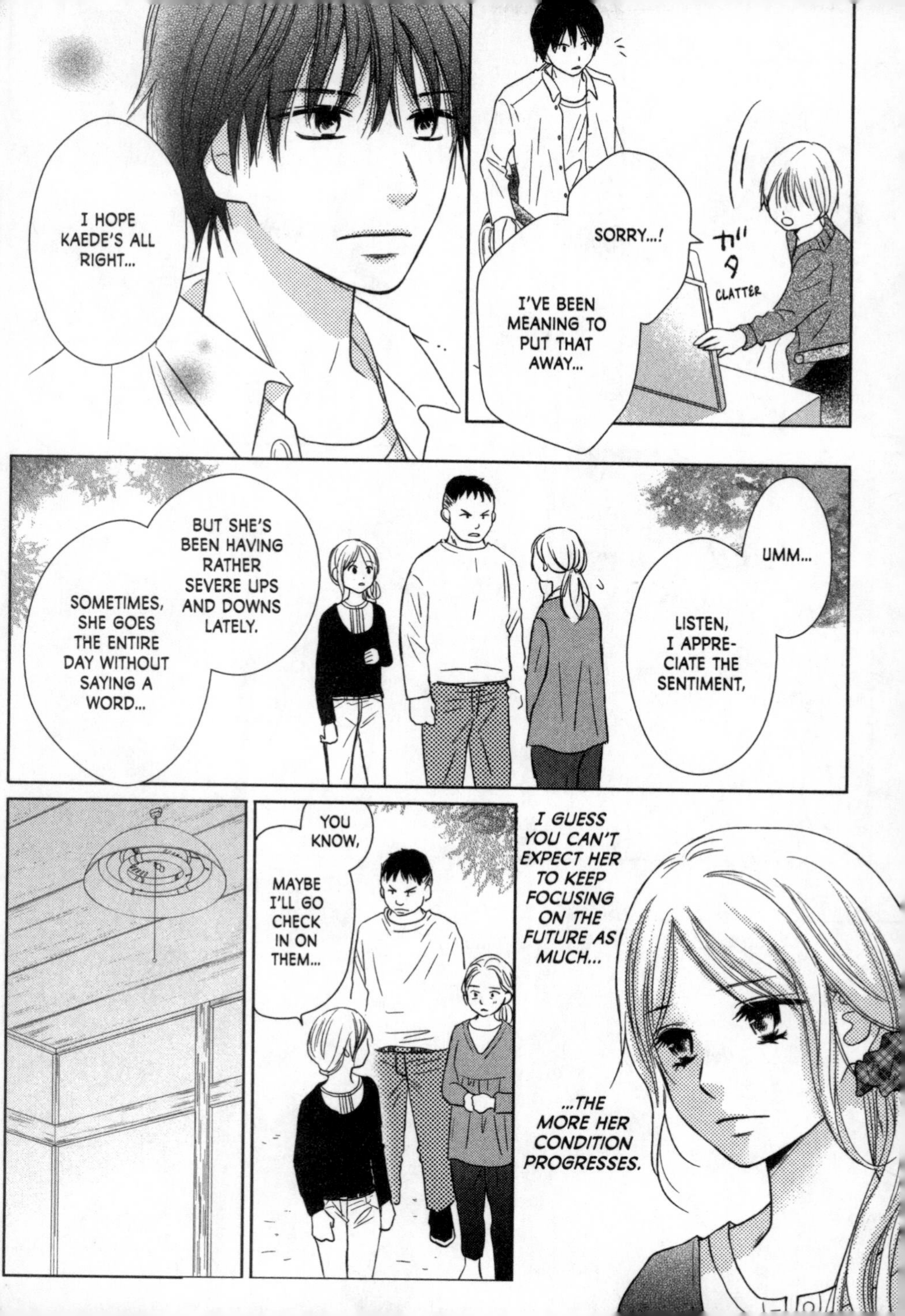

ｶﾞﾀ
CLATTER
SORRY...!
I'VE BEEN MEANING TO PUT THAT AWAY...
I HOPE KAEDE'S ALL RIGHT...
UMM...
LISTEN, I APPRE-CIATE THE SENTIMENT,
BUT SHE'S BEEN HAVING RATHER SEVERE UPS AND DOWNS LATELY.
SOMETIMES, SHE GOES THE ENTIRE DAY WITHOUT SAYING A WORD...
I GUESS YOU CAN'T EXPECT HER TO KEEP FOCUSING ON THE FUTURE AS MUCH...
...THE MORE HER CONDITION PROGRESSES.
YOU KNOW,
MAYBE I'LL GO CHECK IN ON THEM...

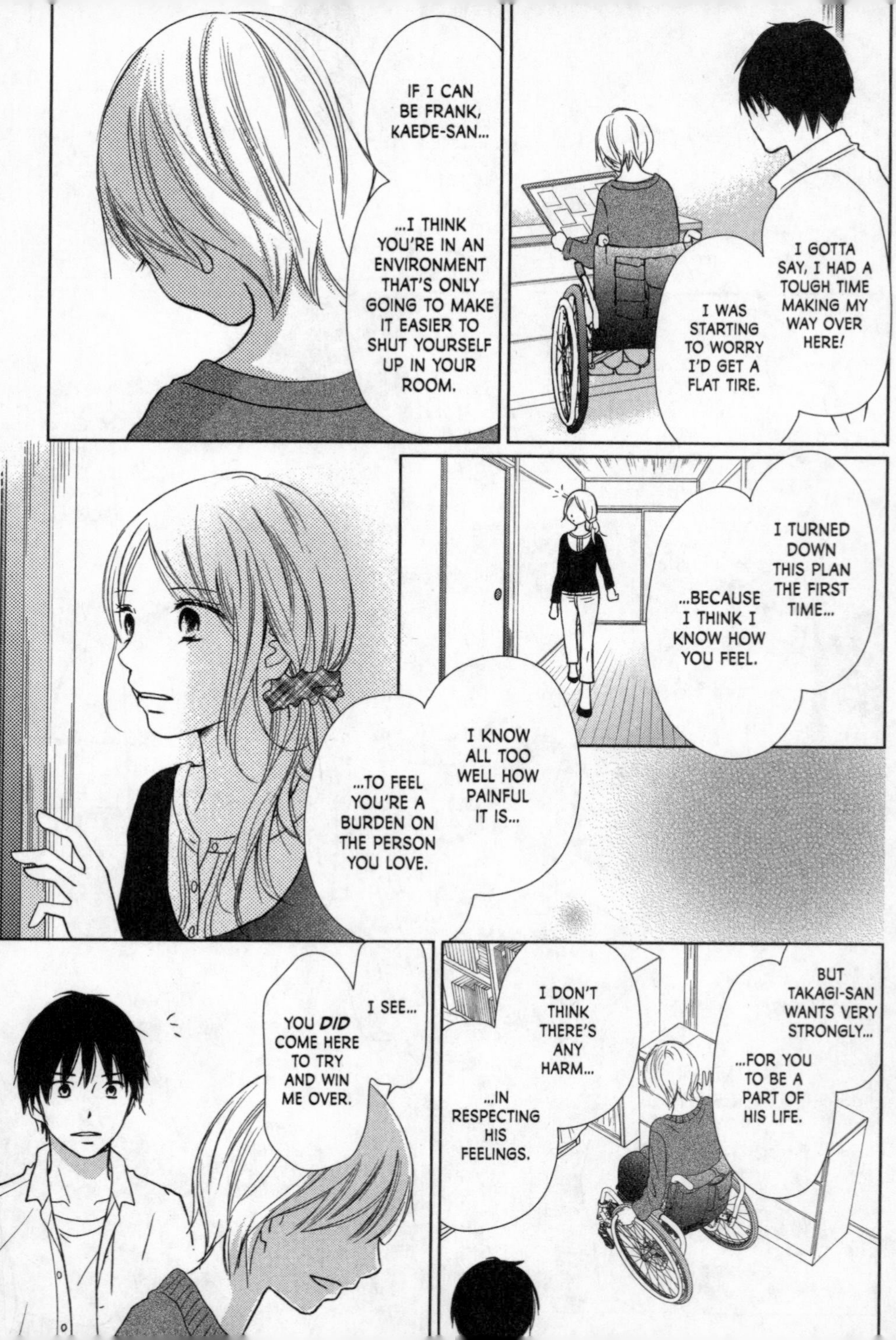
I GOTTA SAY, I HAD A TOUGH TIME MAKING MY WAY OVER HERE!
I WAS STARTING TO WORRY I'D GET A FLAT TIRE.
IF I CAN BE FRANK, KAEDE-SAN...
...I THINK YOU'RE IN AN ENVIRONMENT THAT'S ONLY GOING TO MAKE IT EASIER TO SHUT YOURSELF UP IN YOUR ROOM.
I TURNED DOWN THIS PLAN THE FIRST TIME...
...BECAUSE I THINK I KNOW HOW YOU FEEL.
I KNOW ALL TOO WELL HOW PAINFUL IT IS...
...TO FEEL YOU'RE A BURDEN ON THE PERSON YOU LOVE.
BUT TAKAGI-SAN WANTS VERY STRONGLY...
...FOR YOU TO BE A PART OF HIS LIFE.
I DON'T THINK THERE'S ANY HARM...
...IN RESPECTING HIS FEELINGS.
I SEE...
YOU *DID* COME HERE TO TRY AND WIN ME OVER.

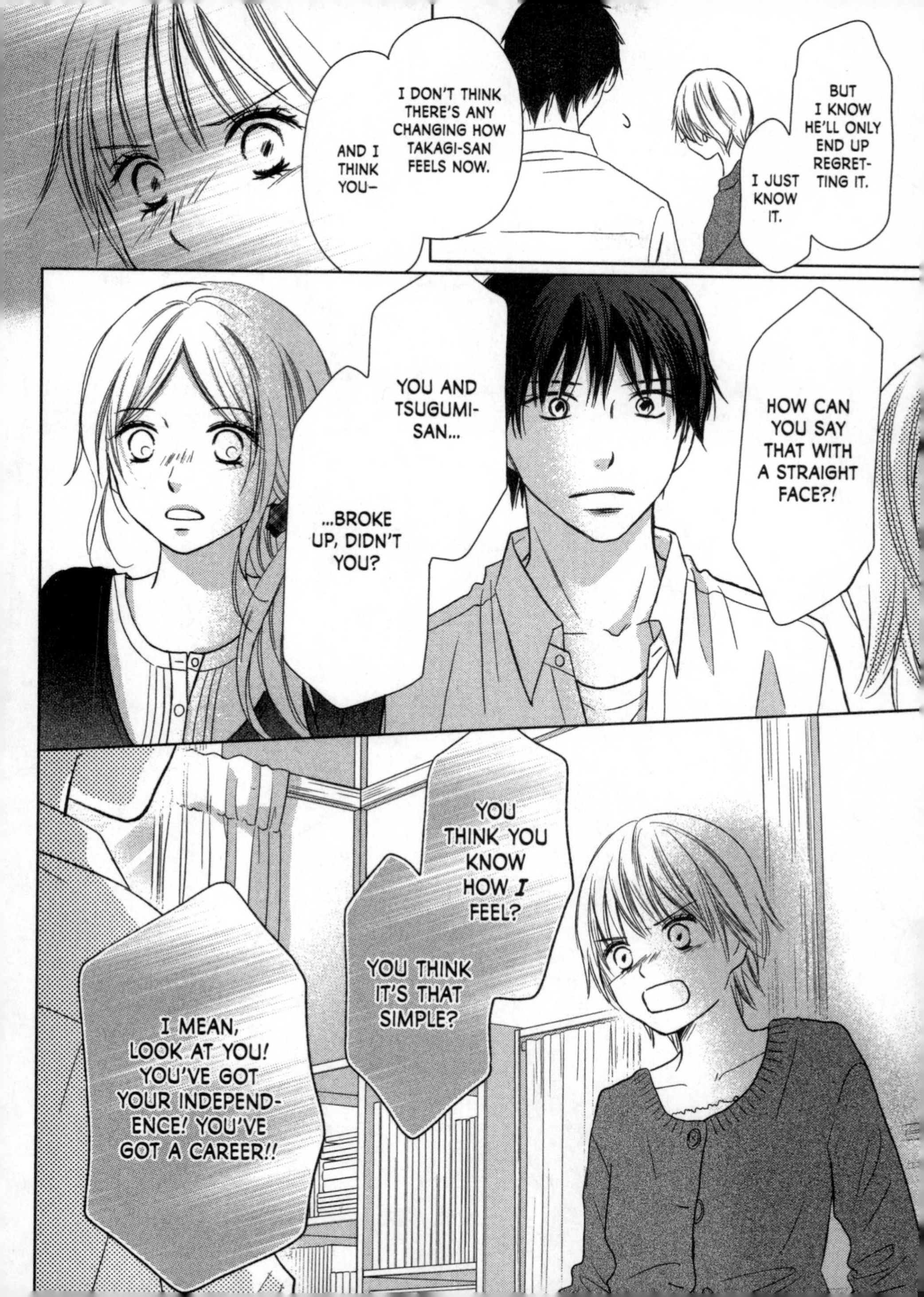
BUT I KNOW HE'LL ONLY END UP REGRET-TING IT.
I JUST KNOW IT.
I DON'T THINK THERE'S ANY CHANGING HOW TAKAGI-SAN FEELS NOW.
AND I THINK YOU–
HOW CAN YOU SAY THAT WITH A STRAIGHT FACE?!
YOU AND TSUGUMI-SAN...
...BROKE UP, DIDN'T YOU?
YOU THINK YOU KNOW HOW *I* FEEL?
YOU THINK IT'S THAT SIMPLE?
I MEAN, LOOK AT YOU! YOU'VE GOT YOUR INDEPEND-ENCE! YOU'VE GOT A CAREER!!

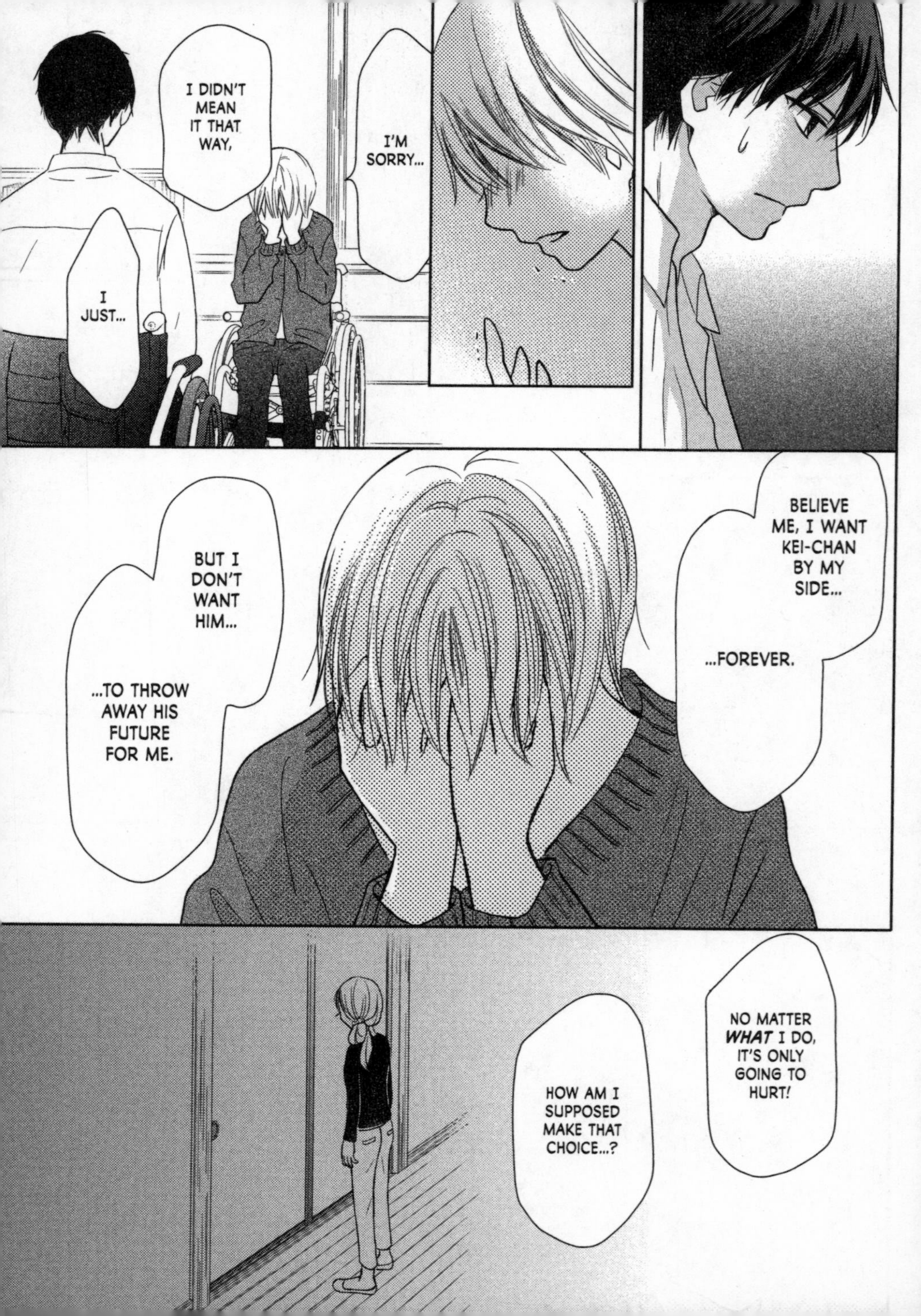
I'M SORRY...
I DIDN'T MEAN IT THAT WAY,
I JUST...
BELIEVE ME, I WANT KEI-CHAN BY MY SIDE...
...FOREVER.
BUT I DON'T WANT HIM...
...TO THROW AWAY HIS FUTURE FOR ME.
NO MATTER *WHAT* I DO, IT'S ONLY GOING TO HURT!
HOW AM I SUPPOSED MAKE THAT CHOICE...?

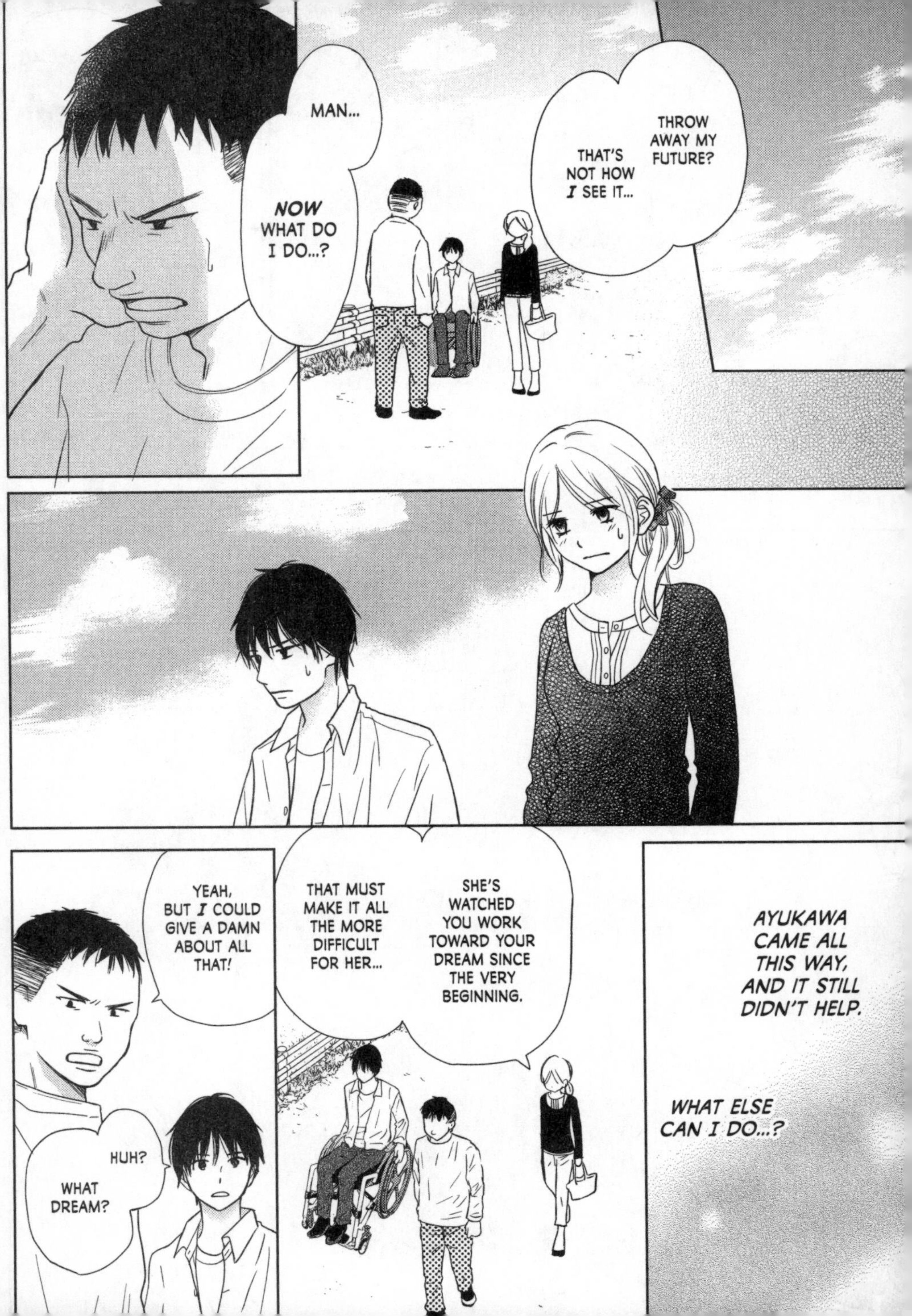
THROW AWAY MY FUTURE? THAT'S NOT HOW *I* SEE IT...
MAN... *NOW* WHAT DO I DO...?
AYUKAWA CAME ALL THIS WAY, AND IT STILL DIDN'T HELP.
WHAT ELSE CAN I DO...?
SHE'S WATCHED YOU WORK TOWARD YOUR DREAM SINCE THE VERY BEGINNING. THAT MUST MAKE IT ALL THE MORE DIFFICULT FOR HER...
YEAH, BUT *I* COULD GIVE A DAMN ABOUT ALL THAT!
HUH? WHAT DREAM?

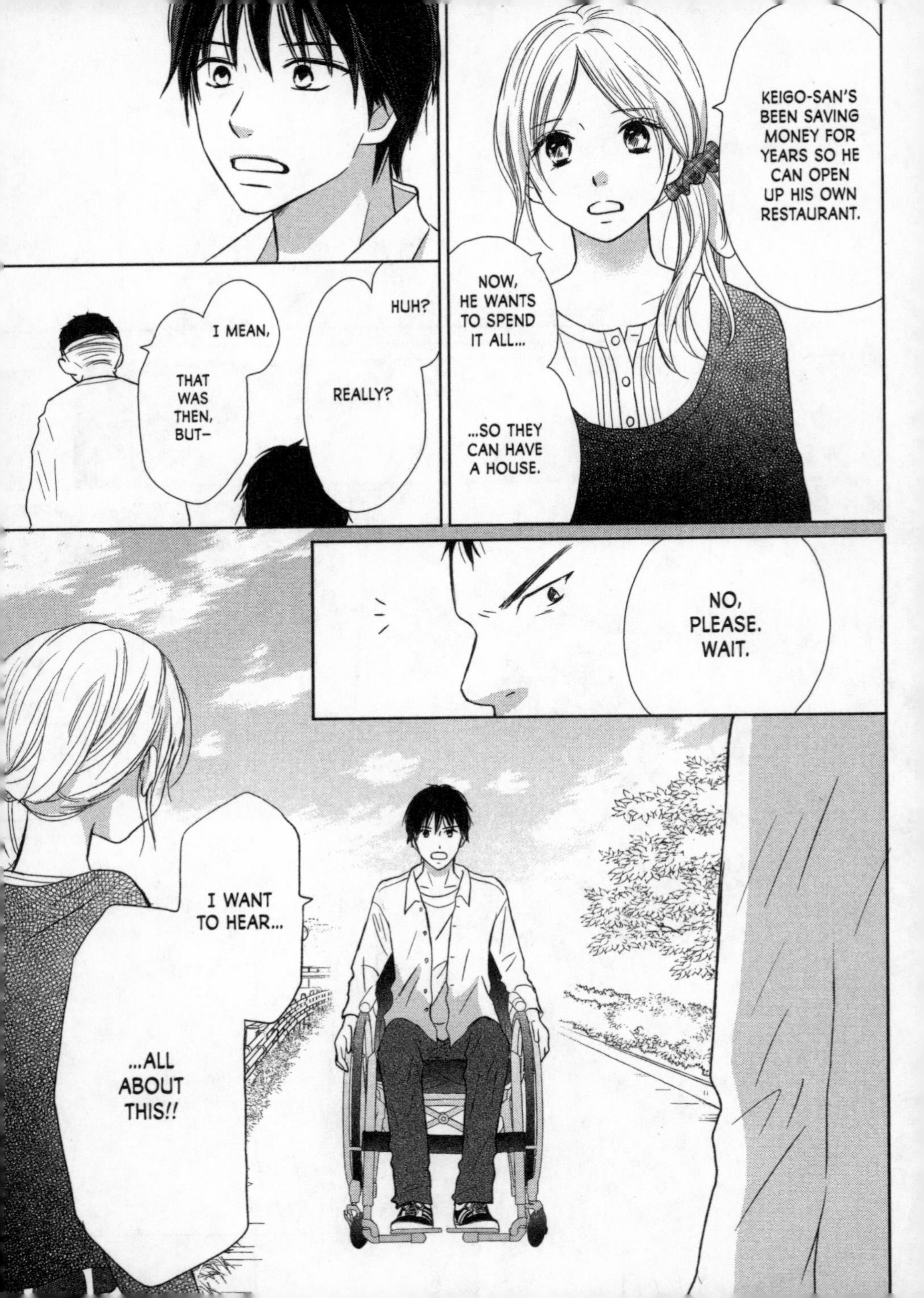
KEIGO-SAN'S BEEN SAVING MONEY FOR YEARS SO HE CAN OPEN UP HIS OWN RESTAURANT.
NOW, HE WANTS TO SPEND IT ALL...
...SO THEY CAN HAVE A HOUSE.
HUH?
REALLY?
I MEAN,
THAT WAS THEN, BUT–
NO, PLEASE. WAIT.
I WANT TO HEAR...
...ALL ABOUT THIS!!

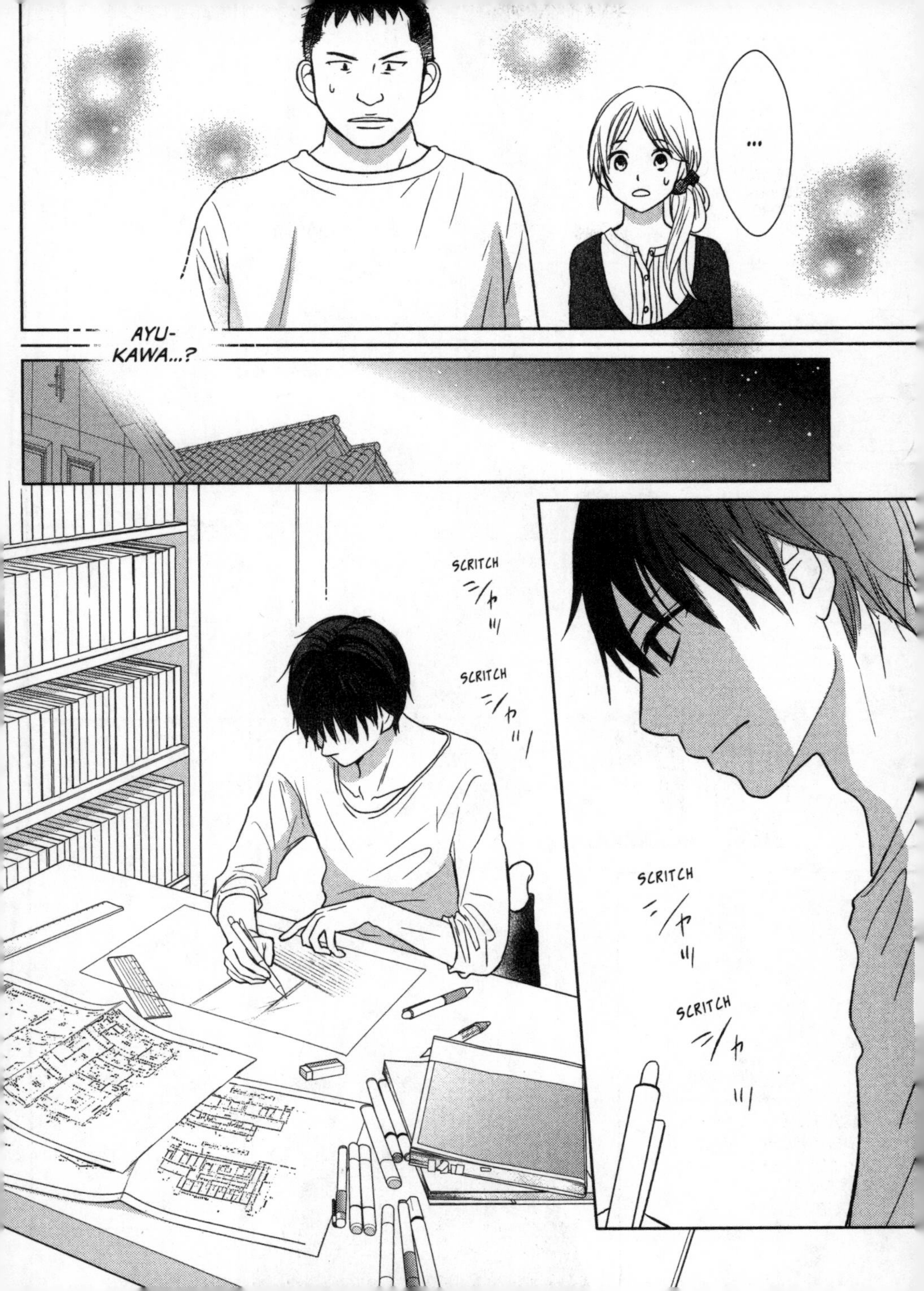
...
AYU-KAWA...?
SCRITCH
SCRITCH
SCRITCH
SCRITCH

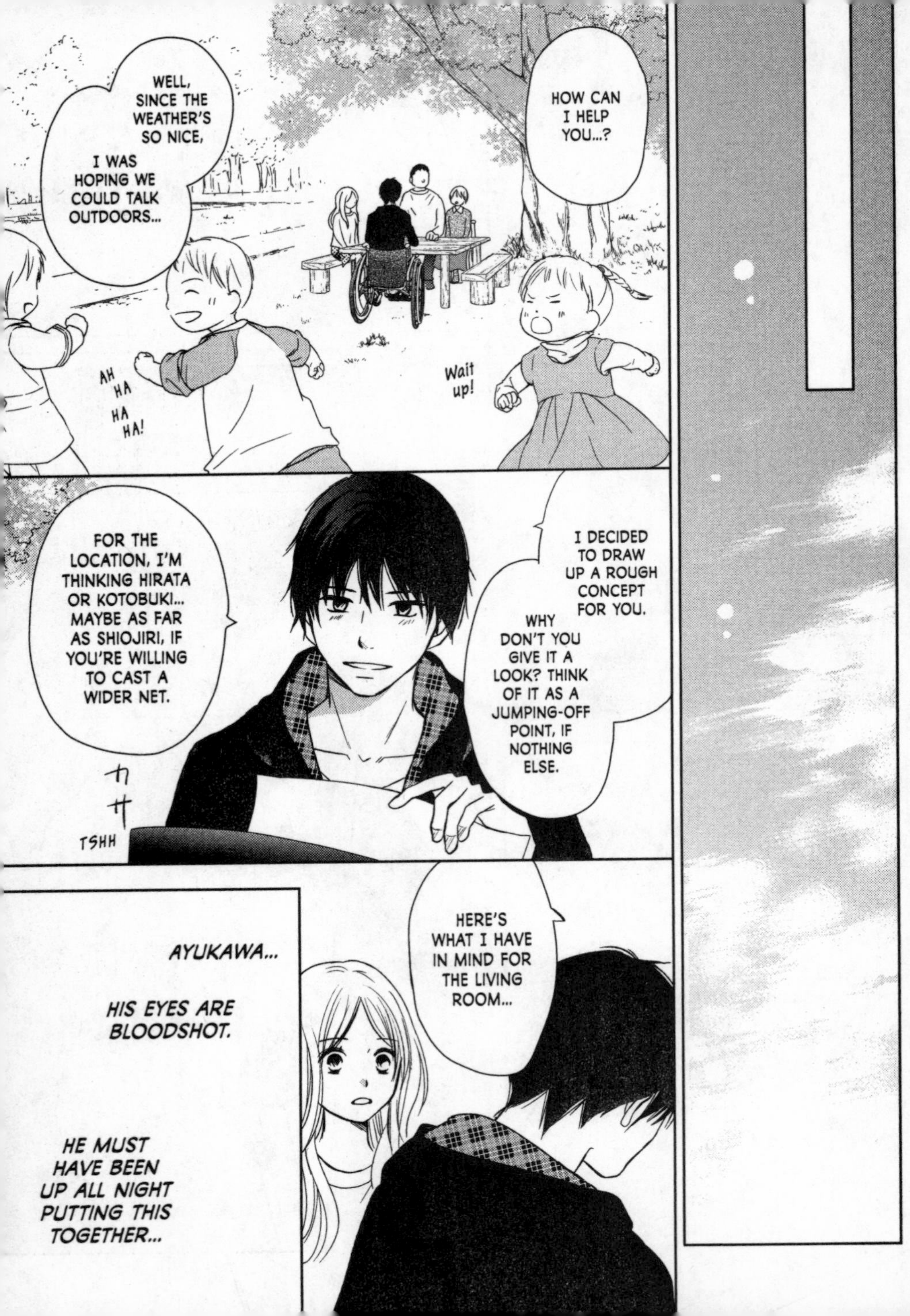
HOW CAN I HELP YOU...?
WELL, SINCE THE WEATHER'S SO NICE,
I WAS HOPING WE COULD TALK OUTDOORS...
Wait up!
AH HA HA HA!
I DECIDED TO DRAW UP A ROUGH CONCEPT FOR YOU.
WHY DON'T YOU GIVE IT A LOOK? THINK OF IT AS A JUMPING-OFF POINT, IF NOTHING ELSE.
FOR THE LOCATION, I'M THINKING HIRATA OR KOTOBUKI... MAYBE AS FAR AS SHIOJIRI, IF YOU'RE WILLING TO CAST A WIDER NET.
カサ
TSHH
HERE'S WHAT I HAVE IN MIND FOR THE LIVING ROOM...
AYUKAWA...
HIS EYES ARE BLOODSHOT.
HE MUST HAVE BEEN UP ALL NIGHT PUTTING THIS TOGETHER...

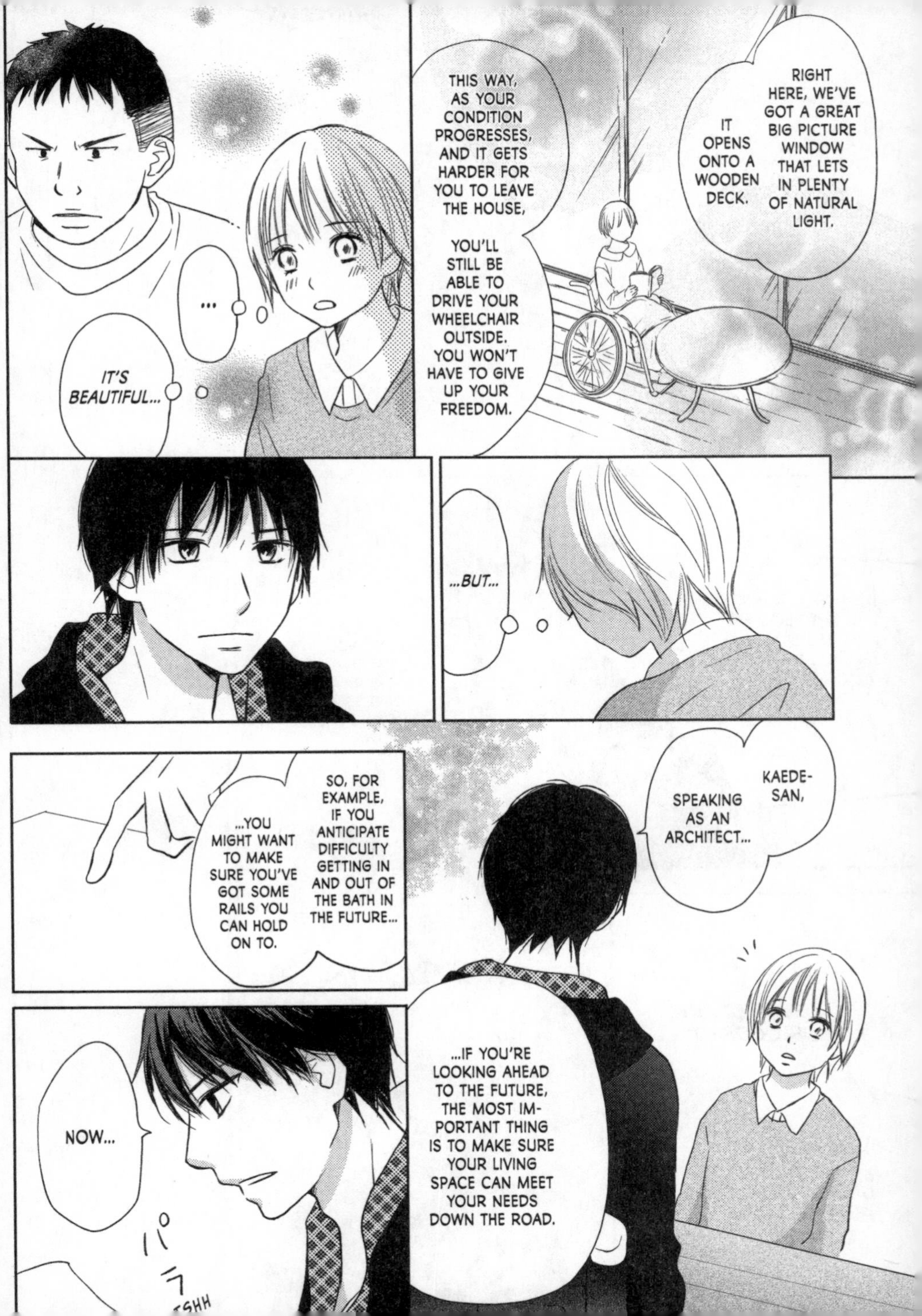
RIGHT HERE, WE'VE GOT A GREAT BIG PICTURE WINDOW THAT LETS IN PLENTY OF NATURAL LIGHT.
IT OPENS ONTO A WOODEN DECK.
THIS WAY, AS YOUR CONDITION PROGRESSES, AND IT GETS HARDER FOR YOU TO LEAVE THE HOUSE,
YOU'LL STILL BE ABLE TO DRIVE YOUR WHEELCHAIR OUTSIDE. YOU WON'T HAVE TO GIVE UP YOUR FREEDOM.
...
IT'S BEAUTIFUL...
...BUT...
KAEDE-SAN,
SPEAKING AS AN ARCHITECT...
SO, FOR EXAMPLE, IF YOU ANTICIPATE DIFFICULTY GETTING IN AND OUT OF THE BATH IN THE FUTURE...
...YOU MIGHT WANT TO MAKE SURE YOU'VE GOT SOME RAILS YOU CAN HOLD ON TO.
...IF YOU'RE LOOKING AHEAD TO THE FUTURE, THE MOST IM-PORTANT THING IS TO MAKE SURE YOUR LIVING SPACE CAN MEET YOUR NEEDS DOWN THE ROAD.
NOW...

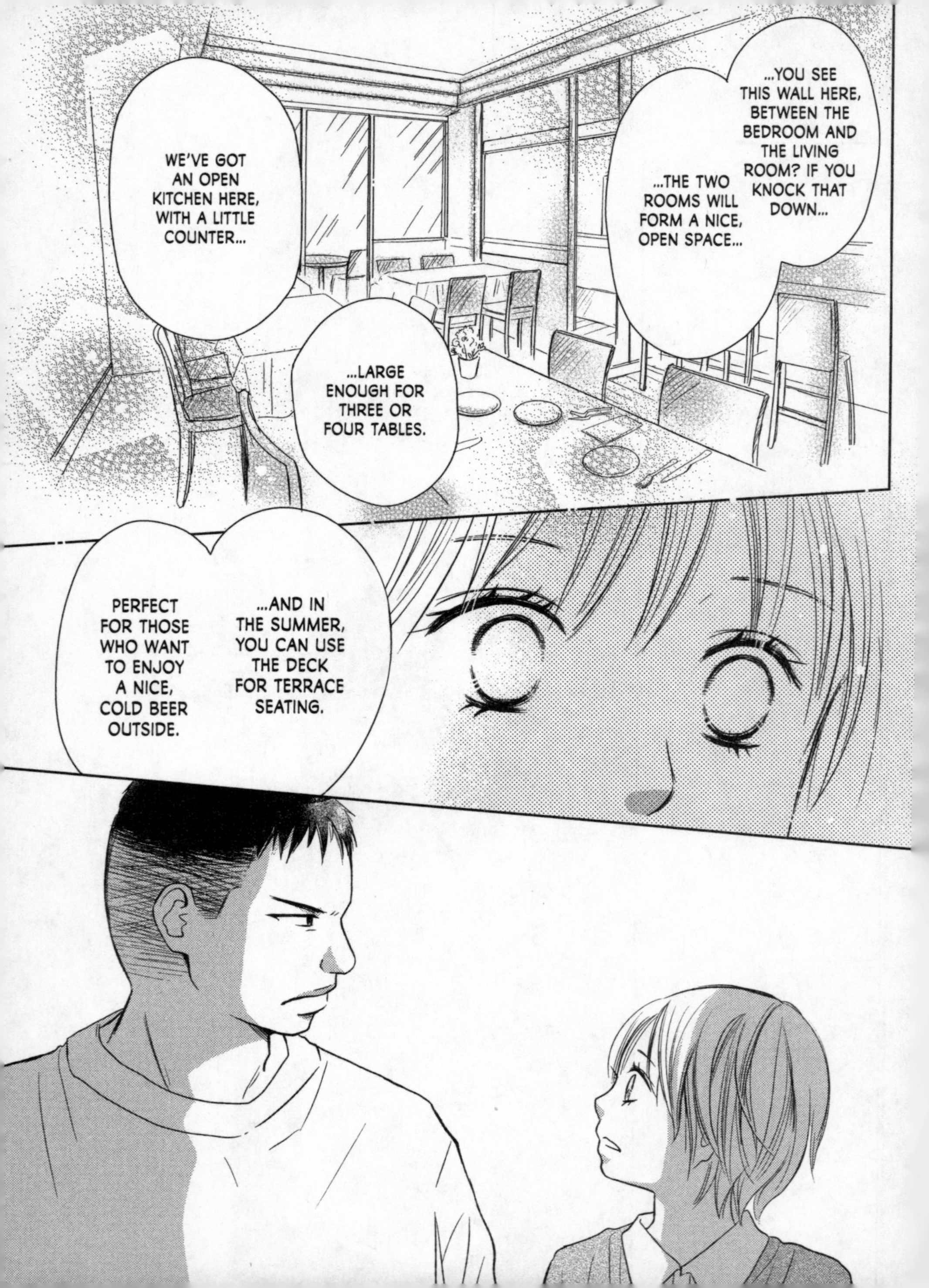
...YOU SEE THIS WALL HERE, BETWEEN THE BEDROOM AND THE LIVING ROOM? IF YOU KNOCK THAT DOWN...
...THE TWO ROOMS WILL FORM A NICE, OPEN SPACE...
WE'VE GOT AN OPEN KITCHEN HERE, WITH A LITTLE COUNTER...
...LARGE ENOUGH FOR THREE OR FOUR TABLES.
...AND IN THE SUMMER, YOU CAN USE THE DECK FOR TERRACE SEATING.
PERFECT FOR THOSE WHO WANT TO ENJOY A NICE, COLD BEER OUTSIDE.

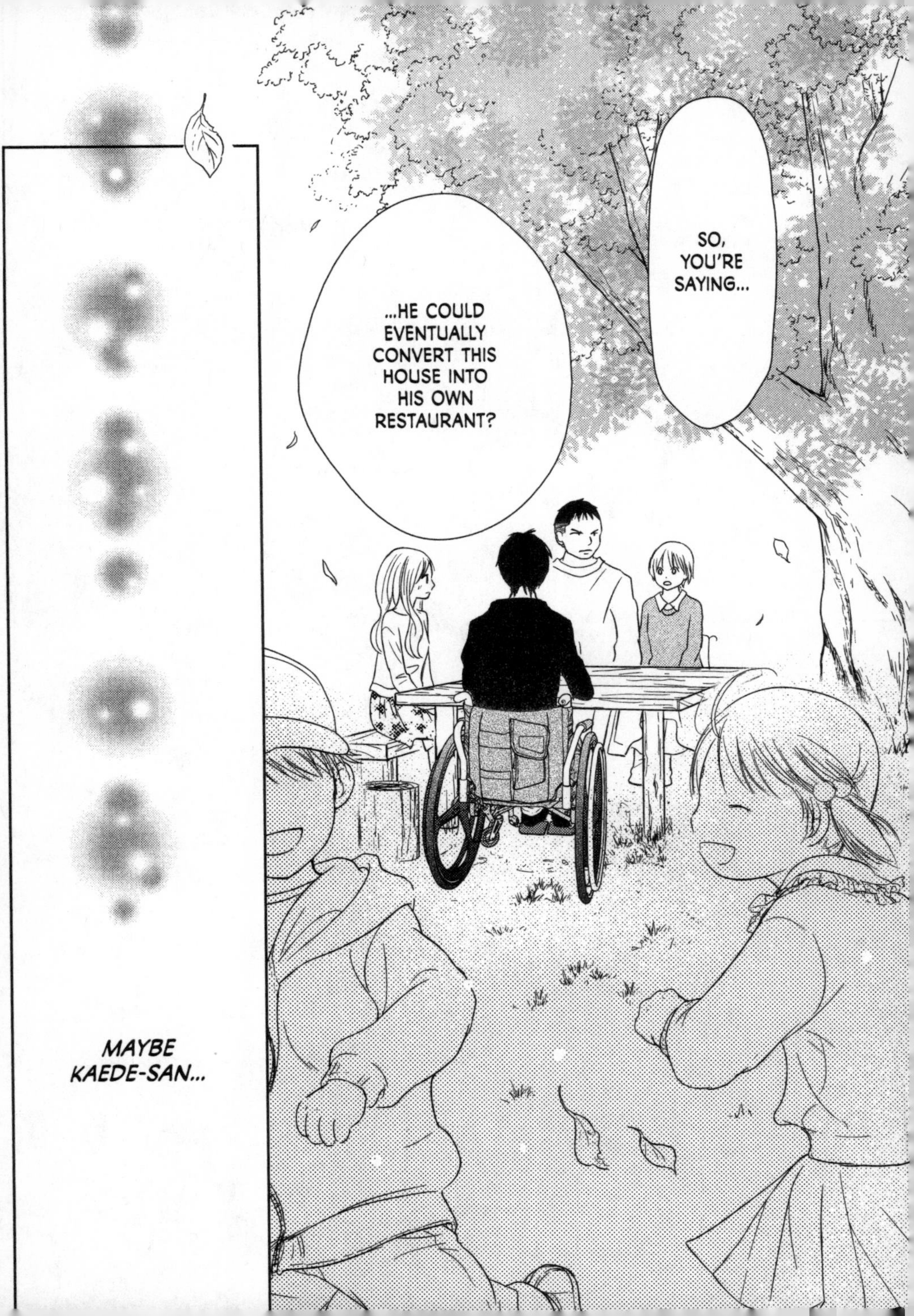
SO, YOU'RE SAYING...
...HE COULD EVENTUALLY CONVERT THIS HOUSE INTO HIS OWN RESTAURANT?
MAYBE KAEDE-SAN...

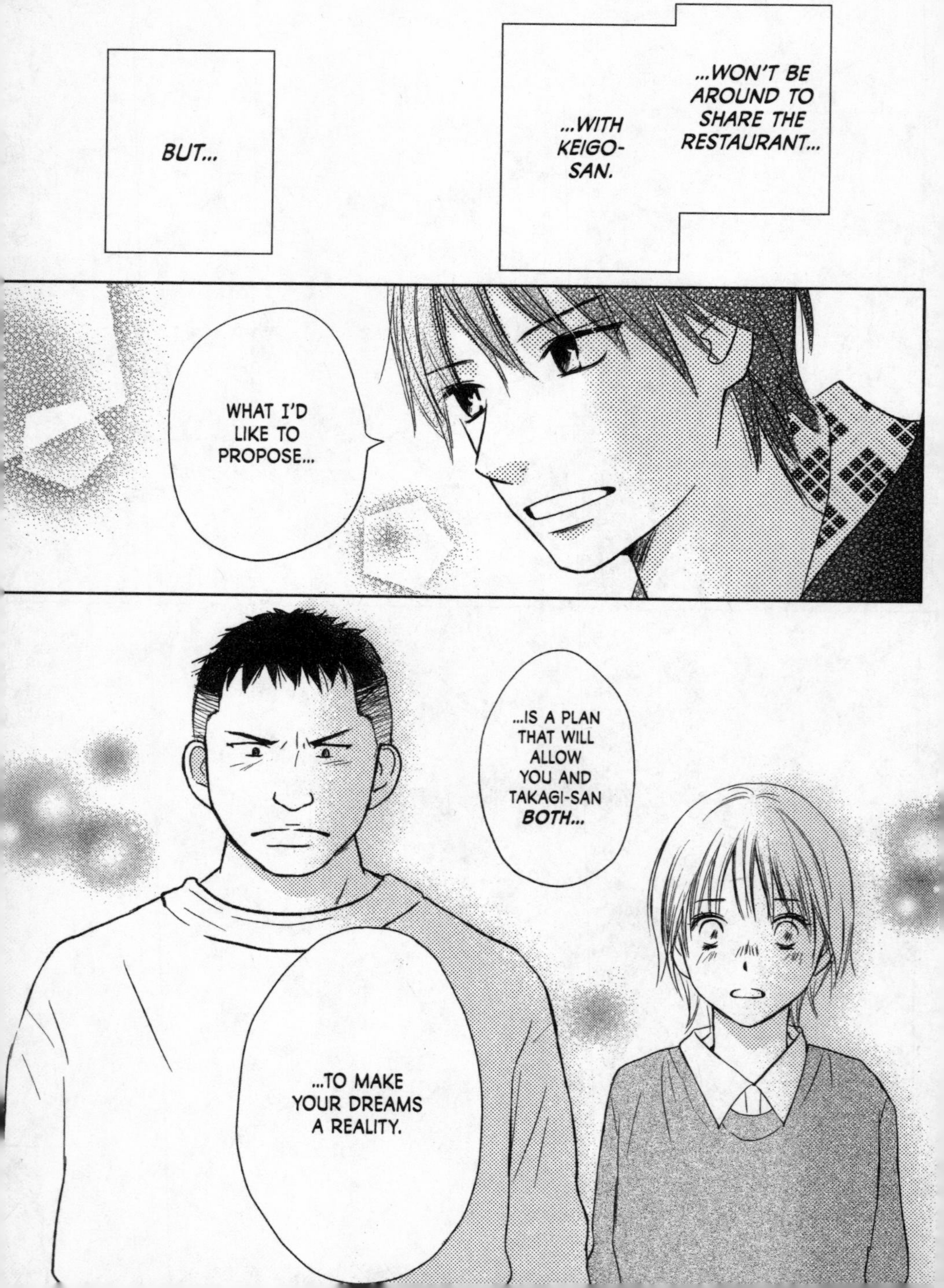
...WON'T BE AROUND TO SHARE THE RESTAURANT...
...WITH KEIGO-SAN.
BUT...
WHAT I'D LIKE TO PROPOSE...
...IS A PLAN THAT WILL ALLOW YOU AND TAKAGI-SAN *BOTH*...
...TO MAKE YOUR DREAMS A REALITY.

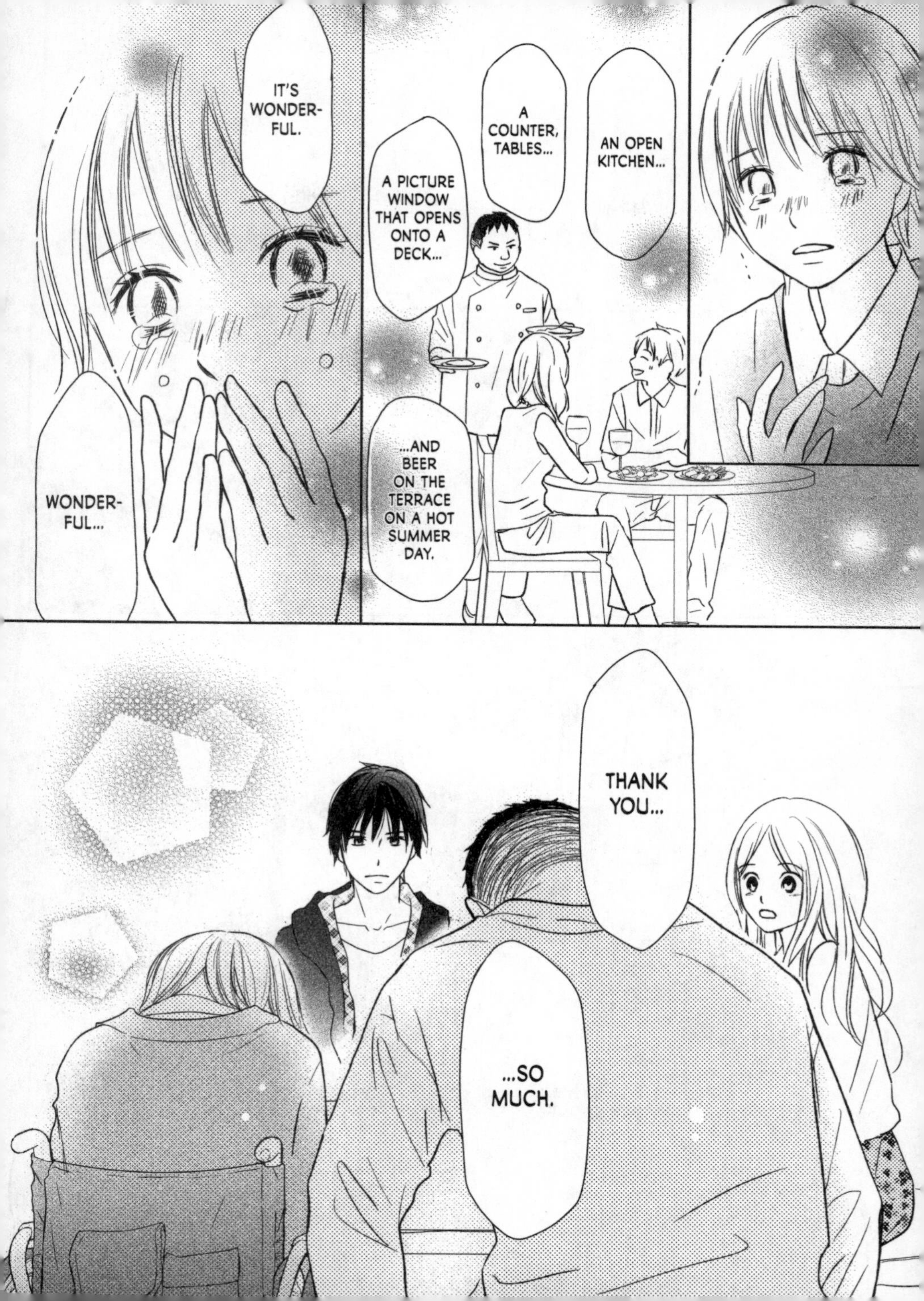
AN OPEN KITCHEN...
A COUNTER, TABLES...
A PICTURE WINDOW THAT OPENS ONTO A DECK...
...AND BEER ON THE TERRACE ON A HOT SUMMER DAY.
IT'S WONDER-FUL.
WONDER-FUL...
THANK YOU...
...SO MUCH.

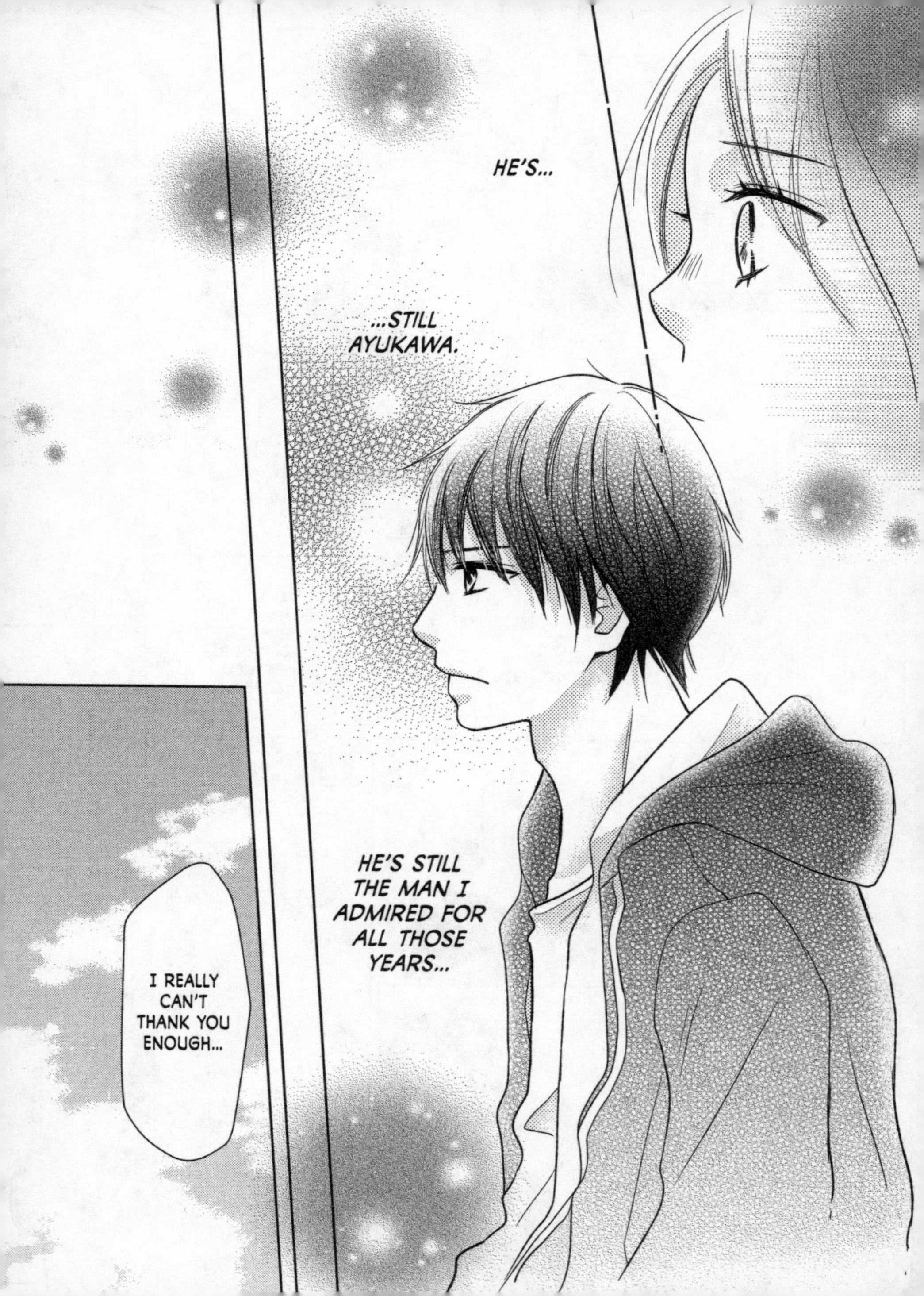
HE'S...
...STILL AYUKAWA.
HE'S STILL THE MAN I ADMIRED FOR ALL THOSE YEARS...
I REALLY CAN'T THANK YOU ENOUGH...

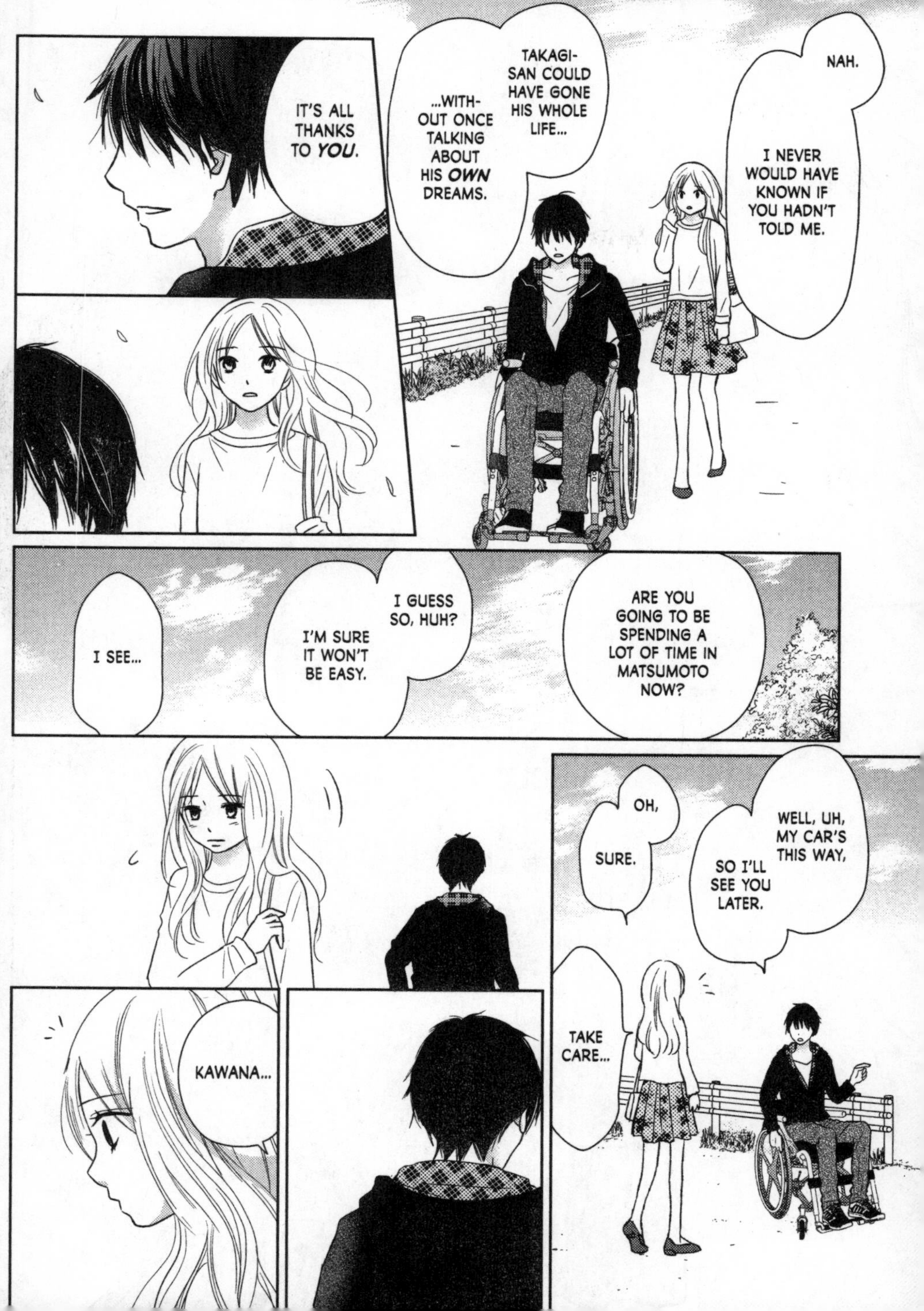
NAH.
I NEVER WOULD HAVE KNOWN IF YOU HADN'T TOLD ME.
TAKAGI-SAN COULD HAVE GONE HIS WHOLE LIFE...
...WITH-OUT ONCE TALKING ABOUT HIS *OWN* DREAMS.
IT'S ALL THANKS TO *YOU*.
ARE YOU GOING TO BE SPENDING A LOT OF TIME IN MATSUMOTO NOW?
I GUESS SO, HUH?
I'M SURE IT WON'T BE EASY.
I SEE...
WELL, UH, MY CAR'S THIS WAY,
SO I'LL SEE YOU LATER.
OH,
SURE.
TAKE CARE...
KAWANA...

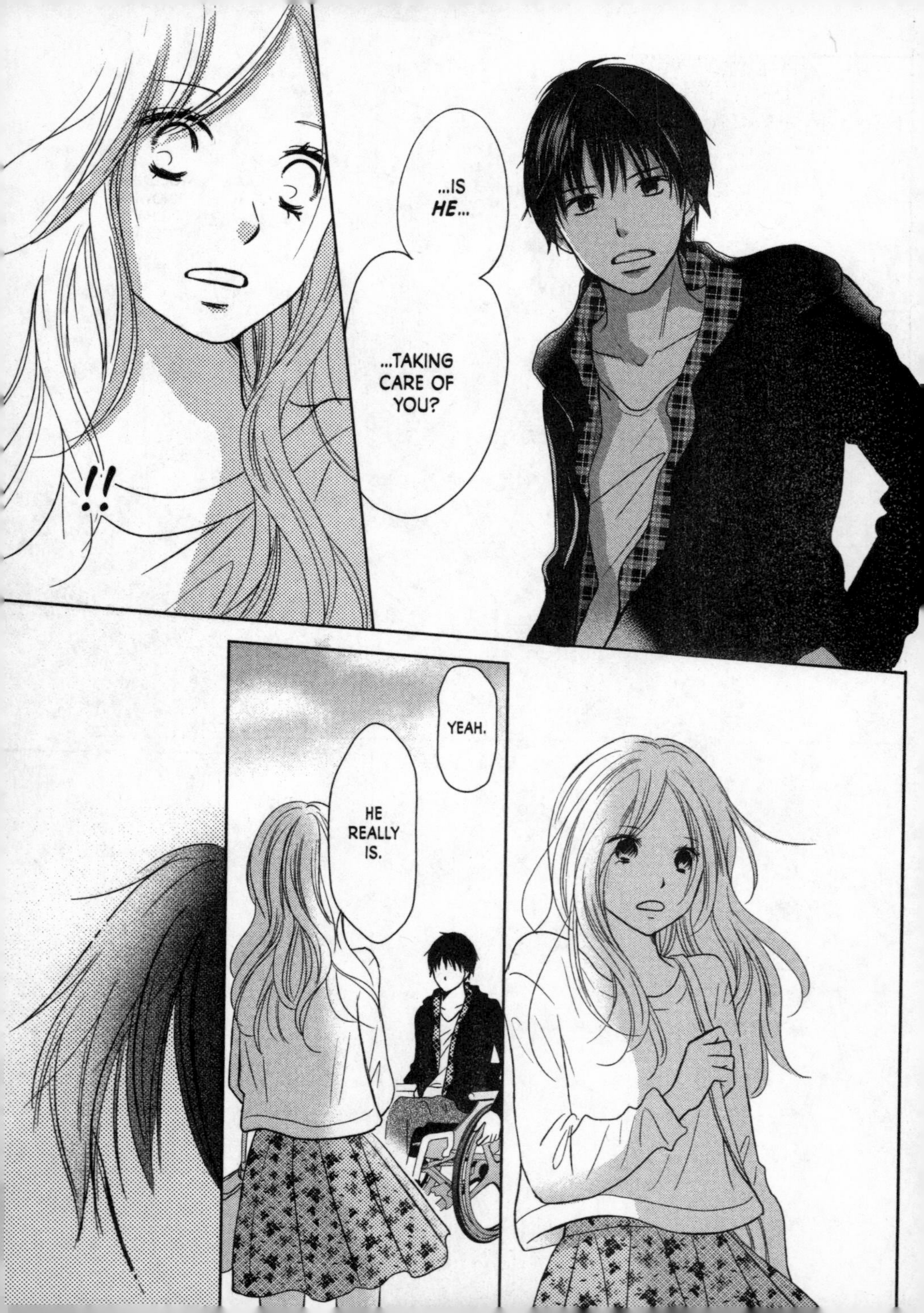
...IS *HE*...
...TAKING CARE OF YOU?
!!
YEAH.
HE REALLY IS.

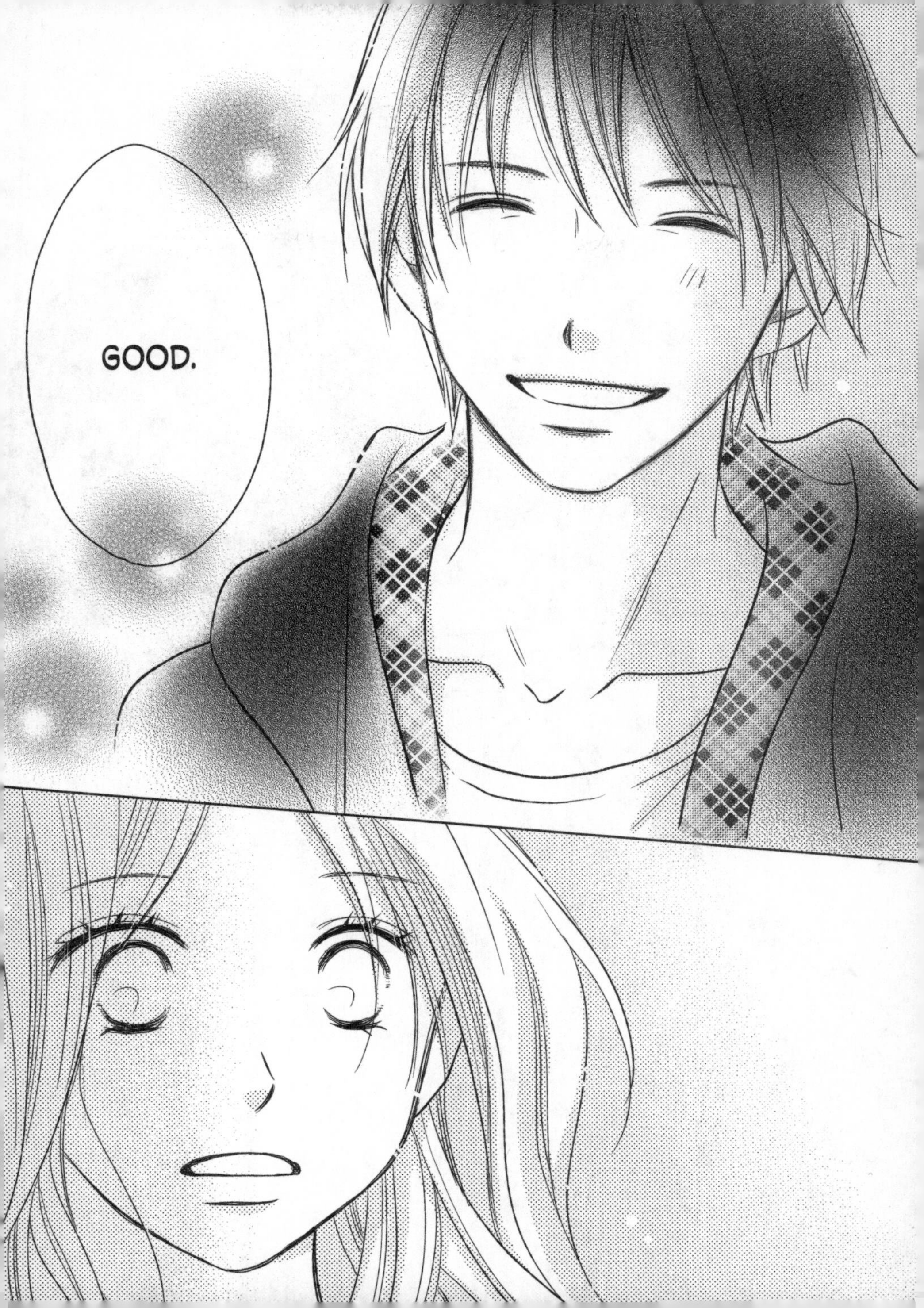
GOOD.

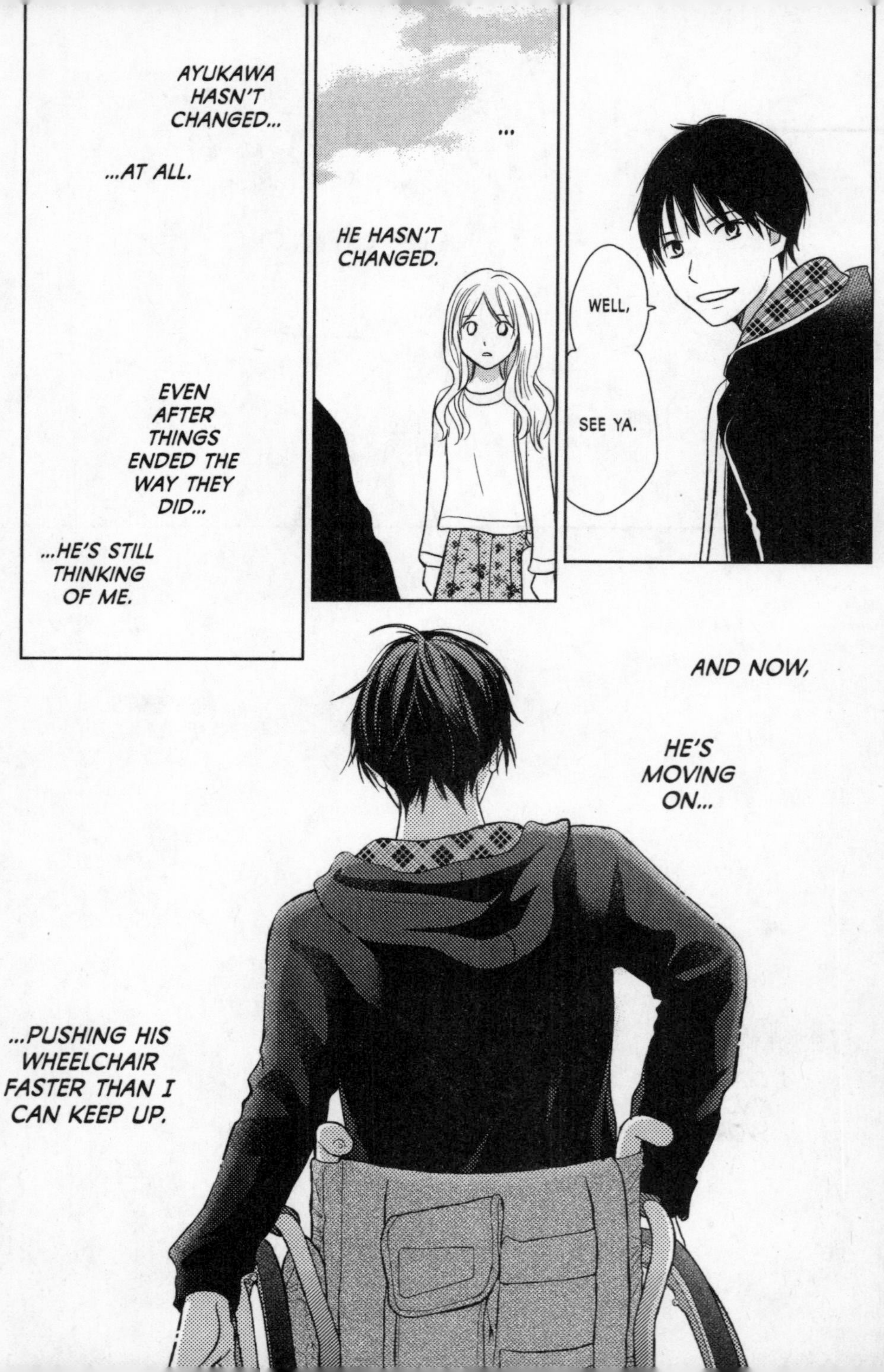
WELL,
SEE YA.
...
HE HASN'T CHANGED.
AYUKAWA HASN'T CHANGED...
...AT ALL.
EVEN AFTER THINGS ENDED THE WAY THEY DID...
...HE'S STILL THINKING OF ME.
AND NOW,
HE'S MOVING ON...
...PUSHING HIS WHEELCHAIR FASTER THAN I CAN KEEP UP.

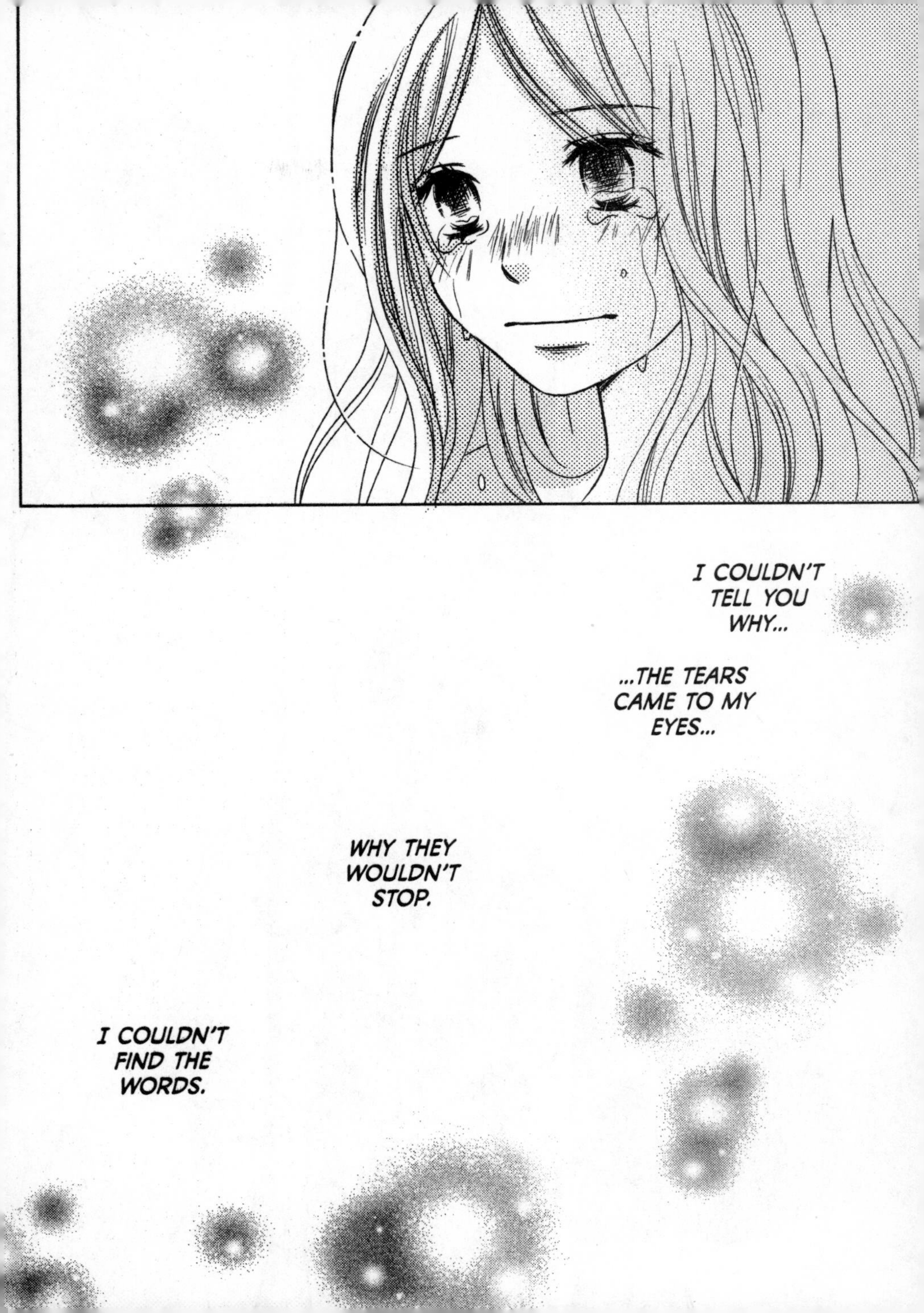
I COULDN'T TELL YOU WHY...
...THE TEARS CAME TO MY EYES...
WHY THEY WOULDN'T STOP.
I COULDN'T FIND THE WORDS.

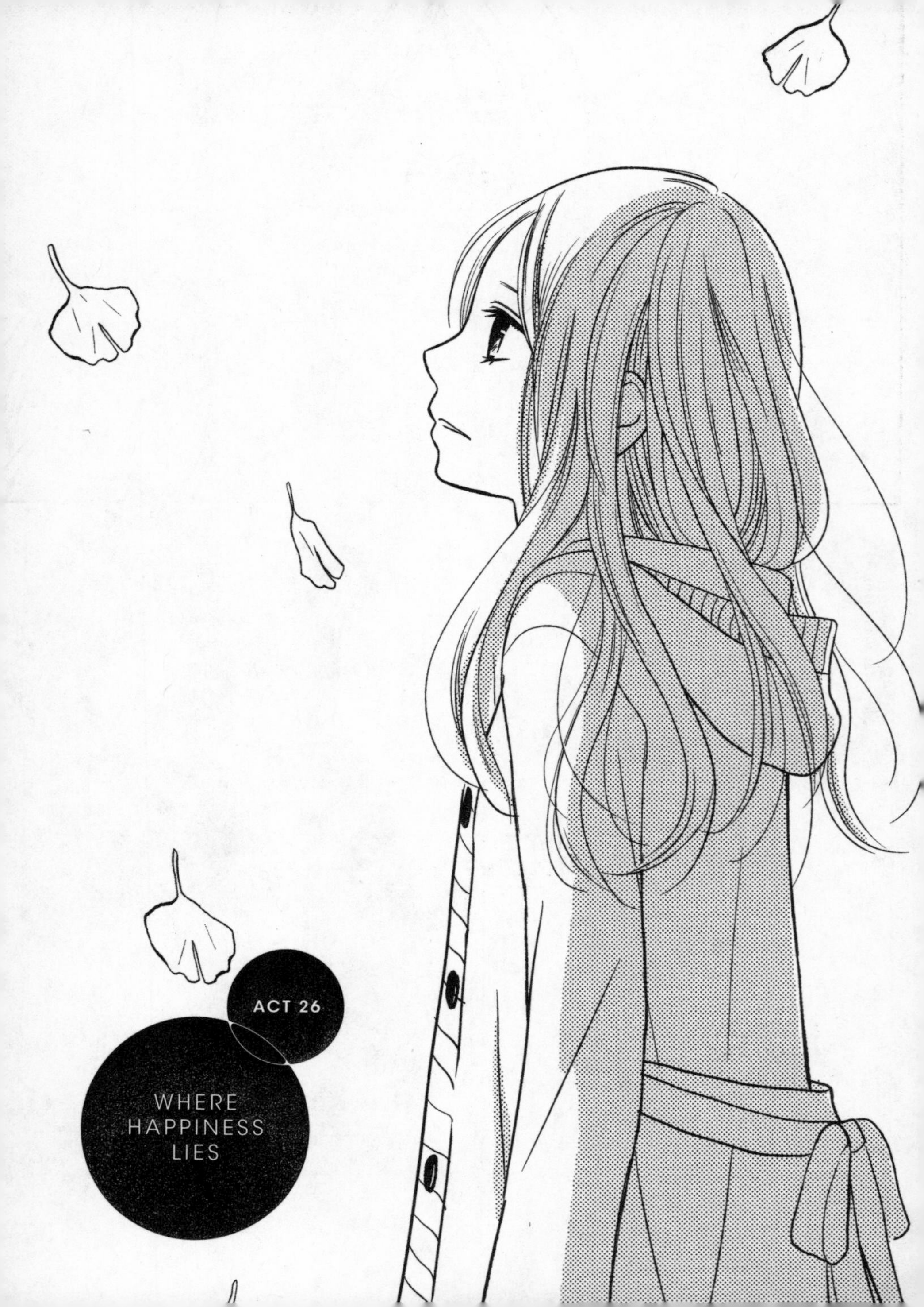
ACT 26
WHERE HAPPINESS LIES

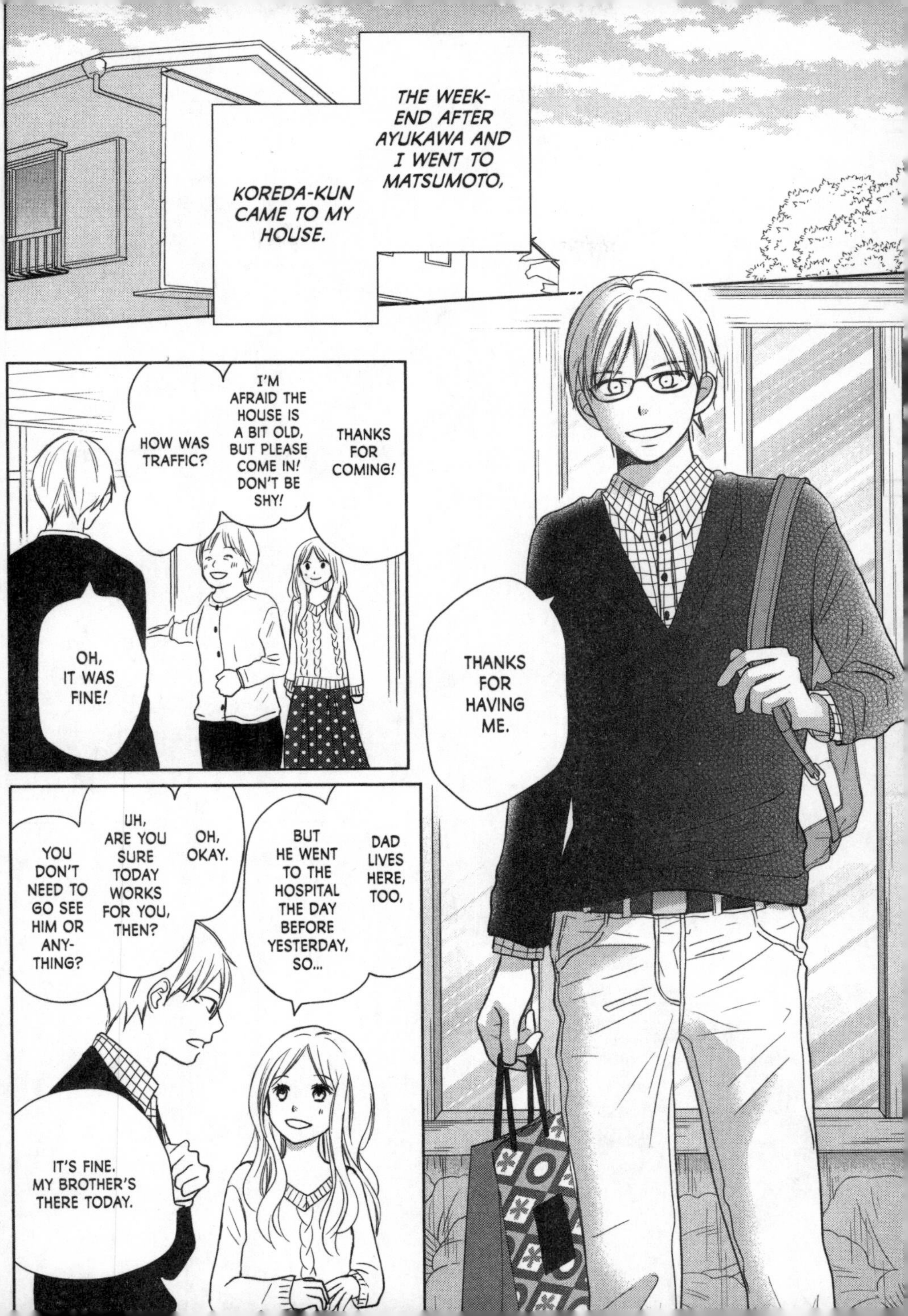
THE WEEK-END AFTER AYUKAWA AND I WENT TO MATSUMOTO,
KOREDA-KUN CAME TO MY HOUSE.
THANKS FOR HAVING ME.
THANKS FOR COMING!
I'M AFRAID THE HOUSE IS A BIT OLD, BUT PLEASE COME IN! DON'T BE SHY!
HOW WAS TRAFFIC?
OH, IT WAS FINE!
DAD LIVES HERE, TOO,
BUT HE WENT TO THE HOSPITAL THE DAY BEFORE YESTERDAY, SO...
OH, OKAY.
UH, ARE YOU SURE TODAY WORKS FOR YOU, THEN?
YOU DON'T NEED TO GO SEE HIM OR ANYTHING?
IT'S FINE. MY BROTHER'S THERE TODAY.

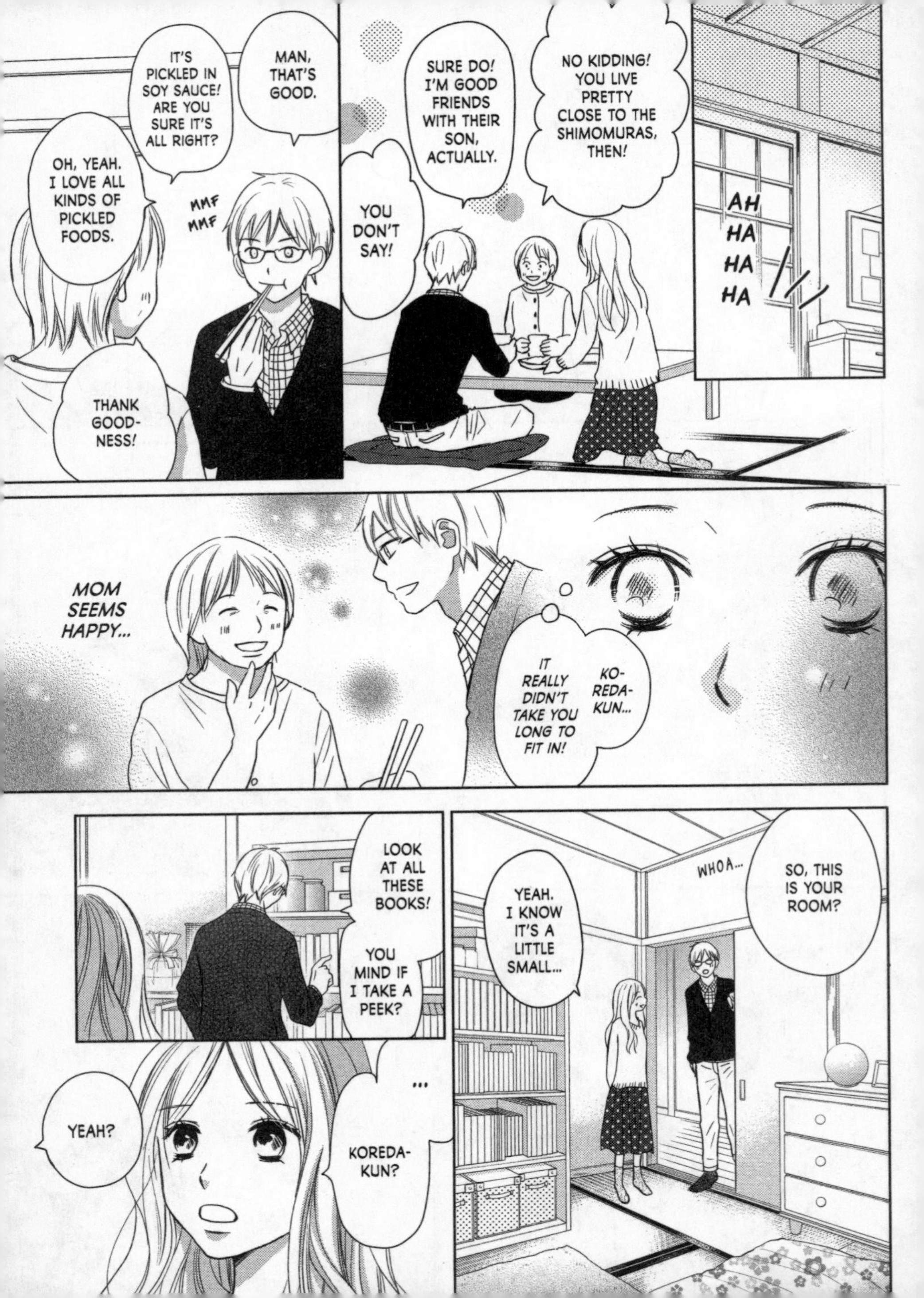
AH HA HA HA
NO KIDDING! YOU LIVE PRETTY CLOSE TO THE SHIMOMURAS, THEN!
SURE DO! I'M GOOD FRIENDS WITH THEIR SON, ACTUALLY.
YOU DON'T SAY!
MAN, THAT'S GOOD.
IT'S PICKLED IN SOY SAUCE! ARE YOU SURE IT'S ALL RIGHT?
OH, YEAH. I LOVE ALL KINDS OF PICKLED FOODS.
MMF MMF
THANK GOOD-NESS!
KO-REDA-KUN...
IT REALLY DIDN'T TAKE YOU LONG TO FIT IN!
MOM SEEMS HAPPY...
SO, THIS IS YOUR ROOM?
WHOA...
YEAH. I KNOW IT'S A LITTLE SMALL...
LOOK AT ALL THESE BOOKS!
YOU MIND IF I TAKE A PEEK?
...
KOREDA-KUN?
YEAH?

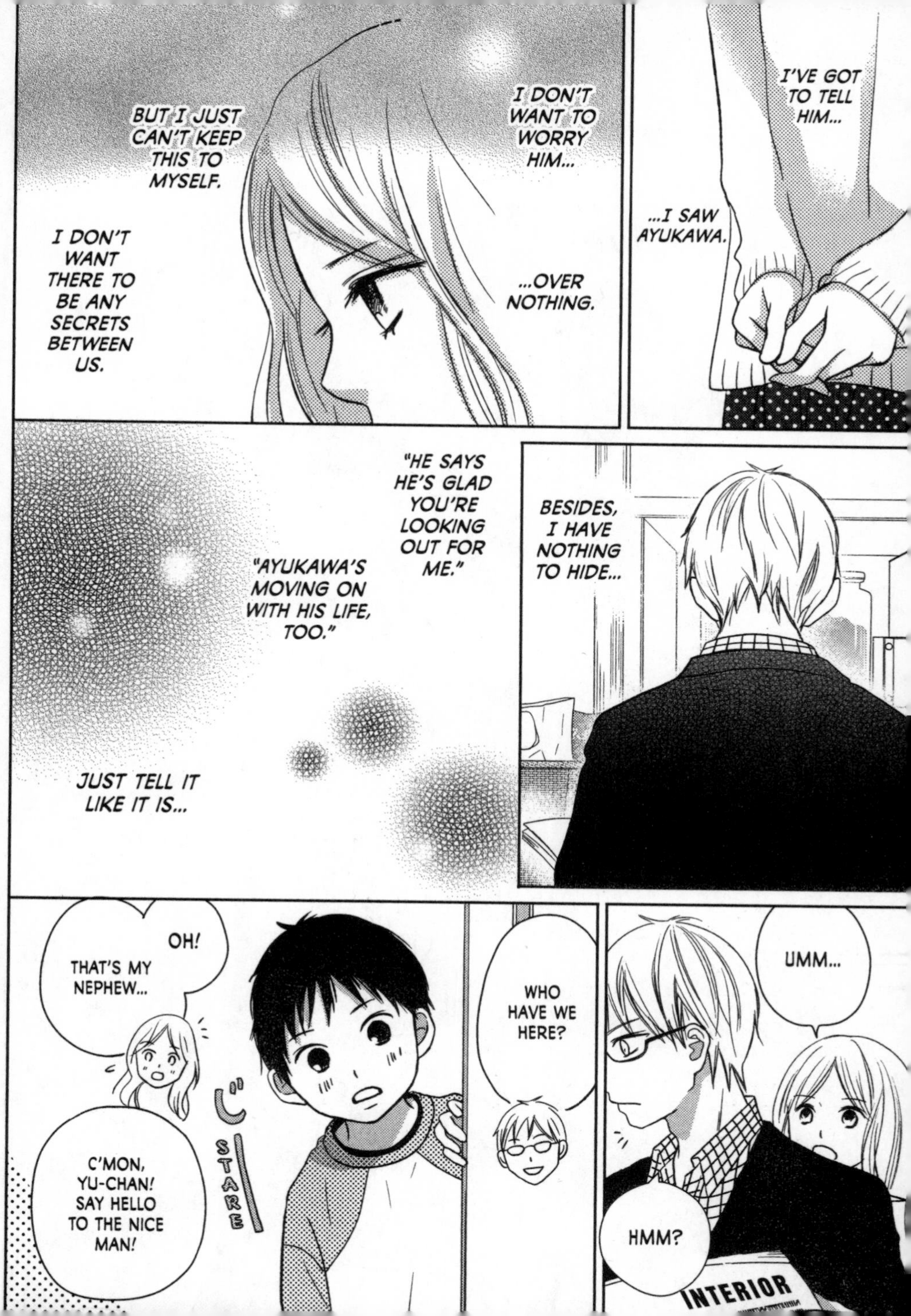
I'VE GOT TO TELL HIM...
...I SAW AYUKAWA.
I DON'T WANT TO WORRY HIM...
...OVER NOTHING.
BUT I JUST CAN'T KEEP THIS TO MYSELF.
I DON'T WANT THERE TO BE ANY SECRETS BETWEEN US.
BESIDES, I HAVE NOTHING TO HIDE...
"HE SAYS HE'S GLAD YOU'RE LOOKING OUT FOR ME."
"AYUKAWA'S MOVING ON WITH HIS LIFE, TOO."
JUST TELL IT LIKE IT IS...
UMM...
HMM?
INTERIOR
WHO HAVE WE HERE?
OH! THAT'S MY NEPHEW...
じ STARE
C'MON, YU-CHAN! SAY HELLO TO THE NICE MAN!

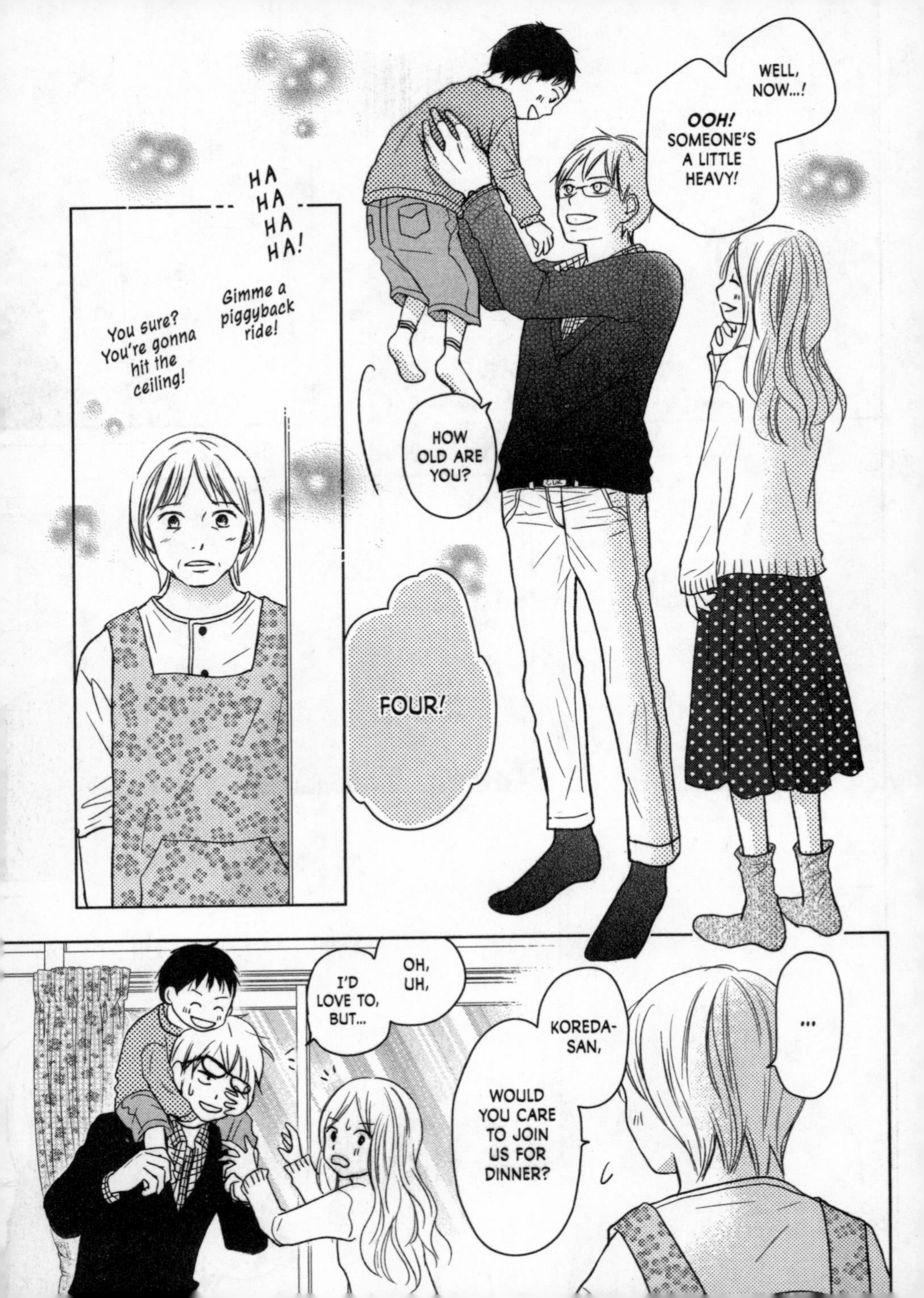
WELL, NOW...!
OOH! SOMEONE'S A LITTLE HEAVY!
HOW OLD ARE YOU?
FOUR!
HA HA HA HA!
Gimme a piggyback ride!
You sure? You're gonna hit the ceiling!
...
KOREDA-SAN,
WOULD YOU CARE TO JOIN US FOR DINNER?
OH, UH,
I'D LOVE TO, BUT...

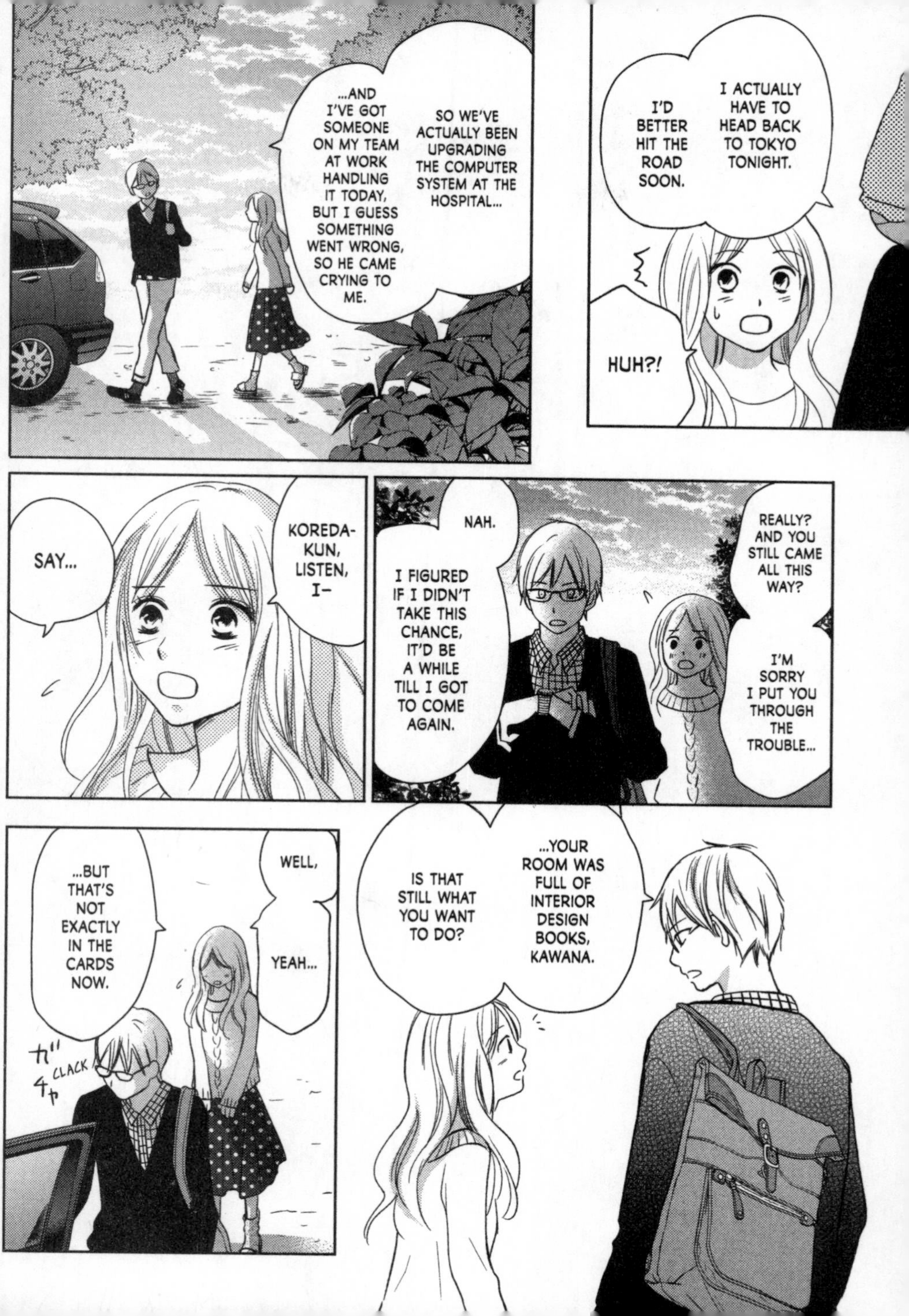
I ACTUALLY HAVE TO HEAD BACK TO TOKYO TONIGHT.
I'D BETTER HIT THE ROAD SOON.
HUH?!
SO WE'VE ACTUALLY BEEN UPGRADING THE COMPUTER SYSTEM AT THE HOSPITAL...
...AND I'VE GOT SOMEONE ON MY TEAM AT WORK HANDLING IT TODAY, BUT I GUESS SOMETHING WENT WRONG, SO HE CAME CRYING TO ME.
REALLY? AND YOU STILL CAME ALL THIS WAY?
I'M SORRY I PUT YOU THROUGH THE TROUBLE...
NAH.
I FIGURED IF I DIDN'T TAKE THIS CHANCE, IT'D BE A WHILE TILL I GOT TO COME AGAIN.
KOREDA-KUN, LISTEN, I—
SAY...
...YOUR ROOM WAS FULL OF INTERIOR DESIGN BOOKS, KAWANA.
IS THAT STILL WHAT YOU WANT TO DO?
WELL,
YEAH...
...BUT THAT'S NOT EXACTLY IN THE CARDS NOW.
ガチャ
CLACK

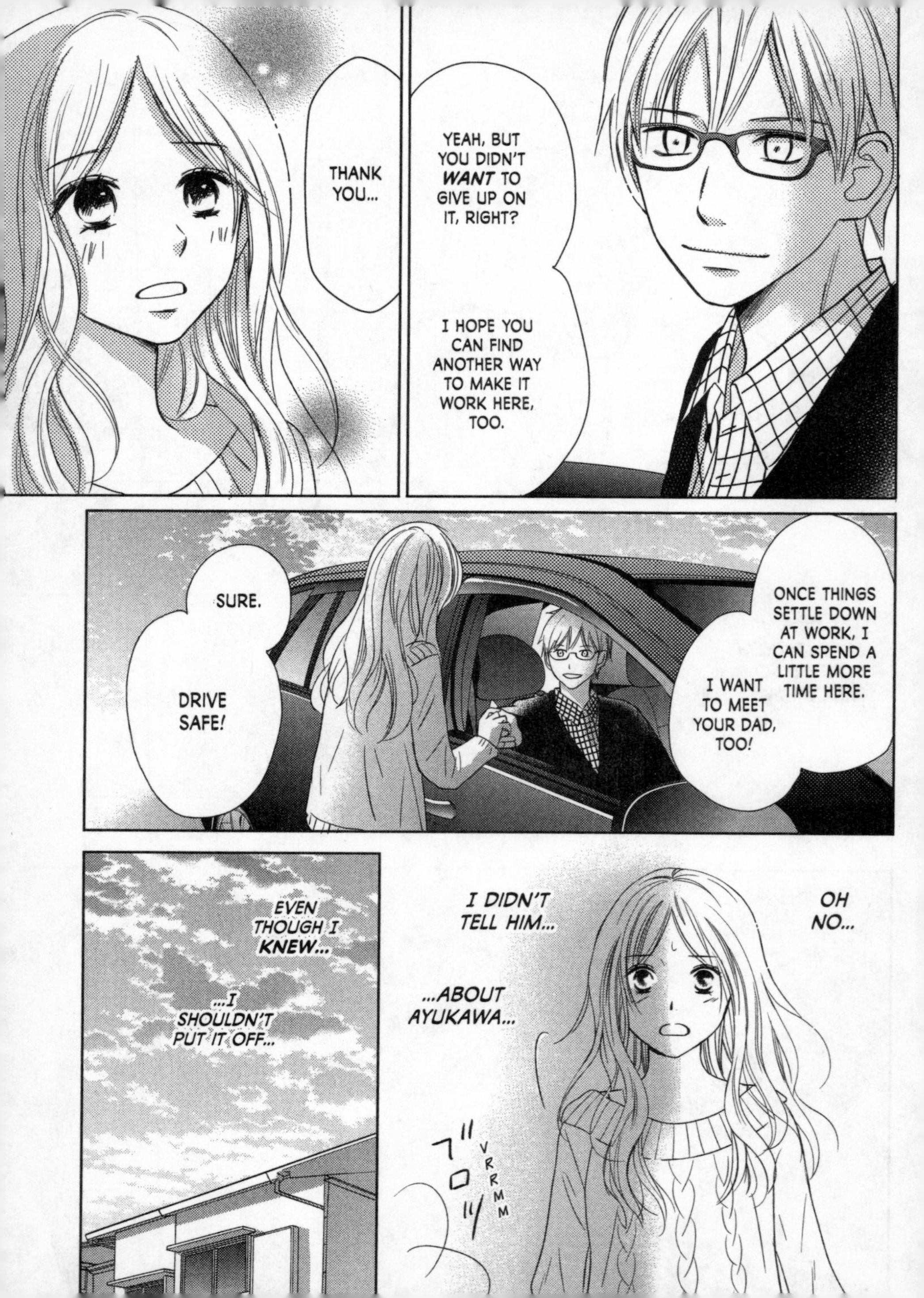
YEAH, BUT YOU DIDN'T *WANT* TO GIVE UP ON IT, RIGHT?
I HOPE YOU CAN FIND ANOTHER WAY TO MAKE IT WORK HERE, TOO.
THANK YOU...
ONCE THINGS SETTLE DOWN AT WORK, I CAN SPEND A LITTLE MORE TIME HERE.
I WANT TO MEET YOUR DAD, TOO!
SURE.
DRIVE SAFE!
OH NO...
I DIDN'T TELL HIM...
...ABOUT AYUKAWA...
VRRMM
EVEN THOUGH I **KNEW**...
...I SHOULDN'T PUT IT OFF...

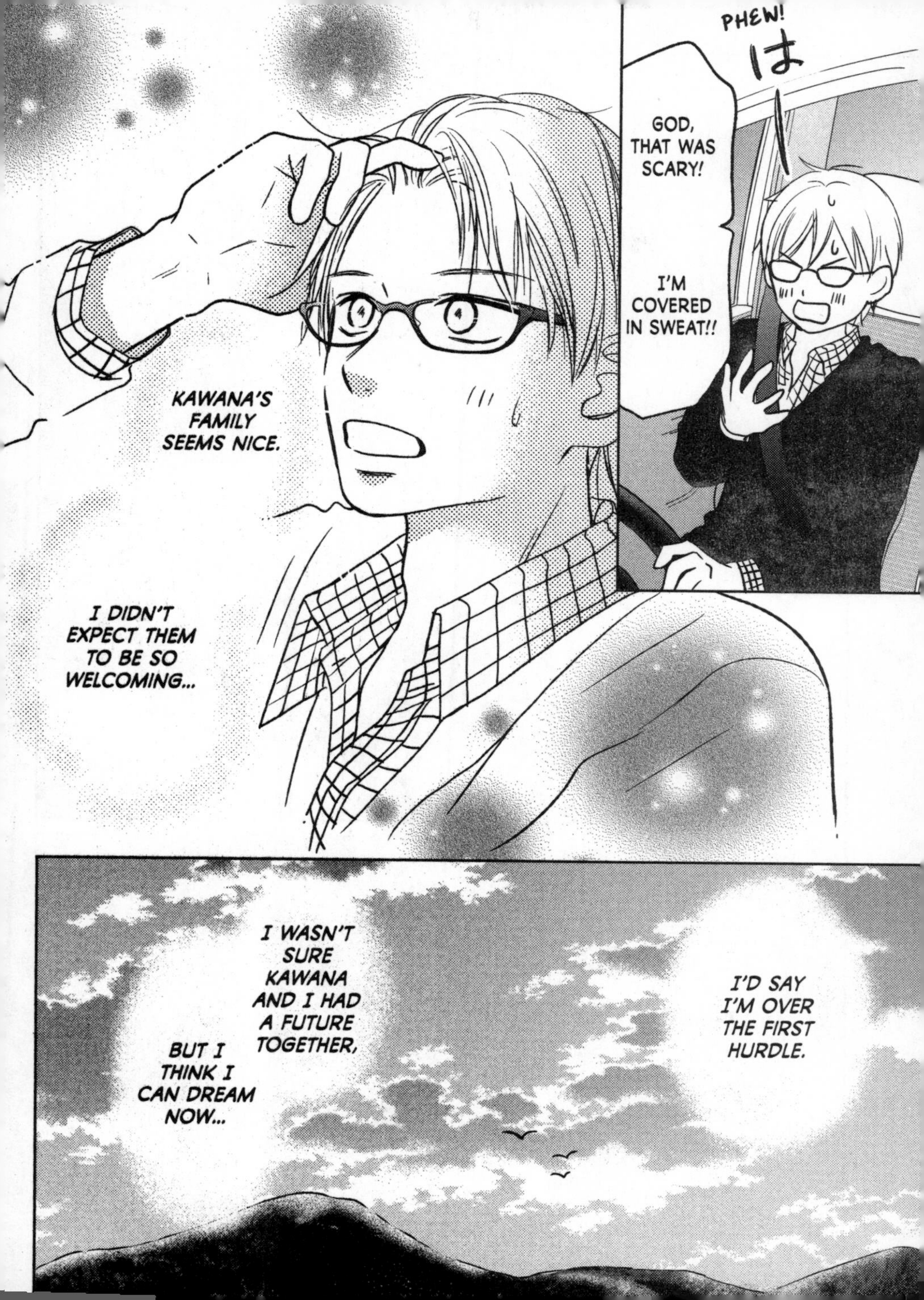
PHEW!
は
GOD, THAT WAS SCARY!
I'M COVERED IN SWEAT!!
KAWANA'S FAMILY SEEMS NICE.
I DIDN'T EXPECT THEM TO BE SO WELCOMING...
I'D SAY I'M OVER THE FIRST HURDLE.
I WASN'T SURE KAWANA AND I HAD A FUTURE TOGETHER,
BUT I THINK I CAN DREAM NOW...

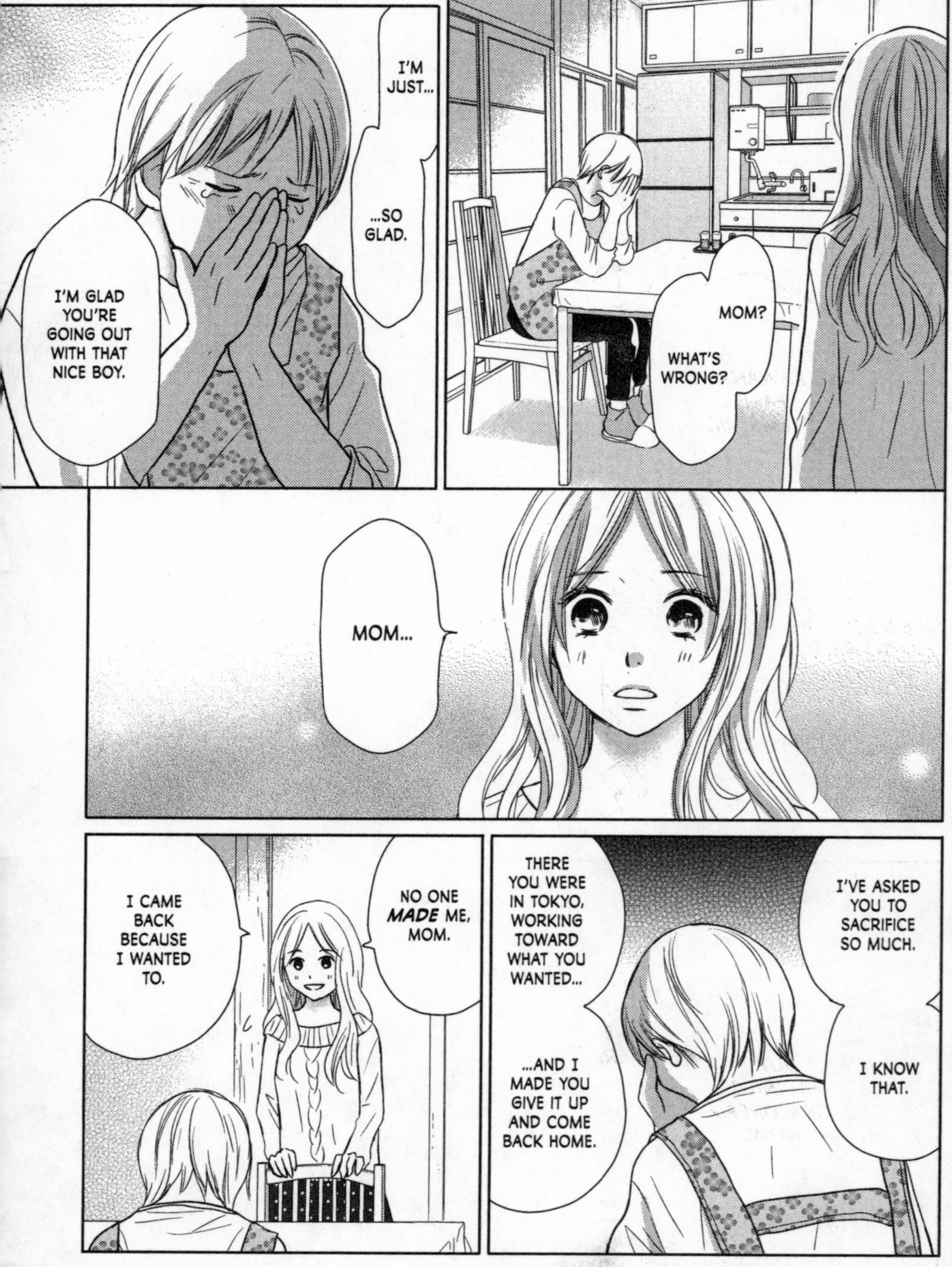
MOM?
WHAT'S WRONG?
I'M JUST...
...SO GLAD.
I'M GLAD YOU'RE GOING OUT WITH THAT NICE BOY.
MOM...
I'VE ASKED YOU TO SACRIFICE SO MUCH.
I KNOW THAT.
THERE YOU WERE IN TOKYO, WORKING TOWARD WHAT YOU WANTED...
...AND I MADE YOU GIVE IT UP AND COME BACK HOME.
NO ONE *MADE* ME, MOM.
I CAME BACK BECAUSE I WANTED TO.

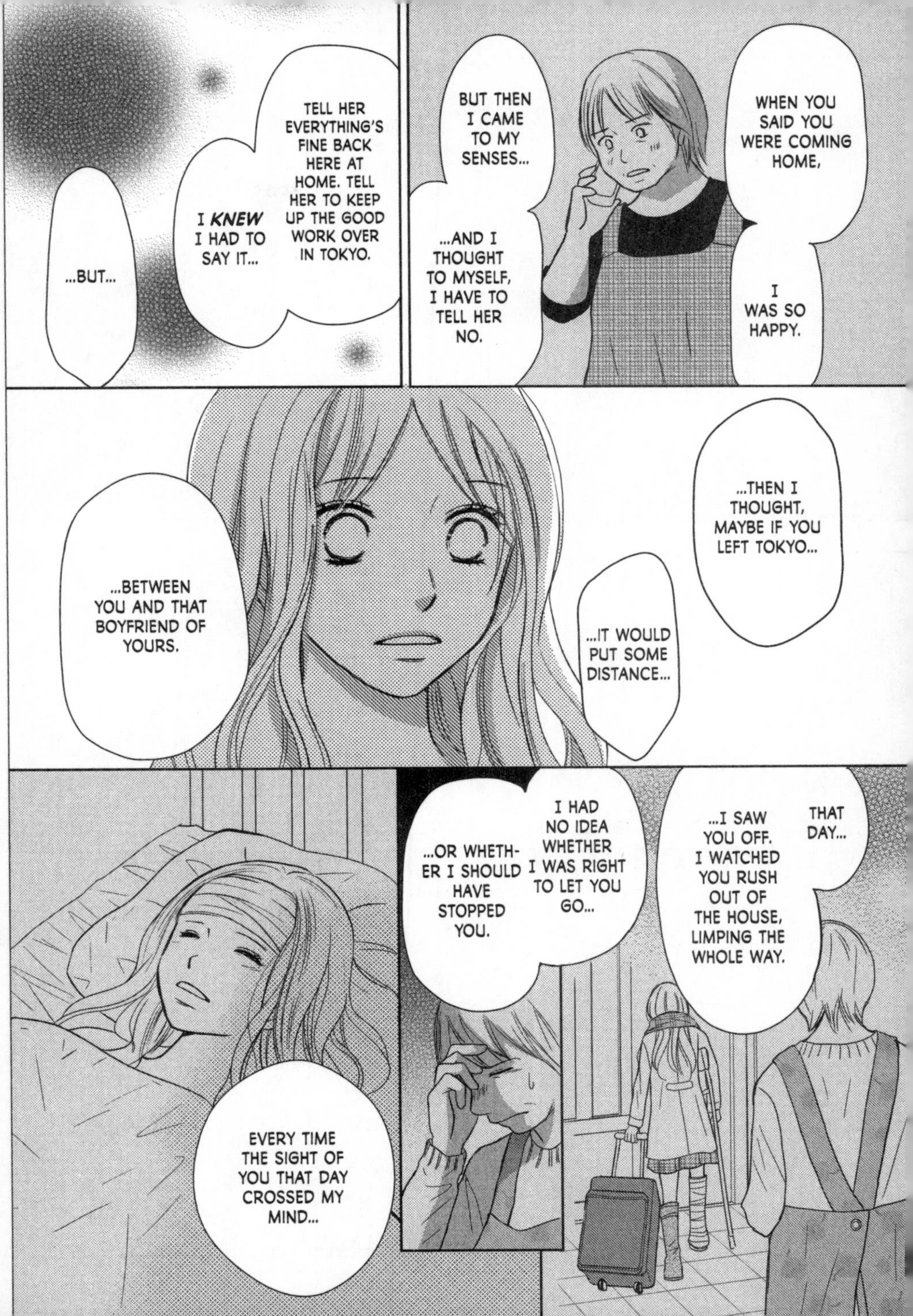
WHEN YOU SAID YOU WERE COMING HOME,
I WAS SO HAPPY.
BUT THEN I CAME TO MY SENSES...
...AND I THOUGHT TO MYSELF, I HAVE TO TELL HER NO.
TELL HER EVERYTHING'S FINE BACK HERE AT HOME. TELL HER TO KEEP UP THE GOOD WORK OVER IN TOKYO.
I *KNEW* I HAD TO SAY IT...
...BUT...
...THEN I THOUGHT, MAYBE IF YOU LEFT TOKYO...
...IT WOULD PUT SOME DISTANCE...
...BETWEEN YOU AND THAT BOYFRIEND OF YOURS.
THAT DAY...
...I SAW YOU OFF. I WATCHED YOU RUSH OUT OF THE HOUSE, LIMPING THE WHOLE WAY.
I HAD NO IDEA WHETHER I WAS RIGHT TO LET YOU GO...
...OR WHETH-ER I SHOULD HAVE STOPPED YOU.
EVERY TIME THE SIGHT OF YOU THAT DAY CROSSED MY MIND...

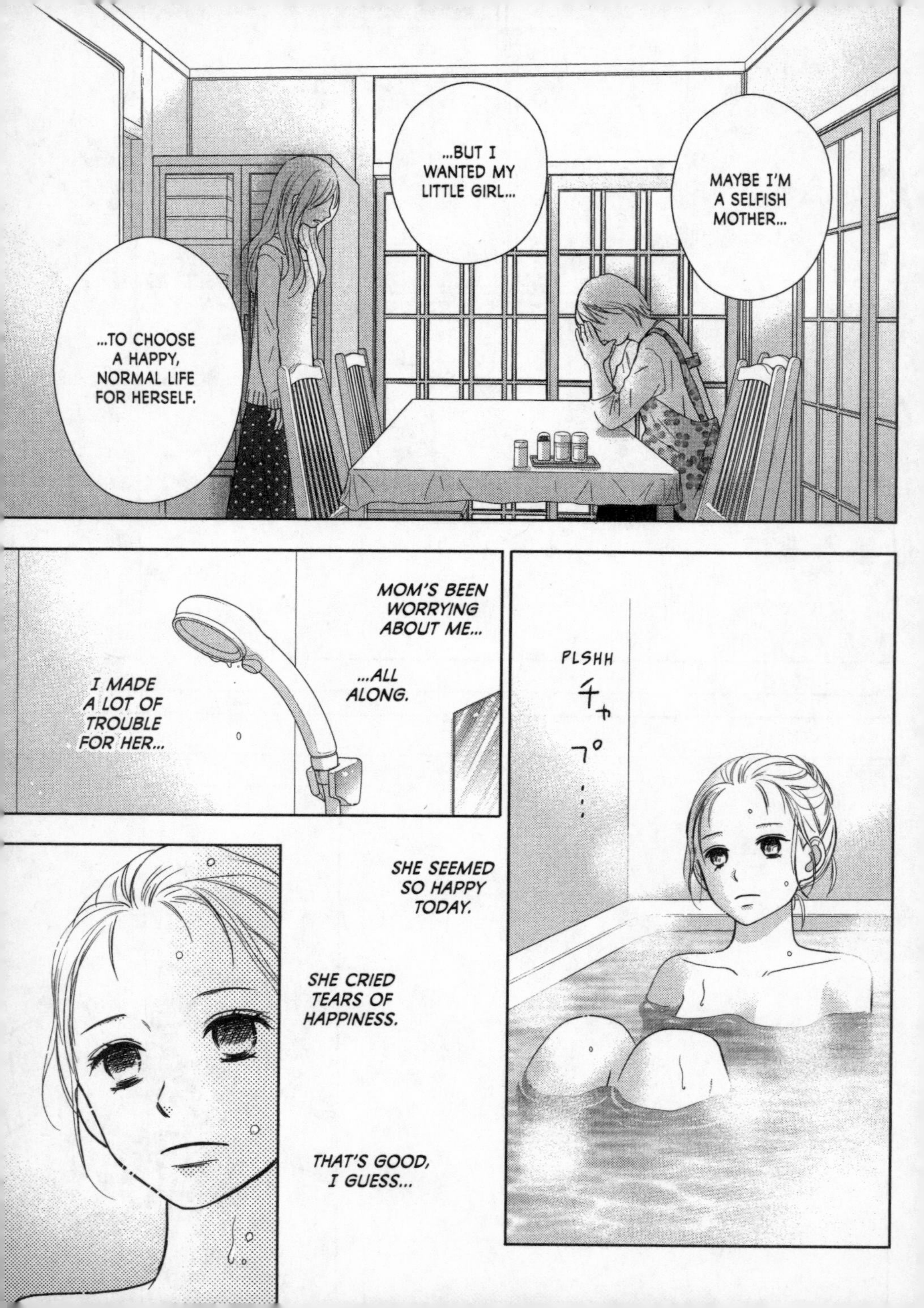
MAYBE I'M A SELFISH MOTHER...
...BUT I WANTED MY LITTLE GIRL...
...TO CHOOSE A HAPPY, NORMAL LIFE FOR HERSELF.
PLSHH
チャプ…
MOM'S BEEN WORRYING ABOUT ME...
...ALL ALONG.
I MADE A LOT OF TROUBLE FOR HER...
SHE SEEMED SO HAPPY TODAY.
SHE CRIED TEARS OF HAPPINESS.
THAT'S GOOD, I GUESS...

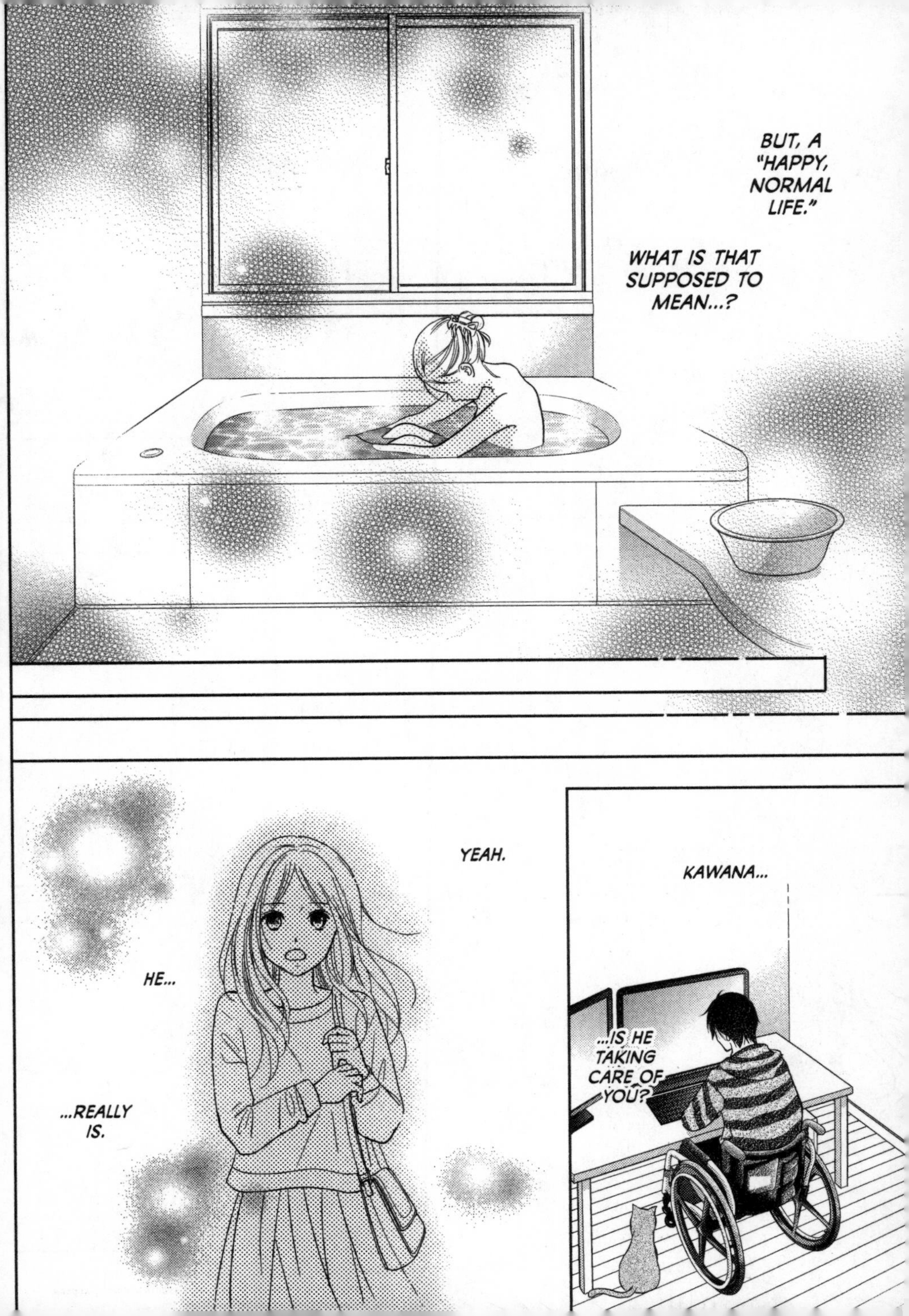
BUT, A "HAPPY, NORMAL LIFE."
WHAT IS THAT SUPPOSED TO MEAN...?
KAWANA...
...IS HE TAKING CARE OF YOU?
YEAH.
HE...
...REALLY IS.

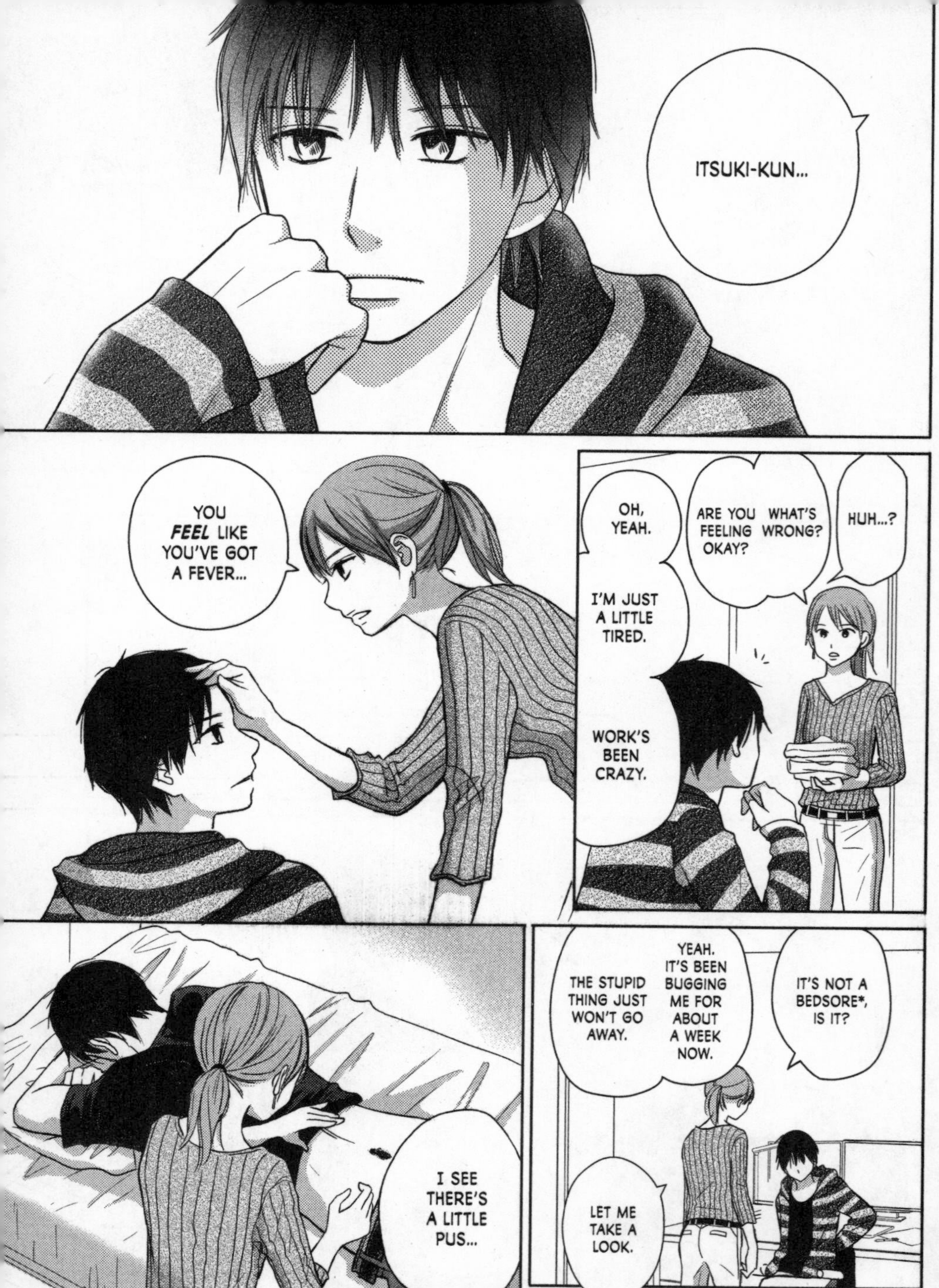
ITSUKI-KUN...
HUH...?
WHAT'S WRONG?
ARE YOU FEELING OKAY?
OH, YEAH.
I'M JUST A LITTLE TIRED.
WORK'S BEEN CRAZY.
YOU FEEL LIKE YOU'VE GOT A FEVER...
IT'S NOT A BEDSORE*, IS IT?
YEAH. IT'S BEEN BUGGING ME FOR ABOUT A WEEK NOW.
THE STUPID THING JUST WON'T GO AWAY.
LET ME TAKE A LOOK.
I SEE THERE'S A LITTLE PUS...

*Bedsore: Necrosis in soft tissue exposed to pressure or friction (for example, by a wheelchair) most often seen in people who spend

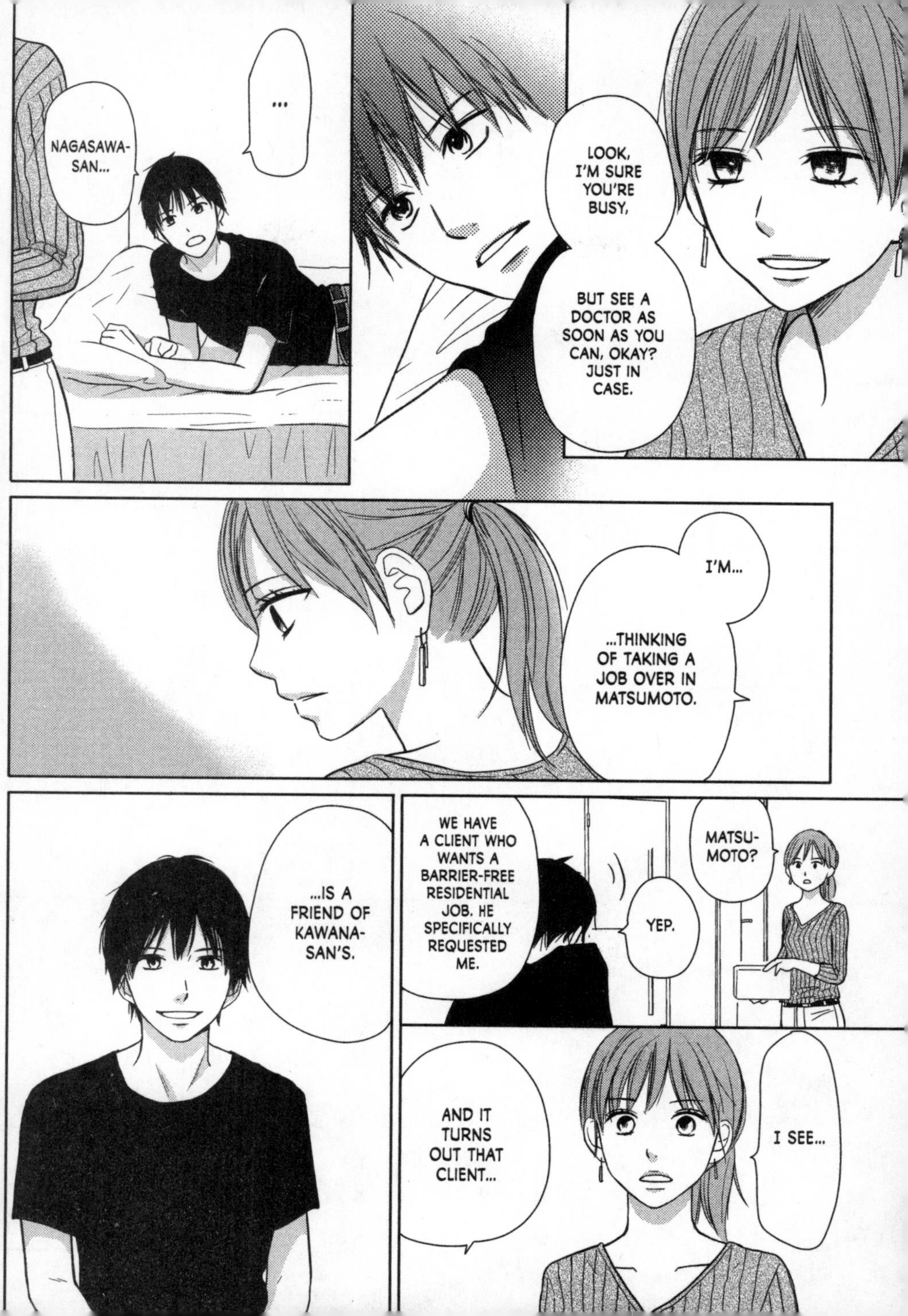
LOOK, I'M SURE YOU'RE BUSY,
BUT SEE A DOCTOR AS SOON AS YOU CAN, OKAY? JUST IN CASE.
...
NAGASAWA-SAN...
I'M...
...THINKING OF TAKING A JOB OVER IN MATSUMOTO.
MATSU-MOTO?
YEP.
WE HAVE A CLIENT WHO WANTS A BARRIER-FREE RESIDENTIAL JOB. HE SPECIFICALLY REQUESTED ME.
I SEE...
AND IT TURNS OUT THAT CLIENT...
...IS A FRIEND OF KAWANA-SAN'S.

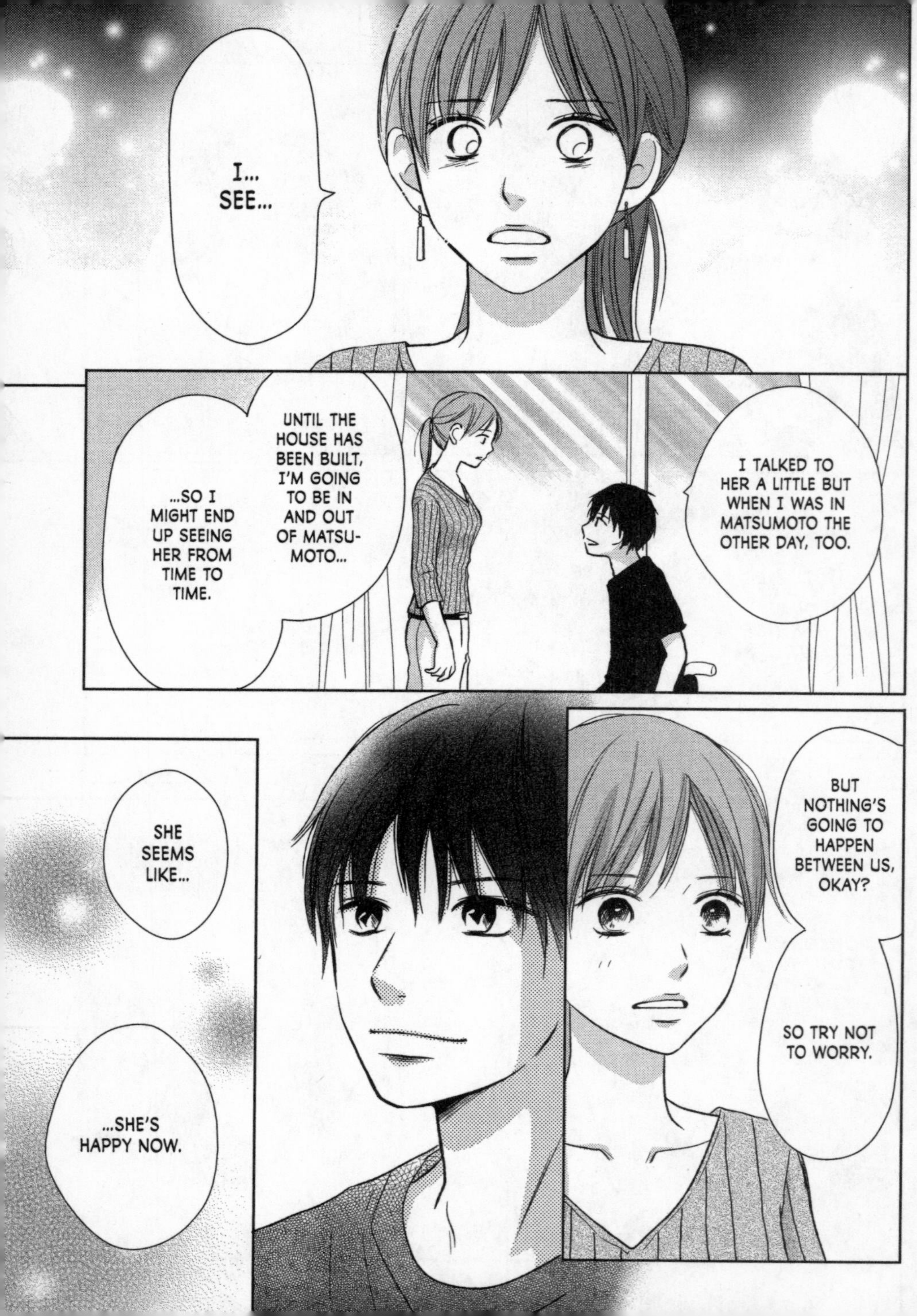
I... SEE...
I TALKED TO HER A LITTLE BUT WHEN I WAS IN MATSUMOTO THE OTHER DAY, TOO.
UNTIL THE HOUSE HAS BEEN BUILT, I'M GOING TO BE IN AND OUT OF MATSU-MOTO...
...SO I MIGHT END UP SEEING HER FROM TIME TO TIME.
BUT NOTHING'S GOING TO HAPPEN BETWEEN US, OKAY?
SO TRY NOT TO WORRY.
SHE SEEMS LIKE...
...SHE'S HAPPY NOW.

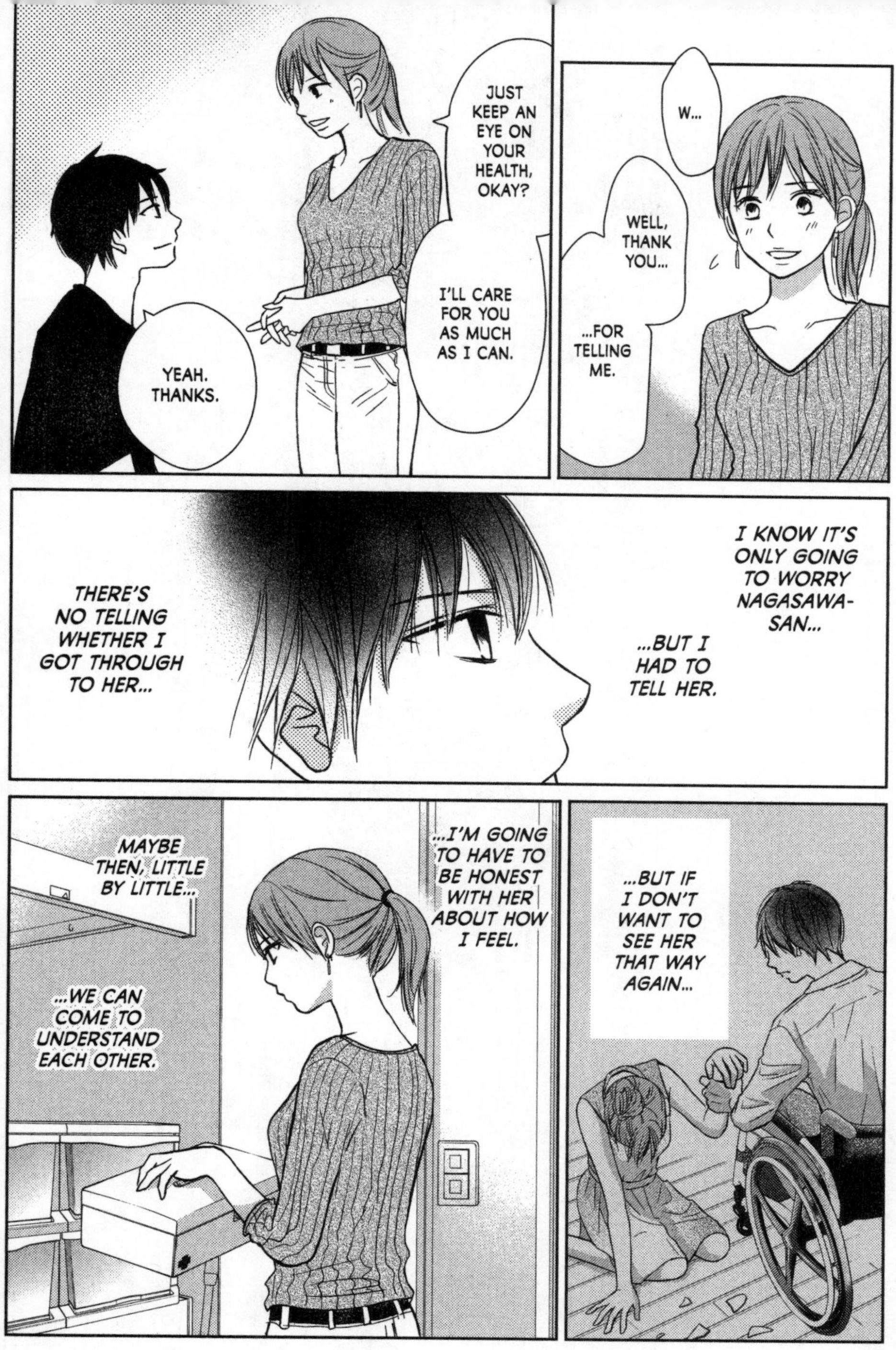
W...
WELL, THANK YOU...
...FOR TELLING ME.
JUST KEEP AN EYE ON YOUR HEALTH, OKAY?
I'LL CARE FOR YOU AS MUCH AS I CAN.
YEAH. THANKS.
I KNOW IT'S ONLY GOING TO WORRY NAGASAWA-SAN...
...BUT I HAD TO TELL HER.
THERE'S NO TELLING WHETHER I GOT THROUGH TO HER...
...BUT IF I DON'T WANT TO SEE HER THAT WAY AGAIN...
...I'M GOING TO HAVE TO BE HONEST WITH HER ABOUT HOW I FEEL.
MAYBE THEN, LITTLE BY LITTLE...
...WE CAN COME TO UNDERSTAND EACH OTHER.

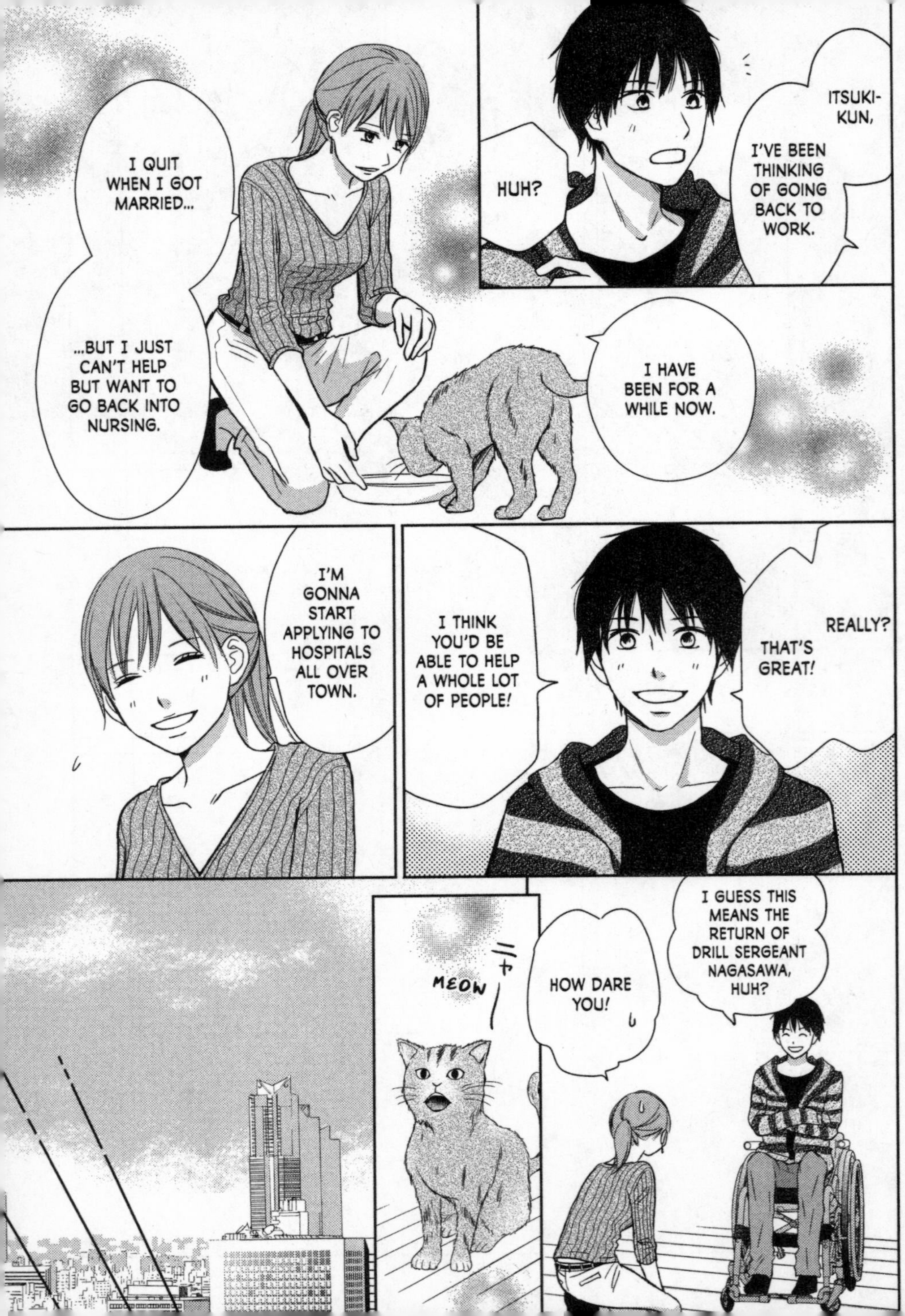
ITSUKI-KUN,
I'VE BEEN THINKING OF GOING BACK TO WORK.
HUH?
I HAVE BEEN FOR A WHILE NOW.
I QUIT WHEN I GOT MARRIED...
...BUT I JUST CAN'T HELP BUT WANT TO GO BACK INTO NURSING.
REALLY?
THAT'S GREAT!
I THINK YOU'D BE ABLE TO HELP A WHOLE LOT OF PEOPLE!
I'M GONNA START APPLYING TO HOSPITALS ALL OVER TOWN.
I GUESS THIS MEANS THE RETURN OF DRILL SERGEANT NAGASAWA, HUH?
HOW DARE YOU!
ニャ
MEOW

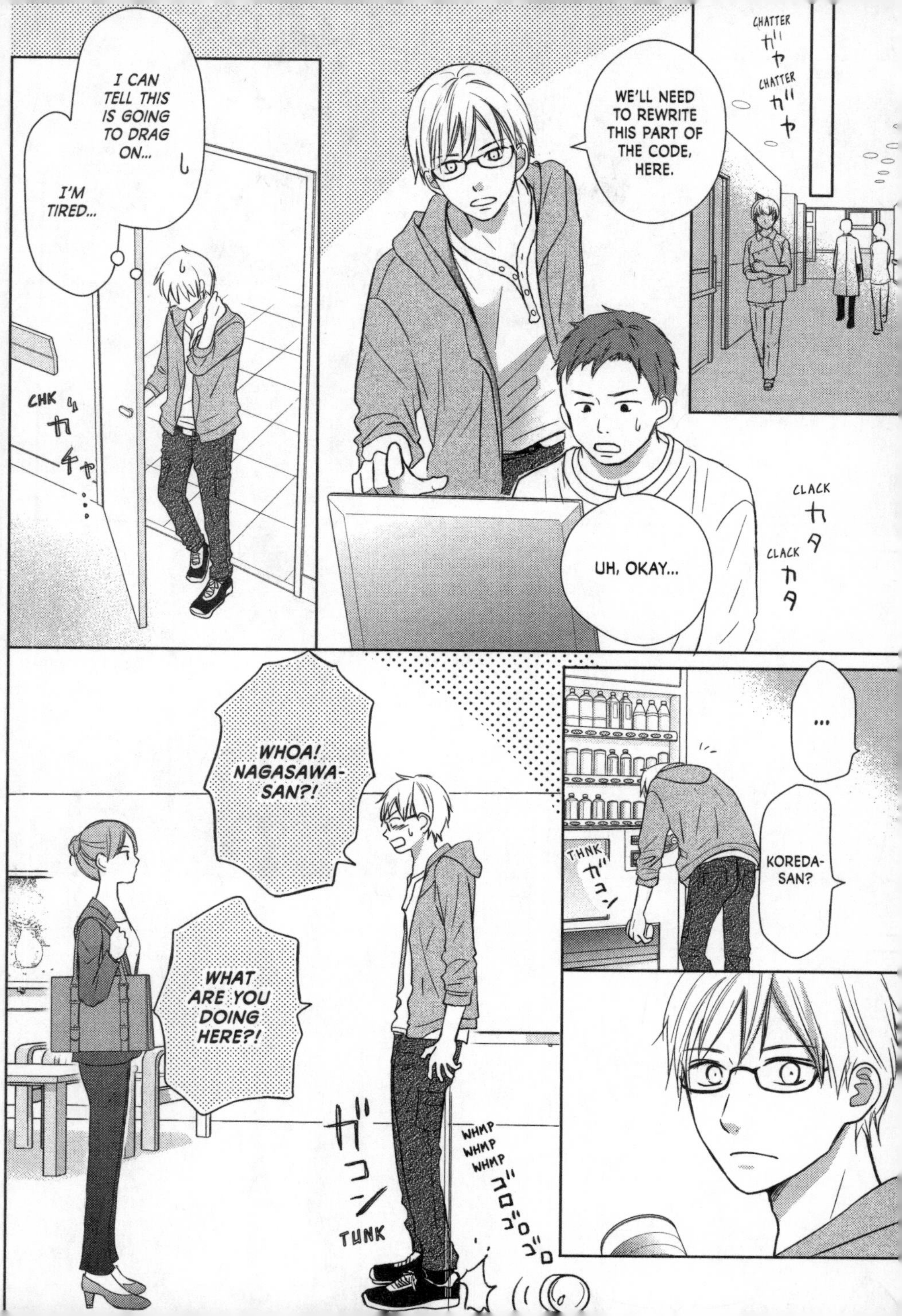
CHATTER
ガヤ
CHATTER
ガヤ
WE'LL NEED TO REWRITE THIS PART OF THE CODE, HERE.
UH, OKAY...
CLACK
カタ
CLACK
カタ
I CAN TELL THIS IS GOING TO DRAG ON...
I'M TIRED...
CHK
カチャ
...
KOREDA-SAN?
THNK
ガコン
WHOA! NAGASAWA-SAN?!
WHAT ARE YOU DOING HERE?!
ガコン
TUNK
WHMP
WHMP
WHMP
ゴロゴロ

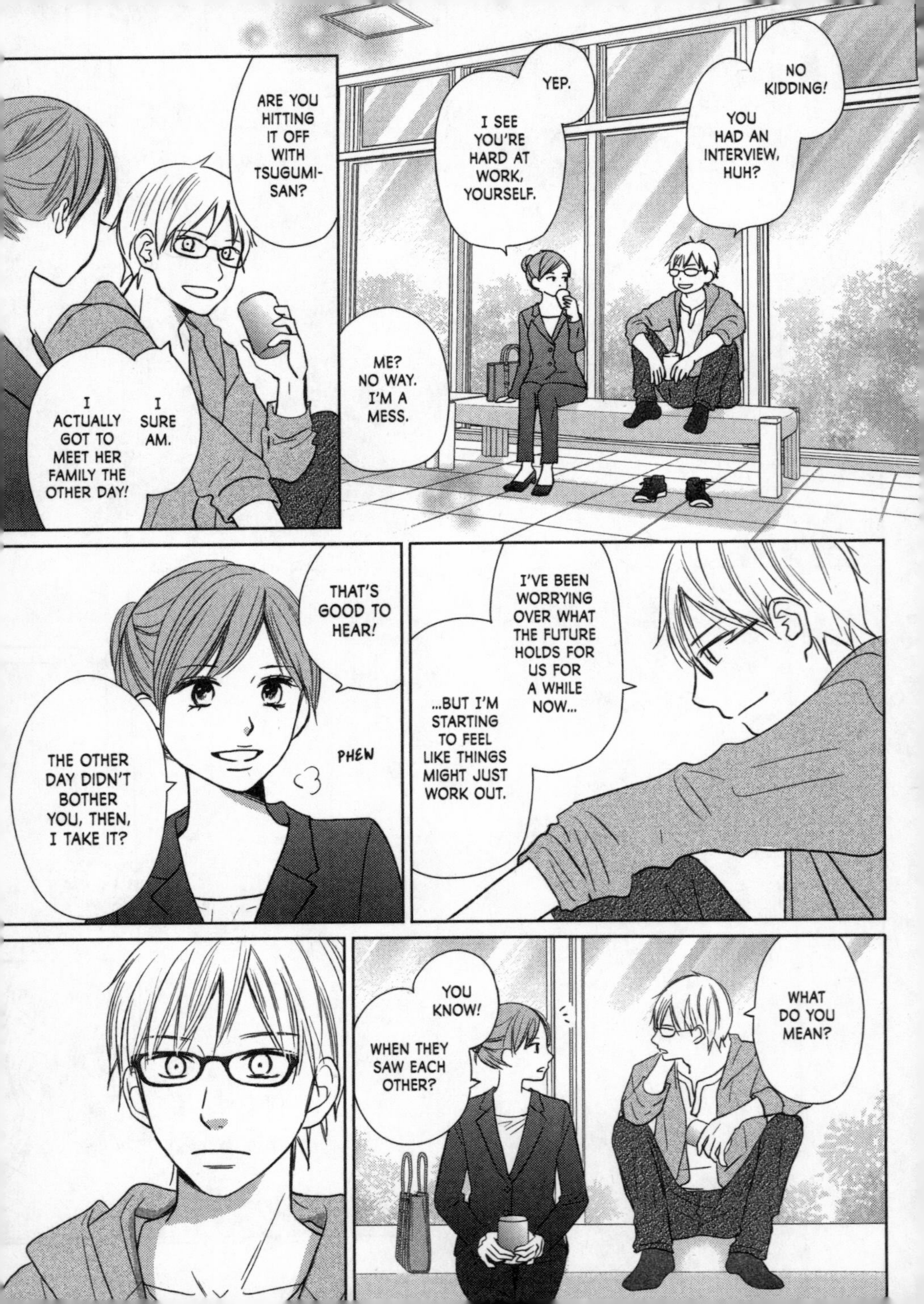
NO KIDDING!
YOU HAD AN INTERVIEW, HUH?
YEP.
I SEE YOU'RE HARD AT WORK, YOURSELF.
ME? NO WAY. I'M A MESS.
ARE YOU HITTING IT OFF WITH TSUGUMI-SAN?
I SURE AM.
I ACTUALLY GOT TO MEET HER FAMILY THE OTHER DAY!
I'VE BEEN WORRYING OVER WHAT THE FUTURE HOLDS FOR US FOR A WHILE NOW...
...BUT I'M STARTING TO FEEL LIKE THINGS MIGHT JUST WORK OUT.
THAT'S GOOD TO HEAR!
PHEW
THE OTHER DAY DIDN'T BOTHER YOU, THEN, I TAKE IT?
WHAT DO YOU MEAN?
YOU KNOW!
WHEN THEY SAW EACH OTHER?

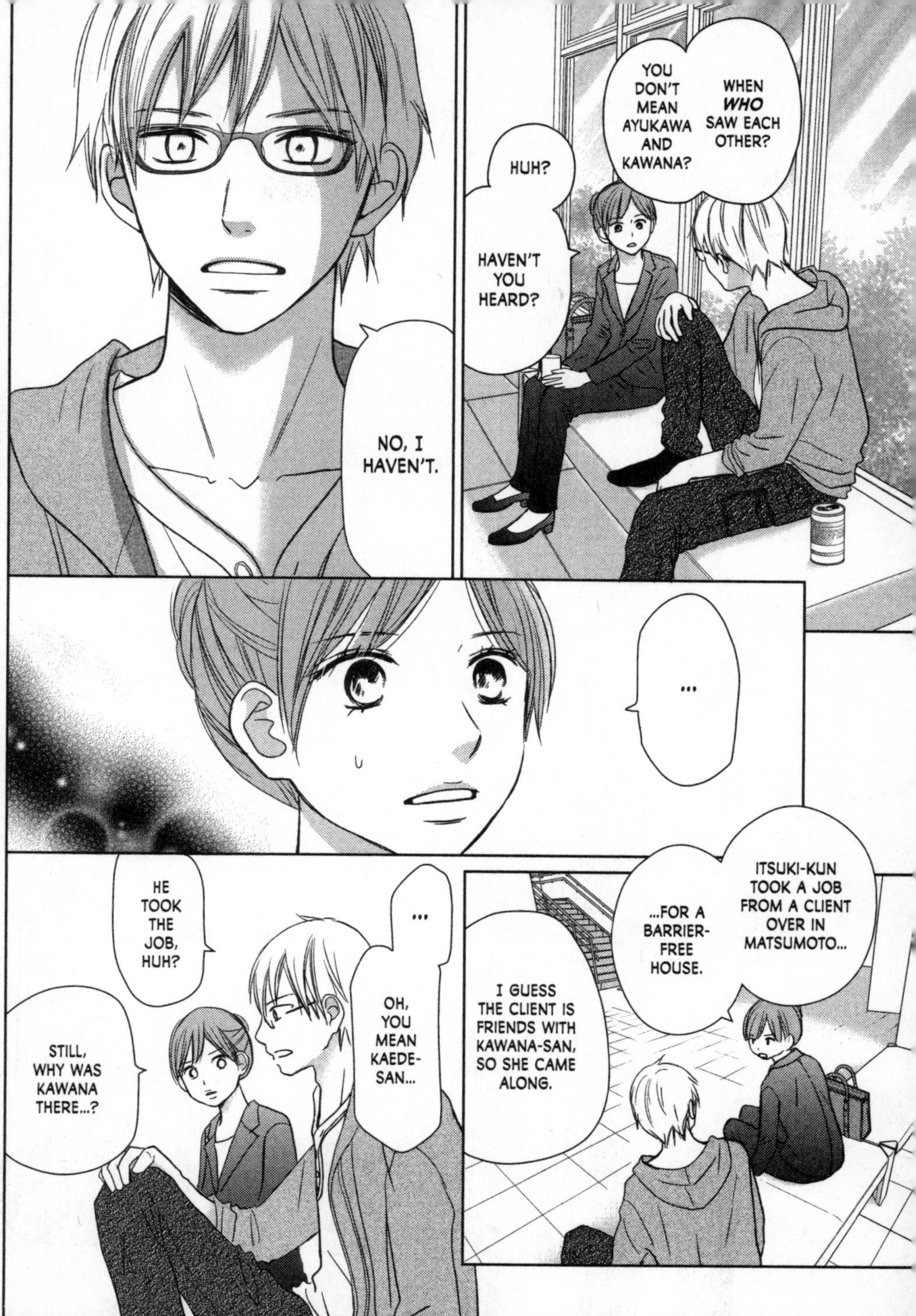
WHEN WHO SAW EACH OTHER?
YOU DON'T MEAN AYUKAWA AND KAWANA?
HUH?
HAVEN'T YOU HEARD?
NO, I HAVEN'T.
...
ITSUKI-KUN TOOK A JOB FROM A CLIENT OVER IN MATSUMOTO...
...FOR A BARRIER-FREE HOUSE.
I GUESS THE CLIENT IS FRIENDS WITH KAWANA-SAN, SO SHE CAME ALONG.
...
HE TOOK THE JOB, HUH?
OH, YOU MEAN KAEDE-SAN...
STILL, WHY WAS KAWANA THERE...?

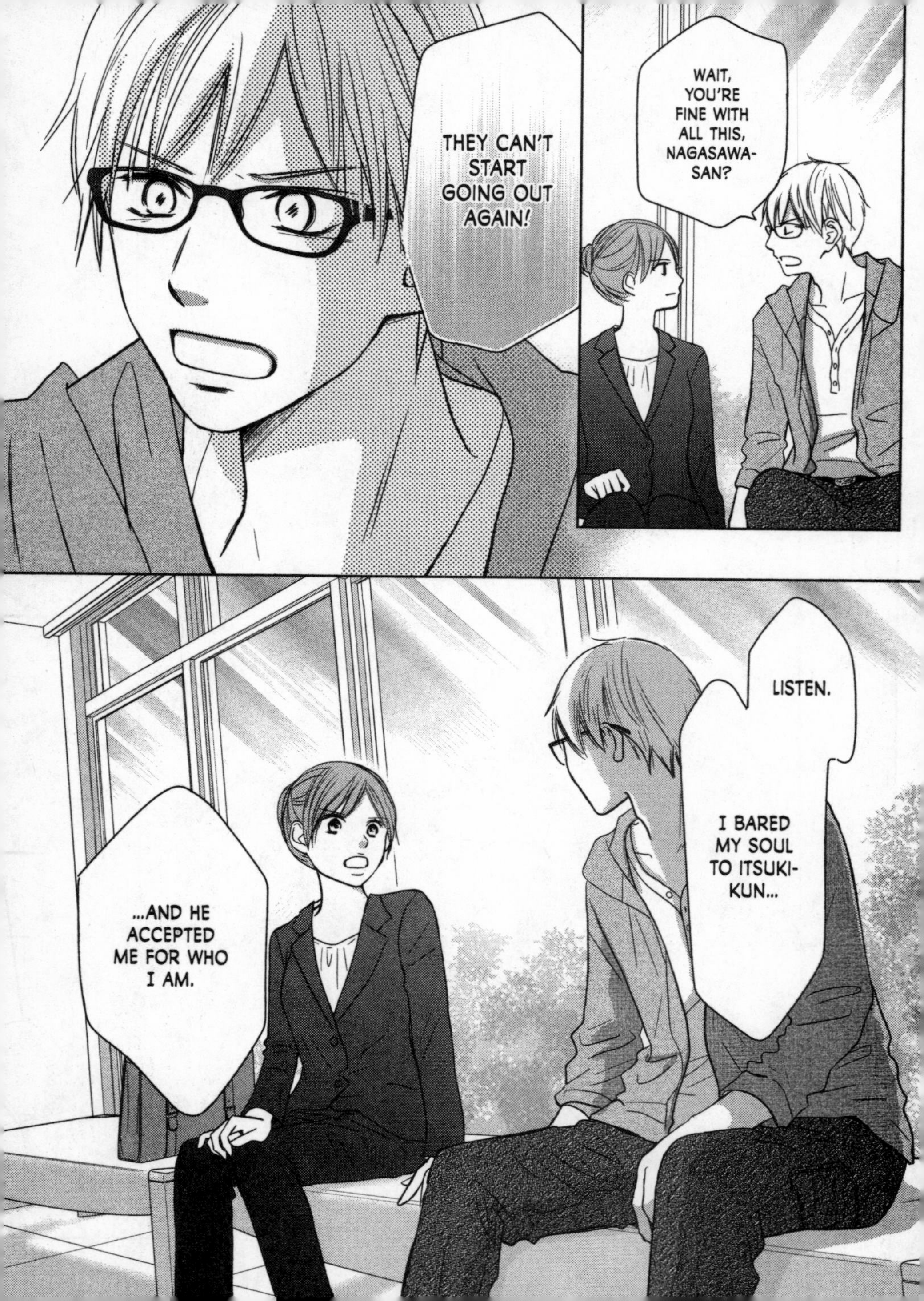
WAIT, YOU'RE FINE WITH ALL THIS, NAGASAWA-SAN?
THEY CAN'T START GOING OUT AGAIN!
LISTEN.
I BARED MY SOUL TO ITSUKI-KUN...
...AND HE ACCEPTED ME FOR WHO I AM.

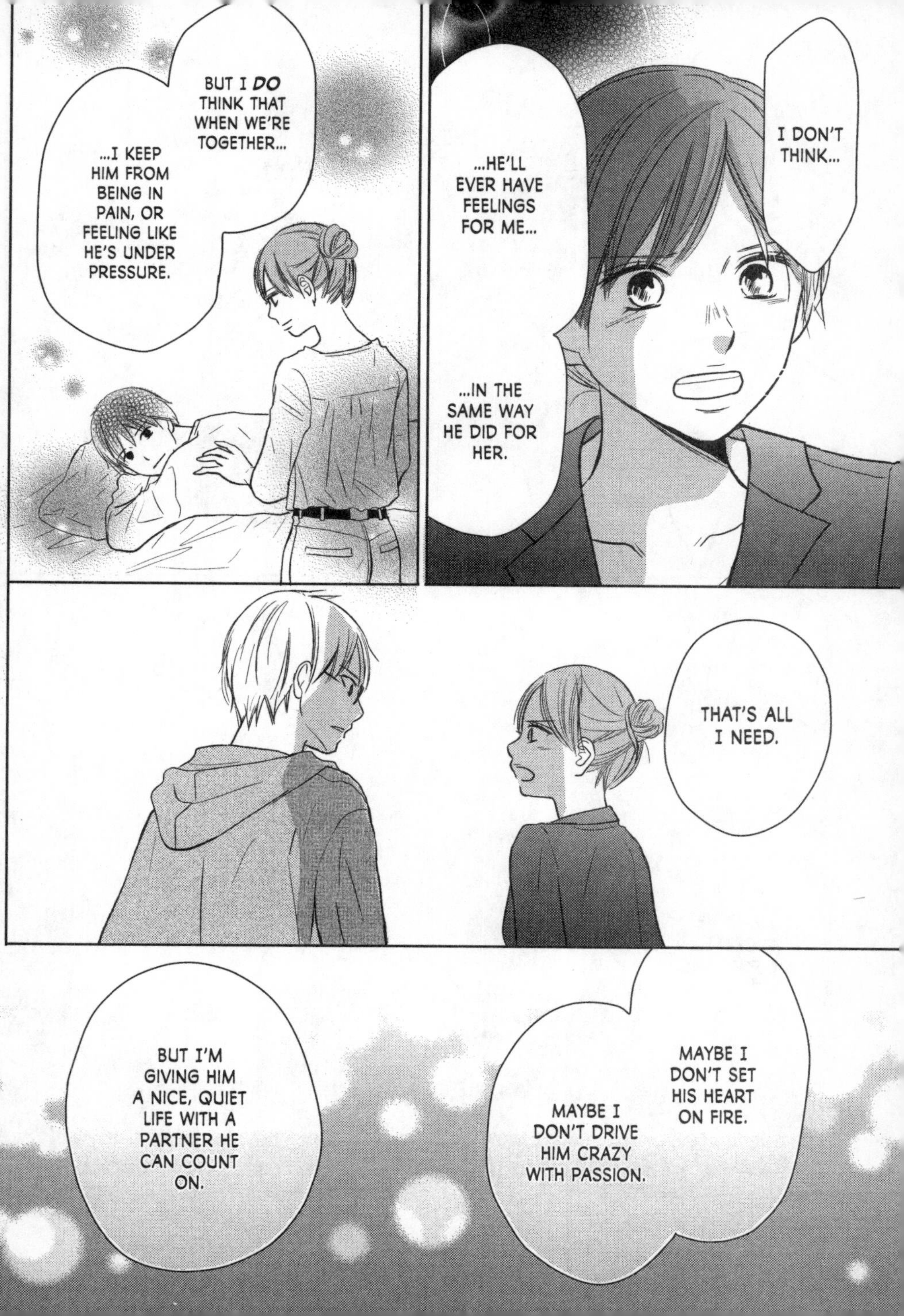
I DON'T THINK...
...HE'LL EVER HAVE FEELINGS FOR ME...
...IN THE SAME WAY HE DID FOR HER.
BUT I DO THINK THAT WHEN WE'RE TOGETHER...
...I KEEP HIM FROM BEING IN PAIN, OR FEELING LIKE HE'S UNDER PRESSURE.
THAT'S ALL I NEED.
MAYBE I DON'T SET HIS HEART ON FIRE.
MAYBE I DON'T DRIVE HIM CRAZY WITH PASSION.
BUT I'M GIVING HIM A NICE, QUIET LIFE WITH A PARTNER HE CAN COUNT ON.

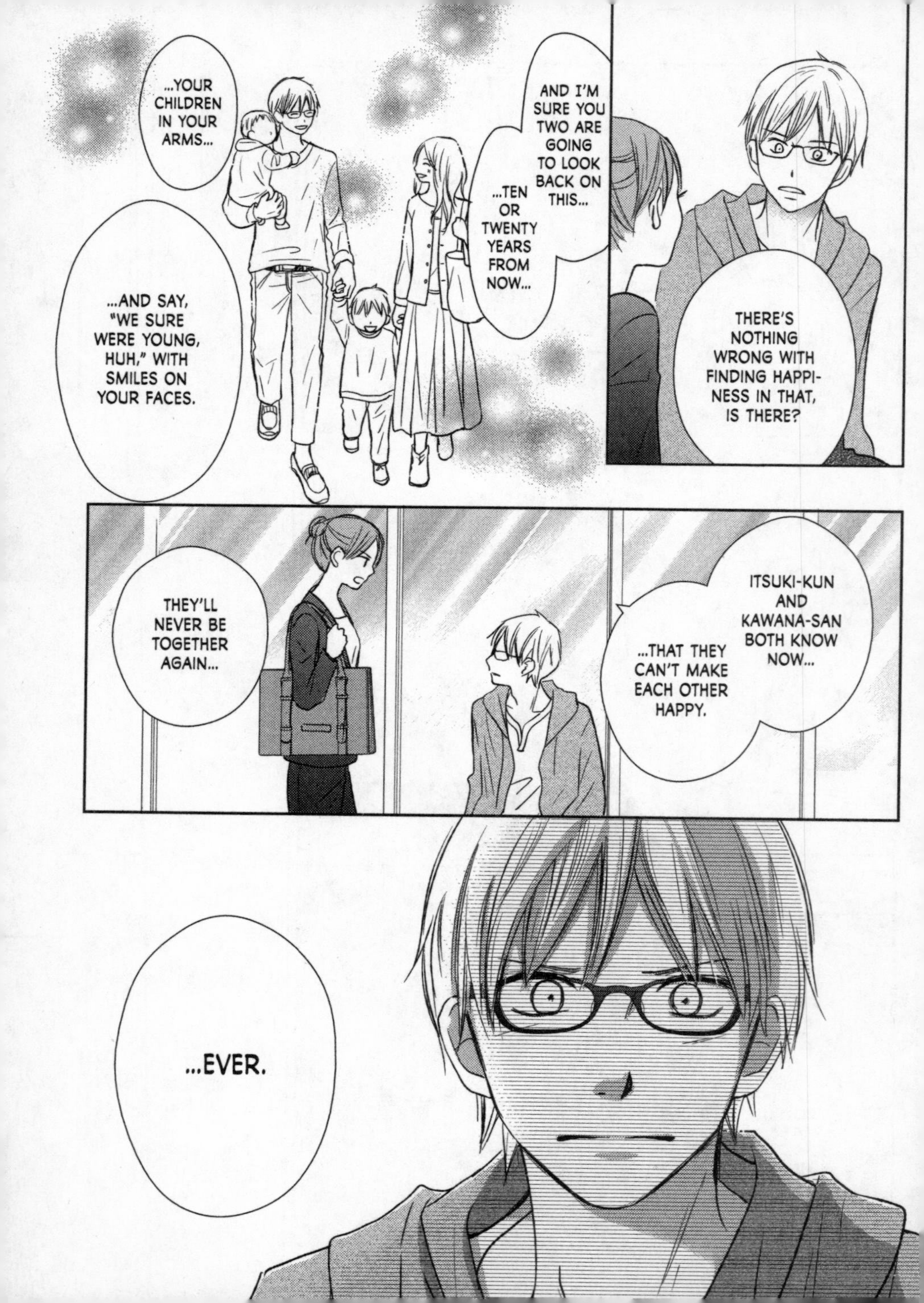
THERE'S NOTHING WRONG WITH FINDING HAPPINESS IN THAT, IS THERE?
AND I'M SURE YOU TWO ARE GOING TO LOOK BACK ON THIS...
...TEN OR TWENTY YEARS FROM NOW...
...YOUR CHILDREN IN YOUR ARMS...
...AND SAY, "WE SURE WERE YOUNG, HUH," WITH SMILES ON YOUR FACES.
ITSUKI-KUN AND KAWANA-SAN BOTH KNOW NOW...
...THAT THEY CAN'T MAKE EACH OTHER HAPPY.
THEY'LL NEVER BE TOGETHER AGAIN...
...EVER.

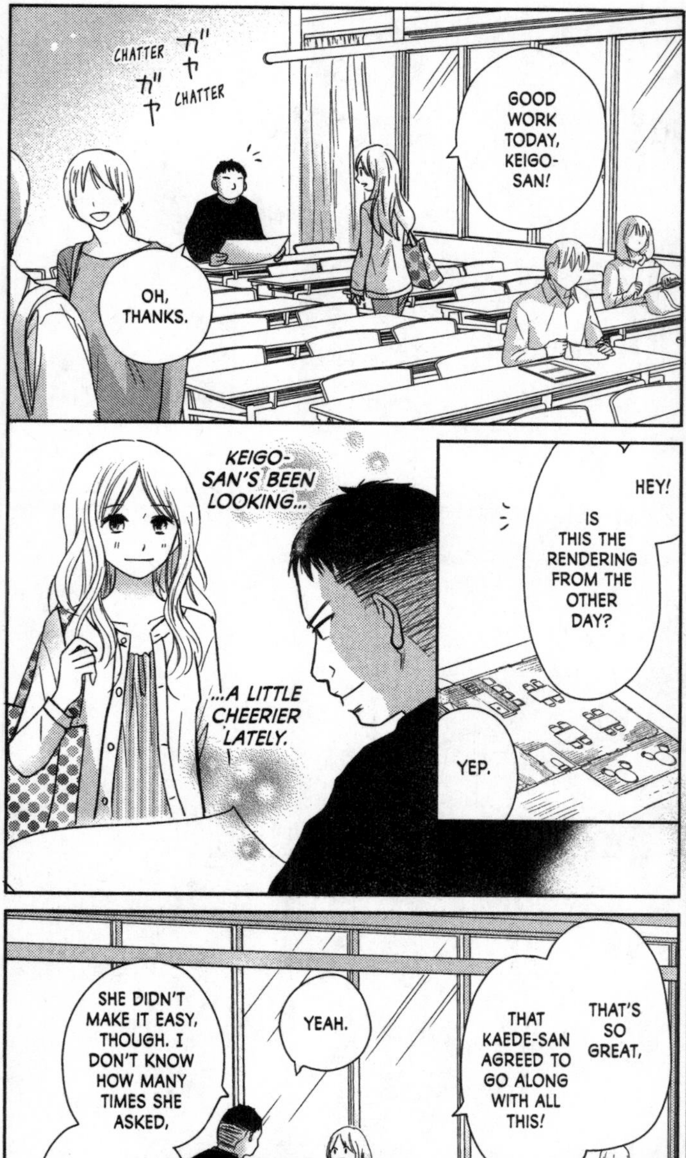
GOOD WORK TODAY, KEIGO-SAN!
CHATTER ガヤ
ガヤ CHATTER
OH, THANKS.
HEY!
IS THIS THE RENDERING FROM THE OTHER DAY?
YEP.
KEIGO-SAN'S BEEN LOOKING...
...A LITTLE CHEERIER LATELY.
THAT'S SO GREAT,
THAT KAEDE-SAN AGREED TO GO ALONG WITH ALL THIS!
YEAH.
SHE DIDN'T MAKE IT EASY, THOUGH. I DON'T KNOW HOW MANY TIMES SHE ASKED,
"ARE YOU REALLY SURE I'M RIGHT FOR YOU?"

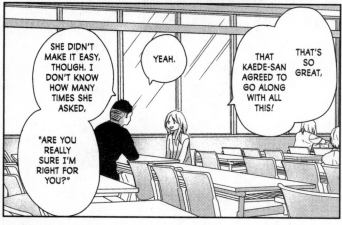

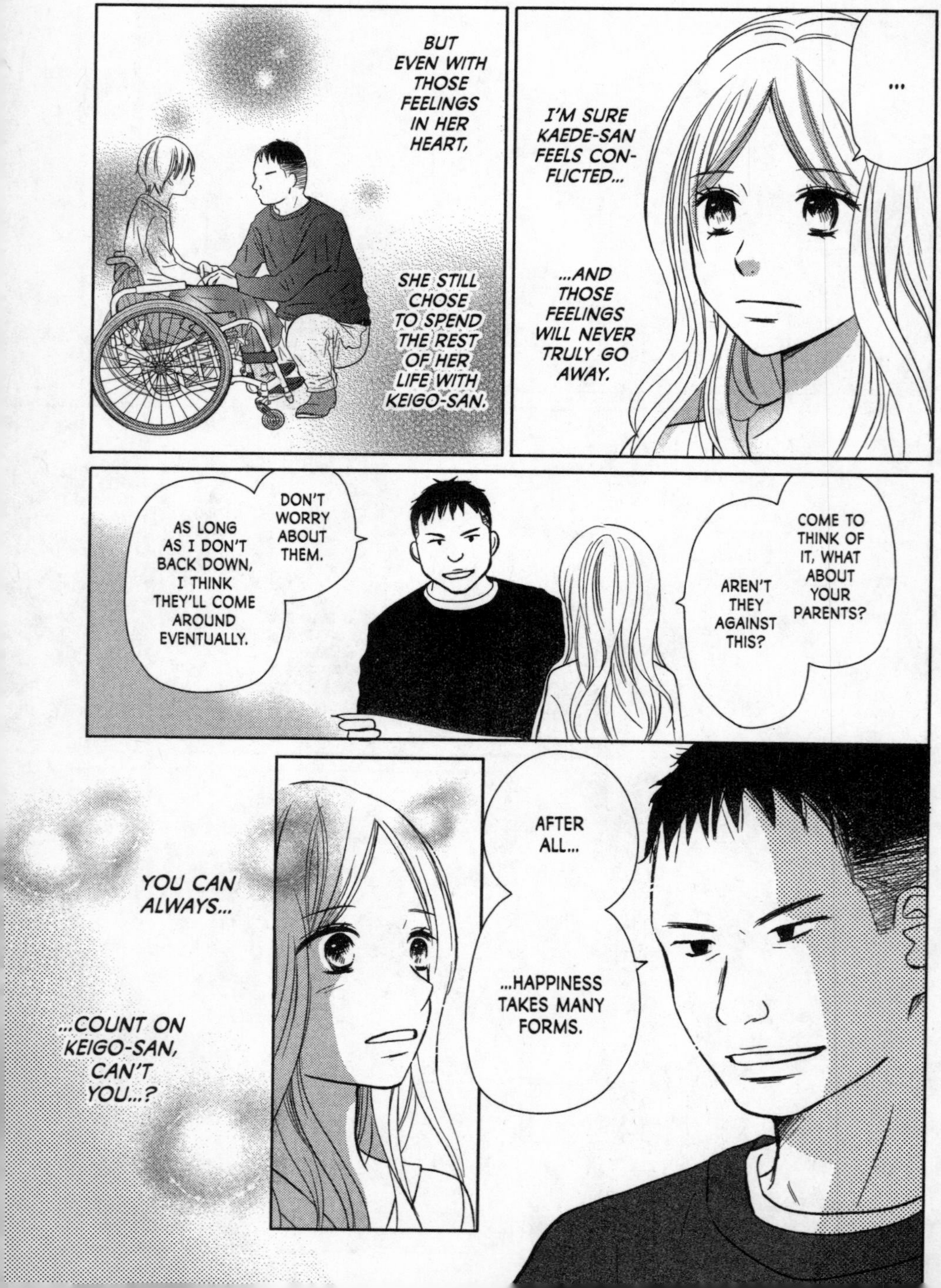
...
I'M SURE KAEDE-SAN FEELS CONFLICTED...
...AND THOSE FEELINGS WILL NEVER TRULY GO AWAY.
BUT EVEN WITH THOSE FEELINGS IN HER HEART,
SHE STILL CHOSE TO SPEND THE REST OF HER LIFE WITH KEIGO-SAN.
COME TO THINK OF IT, WHAT ABOUT YOUR PARENTS?
AREN'T THEY AGAINST THIS?
DON'T WORRY ABOUT THEM.
AS LONG AS I DON'T BACK DOWN, I THINK THEY'LL COME AROUND EVENTUALLY.
AFTER ALL...
...HAPPINESS TAKES MANY FORMS.
YOU CAN ALWAYS...
...COUNT ON KEIGO-SAN, CAN'T YOU...?

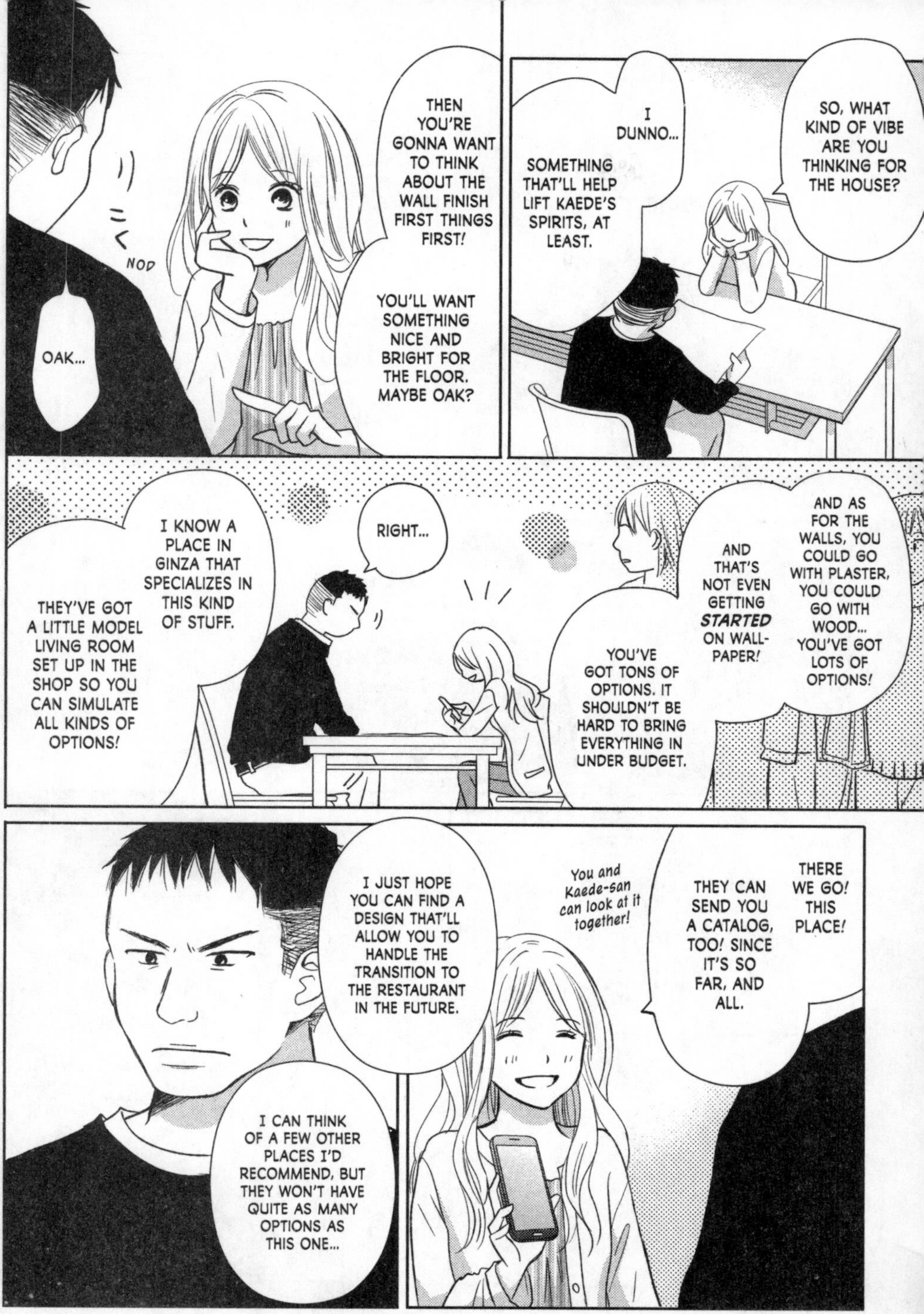
SO, WHAT KIND OF VIBE ARE YOU THINKING FOR THE HOUSE?
I DUNNO...
SOMETHING THAT'LL HELP LIFT KAEDE'S SPIRITS, AT LEAST.
THEN YOU'RE GONNA WANT TO THINK ABOUT THE WALL FINISH FIRST THINGS FIRST!
YOU'LL WANT SOMETHING NICE AND BRIGHT FOR THE FLOOR. MAYBE OAK?
NOD
OAK...
AND AS FOR THE WALLS, YOU COULD GO WITH PLASTER, YOU COULD GO WITH WOOD... YOU'VE GOT LOTS OF OPTIONS!
AND THAT'S NOT EVEN GETTING ***STARTED*** ON WALL-PAPER!
YOU'VE GOT TONS OF OPTIONS. IT SHOULDN'T BE HARD TO BRING EVERYTHING IN UNDER BUDGET.
RIGHT...
I KNOW A PLACE IN GINZA THAT SPECIALIZES IN THIS KIND OF STUFF.
THEY'VE GOT A LITTLE MODEL LIVING ROOM SET UP IN THE SHOP SO YOU CAN SIMULATE ALL KINDS OF OPTIONS!
THERE WE GO! THIS PLACE!
THEY CAN SEND YOU A CATALOG, TOO! SINCE IT'S SO FAR, AND ALL.
You and Kaede-san can look at it together!
I JUST HOPE YOU CAN FIND A DESIGN THAT'LL ALLOW YOU TO HANDLE THE TRANSITION TO THE RESTAURANT IN THE FUTURE.
I CAN THINK OF A FEW OTHER PLACES I'D RECOMMEND, BUT THEY WON'T HAVE QUITE AS MANY OPTIONS AS THIS ONE...

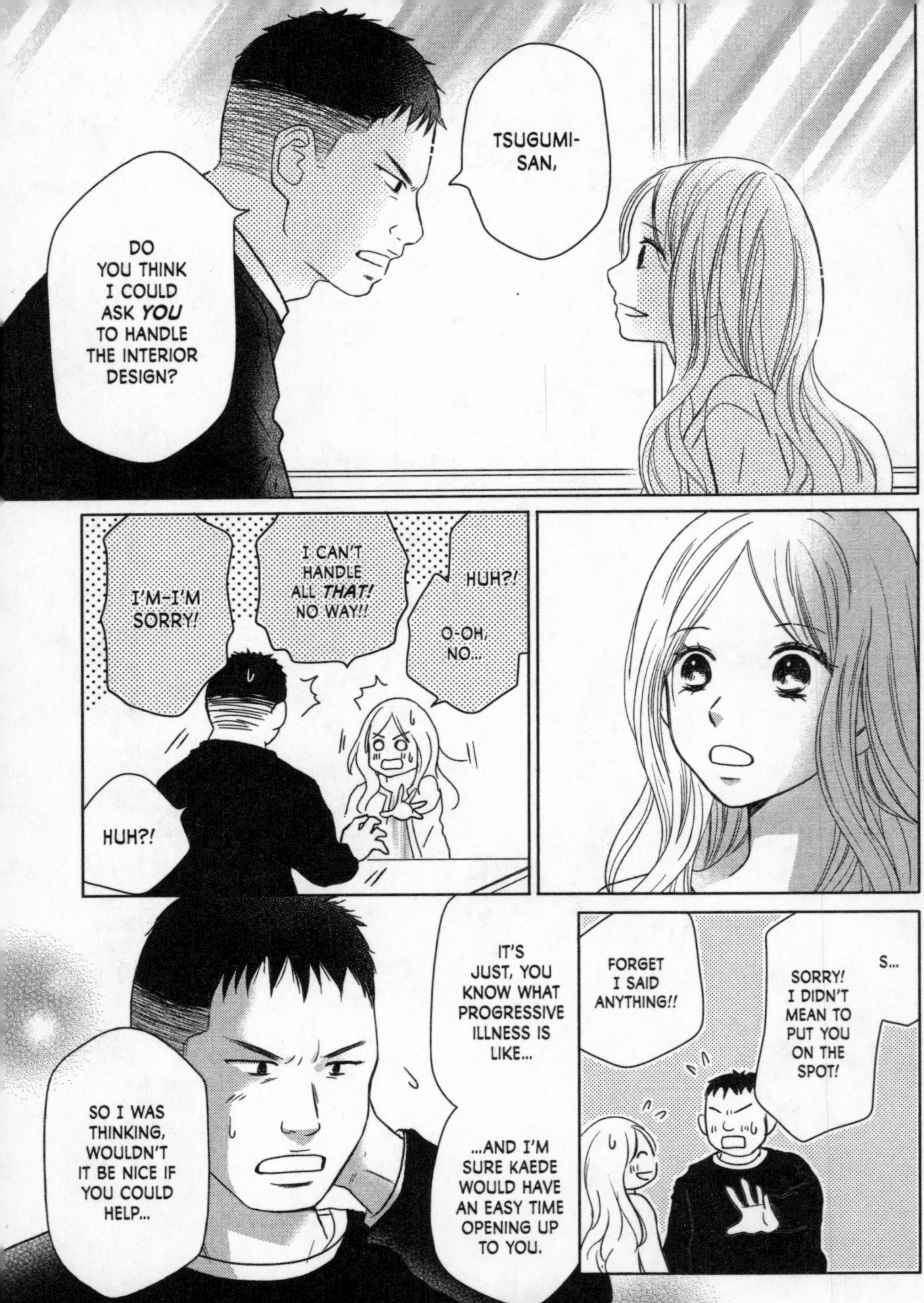
TSUGUMI-SAN,
DO YOU THINK I COULD ASK *YOU* TO HANDLE THE INTERIOR DESIGN?
HUH?!
O-OH, NO...
I CAN'T HANDLE ALL *THAT!* NO WAY!!
I'M-I'M SORRY!
HUH?!
S...
SORRY! I DIDN'T MEAN TO PUT YOU ON THE SPOT!
FORGET I SAID ANYTHING!!
IT'S JUST, YOU KNOW WHAT PROGRESSIVE ILLNESS IS LIKE...
...AND I'M SURE KAEDE WOULD HAVE AN EASY TIME OPENING UP TO YOU.
SO I WAS THINKING, WOULDN'T IT BE NICE IF YOU COULD HELP...

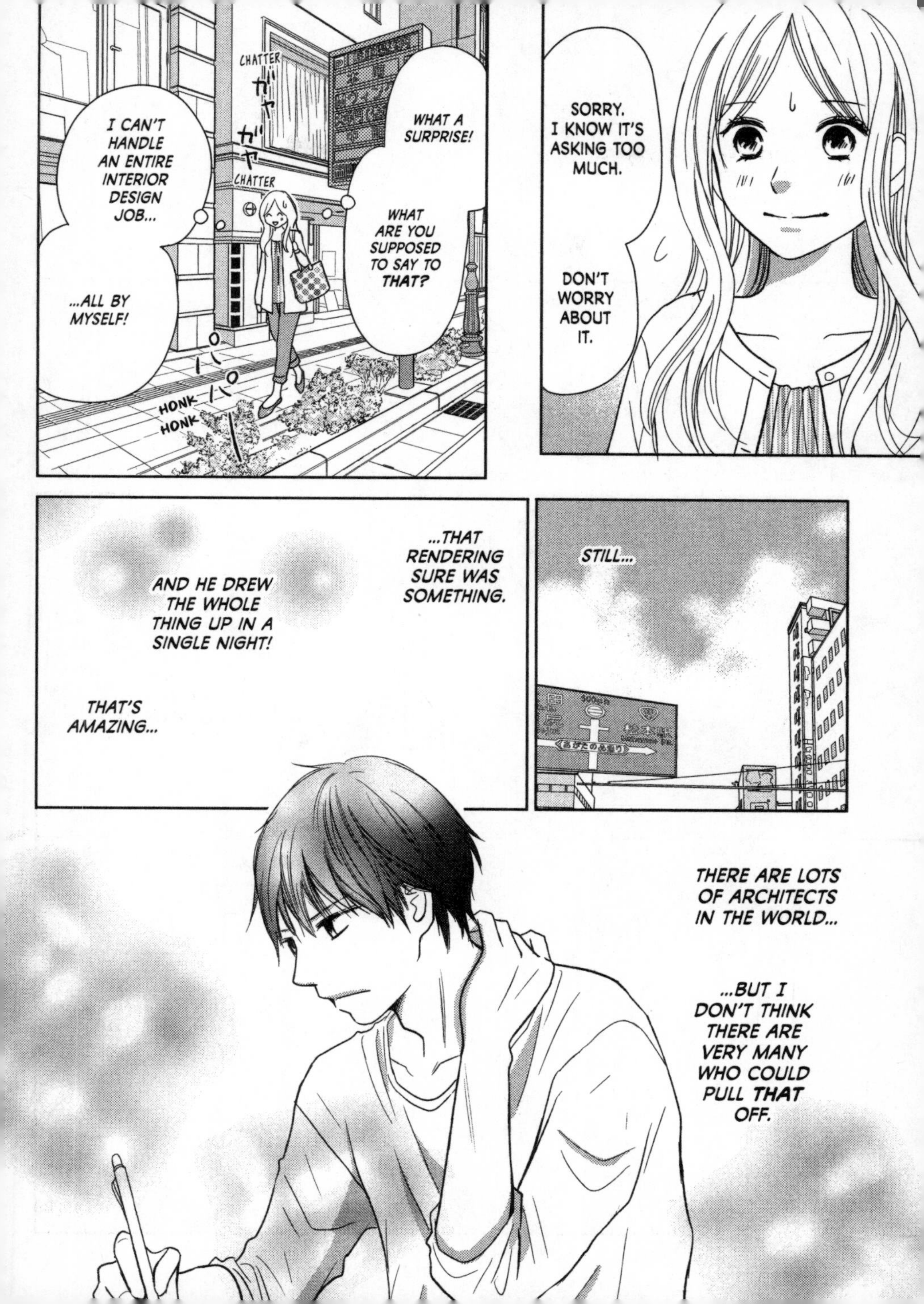
SORRY. I KNOW IT'S ASKING TOO MUCH.
DON'T WORRY ABOUT IT.
WHAT A SURPRISE!
WHAT ARE YOU SUPPOSED TO SAY TO THAT?
CHATTER
ガヤ
ガヤ
CHATTER
I CAN'T HANDLE AN ENTIRE INTERIOR DESIGN JOB...
...ALL BY MYSELF!
パ
パ
HONK
HONK
STILL...
...THAT RENDERING SURE WAS SOMETHING.
AND HE DREW THE WHOLE THING UP IN A SINGLE NIGHT!
THAT'S AMAZING...
THERE ARE LOTS OF ARCHITECTS IN THE WORLD...
...BUT I DON'T THINK THERE ARE VERY MANY WHO COULD PULL THAT OFF.

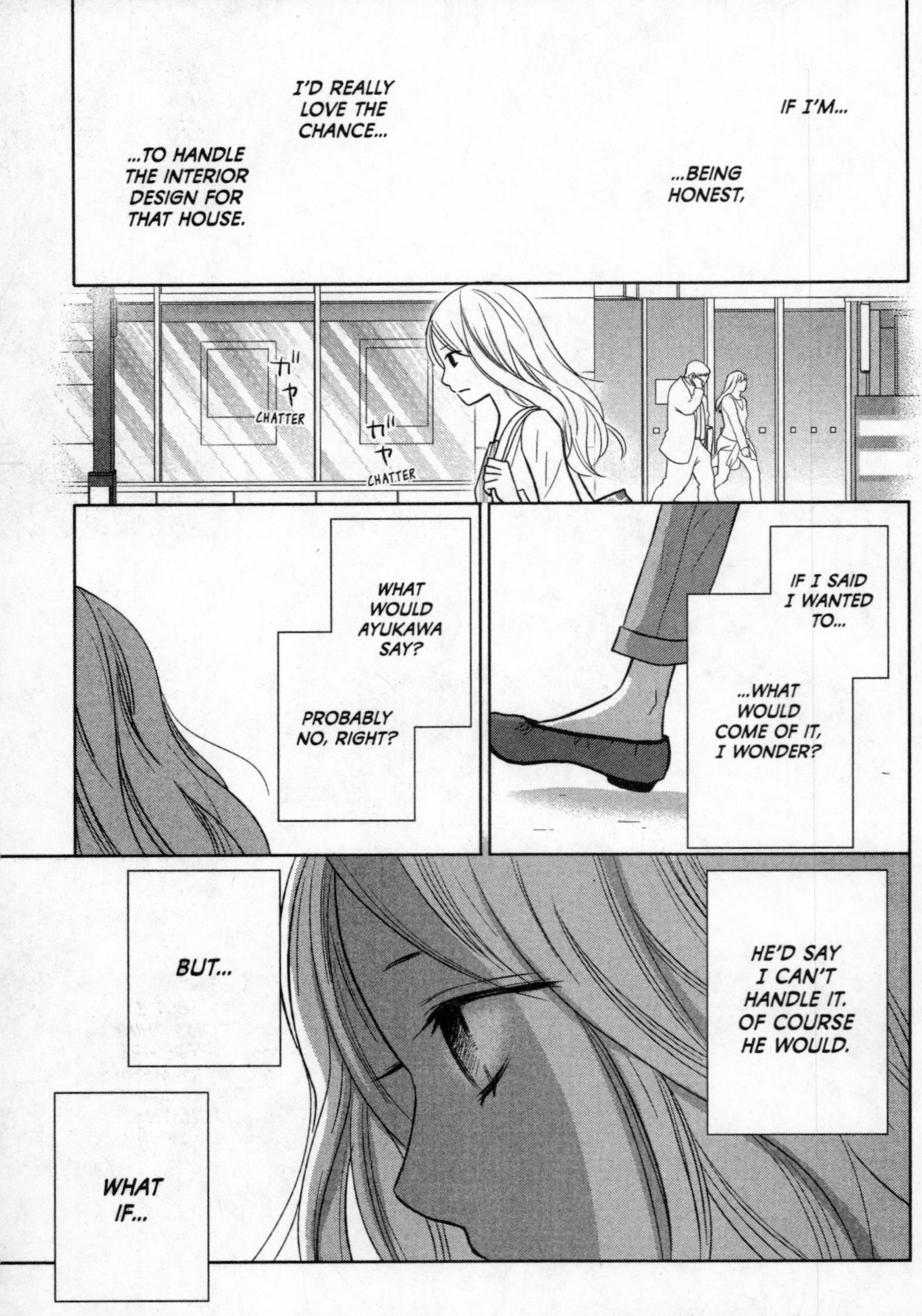

IF I'M...
...BEING HONEST,
I'D REALLY LOVE THE CHANCE...
...TO HANDLE THE INTERIOR DESIGN FOR THAT HOUSE.
ガヤ
CHATTER
ガヤ
CHATTER
IF I SAID I WANTED TO...
...WHAT WOULD COME OF IT, I WONDER?
WHAT WOULD AYUKAWA SAY?
PROBABLY NO, RIGHT?
HE'D SAY I CAN'T HANDLE IT. OF COURSE HE WOULD.
BUT...
WHAT IF...

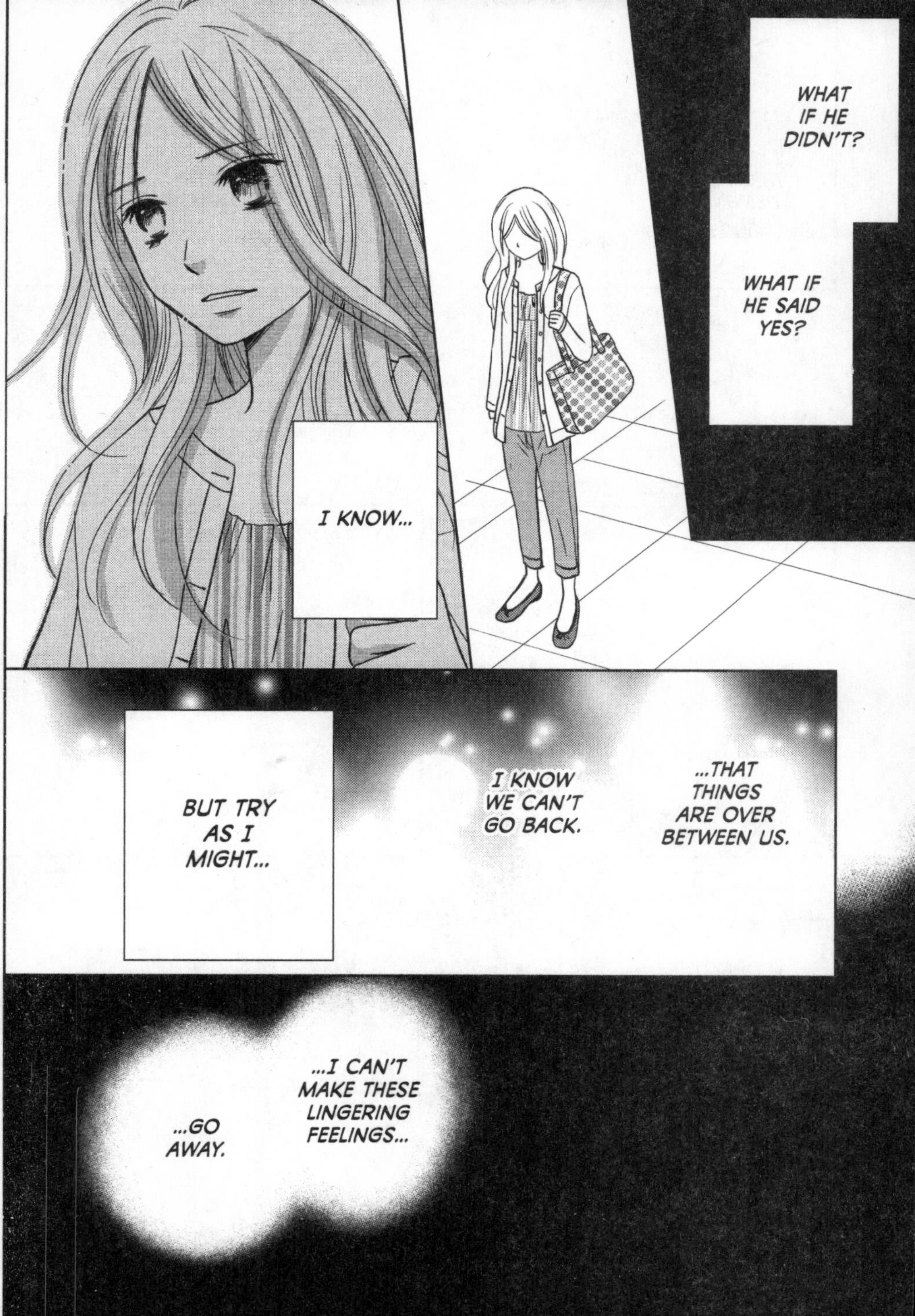
WHAT IF HE DIDN'T?
WHAT IF HE SAID YES?
I KNOW...
...THAT THINGS ARE OVER BETWEEN US.
I KNOW WE CAN'T GO BACK.
BUT TRY AS I MIGHT...
...I CAN'T MAKE THESE LINGERING FEELINGS...
...GO AWAY.

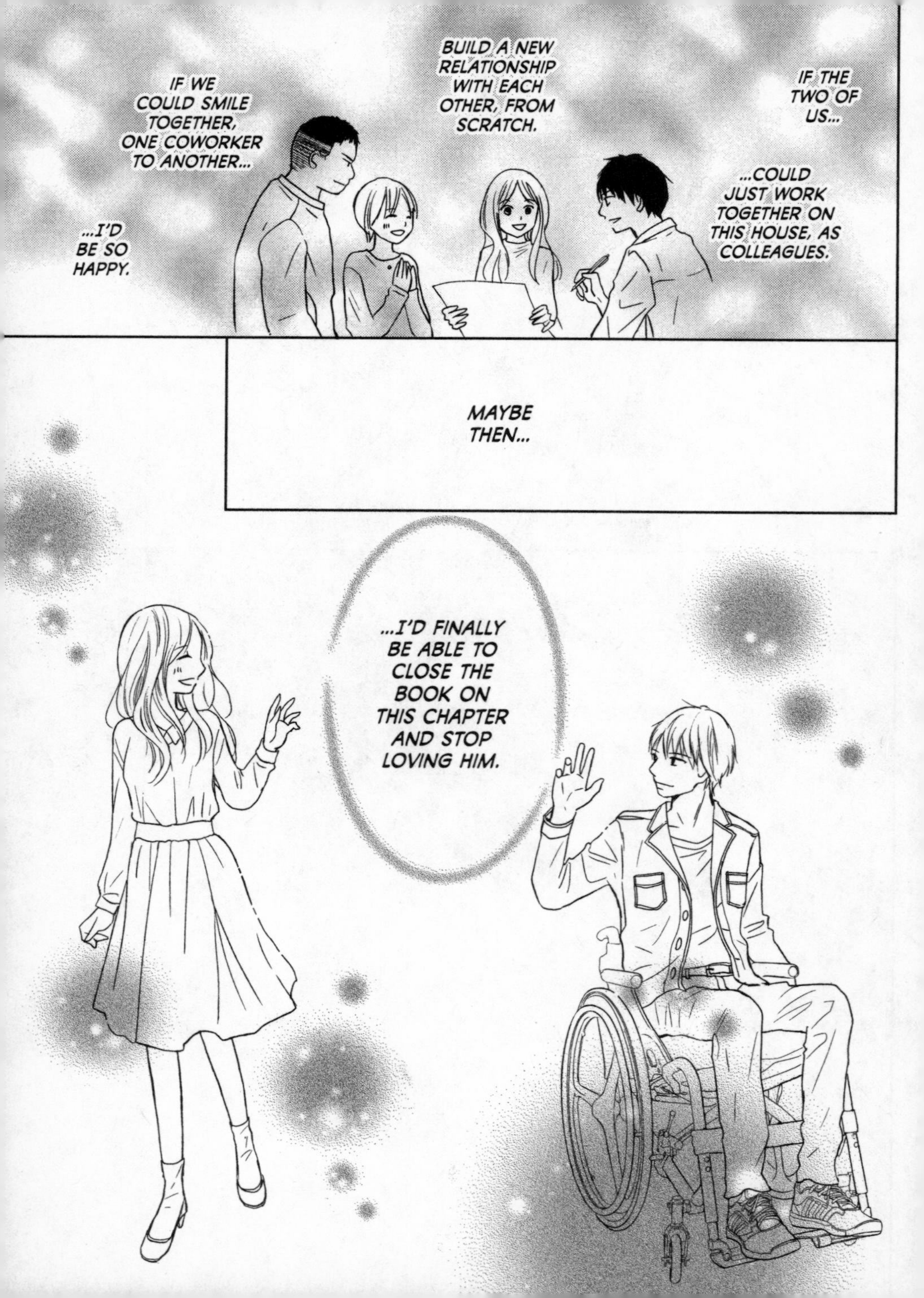
IF THE TWO OF US...
...COULD JUST WORK TOGETHER ON THIS HOUSE, AS COLLEAGUES.
BUILD A NEW RELATIONSHIP WITH EACH OTHER, FROM SCRATCH.
IF WE COULD SMILE TOGETHER, ONE COWORKER TO ANOTHER...
...I'D BE SO HAPPY.
MAYBE THEN...
...I'D FINALLY BE ABLE TO CLOSE THE BOOK ON THIS CHAPTER AND STOP LOVING HIM.

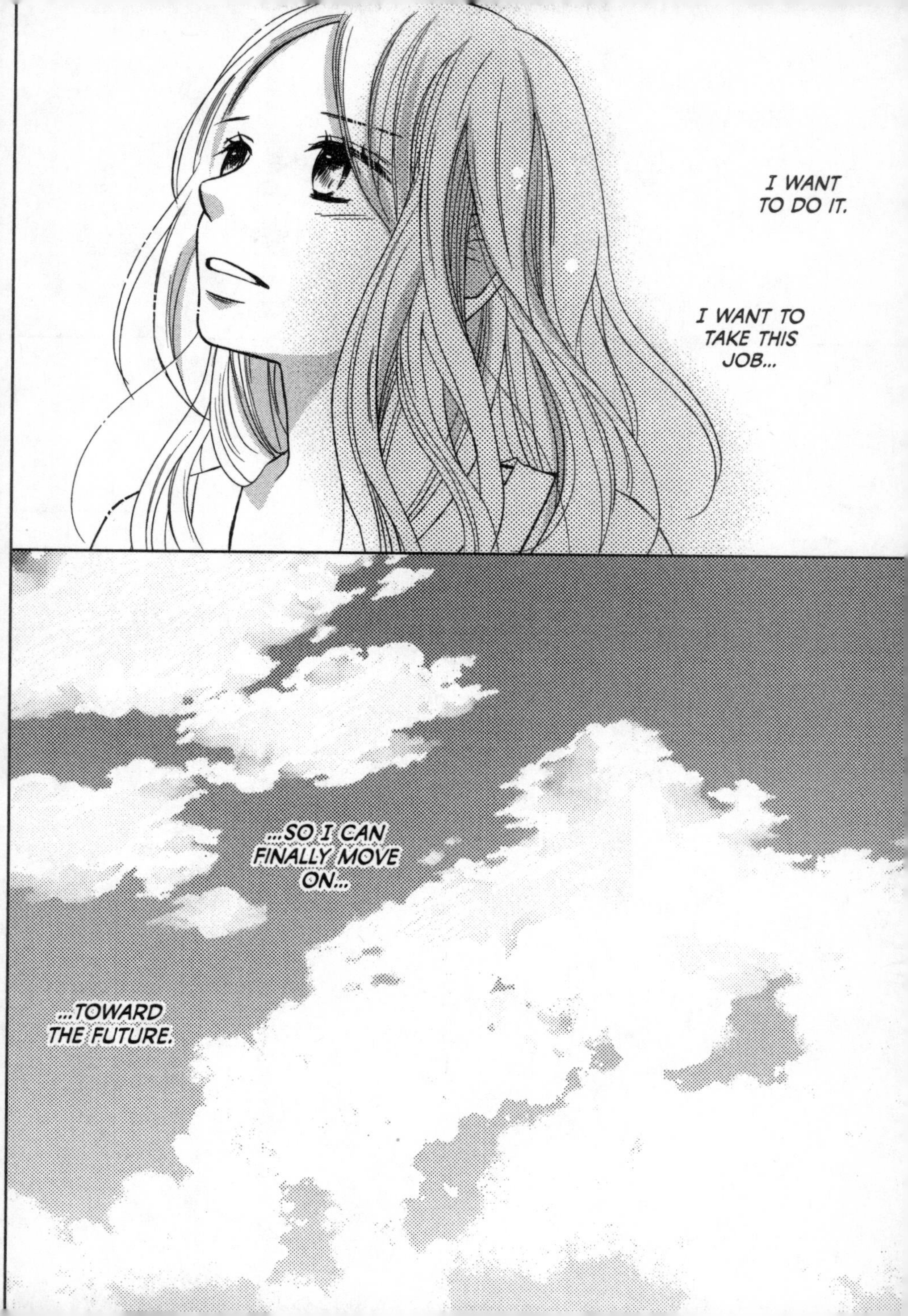
I WANT TO DO IT.
I WANT TO TAKE THIS JOB...
...SO I CAN FINALLY MOVE ON...
...TOWARD THE FUTURE.

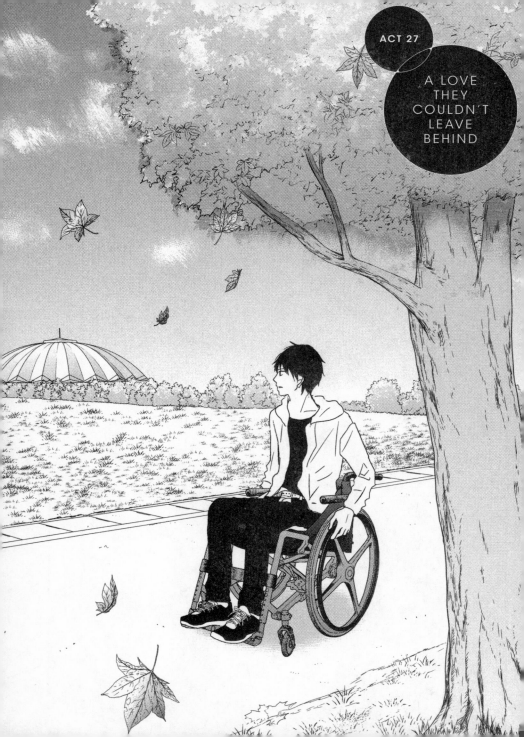

ACT 27

A LOVE
THEY
COULDN'T
LEAVE
BEHIND

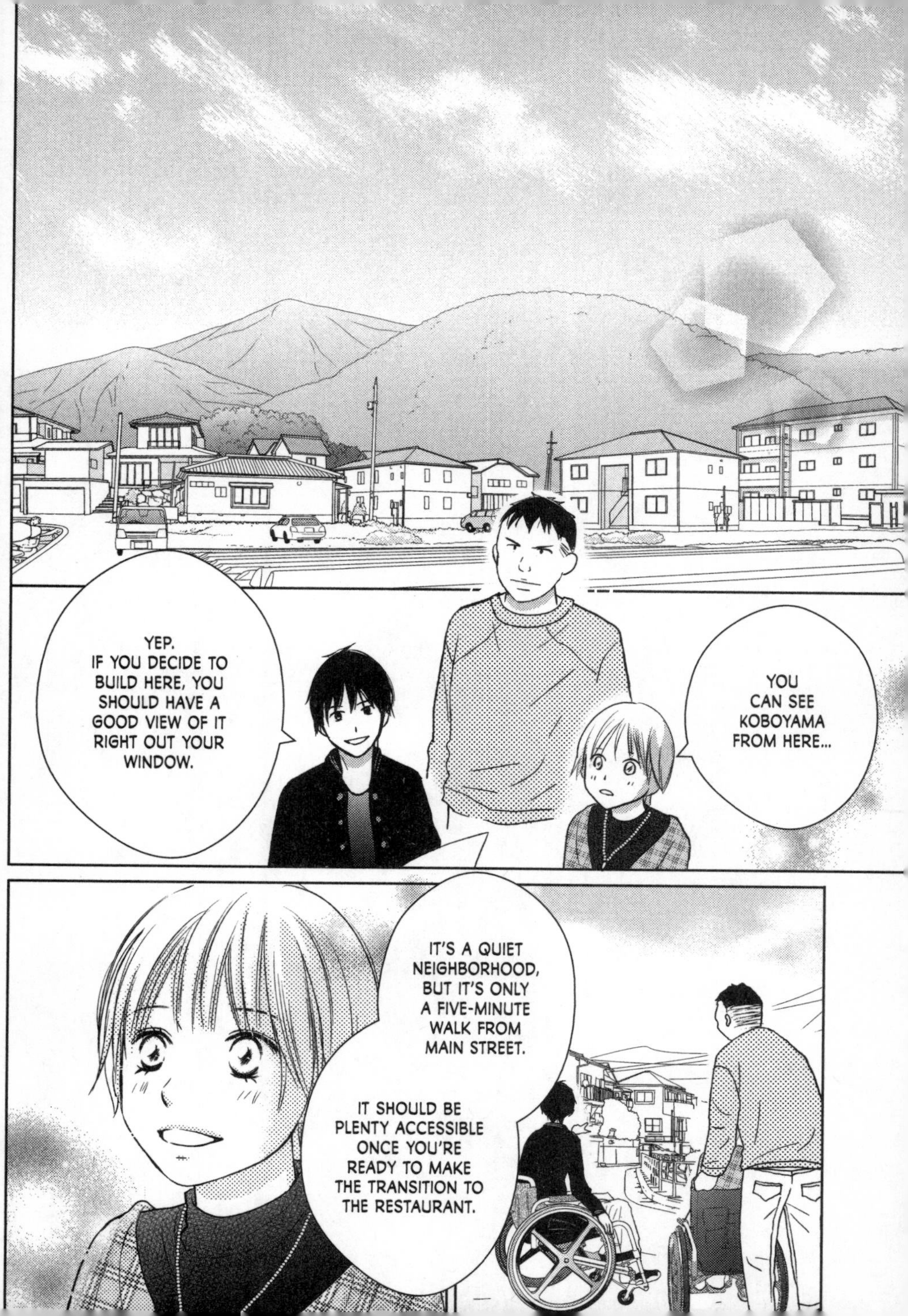
YOU CAN SEE KOBOYAMA FROM HERE...
YEP. IF YOU DECIDE TO BUILD HERE, YOU SHOULD HAVE A GOOD VIEW OF IT RIGHT OUT YOUR WINDOW.
IT'S A QUIET NEIGHBORHOOD, BUT IT'S ONLY A FIVE-MINUTE WALK FROM MAIN STREET.
IT SHOULD BE PLENTY ACCESSIBLE ONCE YOU'RE READY TO MAKE THE TRANSITION TO THE RESTAURANT.

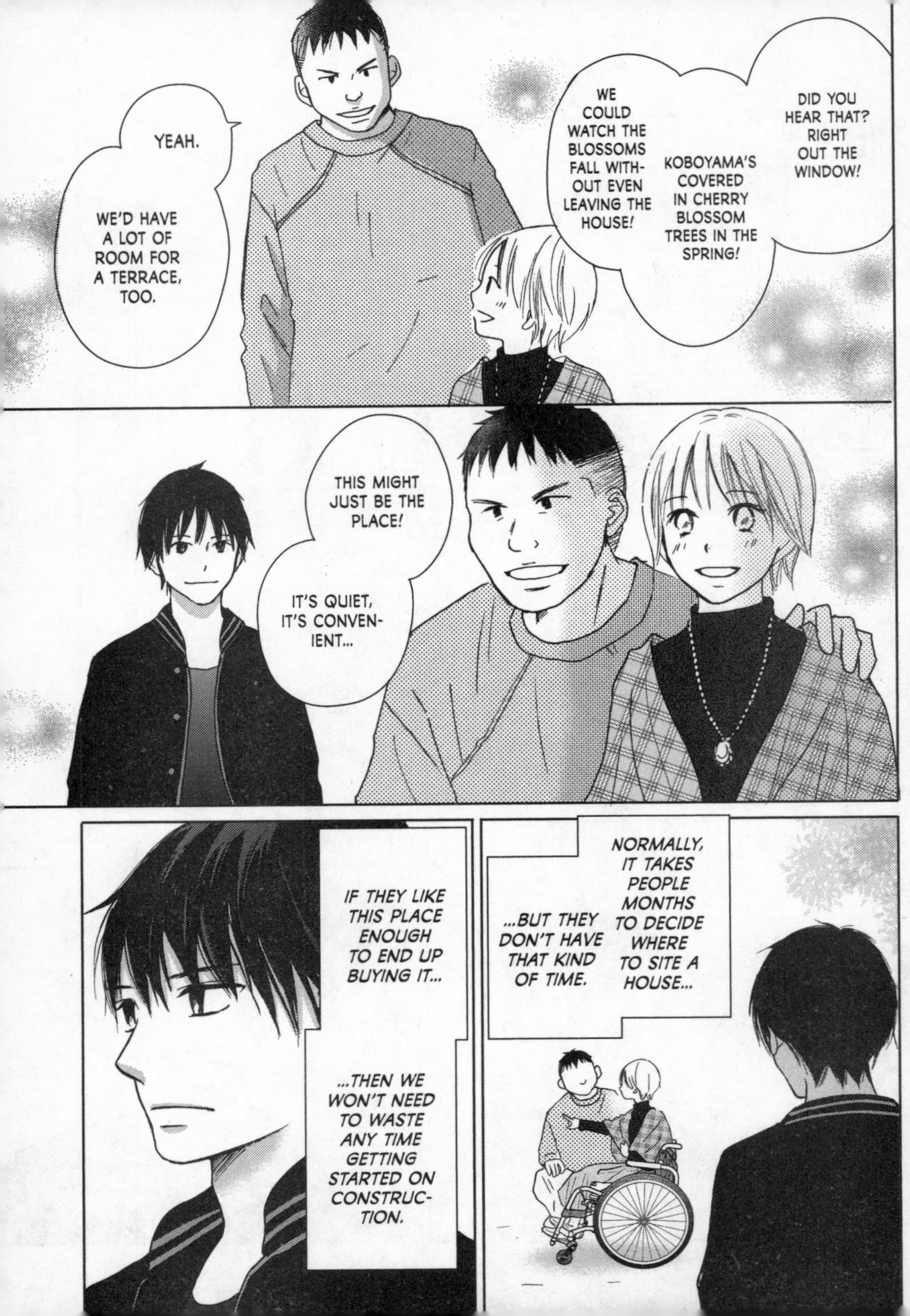
DID YOU HEAR THAT? RIGHT OUT THE WINDOW!
KOBOYAMA'S COVERED IN CHERRY BLOSSOM TREES IN THE SPRING!
WE COULD WATCH THE BLOSSOMS FALL WITHOUT EVEN LEAVING THE HOUSE!
YEAH.
WE'D HAVE A LOT OF ROOM FOR A TERRACE, TOO.
THIS MIGHT JUST BE THE PLACE!
IT'S QUIET, IT'S CONVENIENT...
NORMALLY, IT TAKES PEOPLE MONTHS TO DECIDE WHERE TO SITE A HOUSE...
...BUT THEY DON'T HAVE THAT KIND OF TIME.
IF THEY LIKE THIS PLACE ENOUGH TO END UP BUYING IT...
...THEN WE WON'T NEED TO WASTE ANY TIME GETTING STARTED ON CONSTRUCTION.

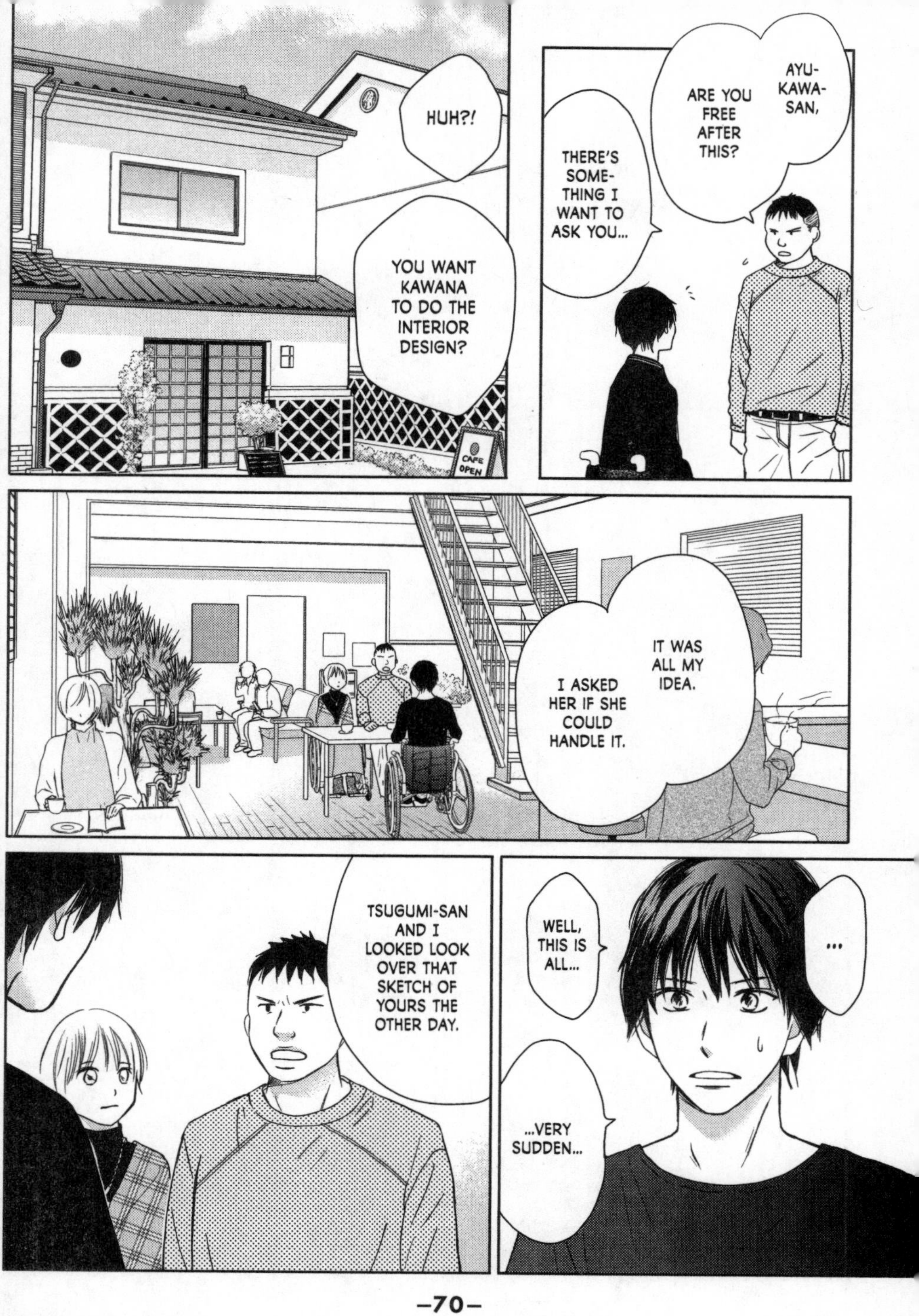
AYU-KAWA-SAN,
ARE YOU FREE AFTER THIS?
THERE'S SOME-THING I WANT TO ASK YOU...
HUH?!
YOU WANT KAWANA TO DO THE INTERIOR DESIGN?
CAFE OPEN
IT WAS ALL MY IDEA.
I ASKED HER IF SHE COULD HANDLE IT.
...
WELL, THIS IS ALL...
...VERY SUDDEN...
TSUGUMI-SAN AND I LOOKED LOOK OVER THAT SKETCH OF YOURS THE OTHER DAY.

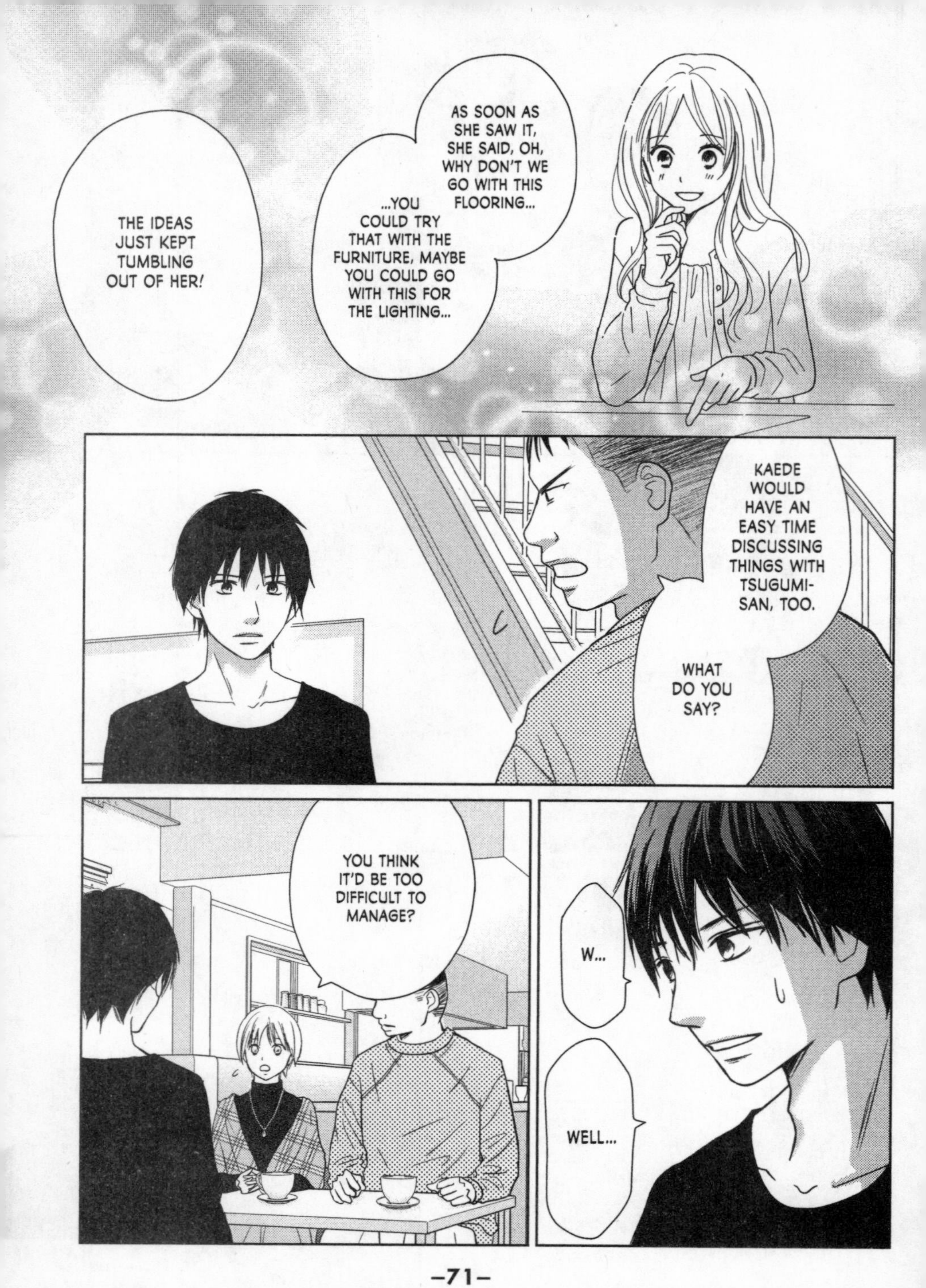
AS SOON AS SHE SAW IT, SHE SAID, OH, WHY DON'T WE GO WITH THIS FLOORING...
...YOU COULD TRY THAT WITH THE FURNITURE, MAYBE YOU COULD GO WITH THIS FOR THE LIGHTING...
THE IDEAS JUST KEPT TUMBLING OUT OF HER!
KAEDE WOULD HAVE AN EASY TIME DISCUSSING THINGS WITH TSUGUMI-SAN, TOO.
WHAT DO YOU SAY?
W...
WELL...
YOU THINK IT'D BE TOO DIFFICULT TO MANAGE?

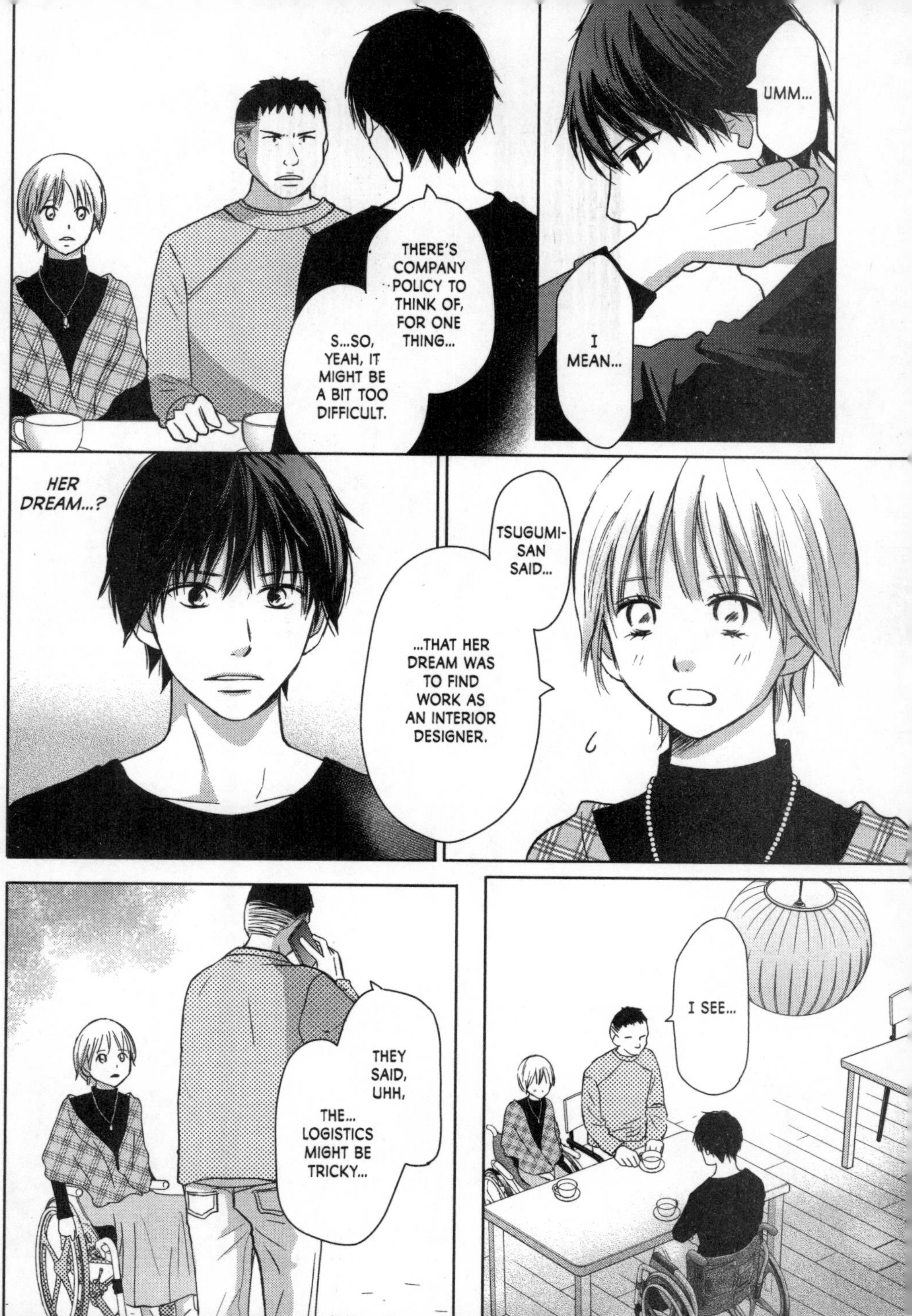
UMM...
I MEAN...
THERE'S COMPANY POLICY TO THINK OF, FOR ONE THING...
S...SO, YEAH, IT MIGHT BE A BIT TOO DIFFICULT.
TSUGUMI-SAN SAID...
...THAT HER DREAM WAS TO FIND WORK AS AN INTERIOR DESIGNER.
HER DREAM...?
I SEE...
THEY SAID, UHH, THE... LOGISTICS MIGHT BE TRICKY...

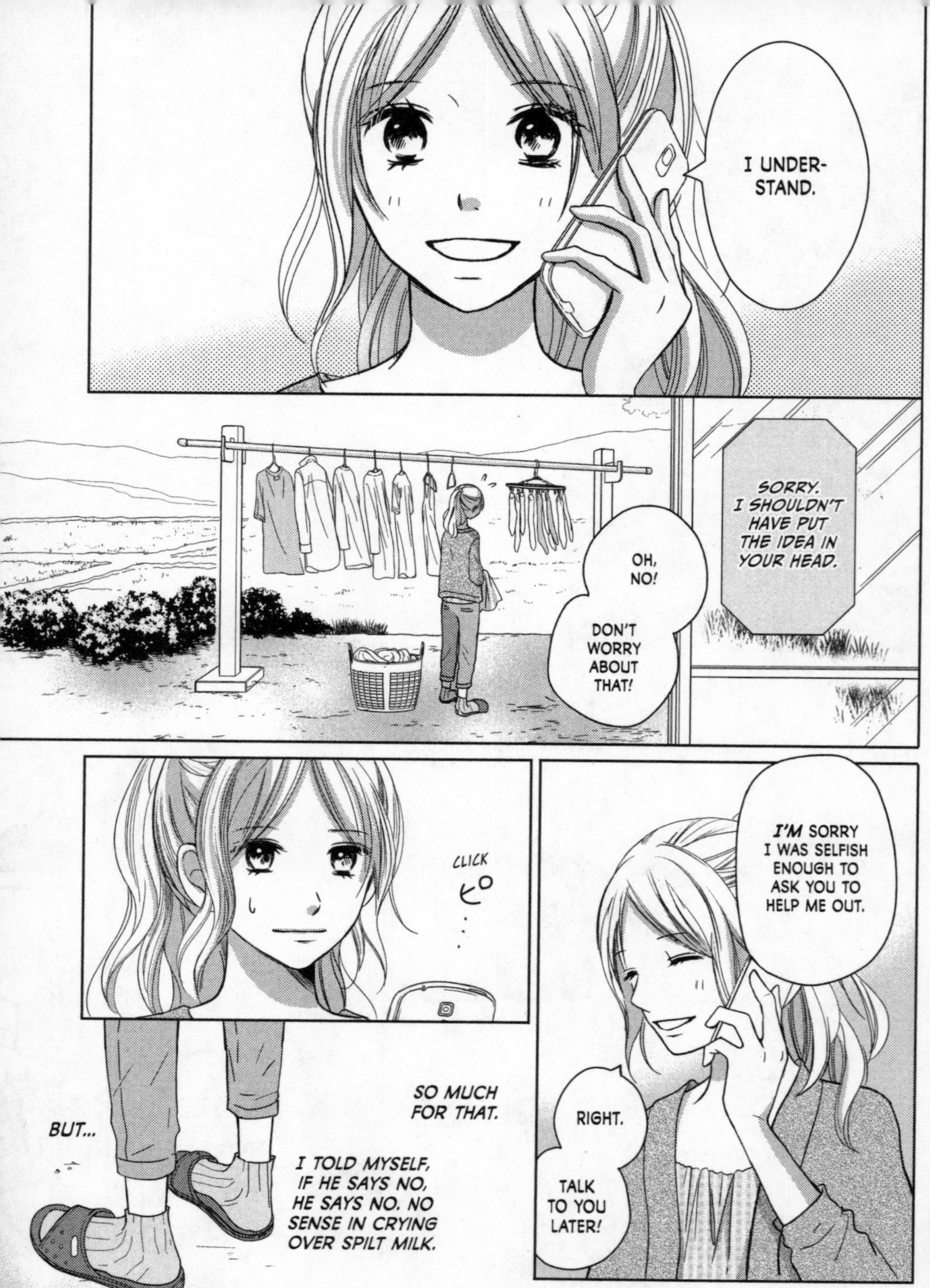
I UNDER-
STAND.
SORRY. I SHOULDN'T HAVE PUT THE IDEA IN YOUR HEAD.
OH, NO!
DON'T WORRY ABOUT THAT!
I'M SORRY I WAS SELFISH ENOUGH TO ASK YOU TO HELP ME OUT.
RIGHT.
TALK TO YOU LATER!
CLICK
ピ
SO MUCH FOR THAT.
I TOLD MYSELF, IF HE SAYS NO, HE SAYS NO. NO SENSE IN CRYING OVER SPILT MILK.
BUT...

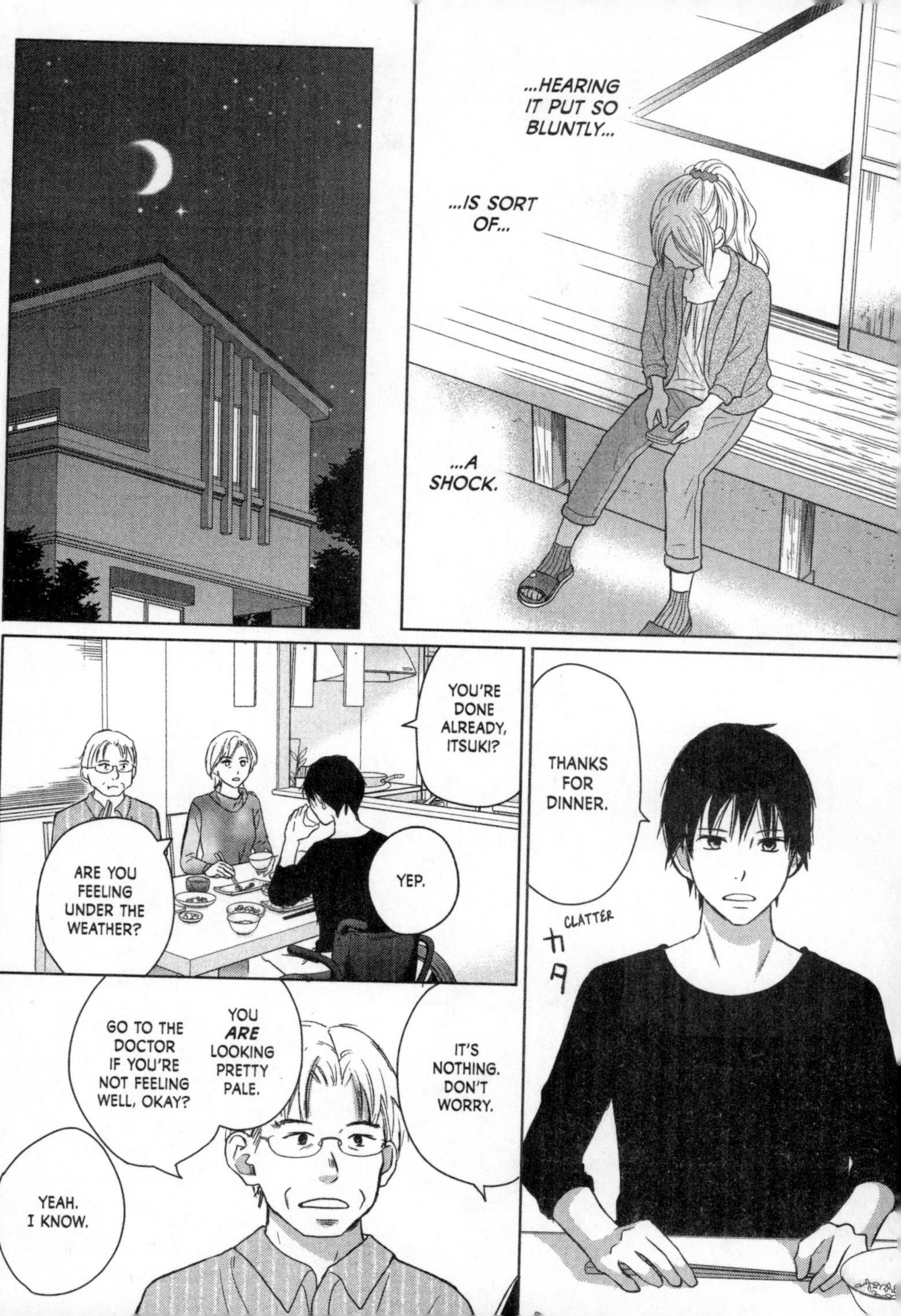
...HEARING IT PUT SO BLUNTLY...
...IS SORT OF...
...A SHOCK.
THANKS FOR DINNER.
CLATTER
カタ
YOU'RE DONE ALREADY, ITSUKI?
YEP.
ARE YOU FEELING UNDER THE WEATHER?
IT'S NOTHING. DON'T WORRY.
YOU *ARE* LOOKING PRETTY PALE.
GO TO THE DOCTOR IF YOU'RE NOT FEELING WELL, OKAY?
YEAH. I KNOW.

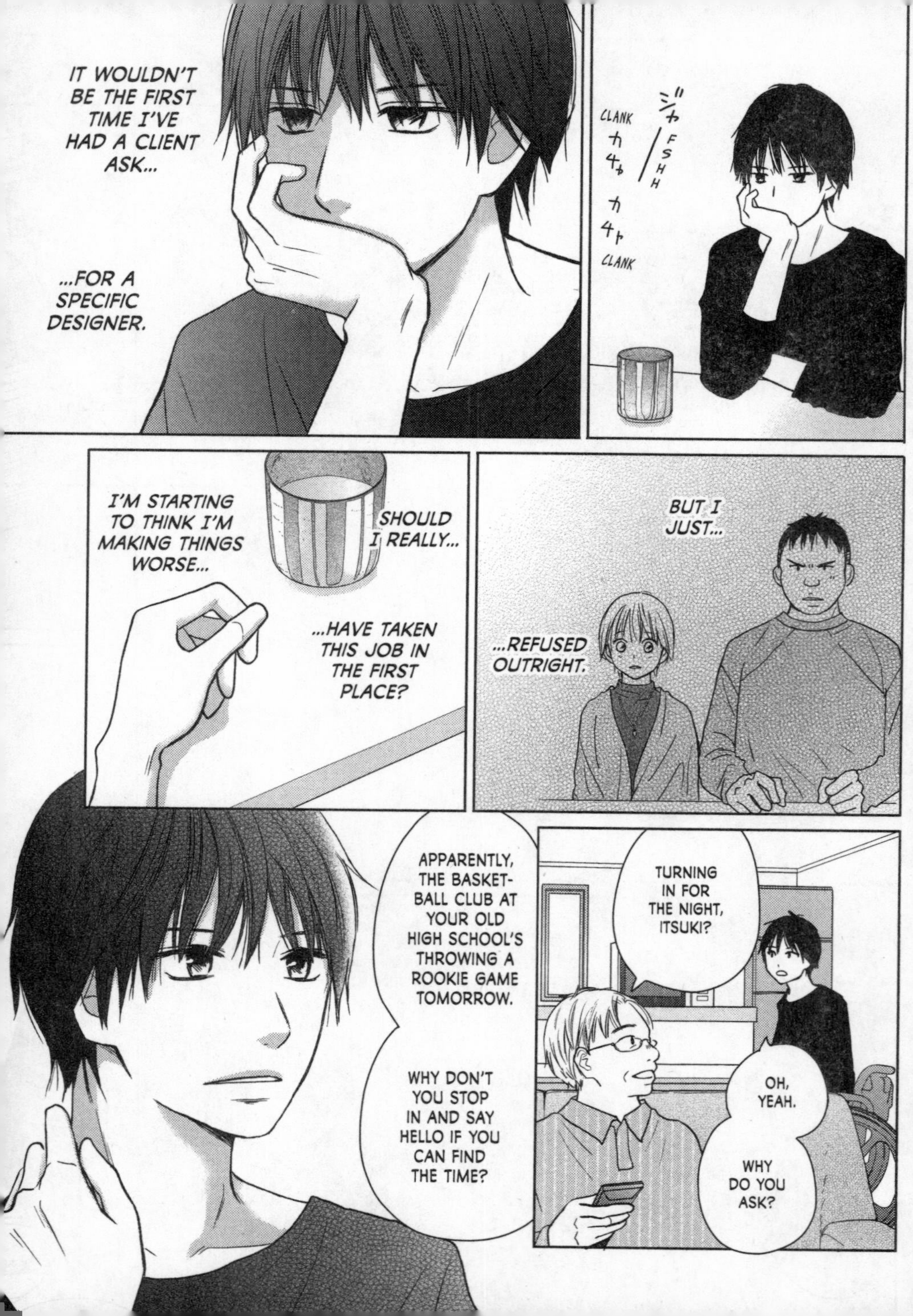

ジャ
FSHH
カチャ
CLANK
カチャ
CLANK
IT WOULDN'T BE THE FIRST TIME I'VE HAD A CLIENT ASK...
...FOR A SPECIFIC DESIGNER.
BUT I JUST...
...REFUSED OUTRIGHT.
SHOULD I REALLY...
...HAVE TAKEN THIS JOB IN THE FIRST PLACE?
I'M STARTING TO THINK I'M MAKING THINGS WORSE...
TURNING IN FOR THE NIGHT, ITSUKI?
OH, YEAH.
WHY DO YOU ASK?
APPARENTLY, THE BASKET-BALL CLUB AT YOUR OLD HIGH SCHOOL'S THROWING A ROOKIE GAME TOMORROW.
WHY DON'T YOU STOP IN AND SAY HELLO IF YOU CAN FIND THE TIME?

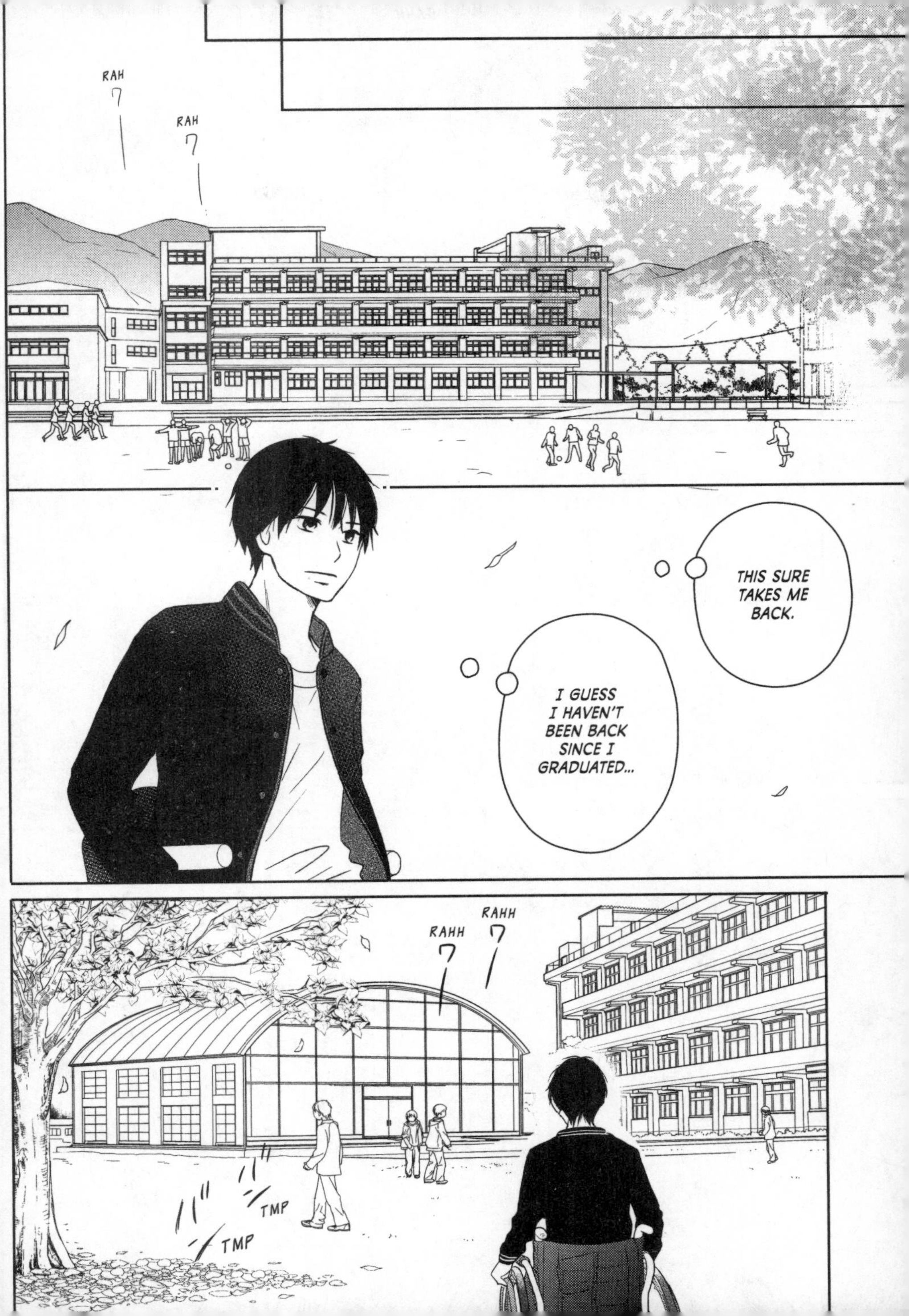
RAH
RAH
THIS SURE TAKES ME BACK.
I GUESS I HAVEN'T BEEN BACK SINCE I GRADUATED...
RAHH
RAHH
TMP
TMP

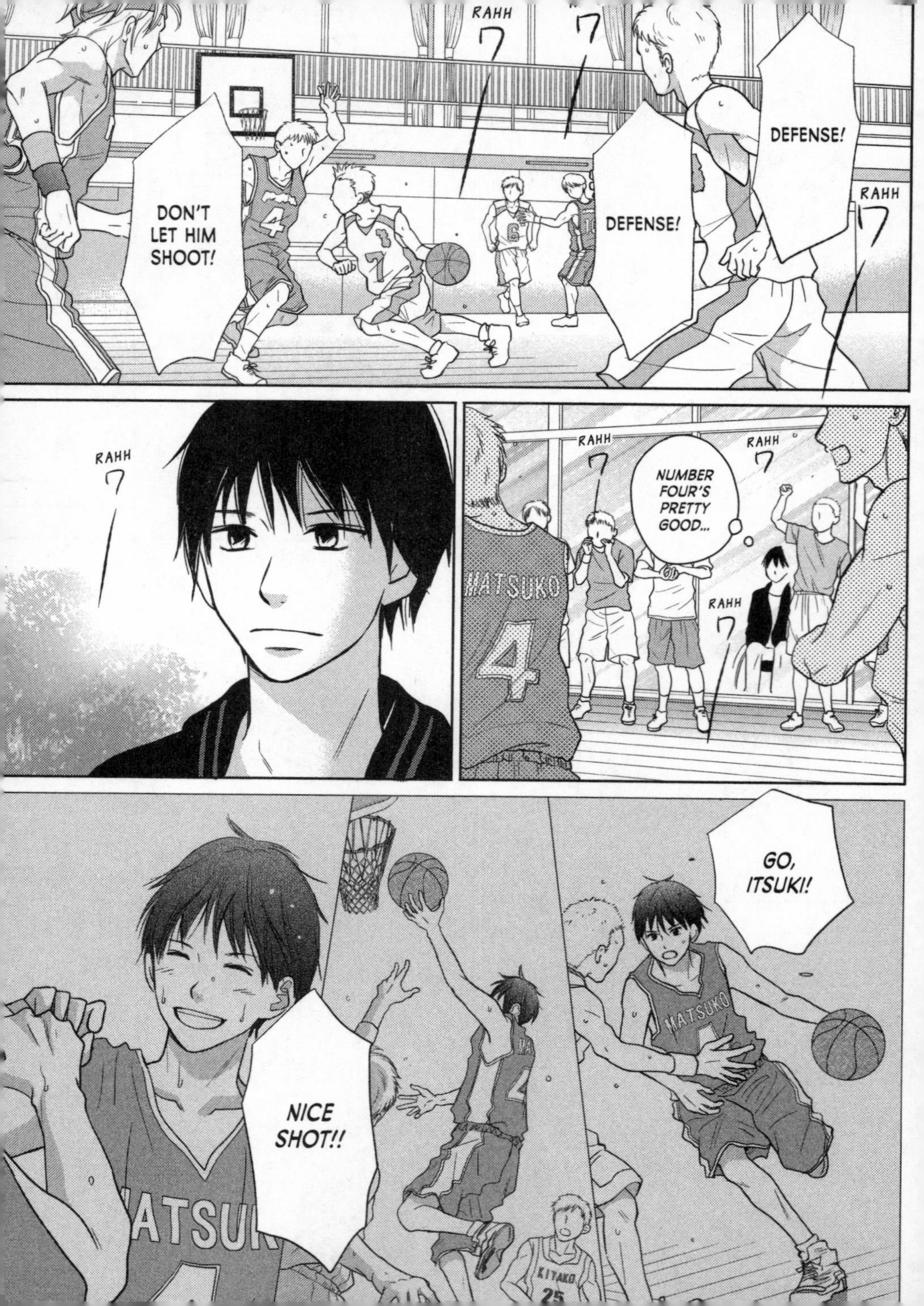
RAHH
DEFENSE!
RAHH
DEFENSE!
RAHH
DON'T LET HIM SHOOT!
RAHH
NUMBER FOUR'S PRETTY GOOD...
RAHH
RAHH
RAHH
GO, ITSUKI!
NICE SHOT!!

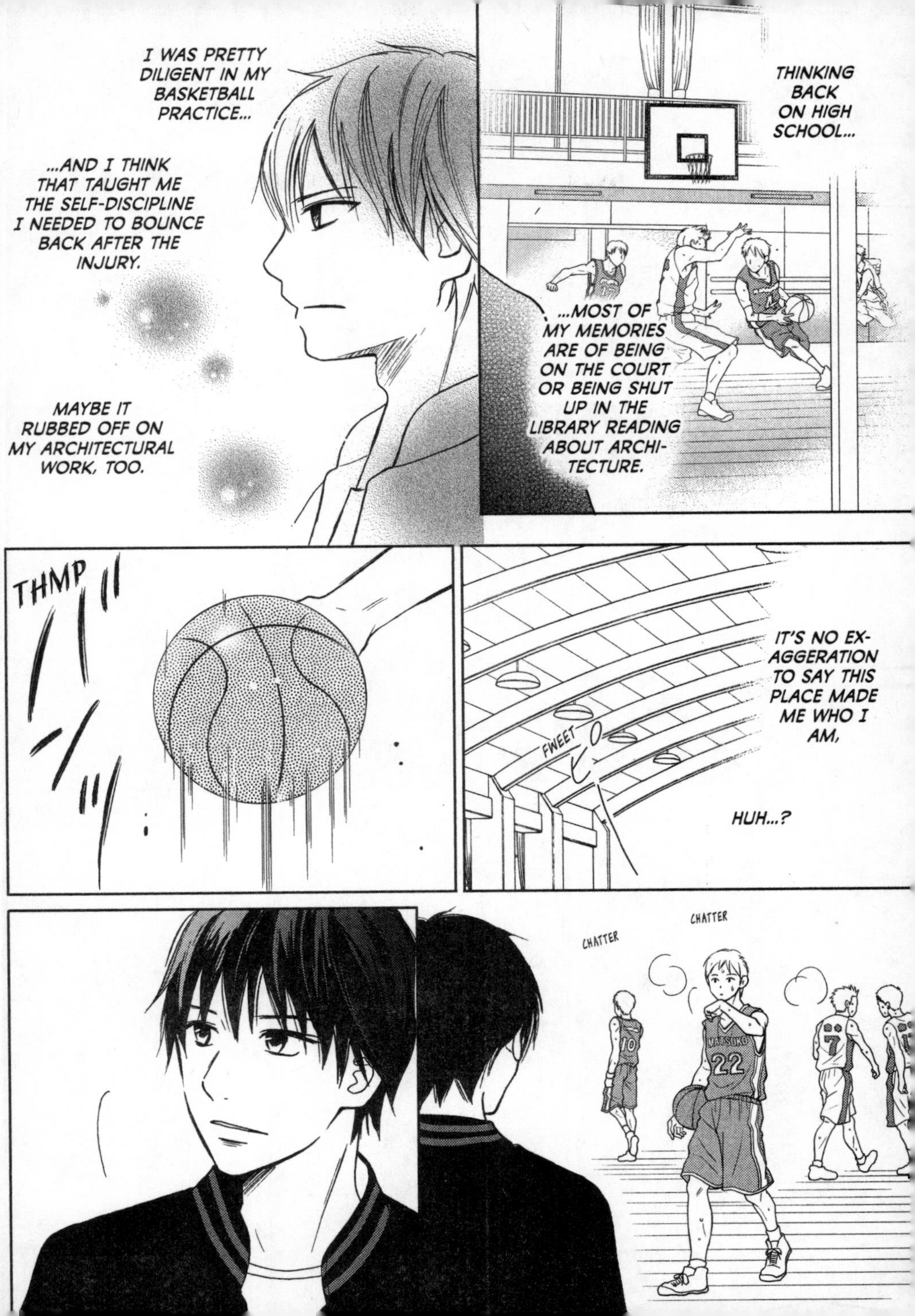
THINKING BACK ON HIGH SCHOOL...
...MOST OF MY MEMORIES ARE OF BEING ON THE COURT OR BEING SHUT UP IN THE LIBRARY READING ABOUT ARCHI-TECTURE.
I WAS PRETTY DILIGENT IN MY BASKETBALL PRACTICE...
...AND I THINK THAT TAUGHT ME THE SELF-DISCIPLINE I NEEDED TO BOUNCE BACK AFTER THE INJURY.
MAYBE IT RUBBED OFF ON MY ARCHITECTURAL WORK, TOO.
IT'S NO EX-AGGERATION TO SAY THIS PLACE MADE ME WHO I AM,
FWEET
HUH...?
THMP
CHATTER
CHATTER

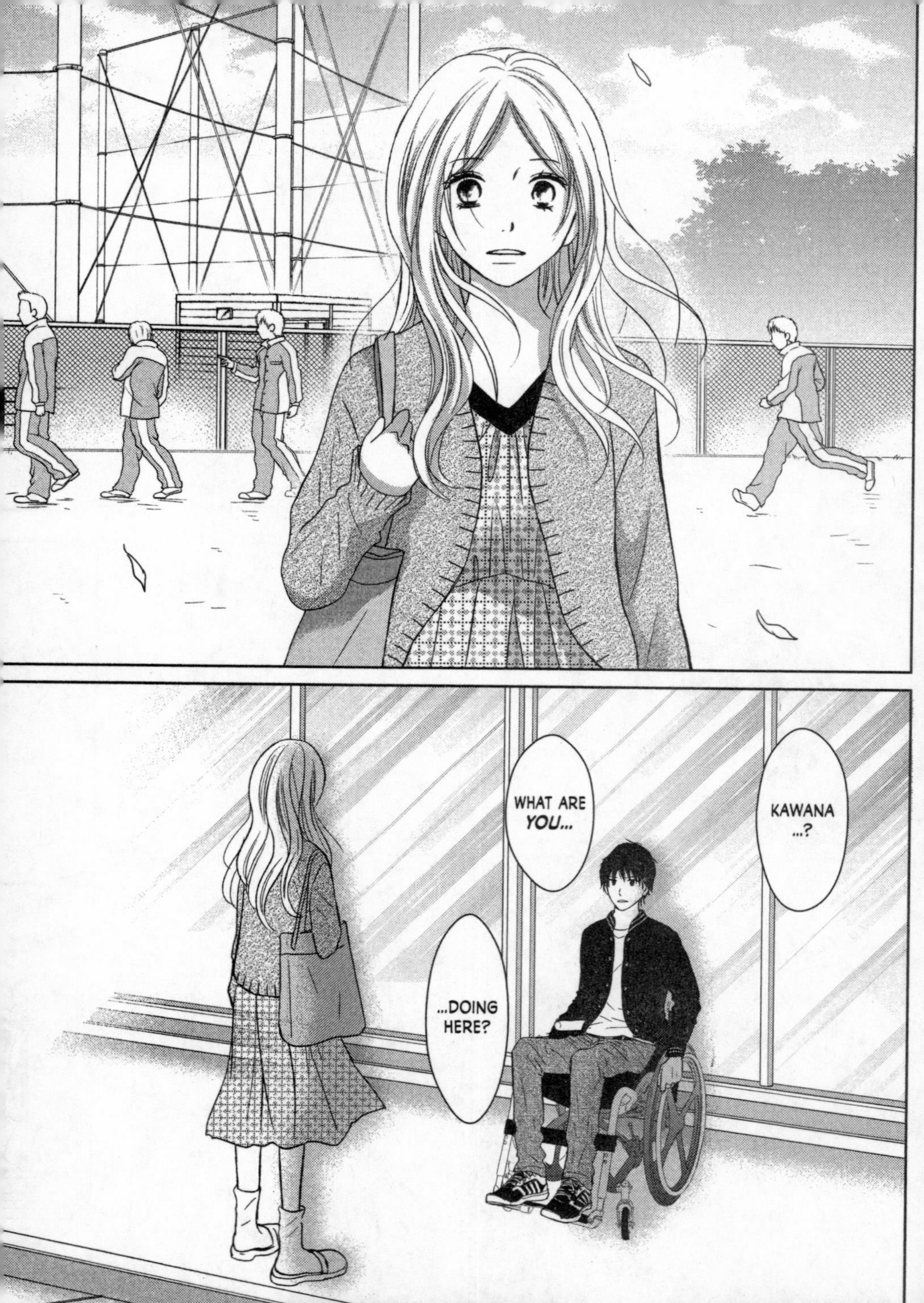
KAWANA ...?
WHAT ARE YOU...
...DOING HERE?

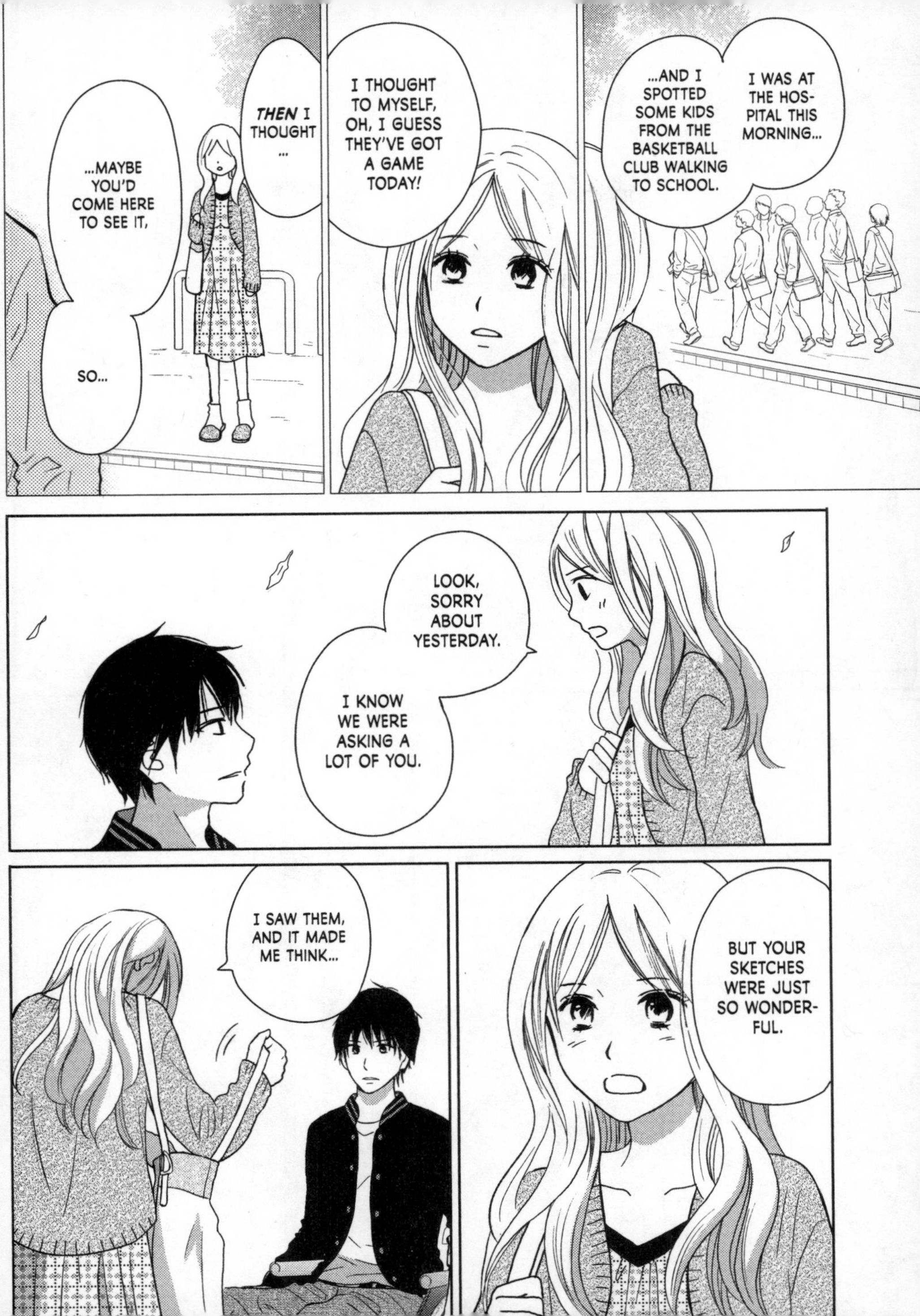
I WAS AT THE HOSPITAL THIS MORNING...
...AND I SPOTTED SOME KIDS FROM THE BASKETBALL CLUB WALKING TO SCHOOL.
I THOUGHT TO MYSELF, OH, I GUESS THEY'VE GOT A GAME TODAY!
THEN I THOUGHT ...
...MAYBE YOU'D COME HERE TO SEE IT,
SO...
LOOK, SORRY ABOUT YESTERDAY.
I KNOW WE WERE ASKING A LOT OF YOU.
BUT YOUR SKETCHES WERE JUST SO WONDERFUL.
I SAW THEM, AND IT MADE ME THINK...

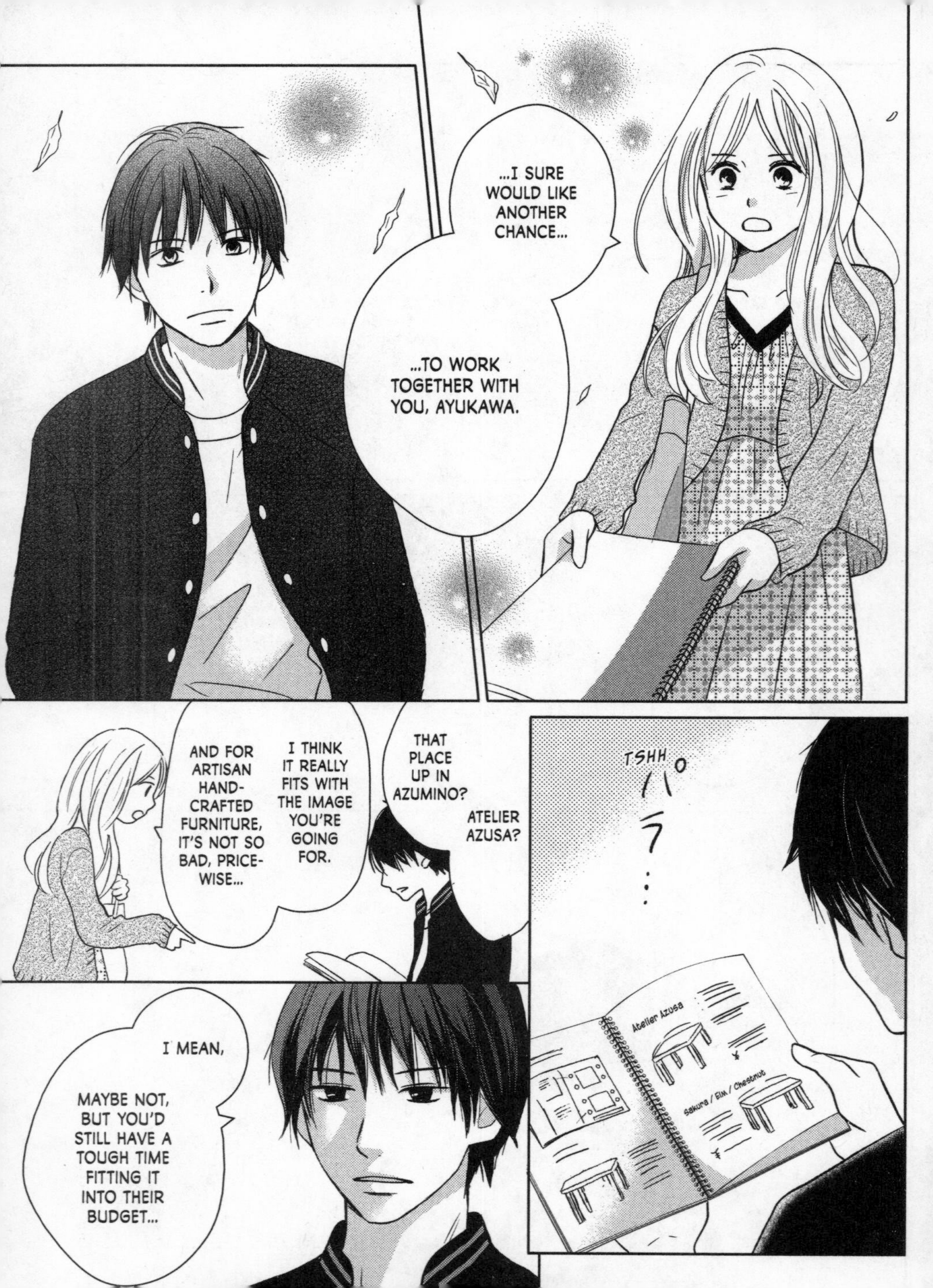
...I SURE WOULD LIKE ANOTHER CHANCE...
...TO WORK TOGETHER WITH YOU, AYUKAWA.
TSHH
パラ…
Atelier Azusa
Sakura / Elm / Chestnut
THAT PLACE UP IN AZUMINO?
ATELIER AZUSA?
I THINK IT REALLY FITS WITH THE IMAGE YOU'RE GOING FOR.
AND FOR ARTISAN HAND-CRAFTED FURNITURE, IT'S NOT SO BAD, PRICE-WISE...
I MEAN,
MAYBE NOT, BUT YOU'D STILL HAVE A TOUGH TIME FITTING IT INTO THEIR BUDGET...

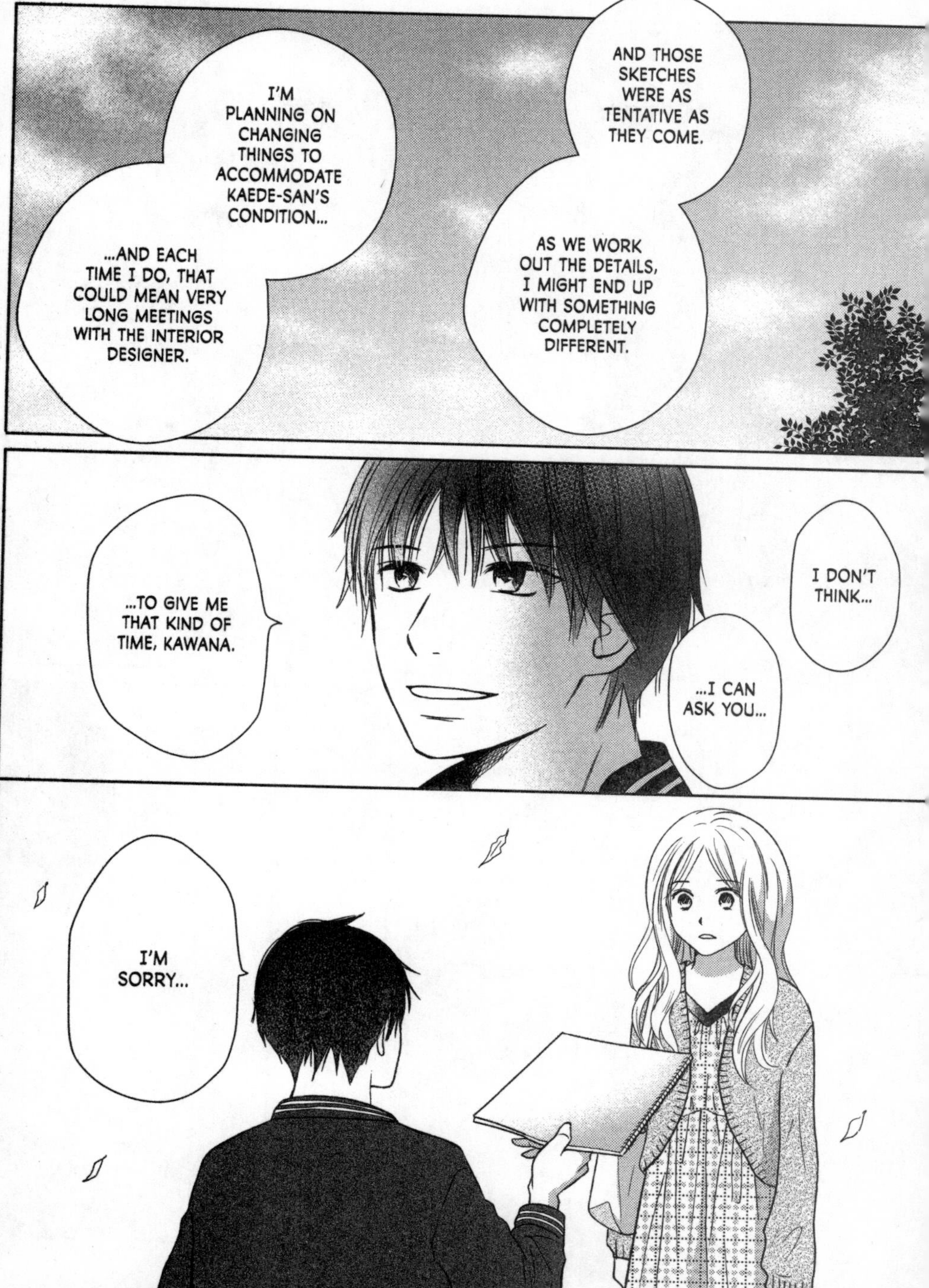
AND THOSE SKETCHES WERE AS TENTATIVE AS THEY COME.
AS WE WORK OUT THE DETAILS, I MIGHT END UP WITH SOMETHING COMPLETELY DIFFERENT.
I'M PLANNING ON CHANGING THINGS TO ACCOMMODATE KAEDE-SAN'S CONDITION...
...AND EACH TIME I DO, THAT COULD MEAN VERY LONG MEETINGS WITH THE INTERIOR DESIGNER.
I DON'T THINK...
...I CAN ASK YOU...
...TO GIVE ME THAT KIND OF TIME, KAWANA.
I'M SORRY...

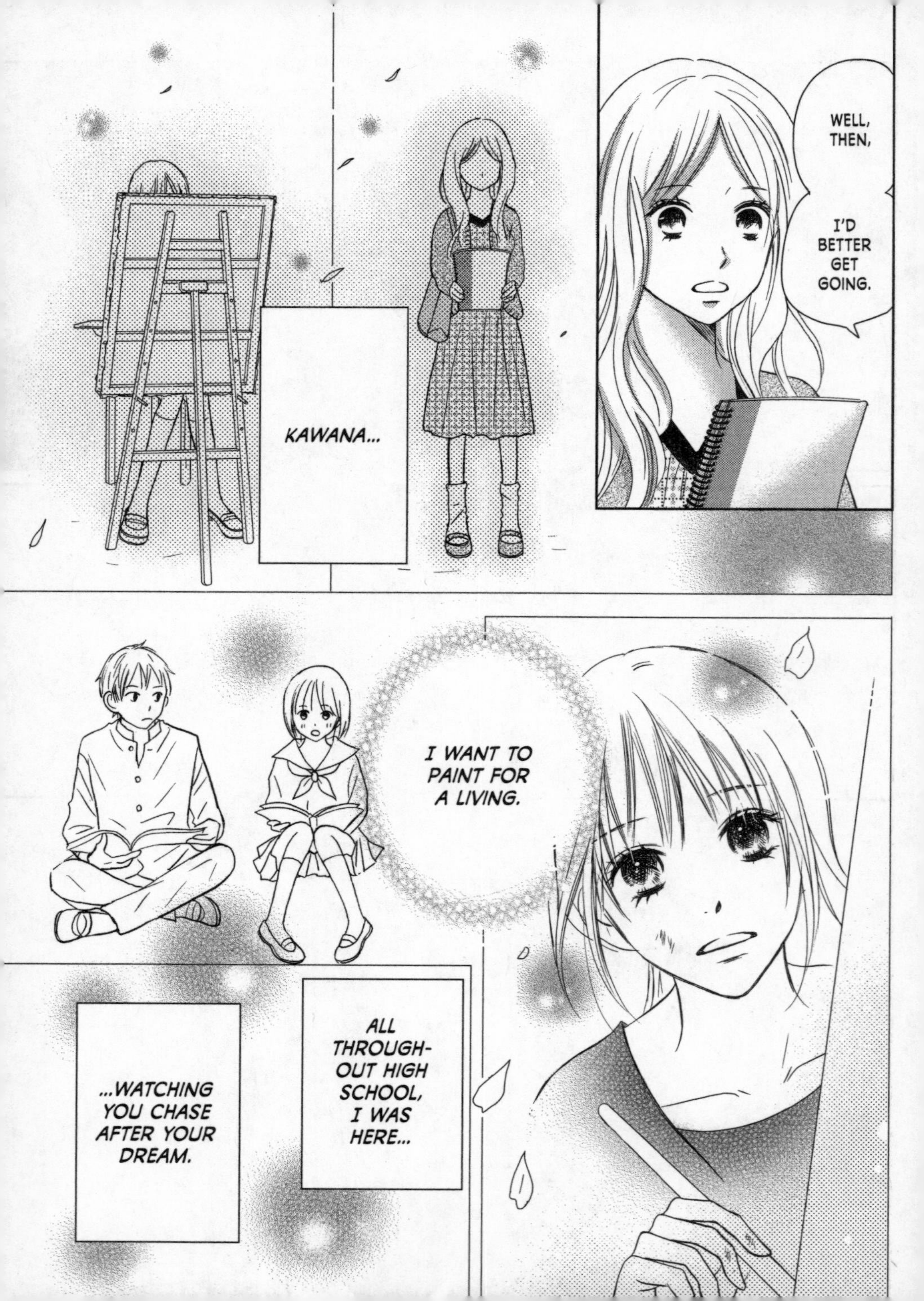
WELL, THEN,
I'D BETTER GET GOING.
KAWANA...
I WANT TO PAINT FOR A LIVING.
ALL THROUGH-OUT HIGH SCHOOL, I WAS HERE...
...WATCHING YOU CHASE AFTER YOUR DREAM.

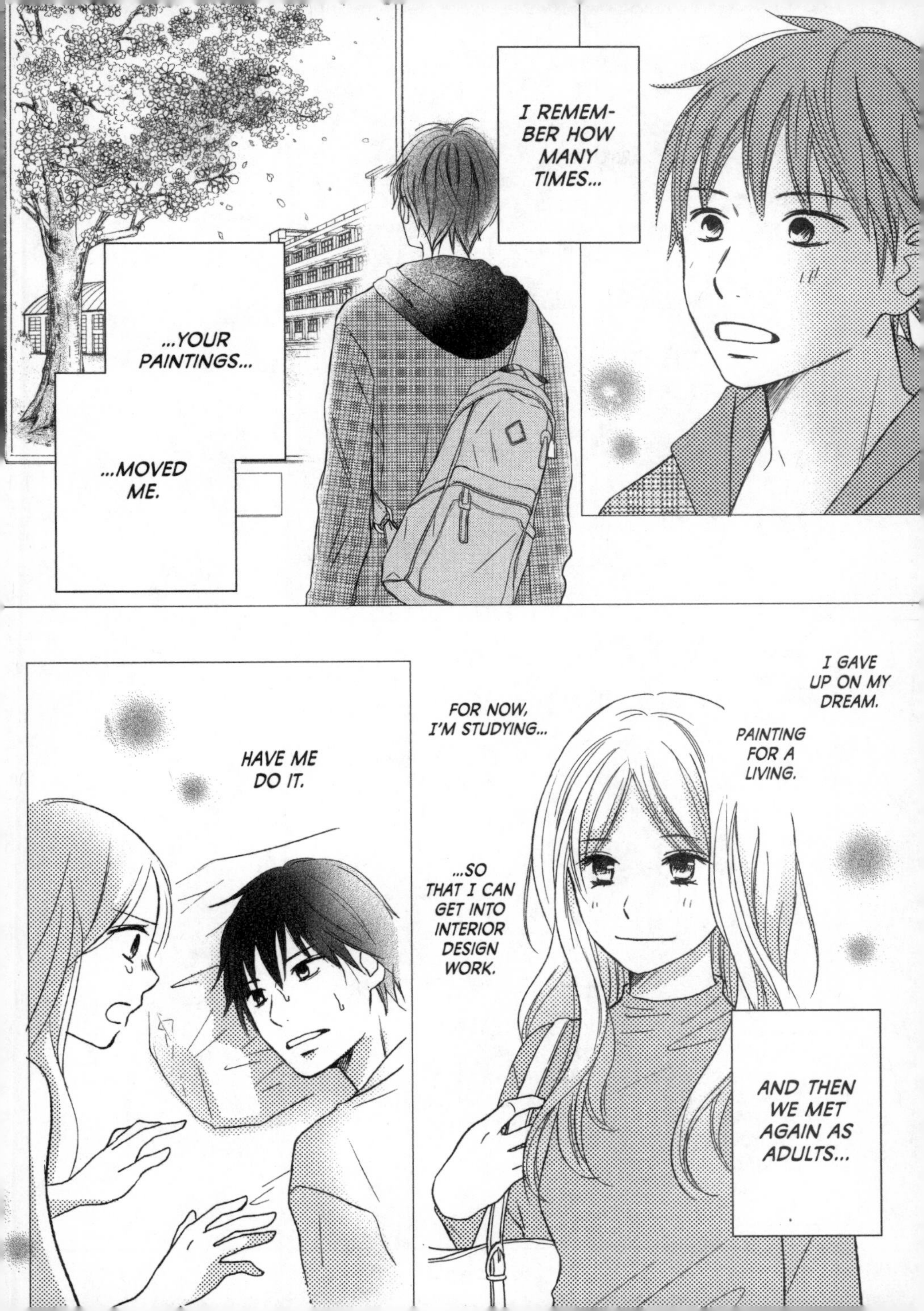
I REMEM-
BER HOW
MANY
TIMES...
...YOUR
PAINTINGS...
...MOVED
ME.
I GAVE
UP ON MY
DREAM.
PAINTING
FOR A
LIVING.
FOR NOW,
I'M STUDYING...
...SO
THAT I CAN
GET INTO
INTERIOR
DESIGN
WORK.
AND THEN
WE MET
AGAIN AS
ADULTS...
HAVE ME
DO IT.

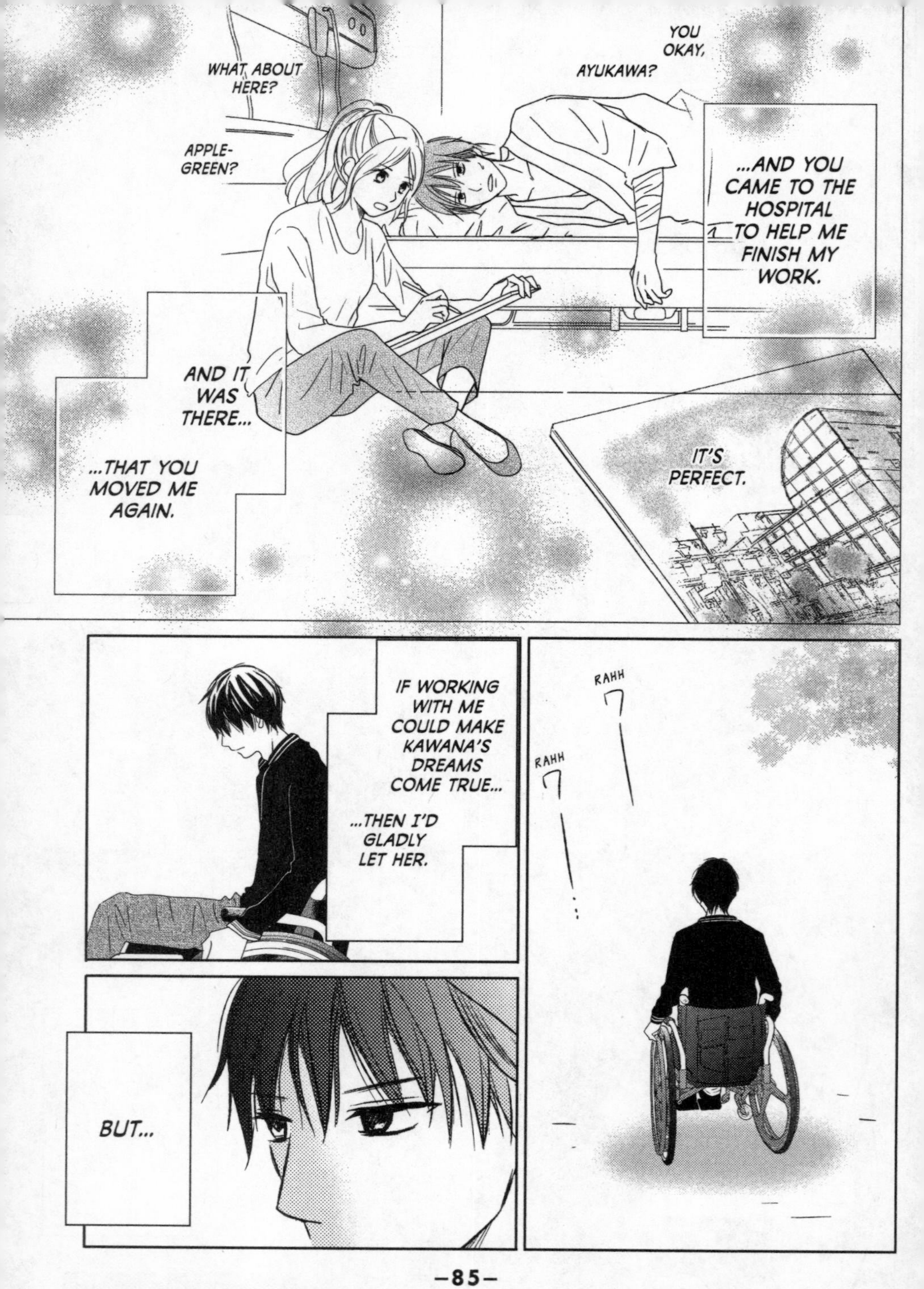
YOU OKAY, AYUKAWA?
...AND YOU CAME TO THE HOSPITAL TO HELP ME FINISH MY WORK.
WHAT ABOUT HERE?
APPLE-GREEN?
IT'S PERFECT.
AND IT WAS THERE...
...THAT YOU MOVED ME AGAIN.
RAHH
RAHH
IF WORKING WITH ME COULD MAKE KAWANA'S DREAMS COME TRUE...
...THEN I'D GLADLY LET HER.
BUT...

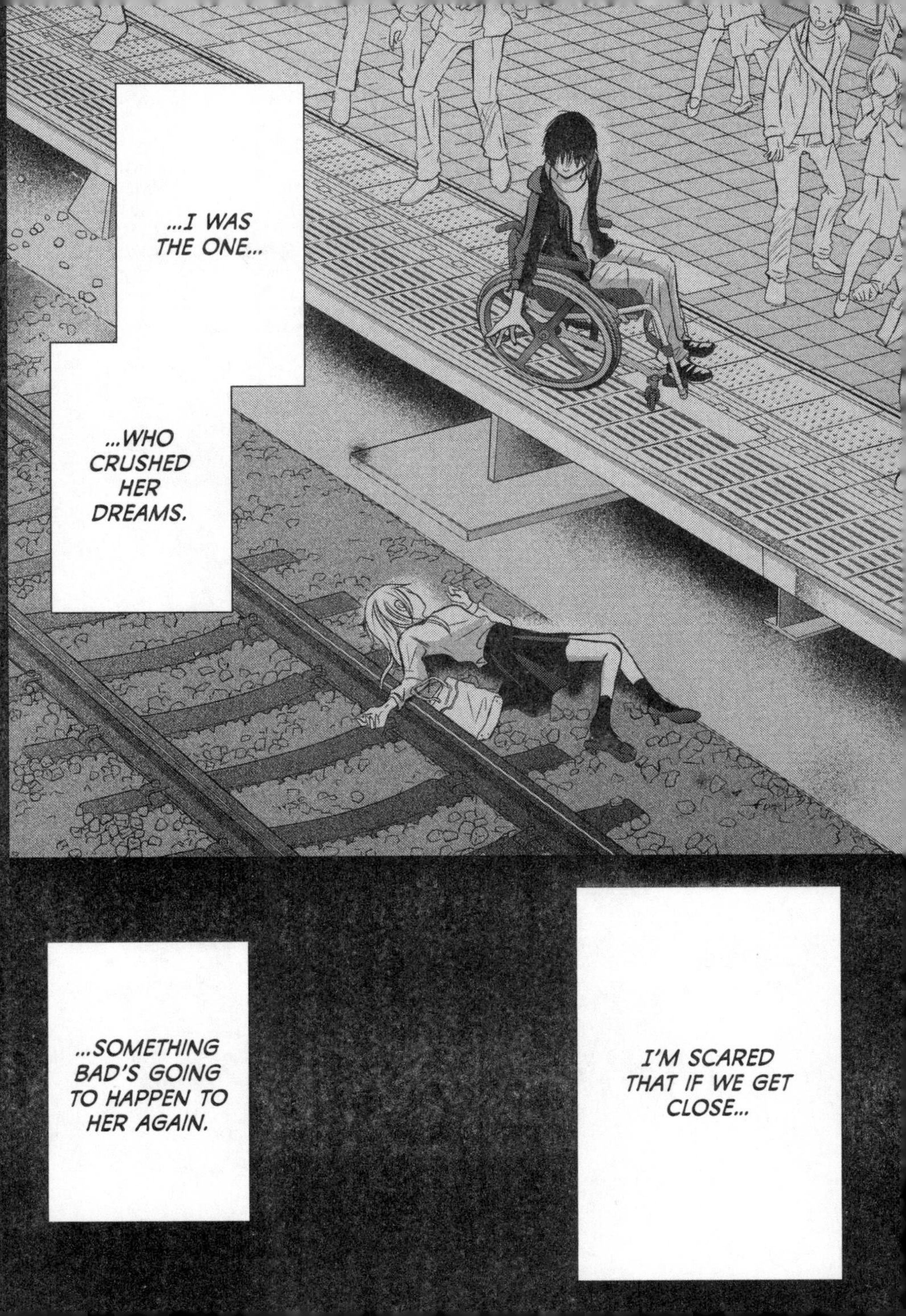
...I WAS THE ONE...
...WHO CRUSHED HER DREAMS.
I'M SCARED THAT IF WE GET CLOSE...
...SOMETHING BAD'S GOING TO HAPPEN TO HER AGAIN.

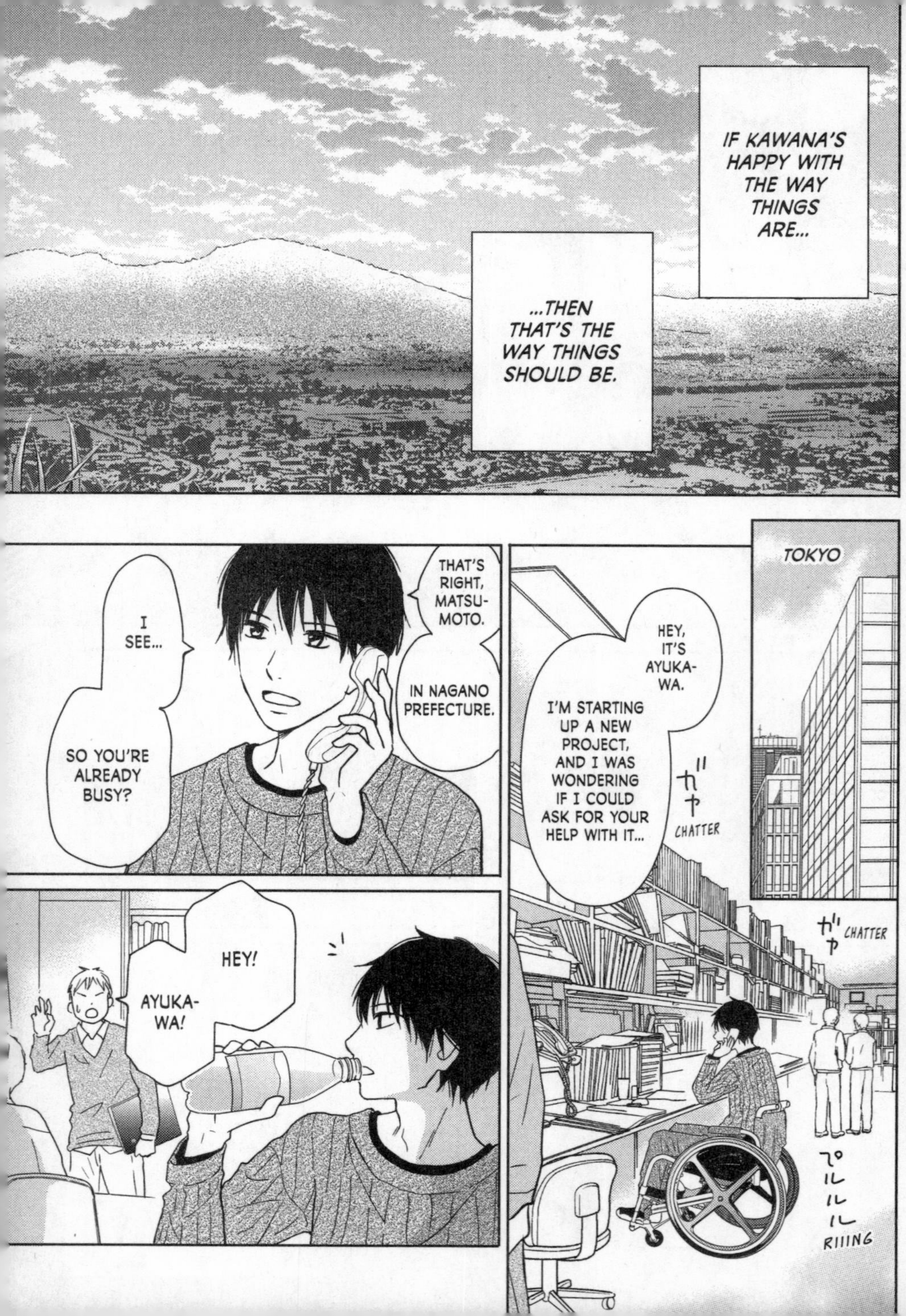
IF KAWANA'S HAPPY WITH THE WAY THINGS ARE...
...THEN THAT'S THE WAY THINGS SHOULD BE.
TOKYO
HEY, IT'S AYUKAWA.
I'M STARTING UP A NEW PROJECT, AND I WAS WONDERING IF I COULD ASK FOR YOUR HELP WITH IT...
ガヤ CHATTER
ガヤ CHATTER
プルルル RIIING
THAT'S RIGHT, MATSUMOTO.
IN NAGANO PREFECTURE.
I SEE...
SO YOU'RE ALREADY BUSY?
HEY!
AYUKAWA!

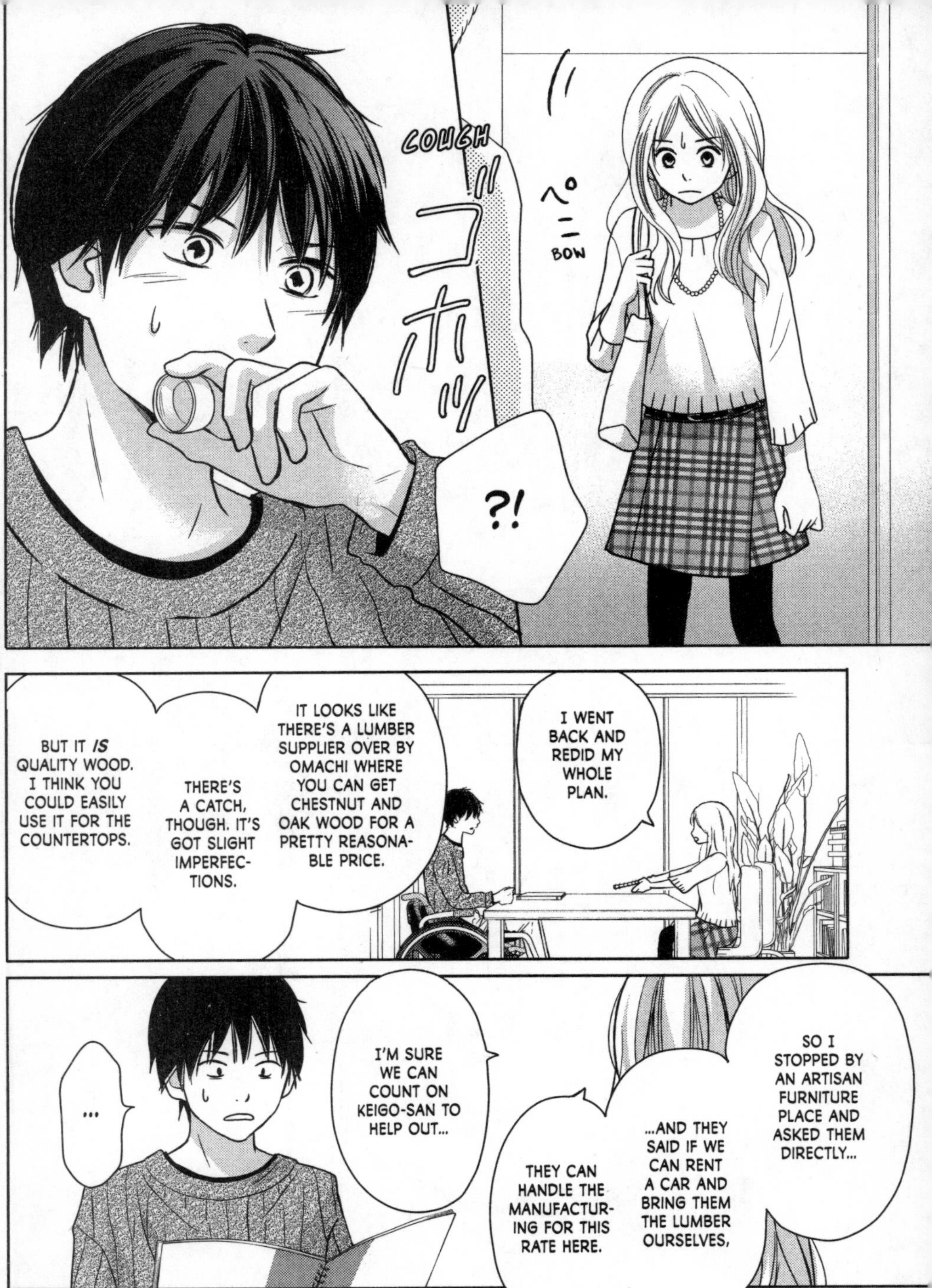
ぺこー
BOW
ゴホッ
COUGH
?!
I WENT BACK AND REDID MY WHOLE PLAN.
IT LOOKS LIKE THERE'S A LUMBER SUPPLIER OVER BY OMACHI WHERE YOU CAN GET CHESTNUT AND OAK WOOD FOR A PRETTY REASONA-BLE PRICE.
THERE'S A CATCH, THOUGH. IT'S GOT SLIGHT IMPERFEC-TIONS.
BUT IT *IS* QUALITY WOOD. I THINK YOU COULD EASILY USE IT FOR THE COUNTERTOPS.
SO I STOPPED BY AN ARTISAN FURNITURE PLACE AND ASKED THEM DIRECTLY...
...AND THEY SAID IF WE CAN RENT A CAR AND BRING THEM THE LUMBER OURSELVES,
THEY CAN HANDLE THE MANUFACTUR-ING FOR THIS RATE HERE.
I'M SURE WE CAN COUNT ON KEIGO-SAN TO HELP OUT...
...

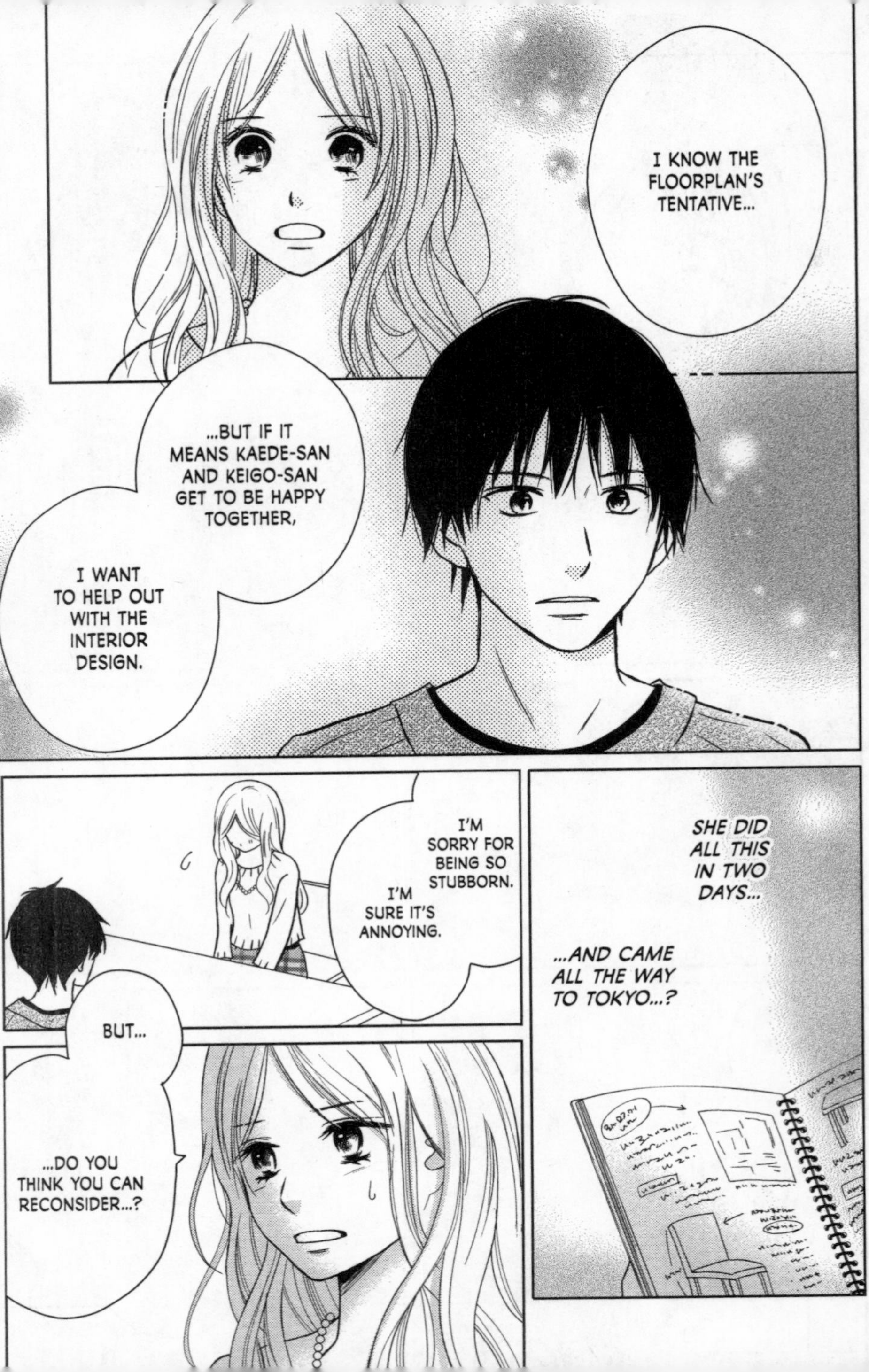
I KNOW THE FLOORPLAN'S TENTATIVE...
...BUT IF IT MEANS KAEDE-SAN AND KEIGO-SAN GET TO BE HAPPY TOGETHER,
I WANT TO HELP OUT WITH THE INTERIOR DESIGN.
SHE DID ALL THIS IN TWO DAYS...
...AND CAME ALL THE WAY TO TOKYO...?
I'M SORRY FOR BEING SO STUBBORN.
I'M SURE IT'S ANNOYING.
BUT...
...DO YOU THINK YOU CAN RECONSIDER...?

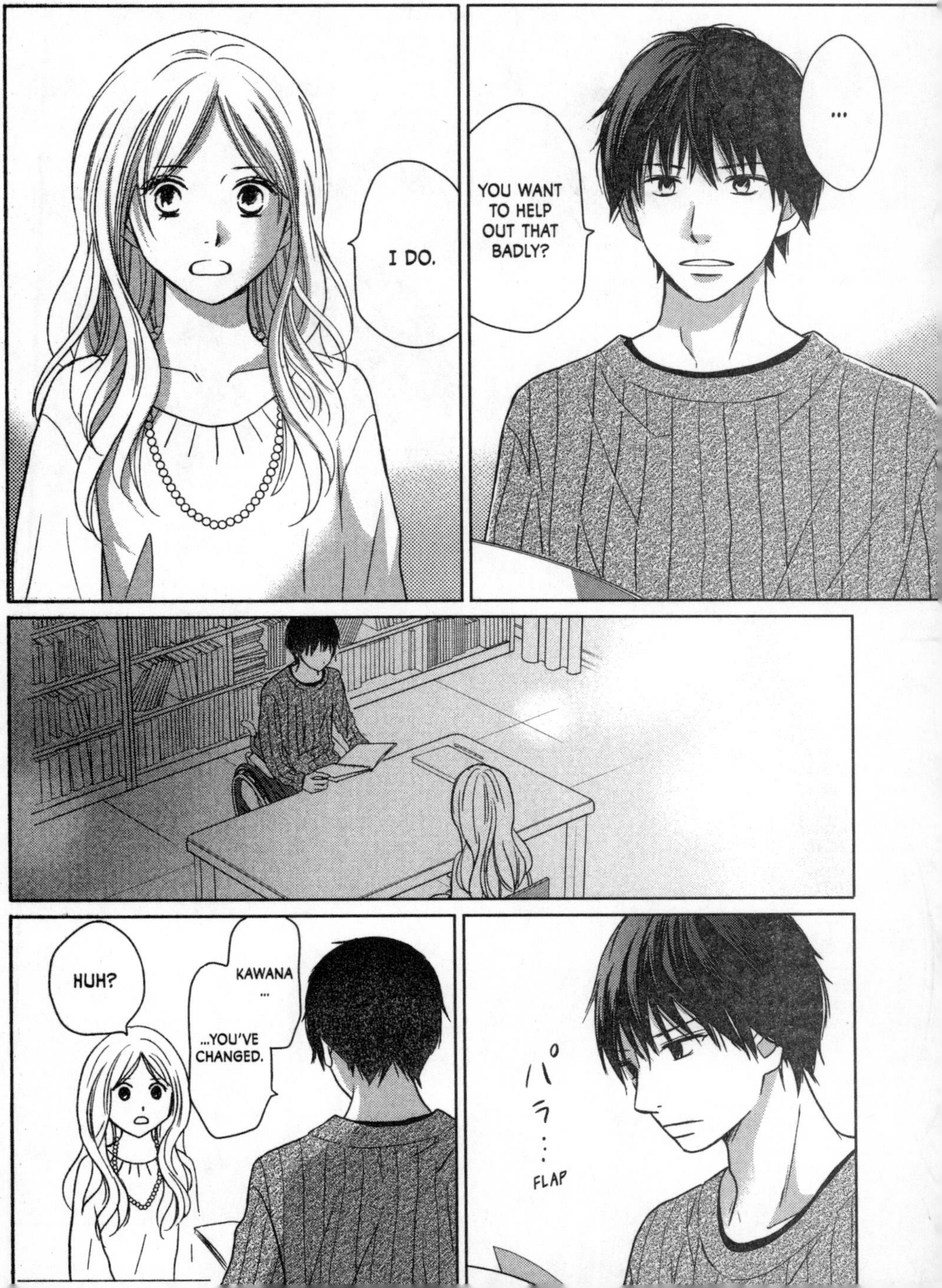
...
YOU WANT TO HELP OUT THAT BADLY?
I DO.
パラ…
FLAP
KAWANA ...
...YOU'VE CHANGED.
HUH?

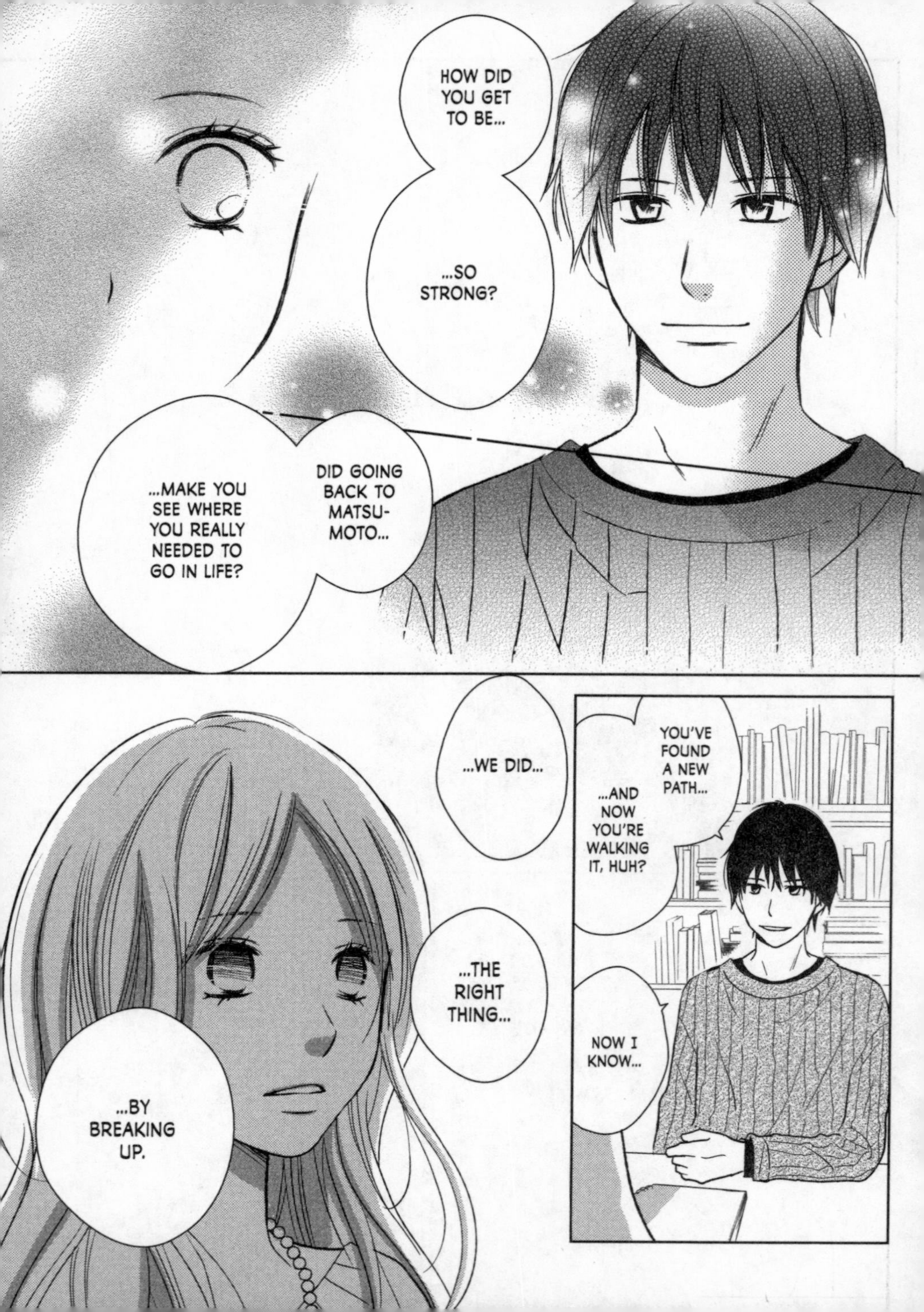
HOW DID YOU GET TO BE...
...SO STRONG?
DID GOING BACK TO MATSU-MOTO...
...MAKE YOU SEE WHERE YOU REALLY NEEDED TO GO IN LIFE?
YOU'VE FOUND A NEW PATH...
...AND NOW YOU'RE WALKING IT, HUH?
NOW I KNOW...
...WE DID...
...THE RIGHT THING...
...BY BREAKING UP.

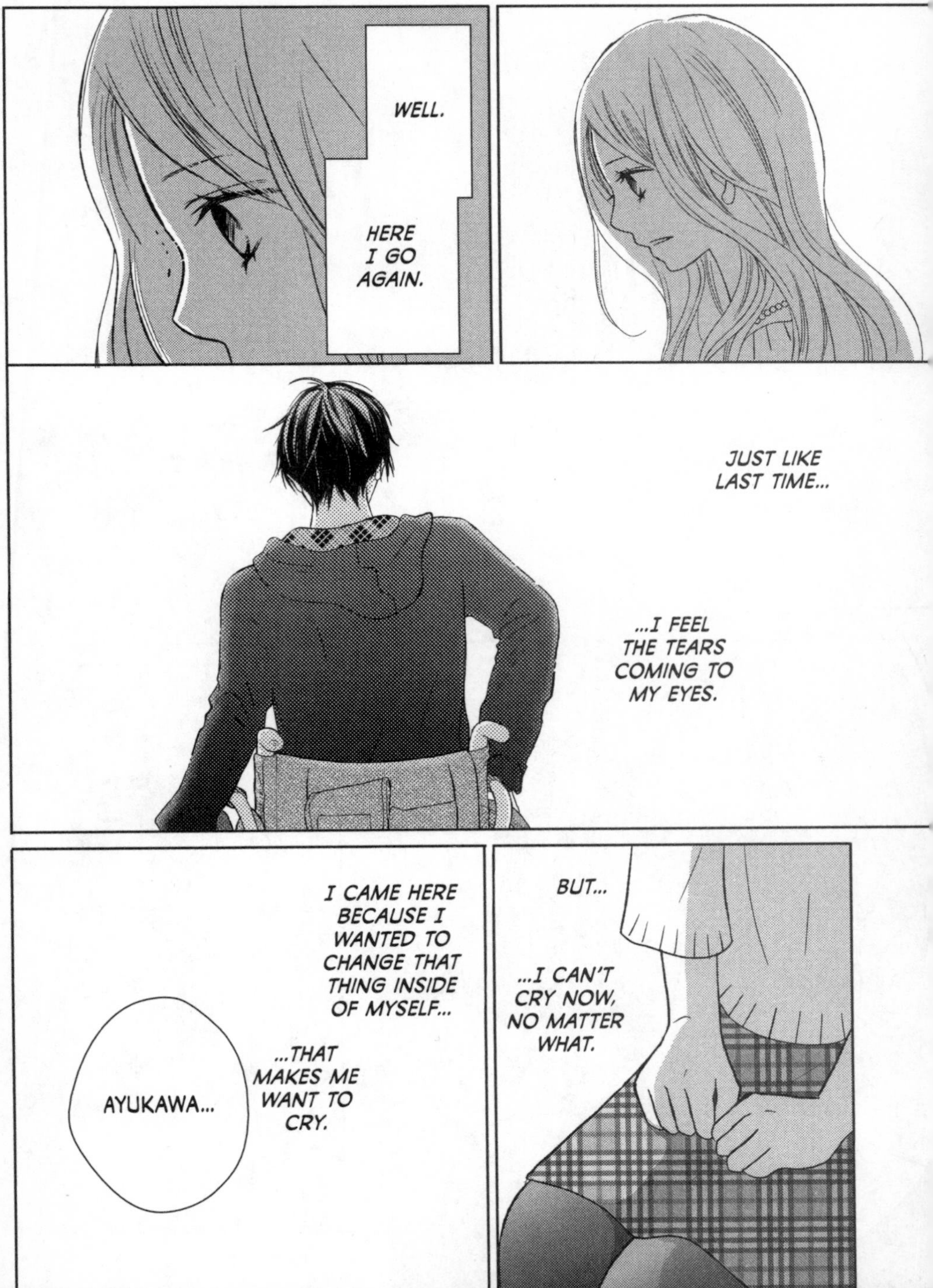
WELL.
HERE I GO AGAIN.
JUST LIKE LAST TIME...
...I FEEL THE TEARS COMING TO MY EYES.
BUT...
...I CAN'T CRY NOW, NO MATTER WHAT.
I CAME HERE BECAUSE I WANTED TO CHANGE THAT THING INSIDE OF MYSELF...
...THAT MAKES ME WANT TO CRY.
AYUKAWA...

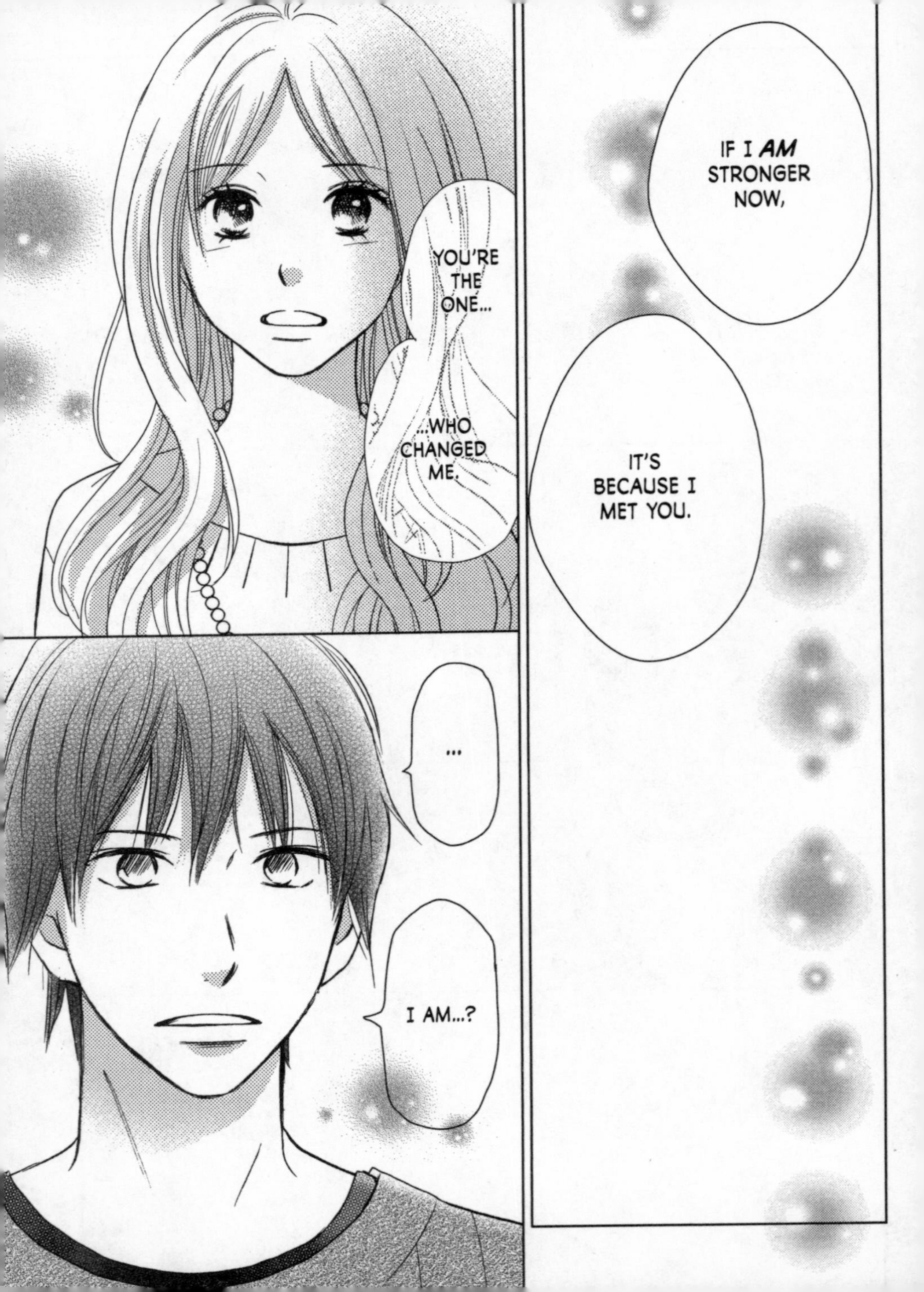
IF I *AM* STRONGER NOW,
IT'S BECAUSE I MET YOU.
YOU'RE THE ONE...
...WHO CHANGED ME.
...
I AM...?

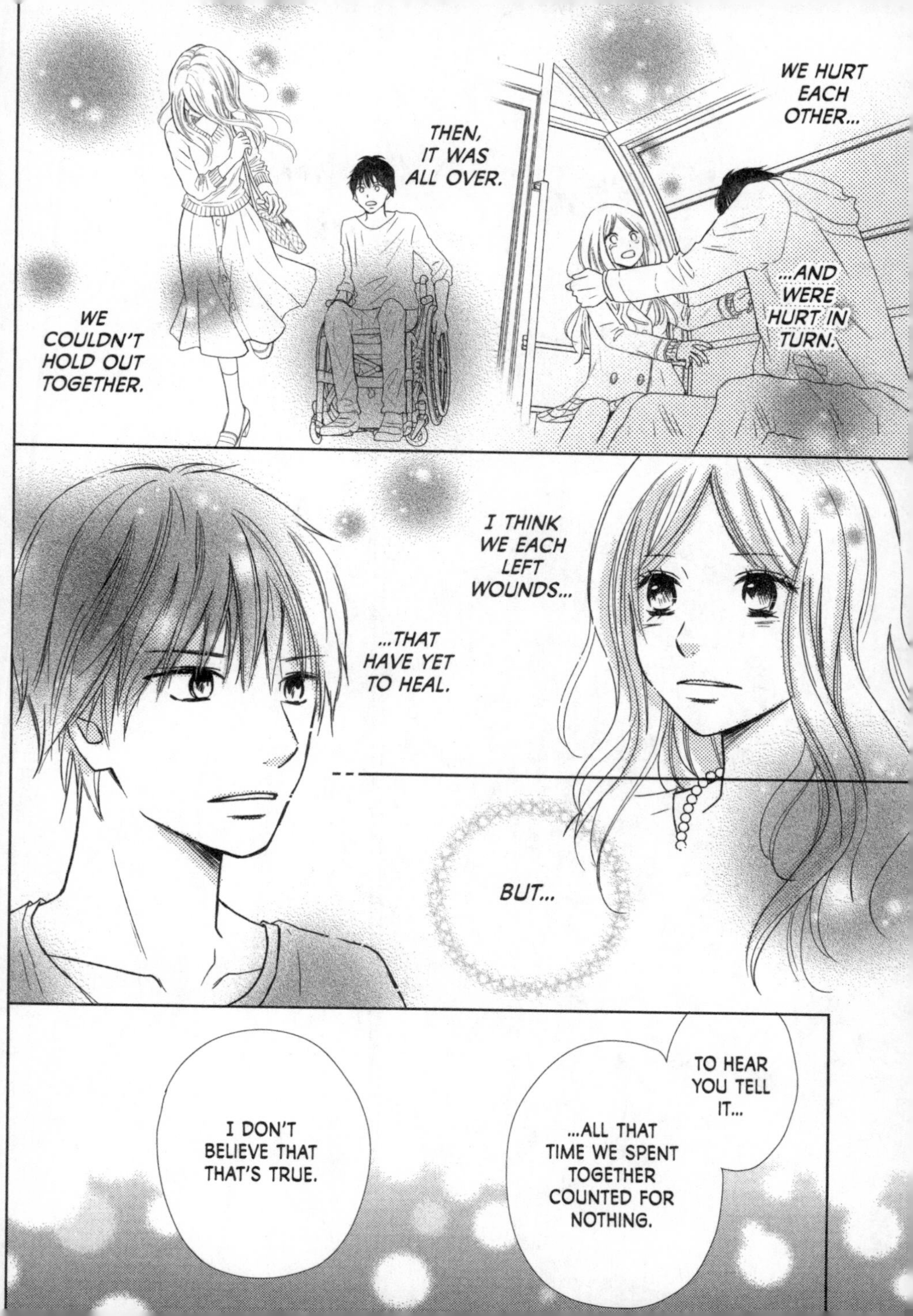
WE HURT EACH OTHER...
...AND WERE HURT IN TURN.
THEN, IT WAS ALL OVER.
WE COULDN'T HOLD OUT TOGETHER.
I THINK WE EACH LEFT WOUNDS...
...THAT HAVE YET TO HEAL.
BUT...
TO HEAR YOU TELL IT...
...ALL THAT TIME WE SPENT TOGETHER COUNTED FOR NOTHING.
I DON'T BELIEVE THAT THAT'S TRUE.

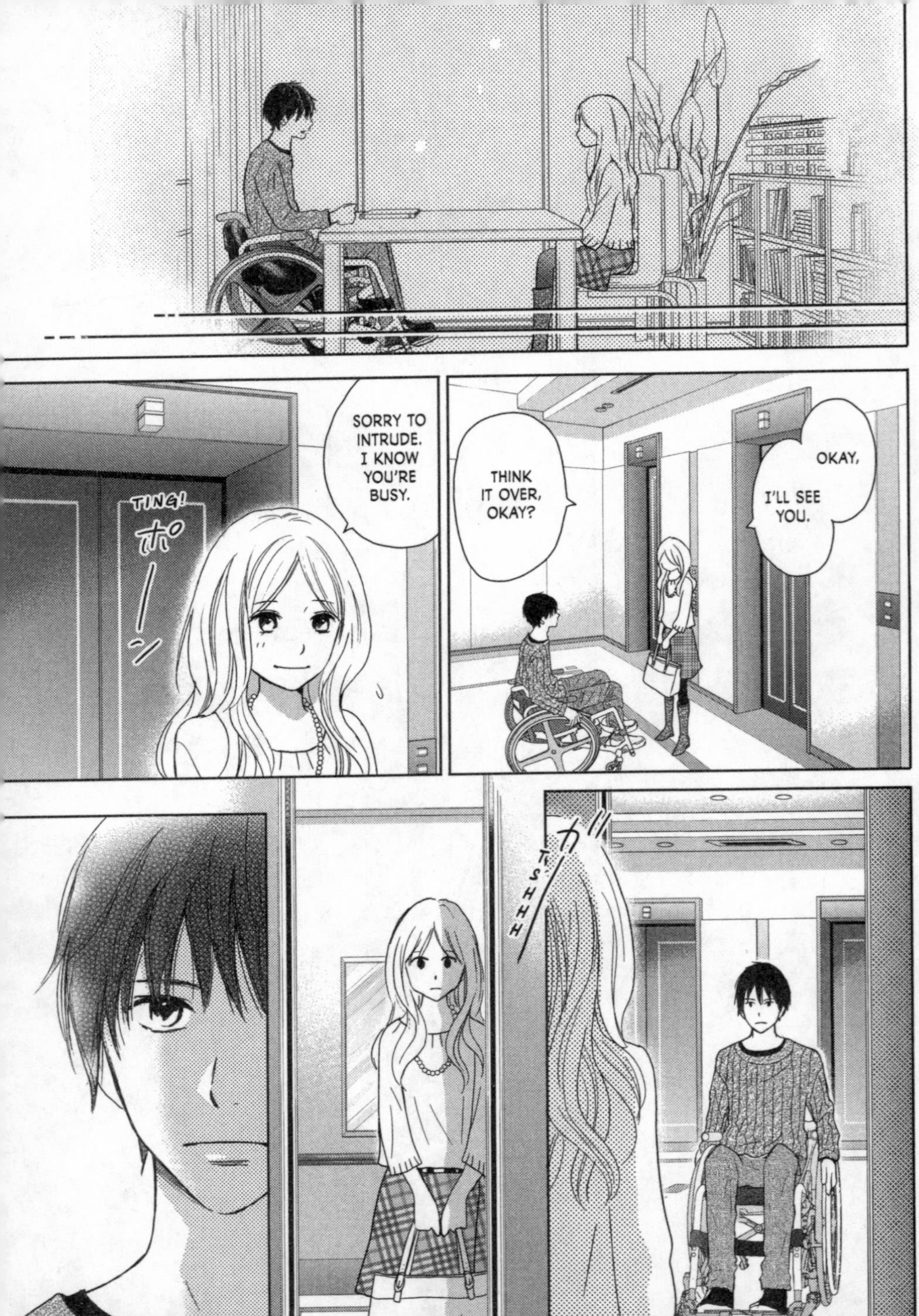
OKAY, I'LL SEE YOU.
THINK IT OVER, OKAY?
SORRY TO INTRUDE. I KNOW YOU'RE BUSY.
TING!
ポーン
TSHHH

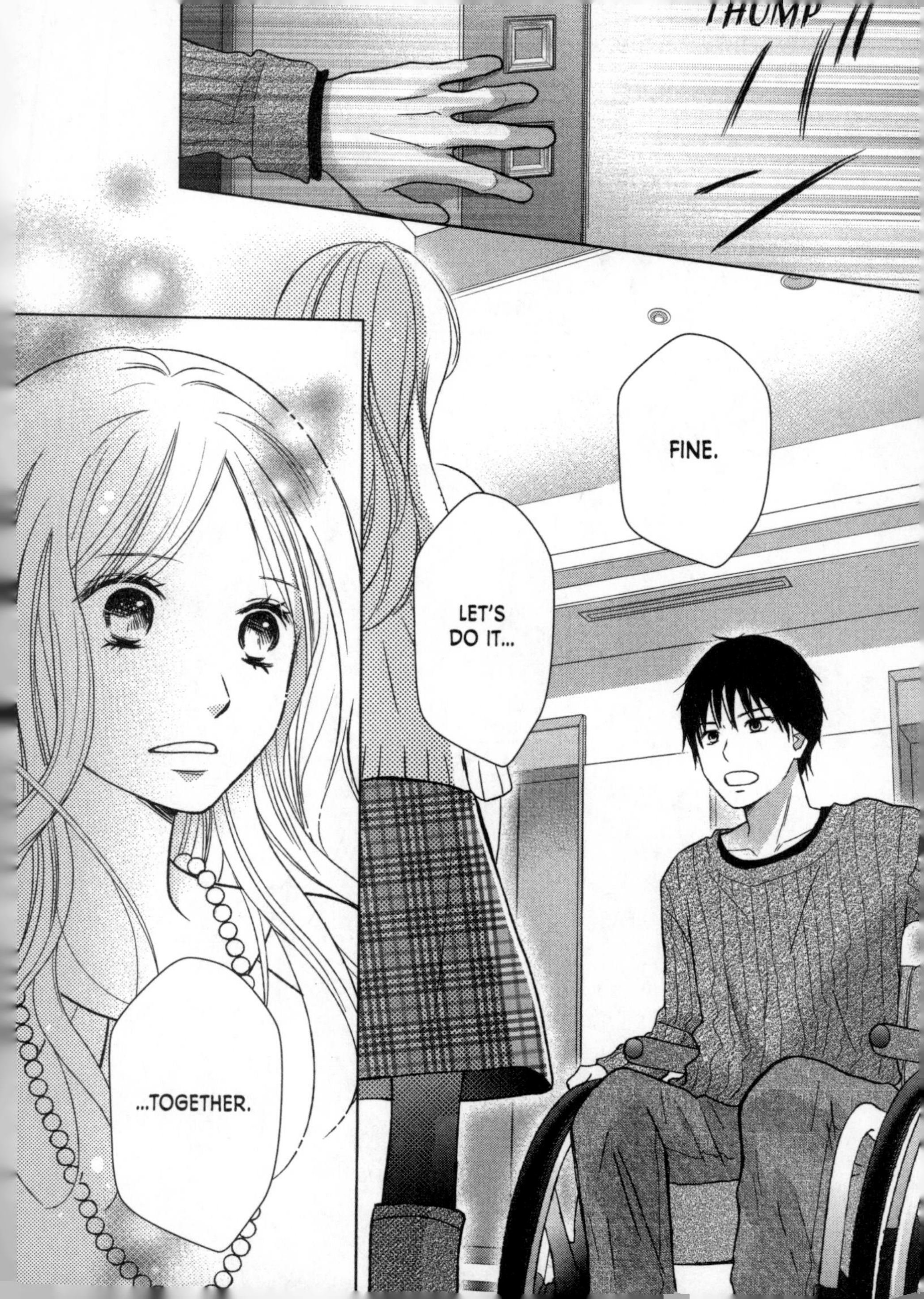
THUMP
FINE.
LET'S DO IT...
...TOGETHER.

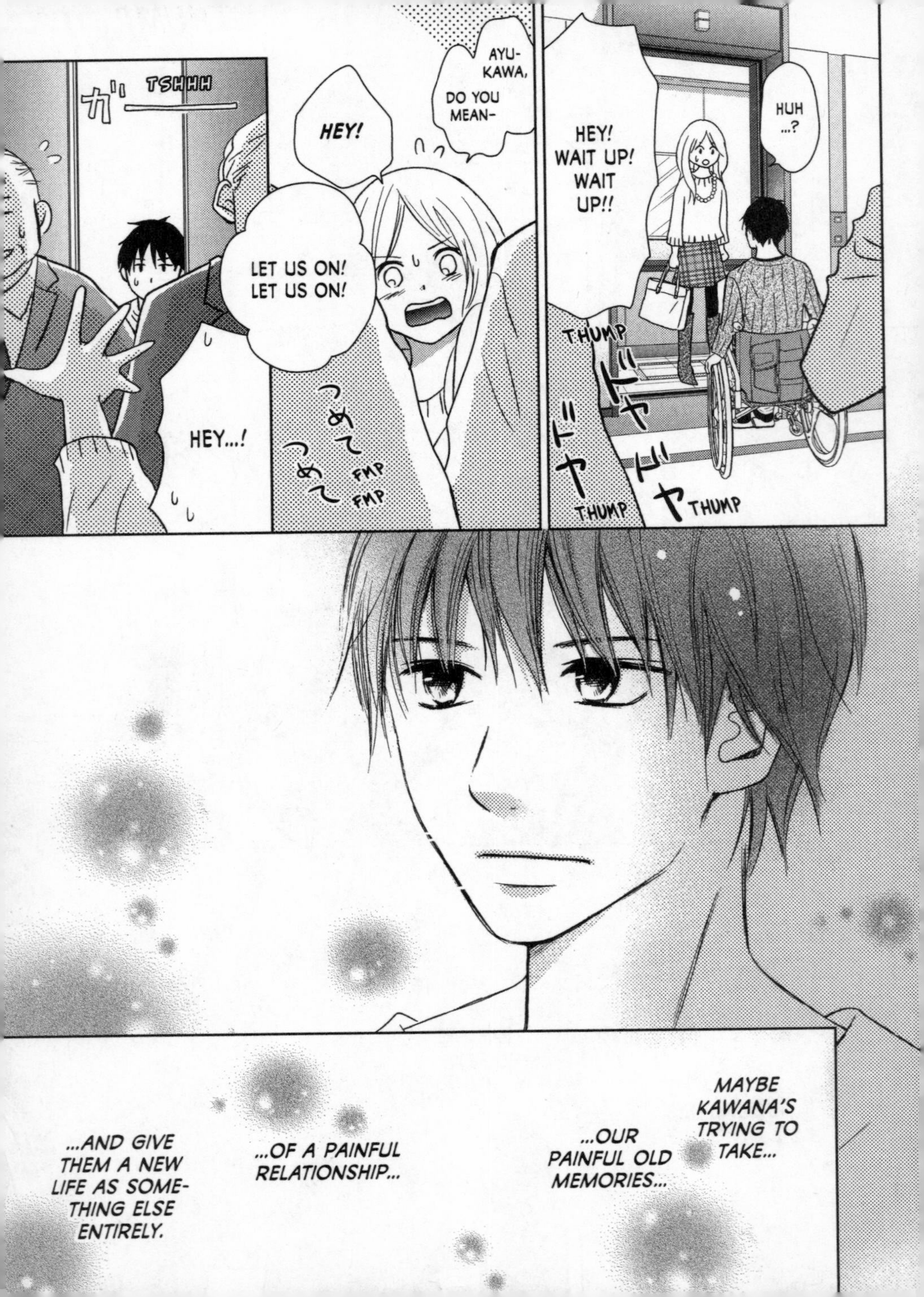

HUH ...?
HEY! WAIT UP! WAIT UP!!
ドヤ
THUMP
ドヤ
THUMP
ドヤ
THUMP
AYU-KAWA, DO YOU MEAN-
HEY!
LET US ON! LET US ON!
つめて
FMP
つめて
FMP
ガー
TSHHH
HEY...!
MAYBE KAWANA'S TRYING TO TAKE...
...OUR PAINFUL OLD MEMORIES...
...OF A PAINFUL RELATIONSHIP...
...AND GIVE THEM A NEW LIFE AS SOME-THING ELSE ENTIRELY.

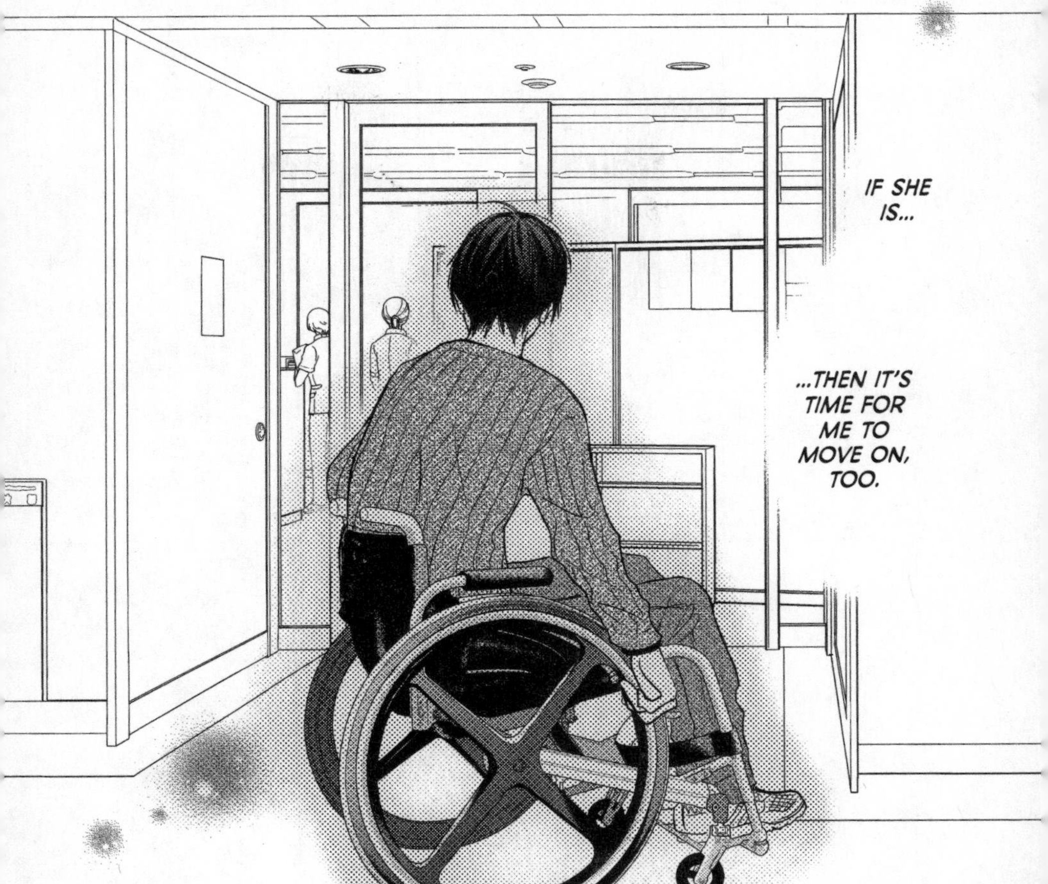
IF SHE IS...
...THEN IT'S TIME FOR ME TO MOVE ON, TOO.

SHE'S RIGHT. I DON'T WANT TO THINK...

...THAT ALL THE TIME WE SPENT TOGETHER...

...COUNTED FOR NOTHING.

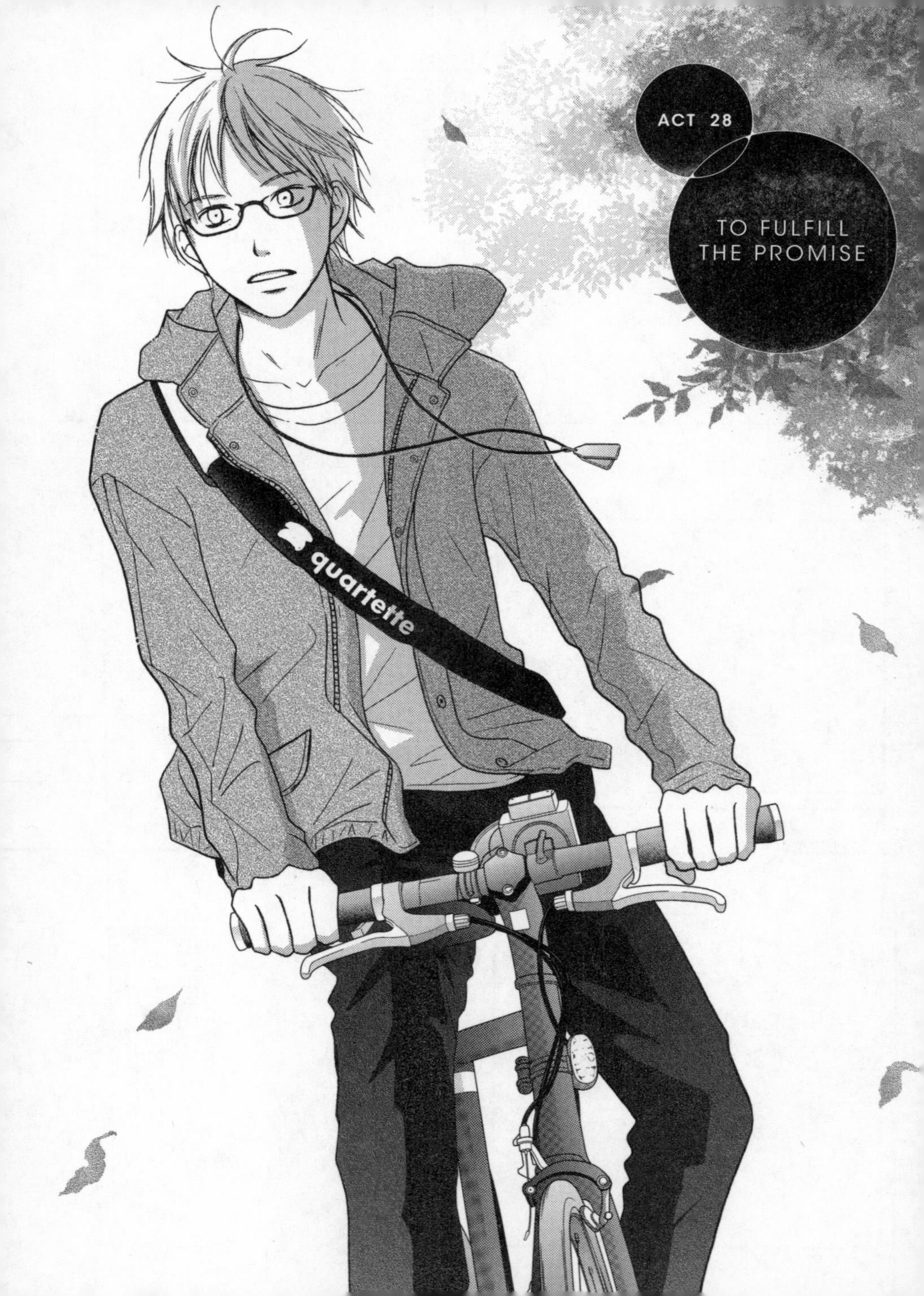
ACT 28
TO FULFILL THE PROMISE
quartette

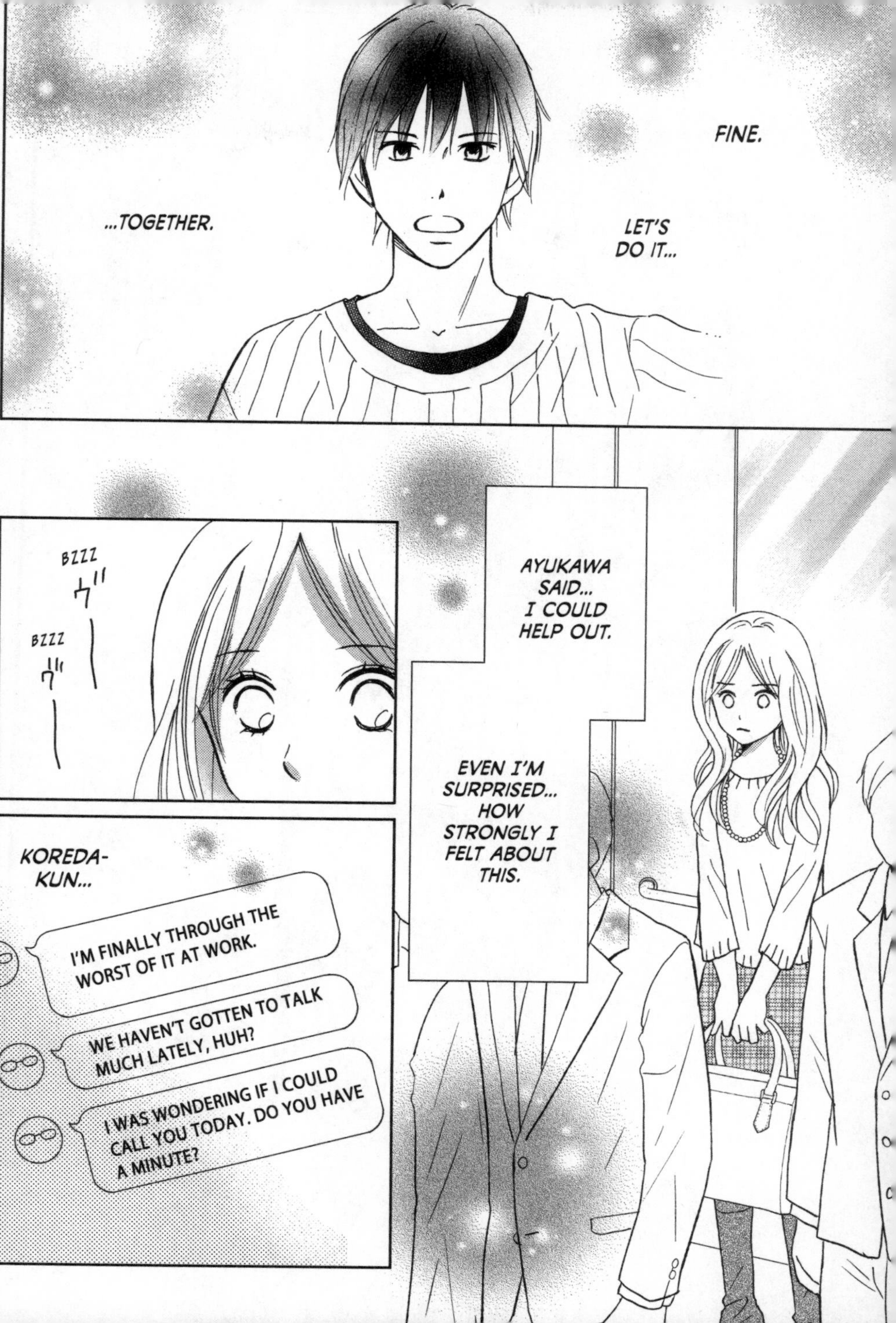
FINE.
LET'S DO IT...
...TOGETHER.
AYUKAWA SAID... I COULD HELP OUT.
EVEN I'M SURPRISED... HOW STRONGLY I FELT ABOUT THIS.
BZZZ
ヴ゛ー
BZZZ
ヴ゛ー
KOREDA-KUN...
I'M FINALLY THROUGH THE WORST OF IT AT WORK.
WE HAVEN'T GOTTEN TO TALK MUCH LATELY, HUH?
I WAS WONDERING IF I COULD CALL YOU TODAY. DO YOU HAVE A MINUTE?

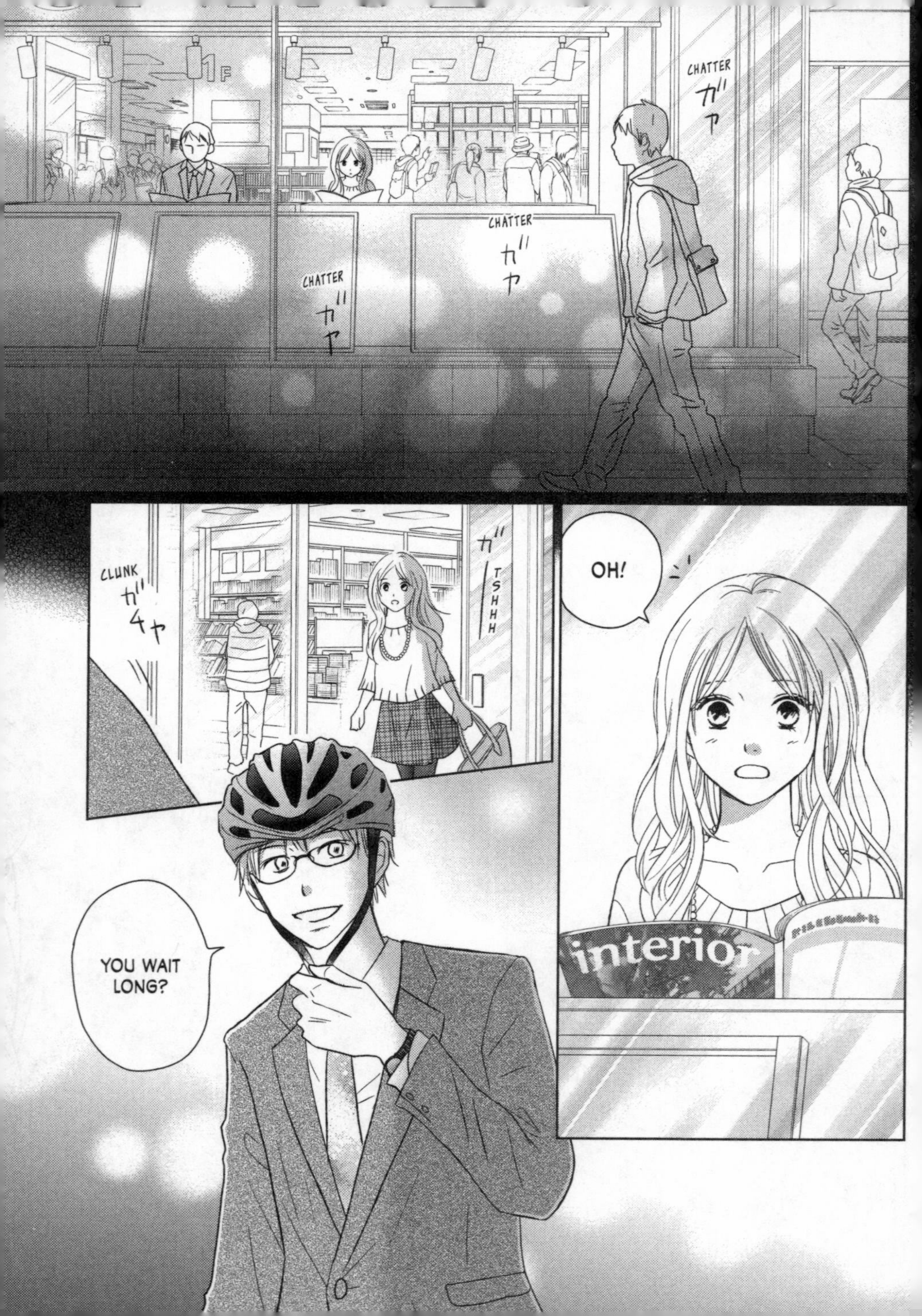
CHATTER ガヤ
CHATTER ガヤ
CHATTER ガヤ
OH!
interior
ガー TSHHH
CLUNK ガチャ
YOU WAIT LONG?

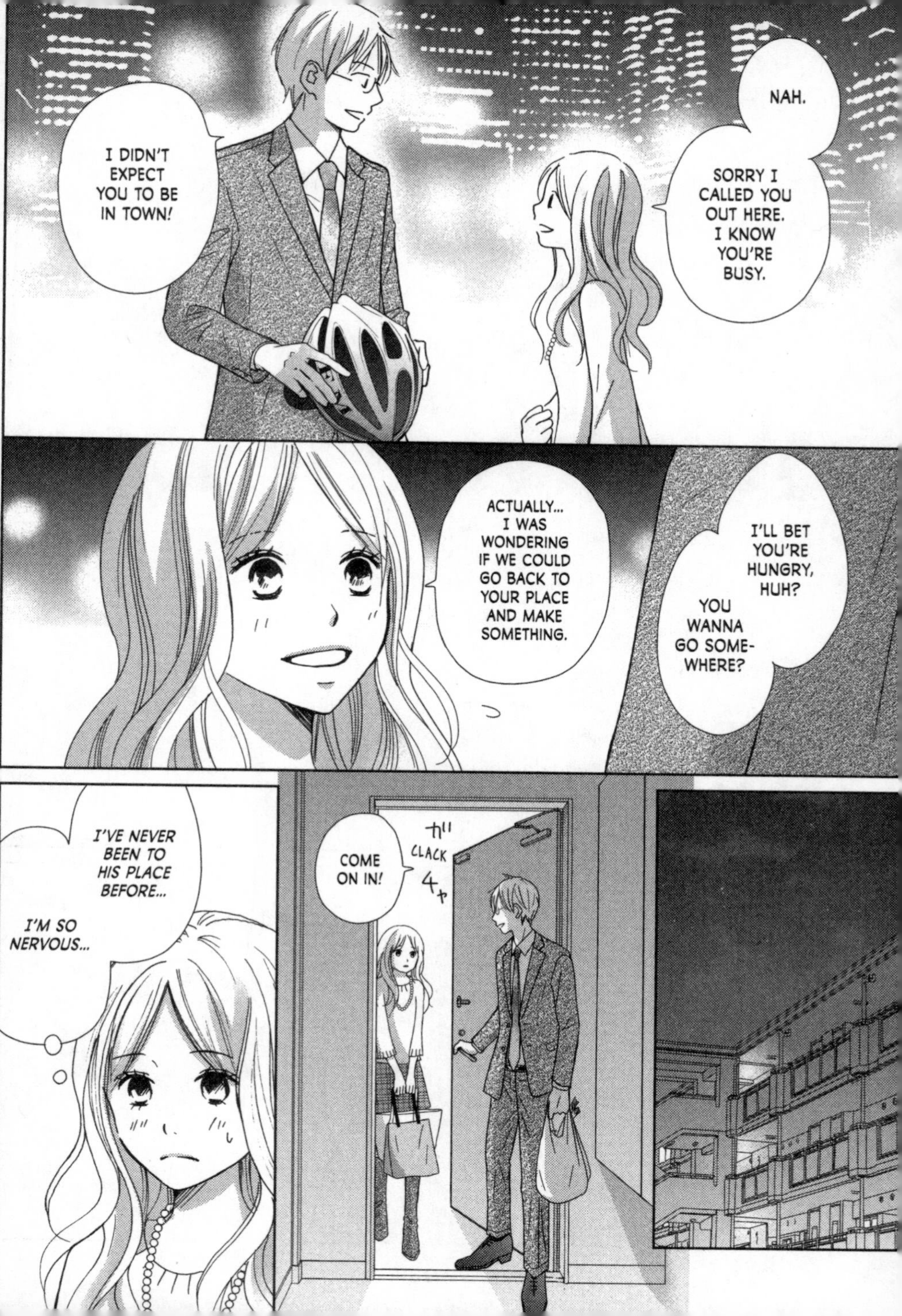
NAH.
SORRY I CALLED YOU OUT HERE. I KNOW YOU'RE BUSY.
I DIDN'T EXPECT YOU TO BE IN TOWN!
I'LL BET YOU'RE HUNGRY, HUH?
YOU WANNA GO SOME-WHERE?
ACTUALLY... I WAS WONDERING IF WE COULD GO BACK TO YOUR PLACE AND MAKE SOMETHING.
CLACK
COME ON IN!
I'VE NEVER BEEN TO HIS PLACE BEFORE...
I'M SO NERVOUS...

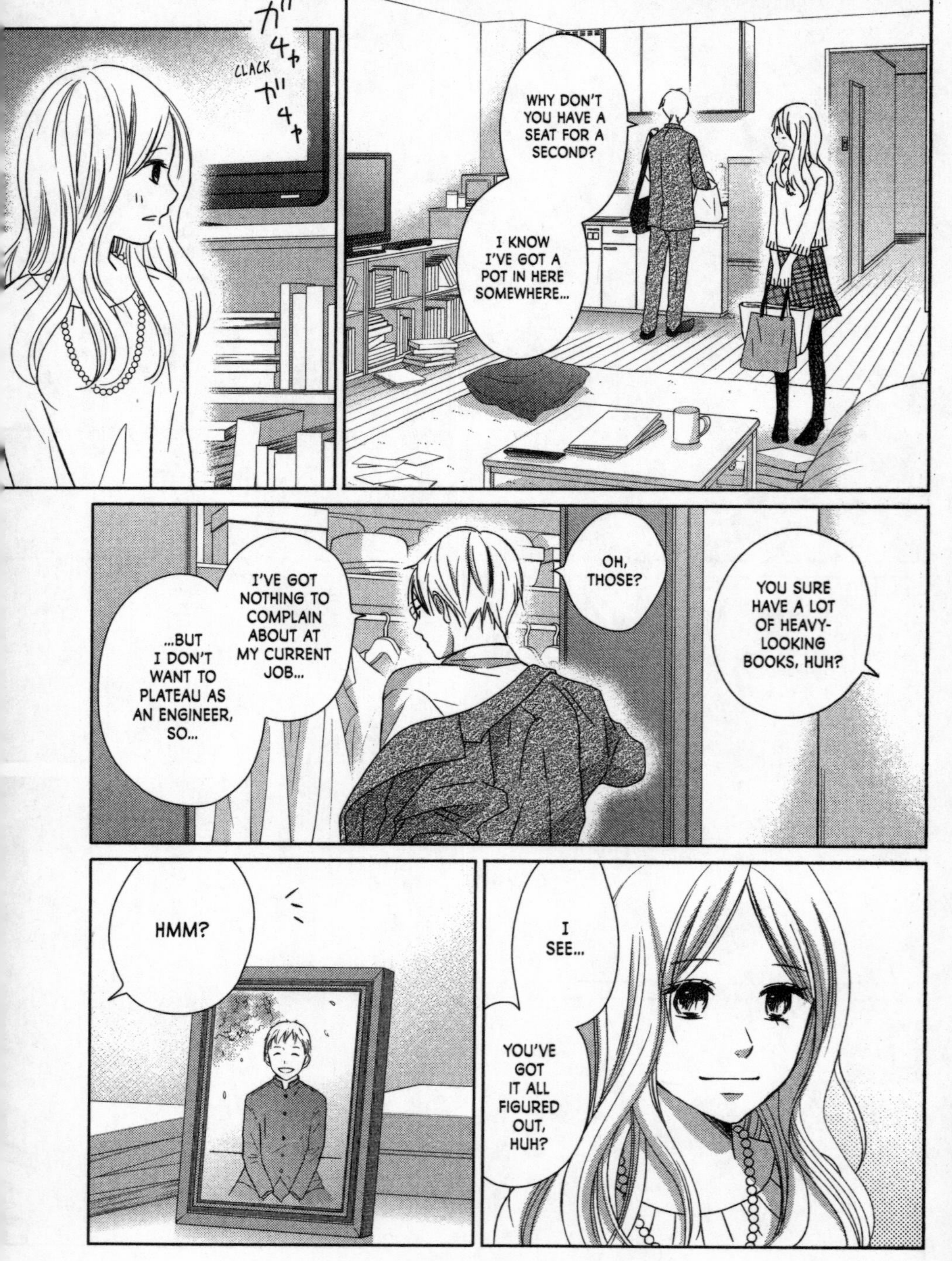
WHY DON'T YOU HAVE A SEAT FOR A SECOND?
I KNOW I'VE GOT A POT IN HERE SOMEWHERE...
CLACK
ガチャ
CLACK
ガチャ
YOU SURE HAVE A LOT OF HEAVY-LOOKING BOOKS, HUH?
OH, THOSE?
I'VE GOT NOTHING TO COMPLAIN ABOUT AT MY CURRENT JOB...
...BUT I DON'T WANT TO PLATEAU AS AN ENGINEER, SO...
I SEE...
YOU'VE GOT IT ALL FIGURED OUT, HUH?
HMM?

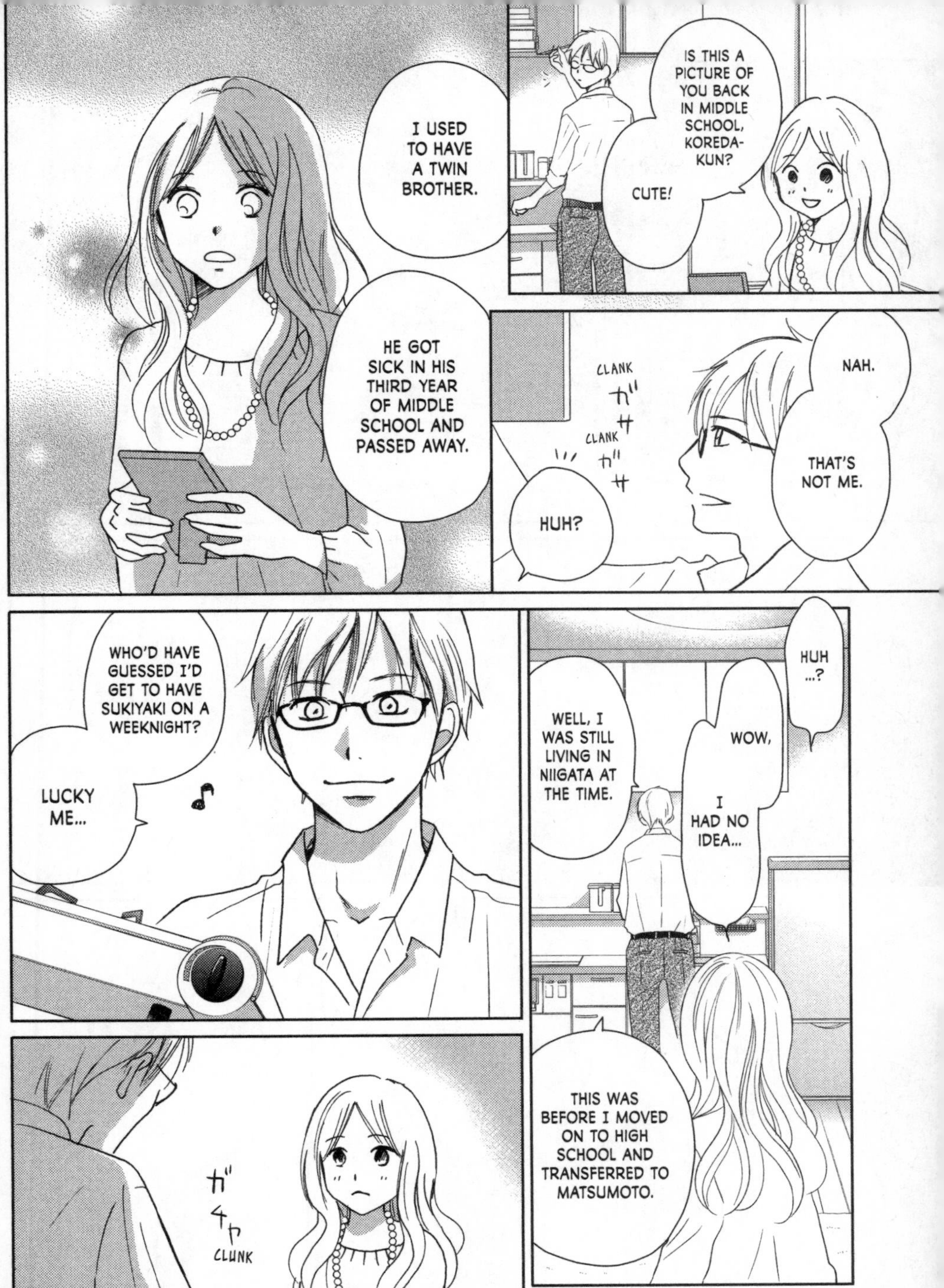
IS THIS A PICTURE OF YOU BACK IN MIDDLE SCHOOL, KOREDA-KUN?
CUTE!
NAH.
THAT'S NOT ME.
CLANK
ガッ
CLANK
ガッ
HUH?
I USED TO HAVE A TWIN BROTHER.
HE GOT SICK IN HIS THIRD YEAR OF MIDDLE SCHOOL AND PASSED AWAY.
HUH ...?
WOW,
I HAD NO IDEA...
WELL, I WAS STILL LIVING IN NIIGATA AT THE TIME.
THIS WAS BEFORE I MOVED ON TO HIGH SCHOOL AND TRANSFERRED TO MATSUMOTO.
WHO'D HAVE GUESSED I'D GET TO HAVE SUKIYAKI ON A WEEKNIGHT?
LUCKY ME...
ガチャ
CLUNK

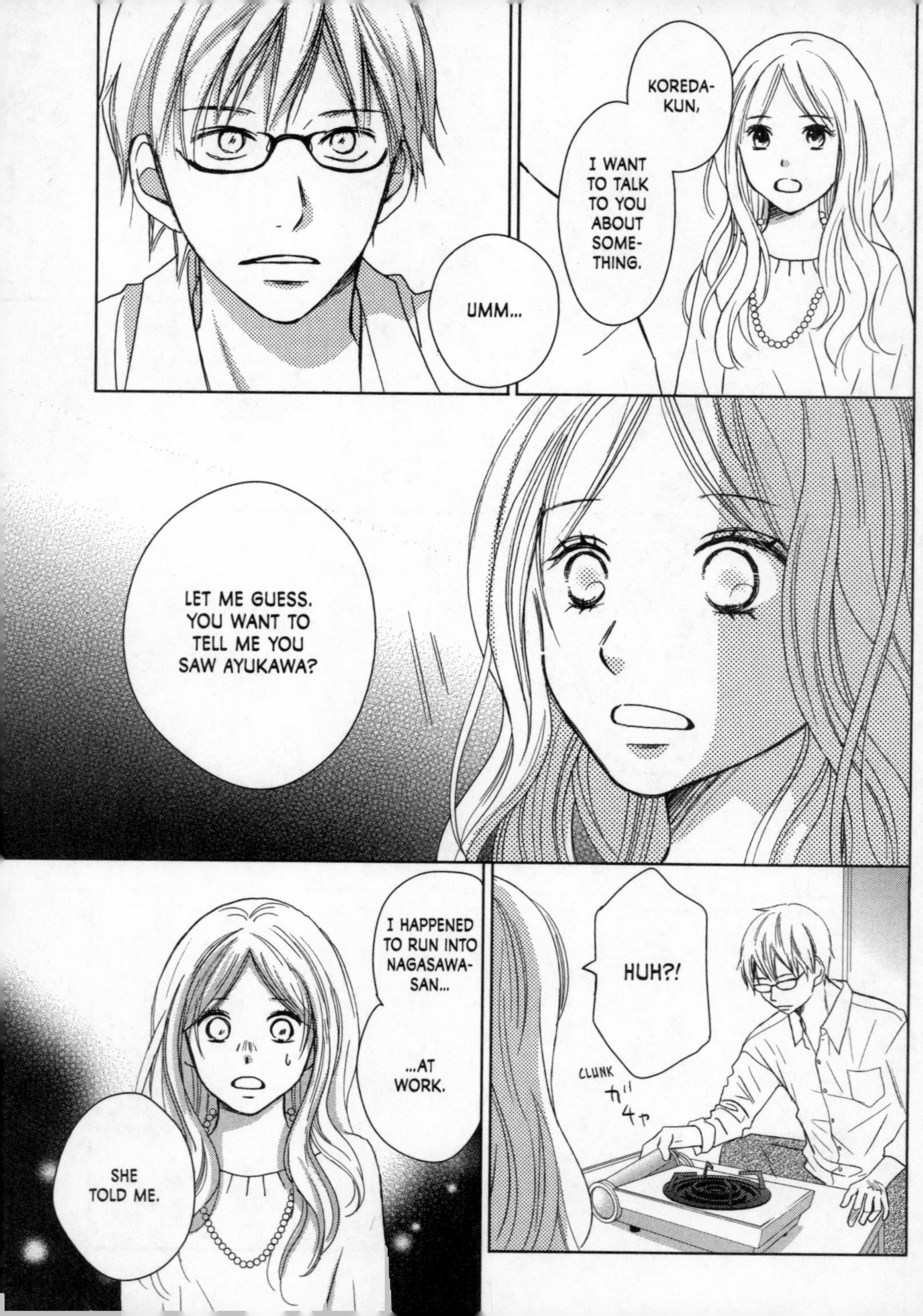
KOREDA-KUN,
I WANT TO TALK TO YOU ABOUT SOMETHING.
UMM...
LET ME GUESS. YOU WANT TO TELL ME YOU SAW AYUKAWA?
HUH?!
CLUNK
I HAPPENED TO RUN INTO NAGASAWA-SAN...
...AT WORK.
SHE TOLD ME.

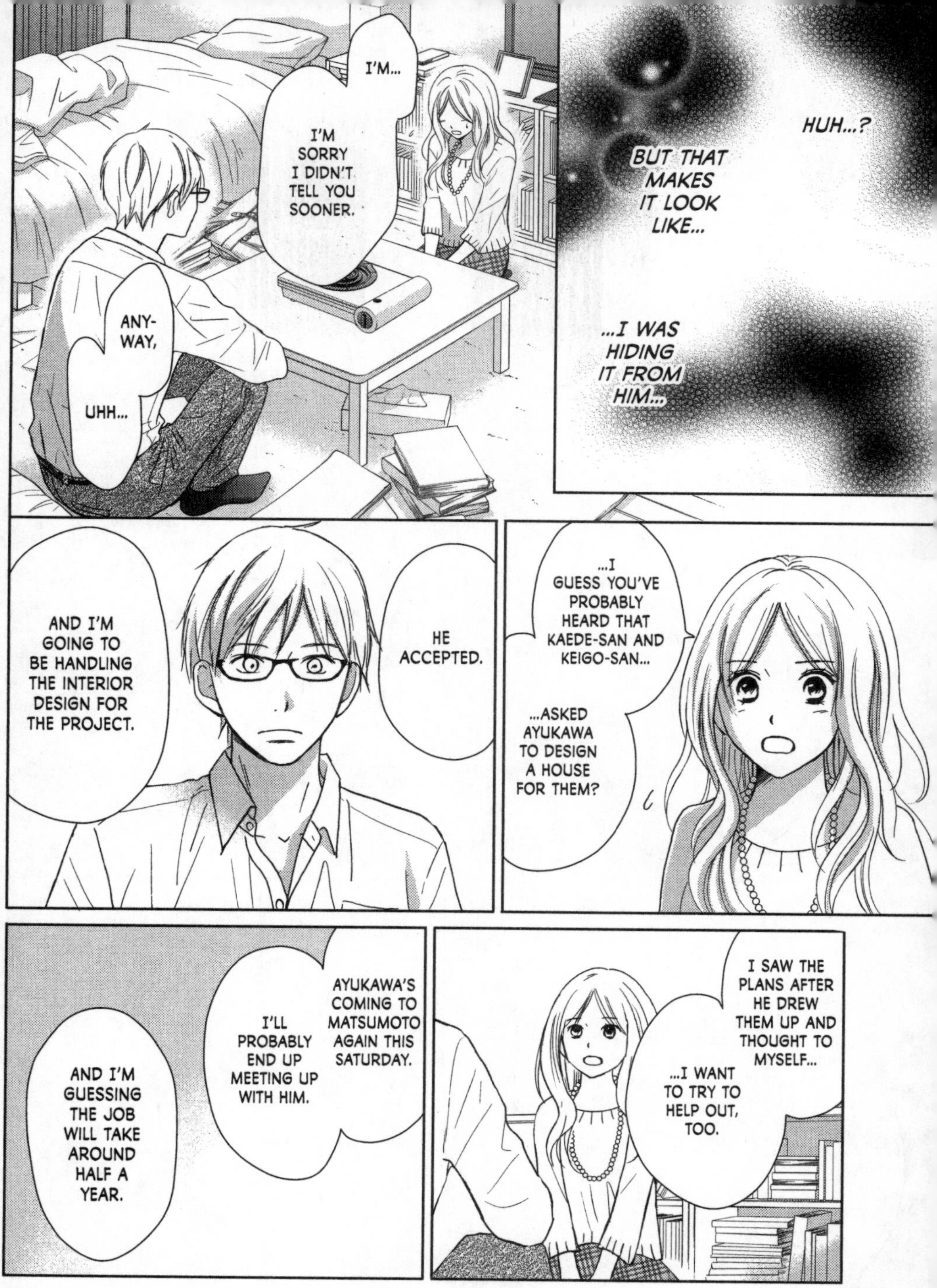
HUH...?
BUT THAT MAKES IT LOOK LIKE...
...I WAS HIDING IT FROM HIM...
I'M...
I'M SORRY I DIDN'T TELL YOU SOONER.
ANY-WAY,
UHH...
...I GUESS YOU'VE PROBABLY HEARD THAT KAEDE-SAN AND KEIGO-SAN...
...ASKED AYUKAWA TO DESIGN A HOUSE FOR THEM?
HE ACCEPTED.
AND I'M GOING TO BE HANDLING THE INTERIOR DESIGN FOR THE PROJECT.
I SAW THE PLANS AFTER HE DREW THEM UP AND THOUGHT TO MYSELF...
...I WANT TO TRY TO HELP OUT, TOO.
AYUKAWA'S COMING TO MATSUMOTO AGAIN THIS SATURDAY.
I'LL PROBABLY END UP MEETING UP WITH HIM.
AND I'M GUESSING THE JOB WILL TAKE AROUND HALF A YEAR.

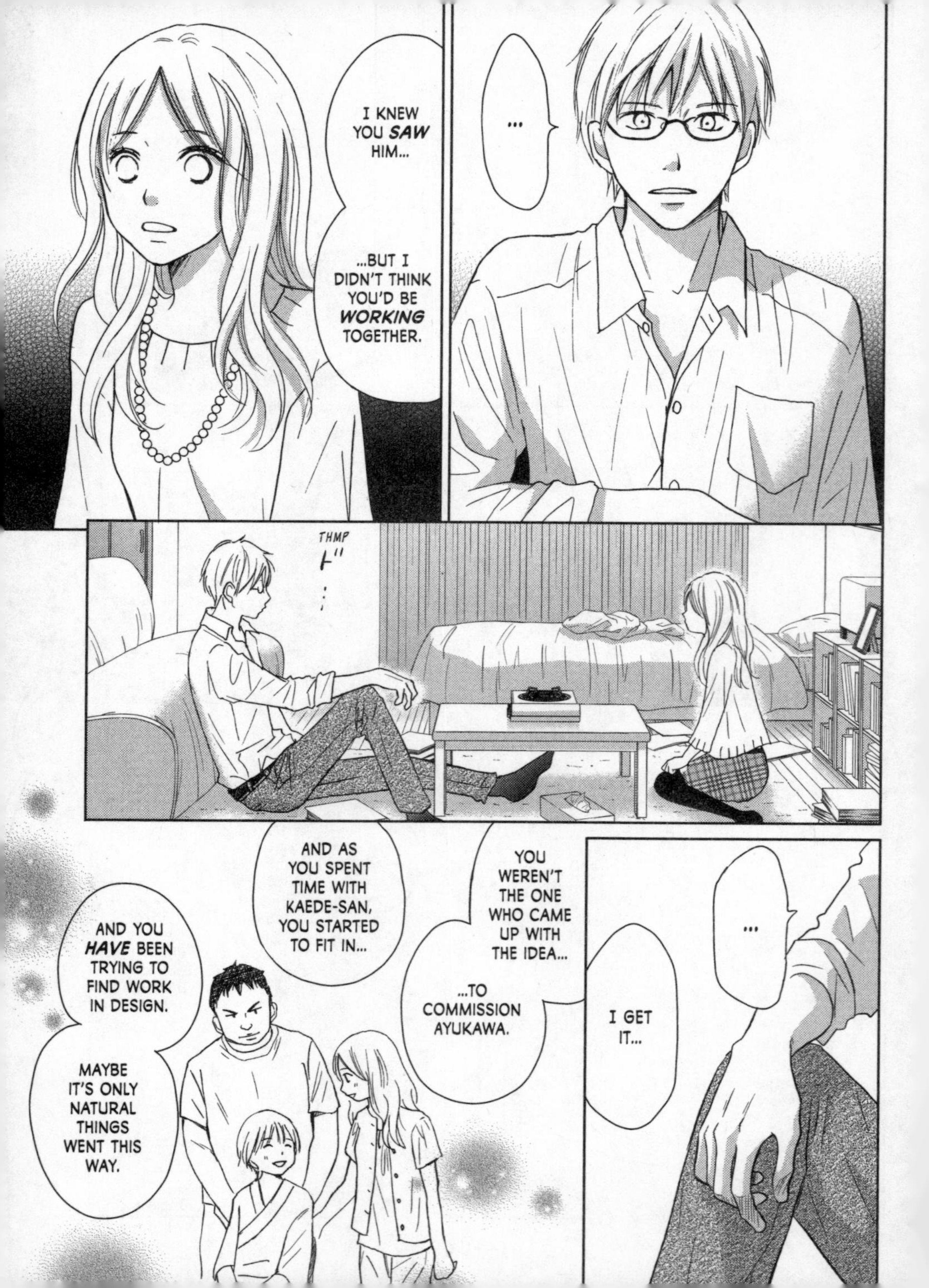
...
I KNEW YOU *SAW* HIM...
...BUT I DIDN'T THINK YOU'D BE *WORKING* TOGETHER.
THMP
ド"
...
I GET IT...
YOU WEREN'T THE ONE WHO CAME UP WITH THE IDEA...
...TO COMMISSION AYUKAWA.
AND AS YOU SPENT TIME WITH KAEDE-SAN, YOU STARTED TO FIT IN...
AND YOU *HAVE* BEEN TRYING TO FIND WORK IN DESIGN.
MAYBE IT'S ONLY NATURAL THINGS WENT THIS WAY.

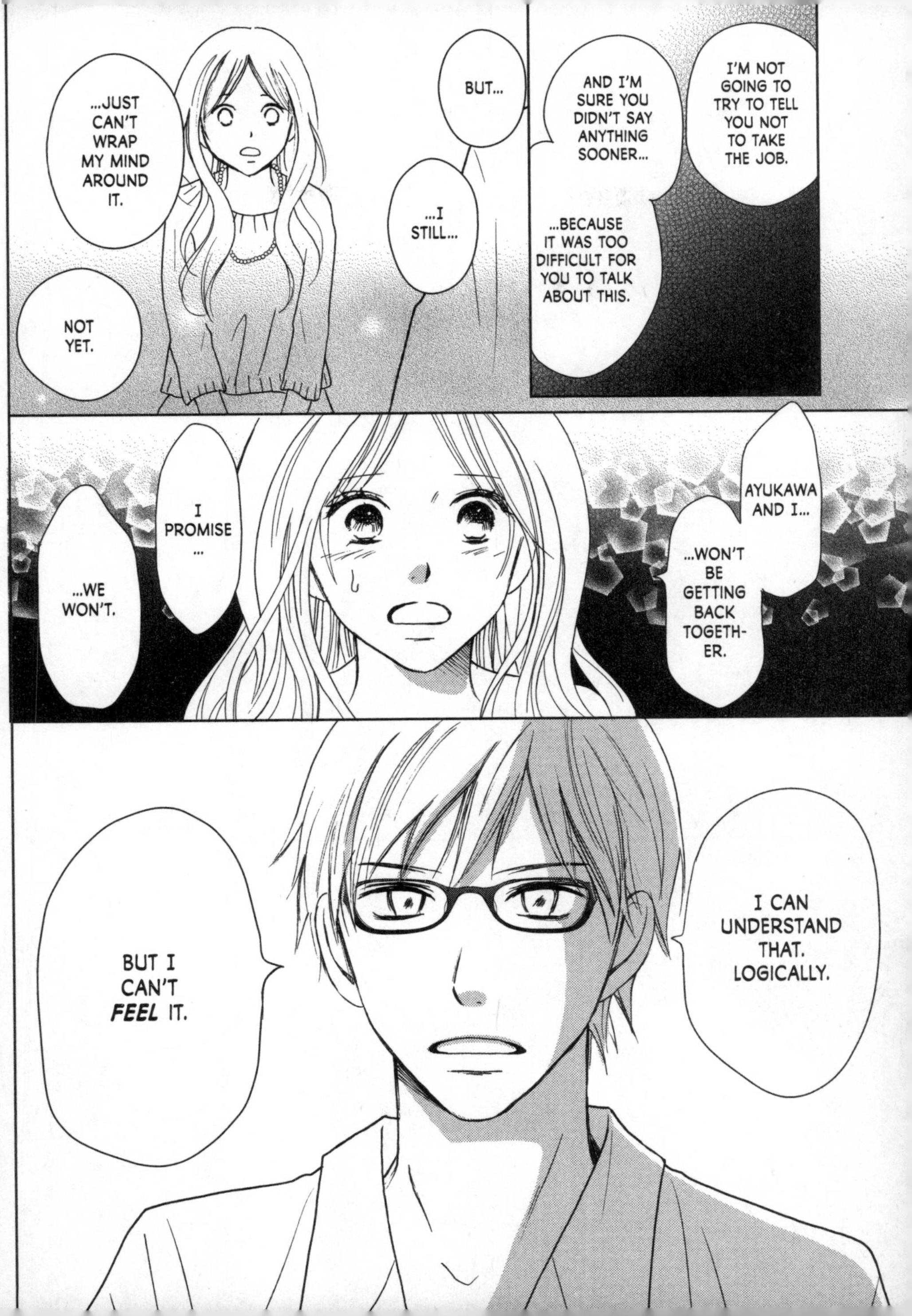
I'M NOT GOING TO TRY TO TELL YOU NOT TO TAKE THE JOB.
AND I'M SURE YOU DIDN'T SAY ANYTHING SOONER...
...BECAUSE IT WAS TOO DIFFICULT FOR YOU TO TALK ABOUT THIS.
BUT...
...I STILL...
...JUST CAN'T WRAP MY MIND AROUND IT.
NOT YET.
AYUKAWA AND I...
...WON'T BE GETTING BACK TOGETHER.
I PROMISE...
...WE WON'T.
I CAN UNDERSTAND THAT. LOGICALLY.
BUT I CAN'T *FEEL* IT.

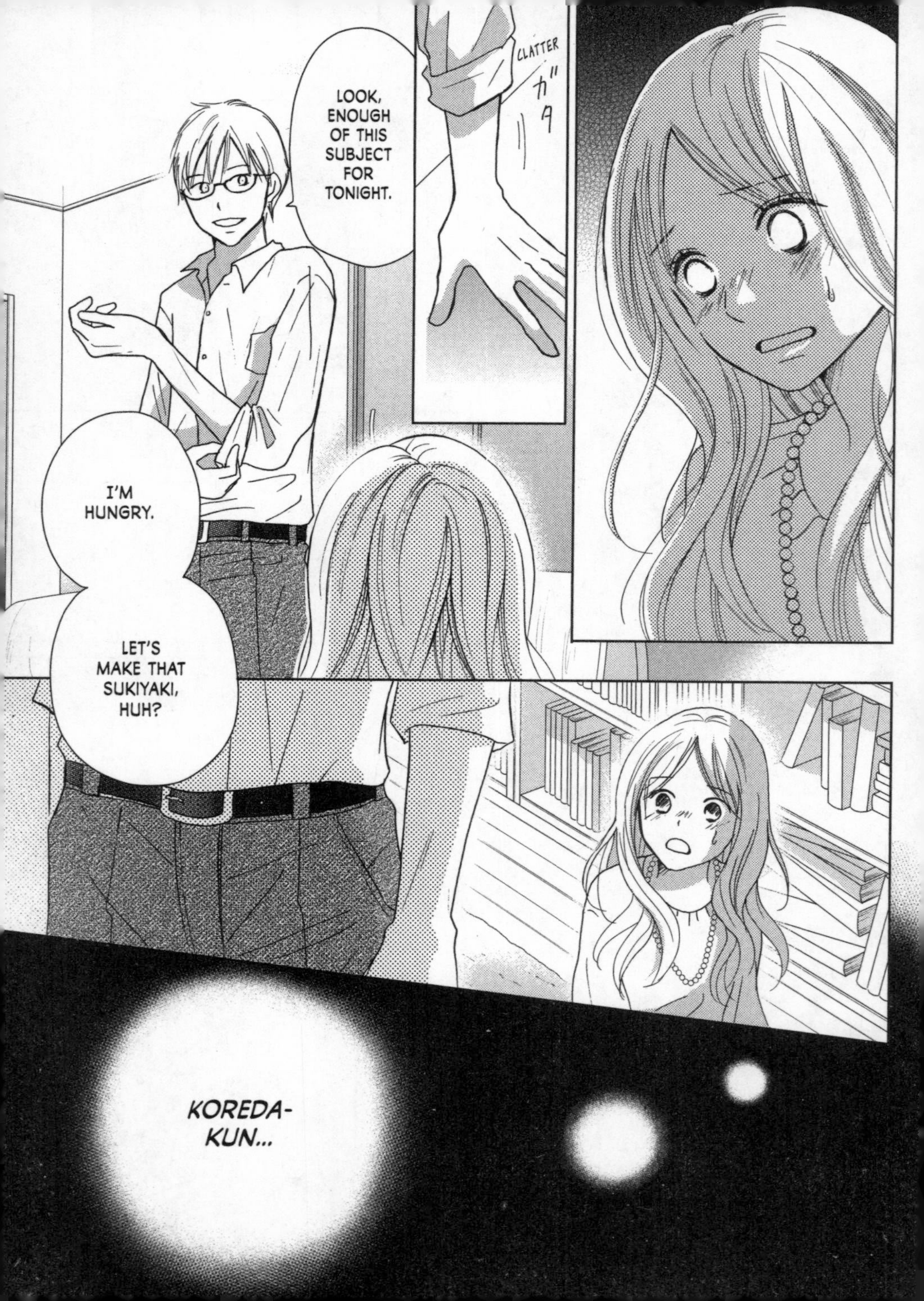
CLATTER
ガタ
LOOK, ENOUGH OF THIS SUBJECT FOR TONIGHT.
I'M HUNGRY.
LET'S MAKE THAT SUKIYAKI, HUH?
KOREDA-KUN...

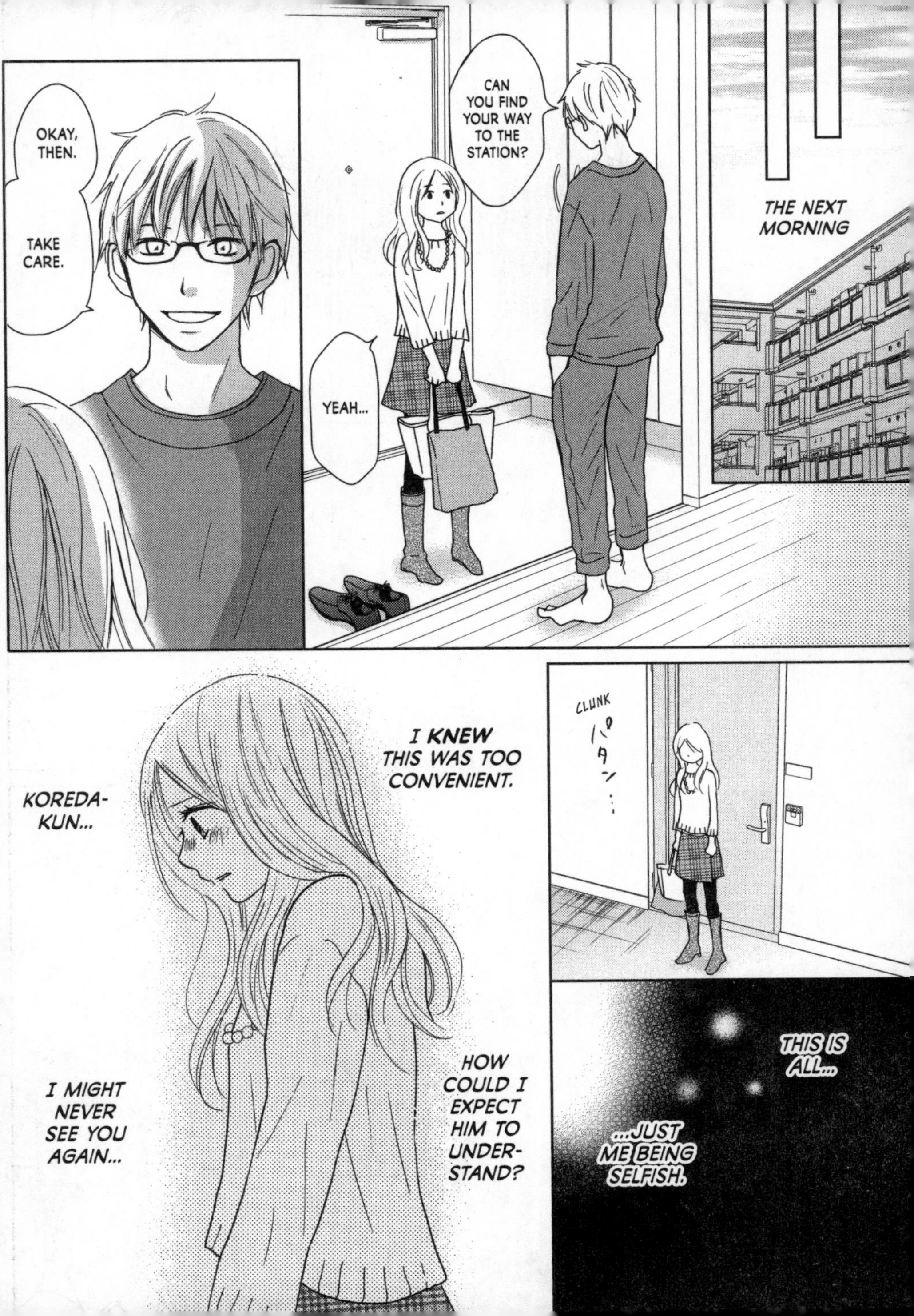
THE NEXT MORNING
CAN YOU FIND YOUR WAY TO THE STATION?
YEAH...
OKAY, THEN.
TAKE CARE.
CLUNK
パタン…
THIS IS ALL...
...JUST ME BEING SELFISH.
I KNEW THIS WAS TOO CONVENIENT.
HOW COULD I EXPECT HIM TO UNDER-STAND?
KOREDA-KUN...
I MIGHT NEVER SEE YOU AGAIN...

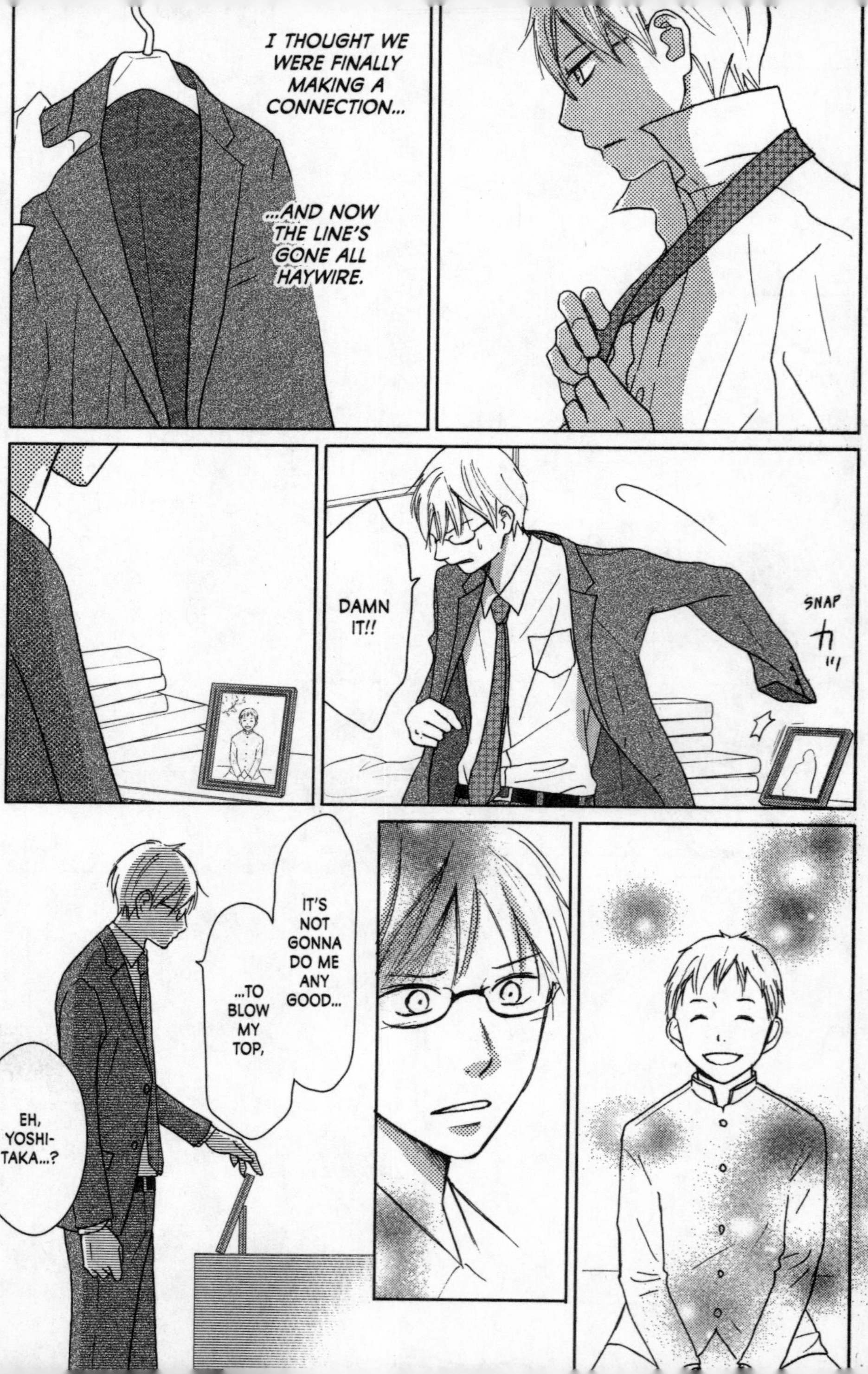
I THOUGHT WE WERE FINALLY MAKING A CONNECTION...
...AND NOW THE LINE'S GONE ALL HAYWIRE.
SNAP
カッ
DAMN IT!!
IT'S NOT GONNA DO ME ANY GOOD...
...TO BLOW MY TOP,
EH, YOSHI-TAKA...?

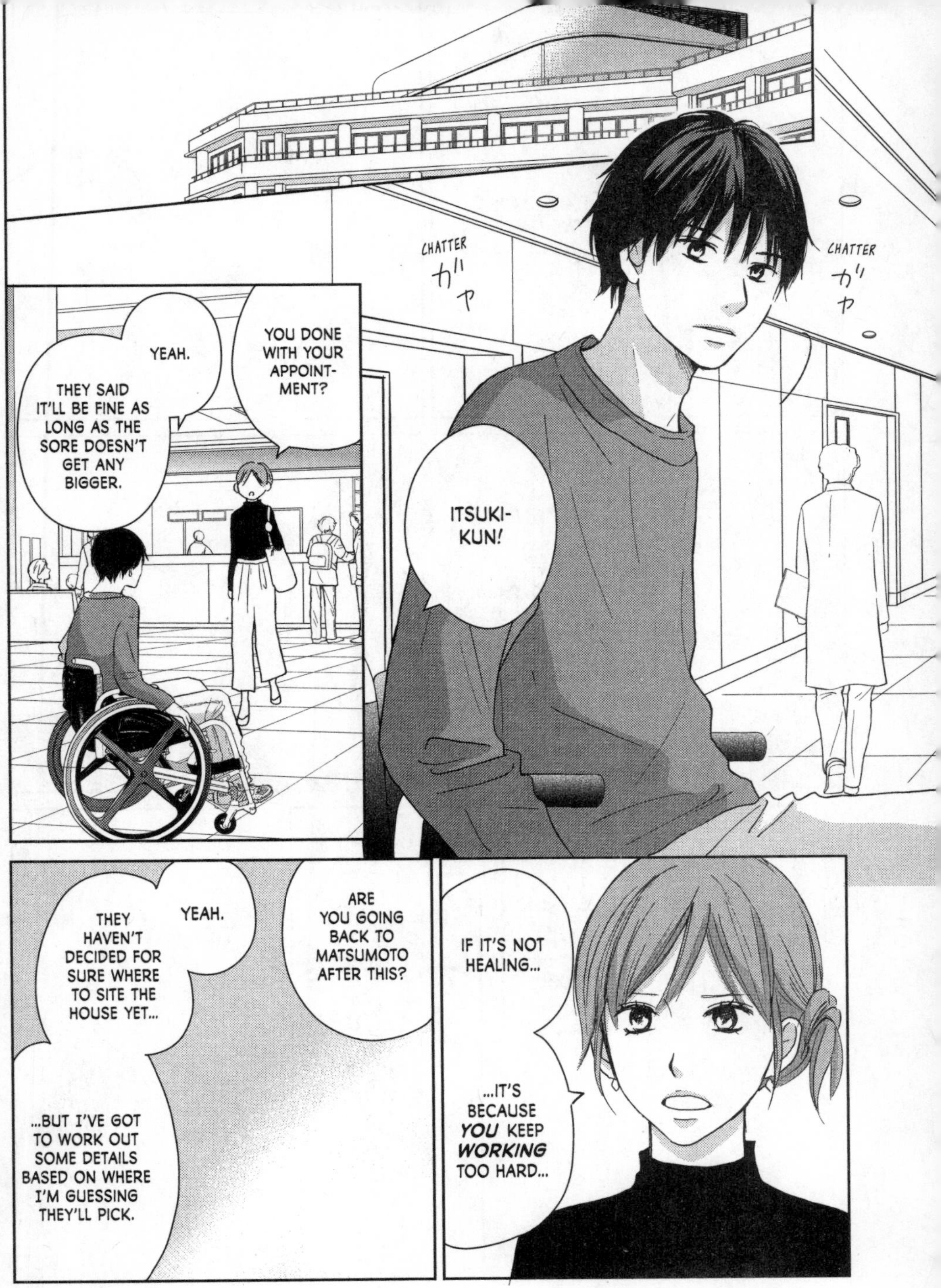
CHATTER
ガヤ
CHATTER
ガヤ
ITSUKI-KUN!
YOU DONE WITH YOUR APPOINTMENT?
YEAH.
THEY SAID IT'LL BE FINE AS LONG AS THE SORE DOESN'T GET ANY BIGGER.
IF IT'S NOT HEALING...
...IT'S BECAUSE ***YOU*** KEEP ***WORKING*** TOO HARD...
ARE YOU GOING BACK TO MATSUMOTO AFTER THIS?
YEAH.
THEY HAVEN'T DECIDED FOR SURE WHERE TO SITE THE HOUSE YET...
...BUT I'VE GOT TO WORK OUT SOME DETAILS BASED ON WHERE I'M GUESSING THEY'LL PICK.

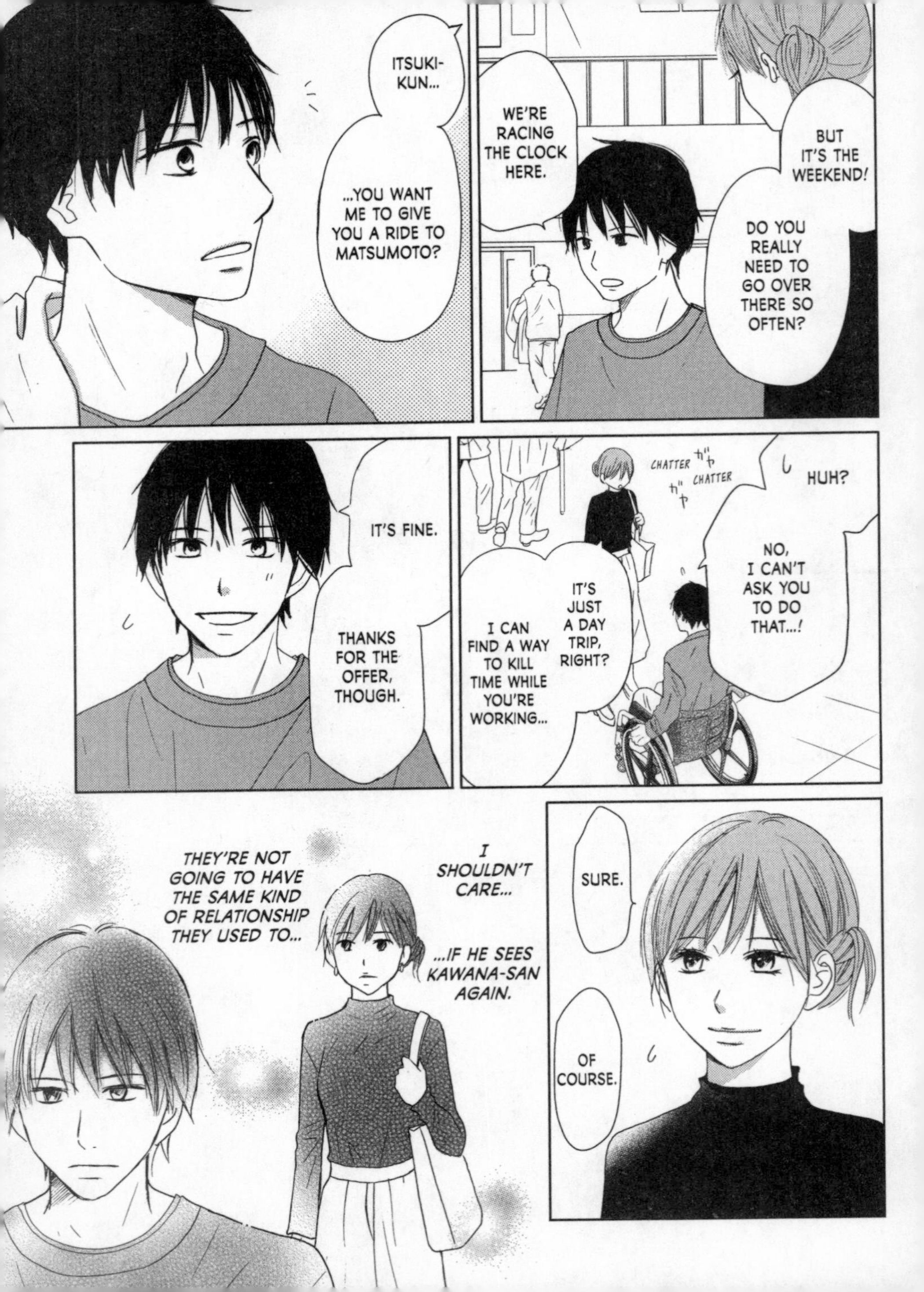
BUT IT'S THE WEEKEND!
DO YOU REALLY NEED TO GO OVER THERE SO OFTEN?
WE'RE RACING THE CLOCK HERE.
ITSUKI-KUN...
...YOU WANT ME TO GIVE YOU A RIDE TO MATSUMOTO?
HUH?
NO, I CAN'T ASK YOU TO DO THAT...!
ガヤ CHATTER
ガヤ CHATTER
IT'S JUST A DAY TRIP, RIGHT?
I CAN FIND A WAY TO KILL TIME WHILE YOU'RE WORKING...
IT'S FINE.
THANKS FOR THE OFFER, THOUGH.
SURE.
OF COURSE.
I SHOULDN'T CARE...
...IF HE SEES KAWANA-SAN AGAIN.
THEY'RE NOT GOING TO HAVE THE SAME KIND OF RELATIONSHIP THEY USED TO...

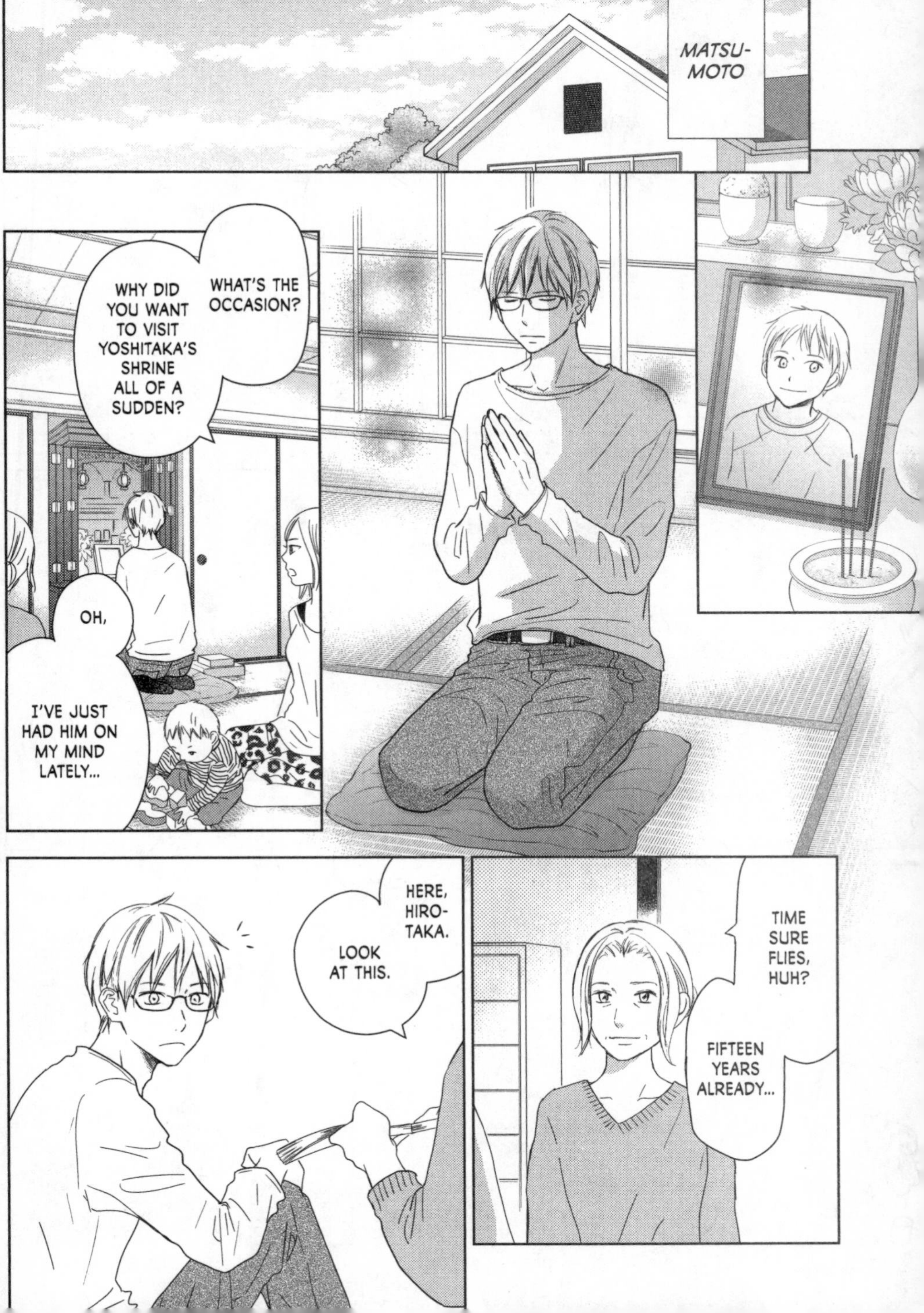
MATSU-
MOTO
WHAT'S THE OCCASION?
WHY DID YOU WANT TO VISIT YOSHITAKA'S SHRINE ALL OF A SUDDEN?
OH,
I'VE JUST HAD HIM ON MY MIND LATELY...
TIME SURE FLIES, HUH?
FIFTEEN YEARS ALREADY...
HERE, HIRO-
TAKA.
LOOK AT THIS.

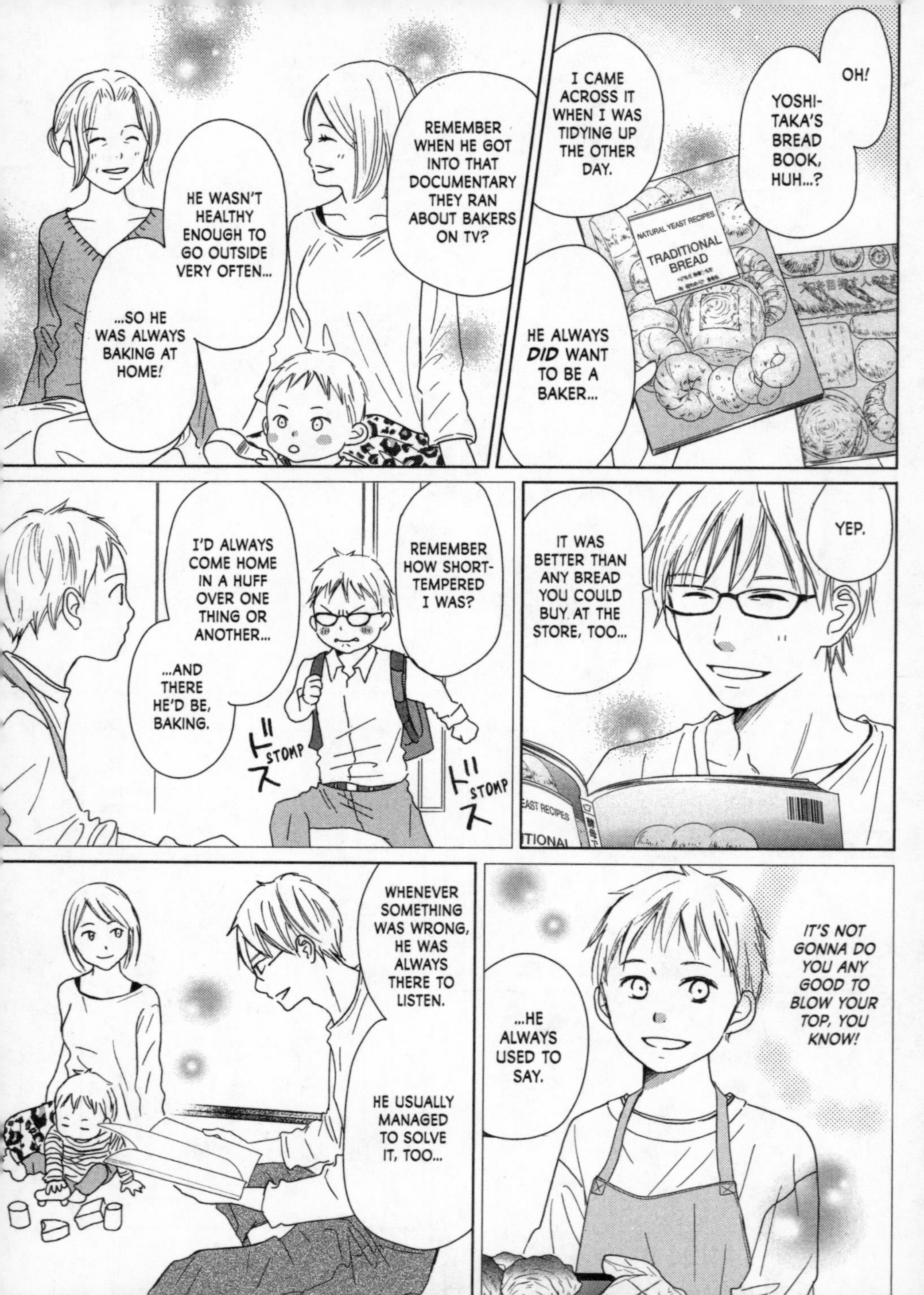
OH! YOSHI-TAKA'S BREAD BOOK, HUH...?
I CAME ACROSS IT WHEN I WAS TIDYING UP THE OTHER DAY.
NATURAL YEAST RECIPES
TRADITIONAL BREAD
HE ALWAYS *DID* WANT TO BE A BAKER...
REMEMBER WHEN HE GOT INTO THAT DOCUMENTARY THEY RAN ABOUT BAKERS ON TV?
HE WASN'T HEALTHY ENOUGH TO GO OUTSIDE VERY OFTEN...
...SO HE WAS ALWAYS BAKING AT HOME!
YEP.
IT WAS BETTER THAN ANY BREAD YOU COULD BUY AT THE STORE, TOO...
EAST RECIPES
TIONAL
REMEMBER HOW SHORT-TEMPERED I WAS?
I'D ALWAYS COME HOME IN A HUFF OVER ONE THING OR ANOTHER...
...AND THERE HE'D BE, BAKING.
ドス STOMP
ドス STOMP
IT'S NOT GONNA DO YOU ANY GOOD TO BLOW YOUR TOP, YOU KNOW!
...HE ALWAYS USED TO SAY.
WHENEVER SOMETHING WAS WRONG, HE WAS ALWAYS THERE TO LISTEN.
HE USUALLY MANAGED TO SOLVE IT, TOO...

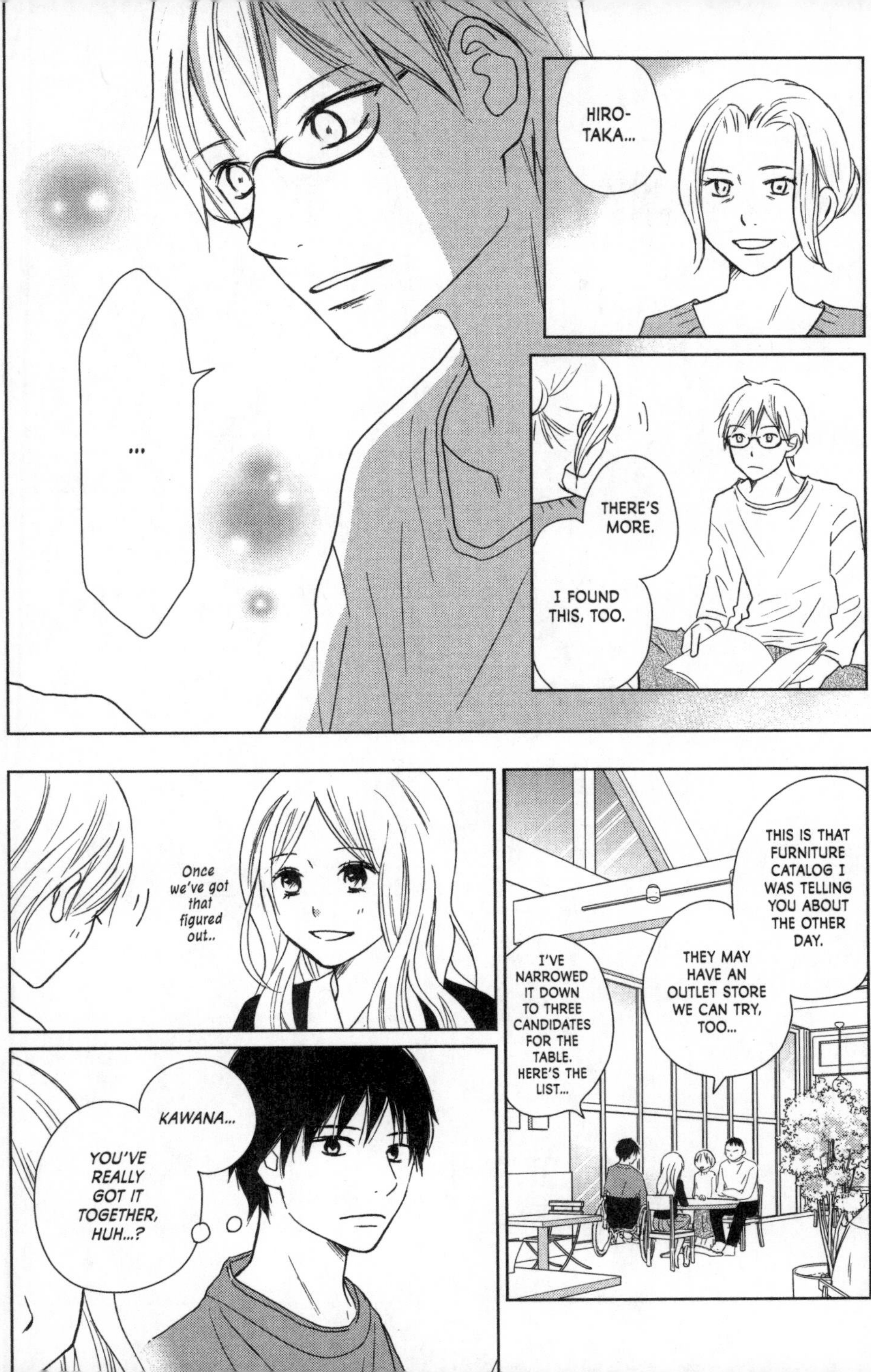
HIRO-TAKA...
THERE'S MORE.
I FOUND THIS, TOO.
...
THIS IS THAT FURNITURE CATALOG I WAS TELLING YOU ABOUT THE OTHER DAY.
THEY MAY HAVE AN OUTLET STORE WE CAN TRY, TOO...
I'VE NARROWED IT DOWN TO THREE CANDIDATES FOR THE TABLE. HERE'S THE LIST...
Once we've got that figured out..
KAWANA...
YOU'VE REALLY GOT IT TOGETHER, HUH...?

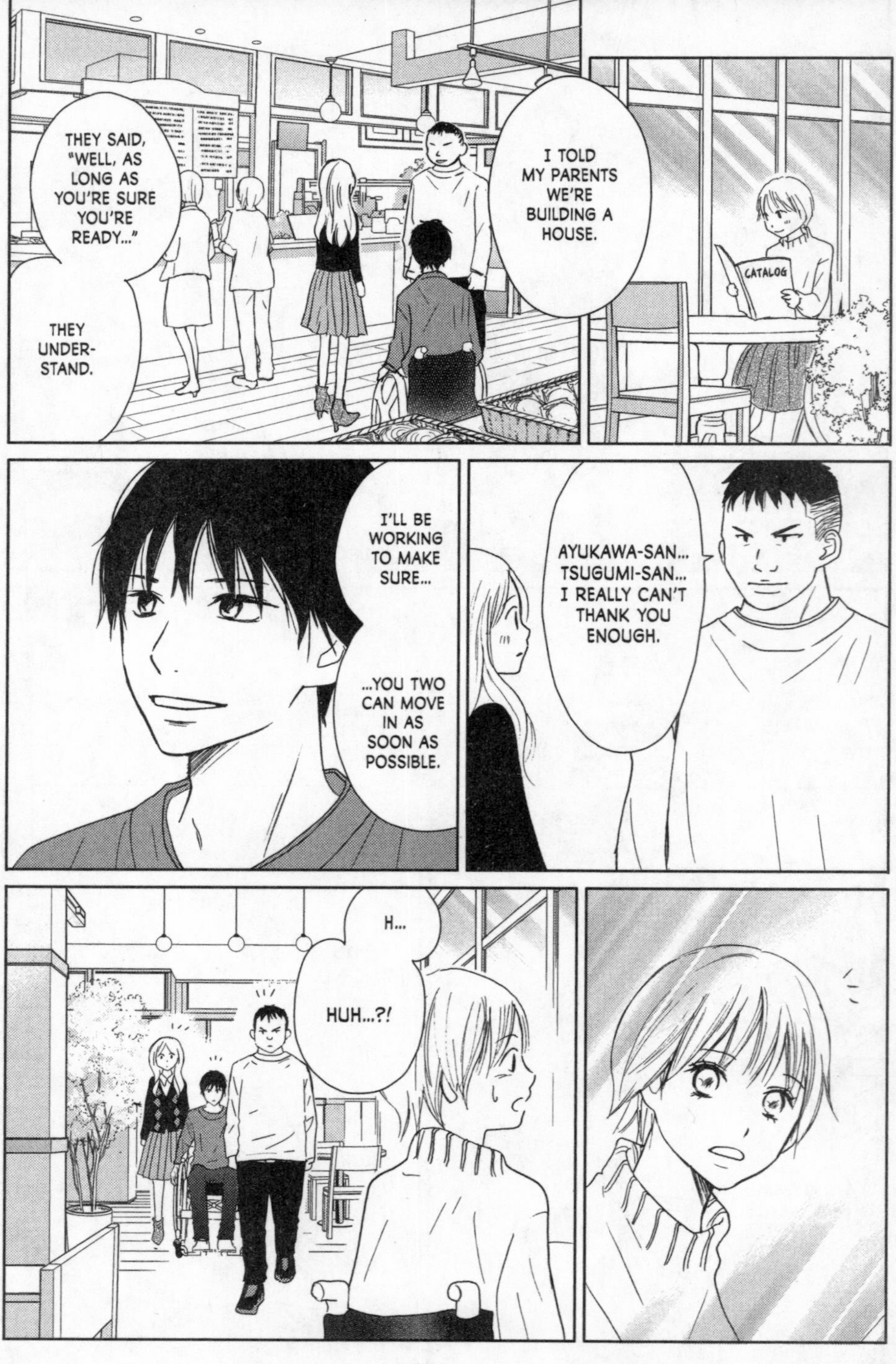
CATALOG
I TOLD MY PARENTS WE'RE BUILDING A HOUSE.
THEY SAID, "WELL, AS LONG AS YOU'RE SURE YOU'RE READY..."
THEY UNDER-STAND.
AYUKAWA-SAN... TSUGUMI-SAN... I REALLY CAN'T THANK YOU ENOUGH.
I'LL BE WORKING TO MAKE SURE...
...YOU TWO CAN MOVE IN AS SOON AS POSSIBLE.
H...
HUH...?!

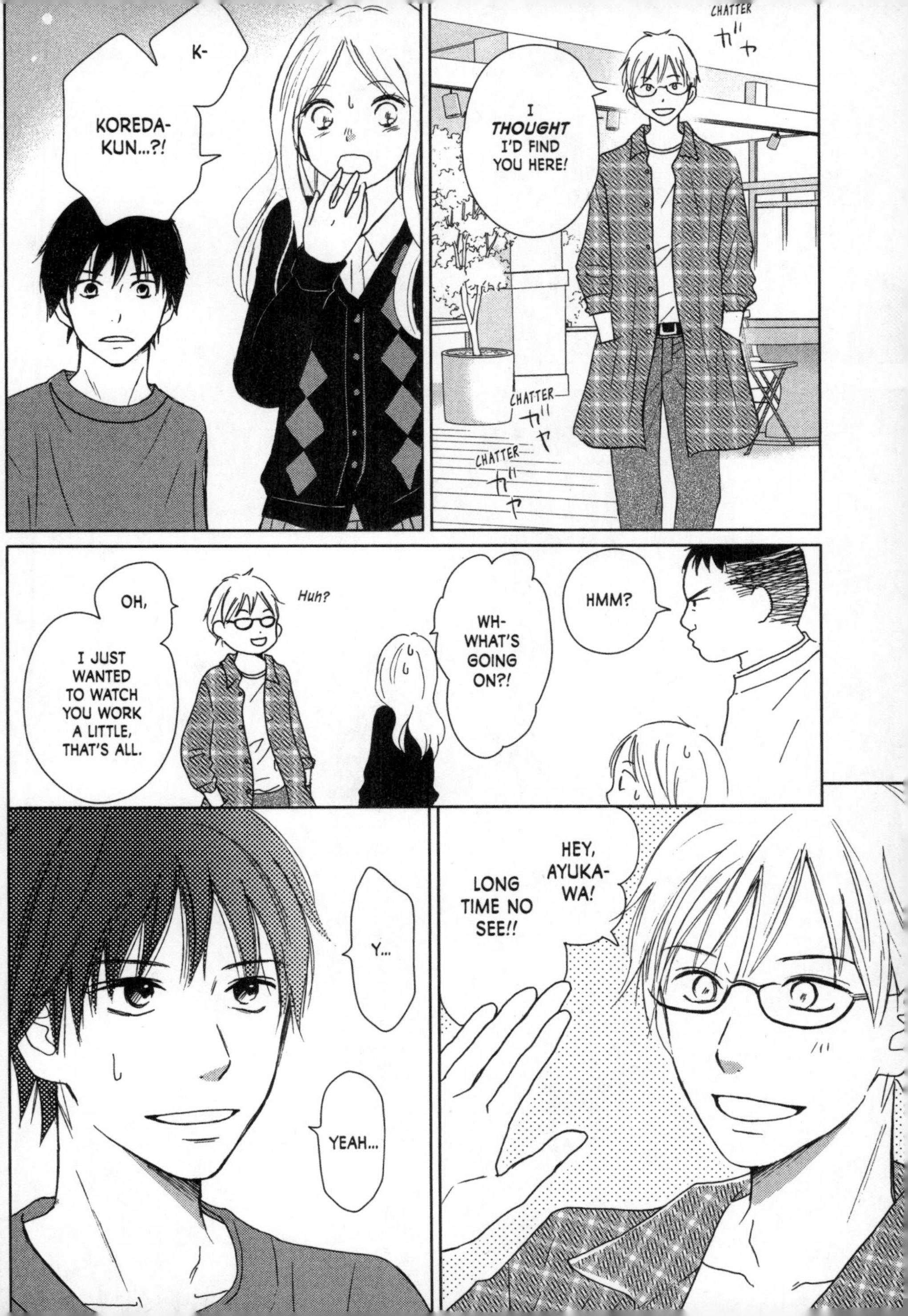
CHATTER
ガヤ
I THOUGHT I'D FIND YOU HERE!
CHATTER
ガヤ
CHATTER
ガヤ
K-
KOREDA-KUN...?!
HMM?
WH- WHAT'S GOING ON?!
Huh?
OH,
I JUST WANTED TO WATCH YOU WORK A LITTLE, THAT'S ALL.
HEY, AYUKAWA!
LONG TIME NO SEE!!
Y...
YEAH...

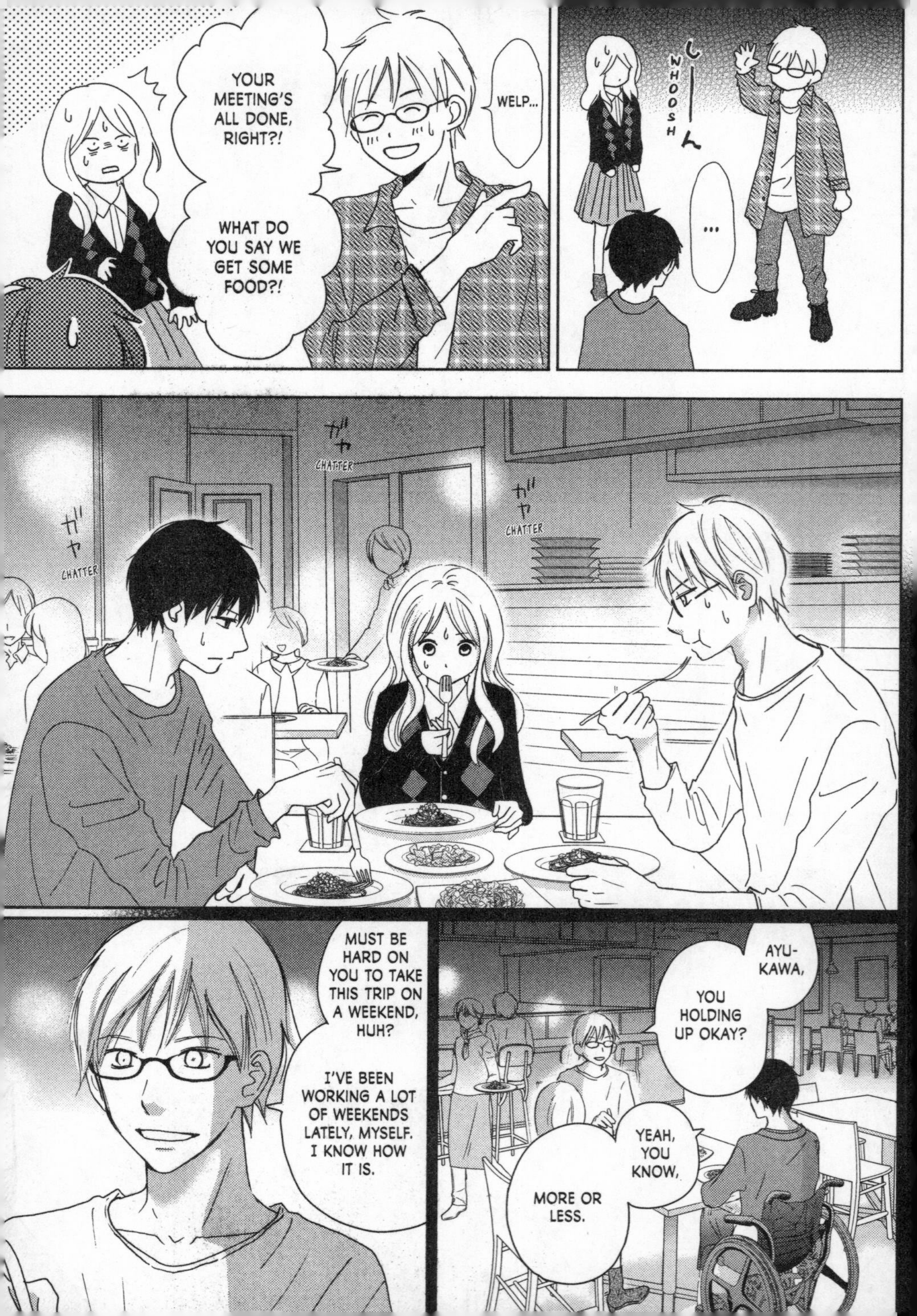

WHOOSH
...
WELP...
YOUR MEETING'S ALL DONE, RIGHT?!
WHAT DO YOU SAY WE GET SOME FOOD?!
CHATTER
CHATTER
CHATTER
AYU-KAWA,
YOU HOLDING UP OKAY?
YEAH, YOU KNOW,
MORE OR LESS.
MUST BE HARD ON YOU TO TAKE THIS TRIP ON A WEEKEND, HUH?
I'VE BEEN WORKING A LOT OF WEEKENDS LATELY, MYSELF. I KNOW HOW IT IS.

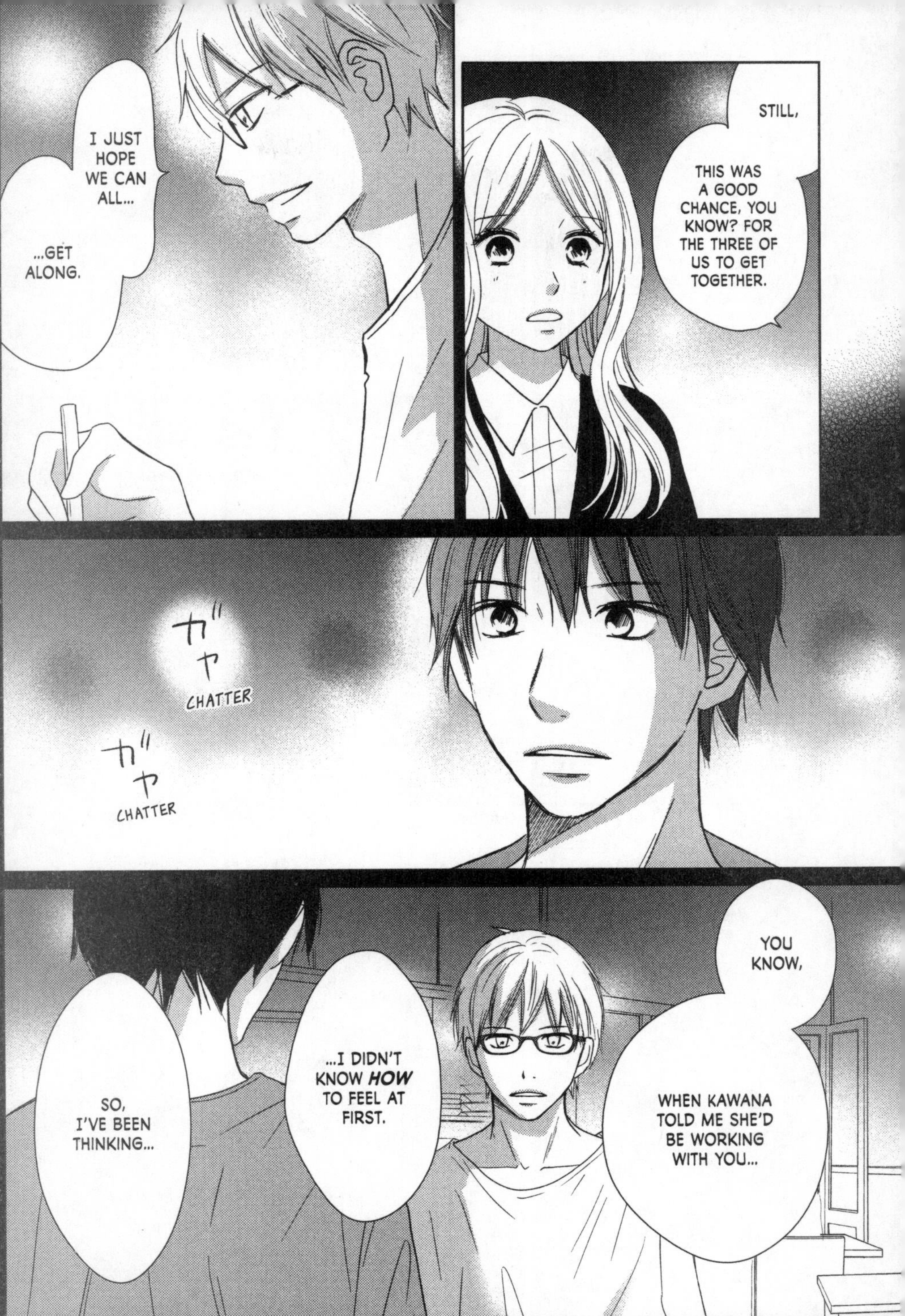
STILL,
THIS WAS A GOOD CHANCE, YOU KNOW? FOR THE THREE OF US TO GET TOGETHER.
I JUST HOPE WE CAN ALL...
...GET ALONG.
ガヤ
CHATTER
ガヤ
CHATTER
YOU KNOW,
WHEN KAWANA TOLD ME SHE'D BE WORKING WITH YOU...
...I DIDN'T KNOW *HOW* TO FEEL AT FIRST.
SO, I'VE BEEN THINKING...

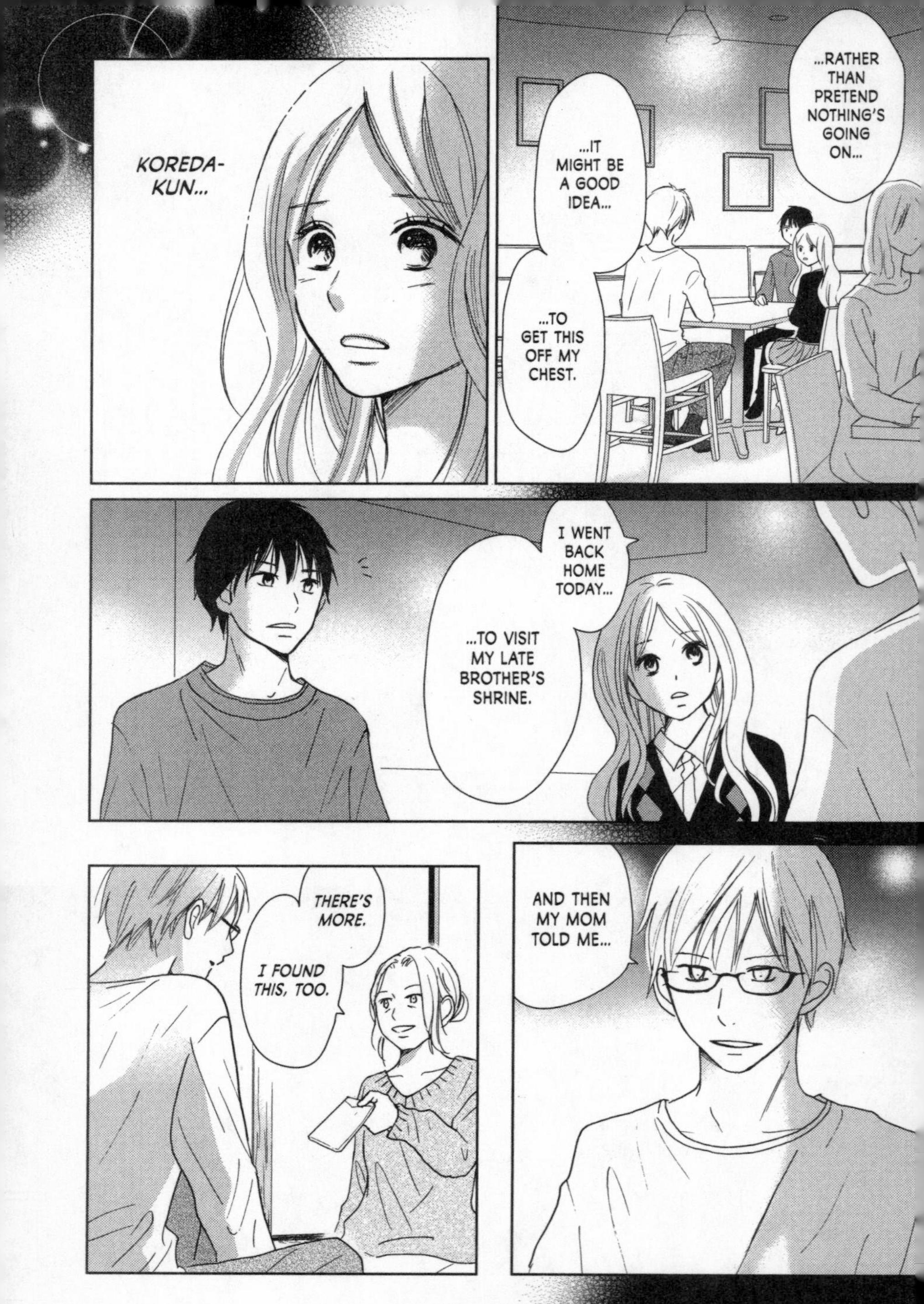
...RATHER THAN PRETEND NOTHING'S GOING ON...
...IT MIGHT BE A GOOD IDEA...
...TO GET THIS OFF MY CHEST.
KOREDA-KUN...
I WENT BACK HOME TODAY...
...TO VISIT MY LATE BROTHER'S SHRINE.
AND THEN MY MOM TOLD ME...
THERE'S MORE.
I FOUND THIS, TOO.

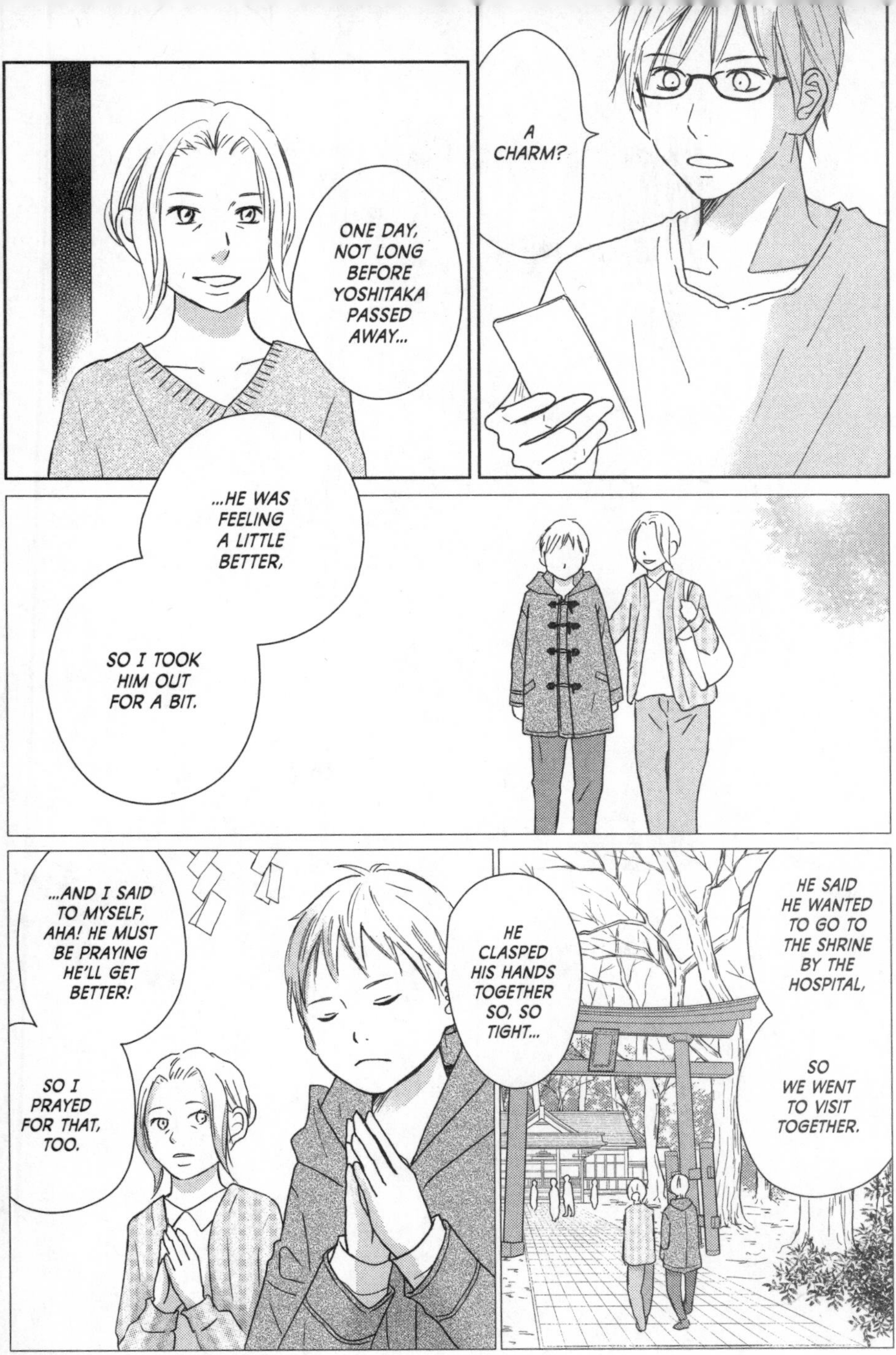
A CHARM?
ONE DAY, NOT LONG BEFORE YOSHITAKA PASSED AWAY...
...HE WAS FEELING A LITTLE BETTER,
SO I TOOK HIM OUT FOR A BIT.
HE SAID HE WANTED TO GO TO THE SHRINE BY THE HOSPITAL,
SO WE WENT TO VISIT TOGETHER.
HE CLASPED HIS HANDS TOGETHER SO, SO TIGHT...
...AND I SAID TO MYSELF, AHA! HE MUST BE PRAYING HE'LL GET BETTER!
SO I PRAYED FOR THAT, TOO.

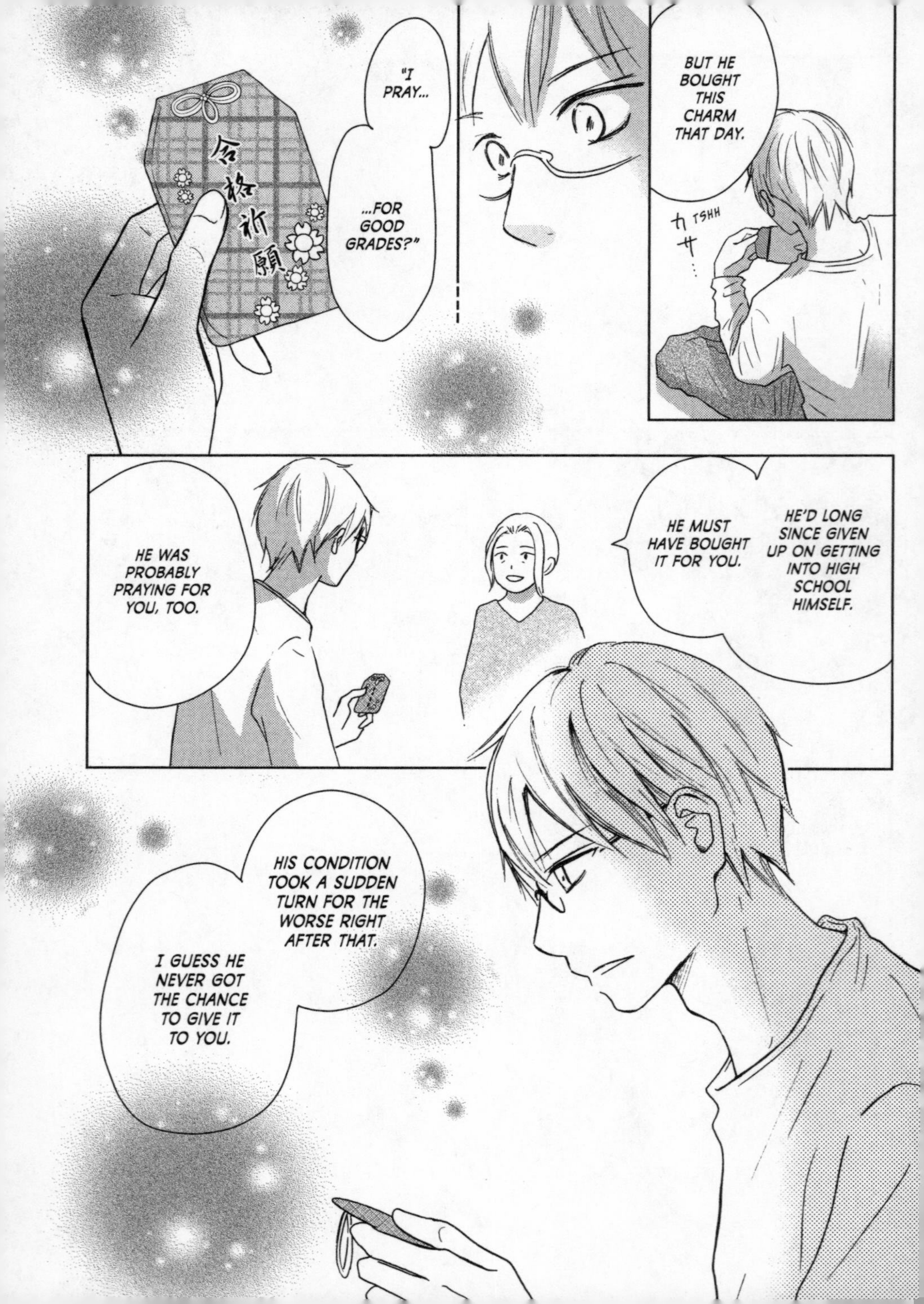
BUT HE BOUGHT THIS CHARM THAT DAY.
カサ…
TSHH
合格祈願
"I PRAY...
...FOR GOOD GRADES?"
HE'D LONG SINCE GIVEN UP ON GETTING INTO HIGH SCHOOL HIMSELF.
HE MUST HAVE BOUGHT IT FOR YOU.
HE WAS PROBABLY PRAYING FOR YOU, TOO.
HIS CONDITION TOOK A SUDDEN TURN FOR THE WORSE RIGHT AFTER THAT.
I GUESS HE NEVER GOT THE CHANCE TO GIVE IT TO YOU.

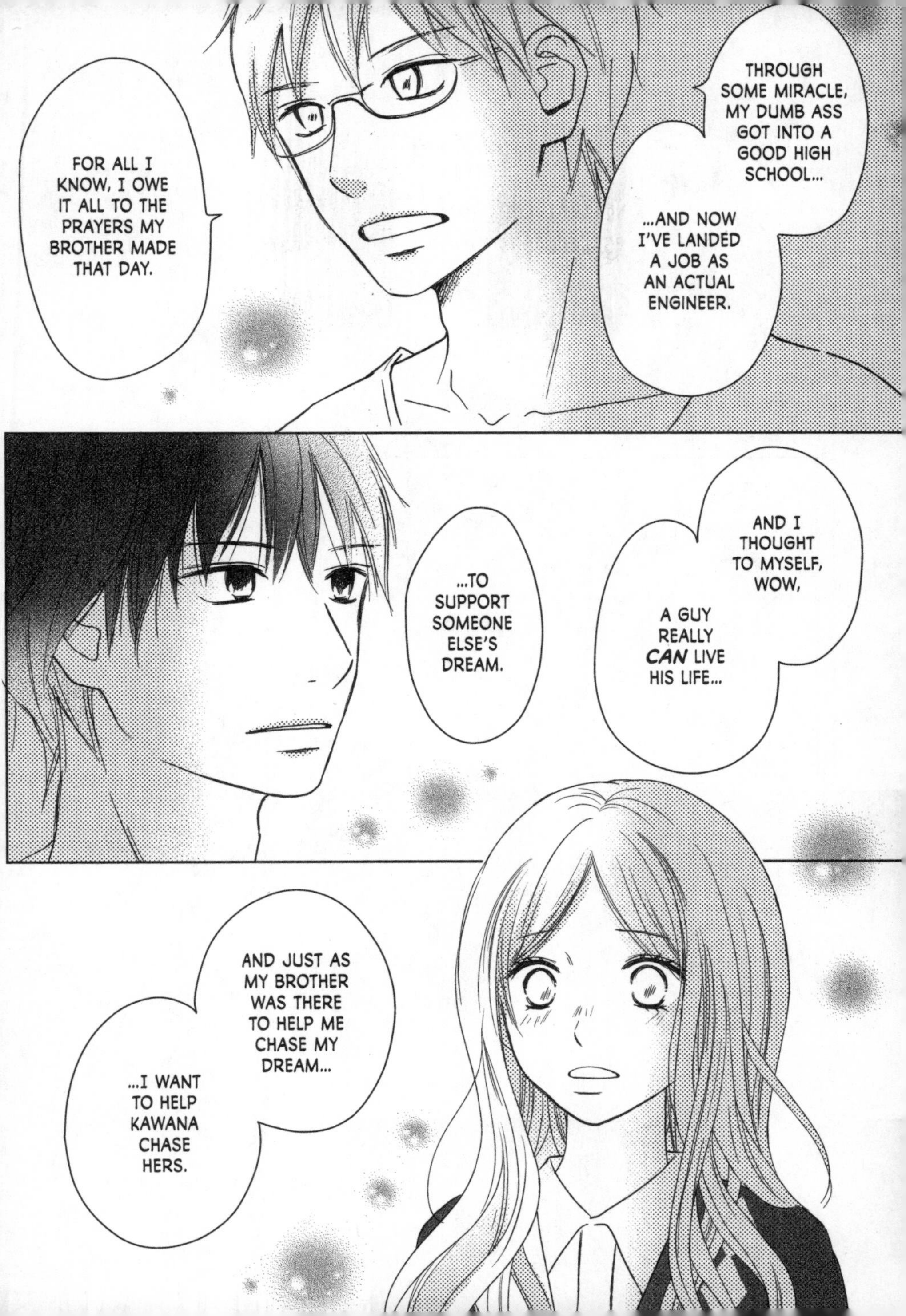
THROUGH SOME MIRACLE, MY DUMB ASS GOT INTO A GOOD HIGH SCHOOL...
...AND NOW I'VE LANDED A JOB AS AN ACTUAL ENGINEER.
FOR ALL I KNOW, I OWE IT ALL TO THE PRAYERS MY BROTHER MADE THAT DAY.
AND I THOUGHT TO MYSELF, WOW,
A GUY REALLY *CAN* LIVE HIS LIFE...
...TO SUPPORT SOMEONE ELSE'S DREAM.
AND JUST AS MY BROTHER WAS THERE TO HELP ME CHASE MY DREAM...
...I WANT TO HELP KAWANA CHASE HERS.

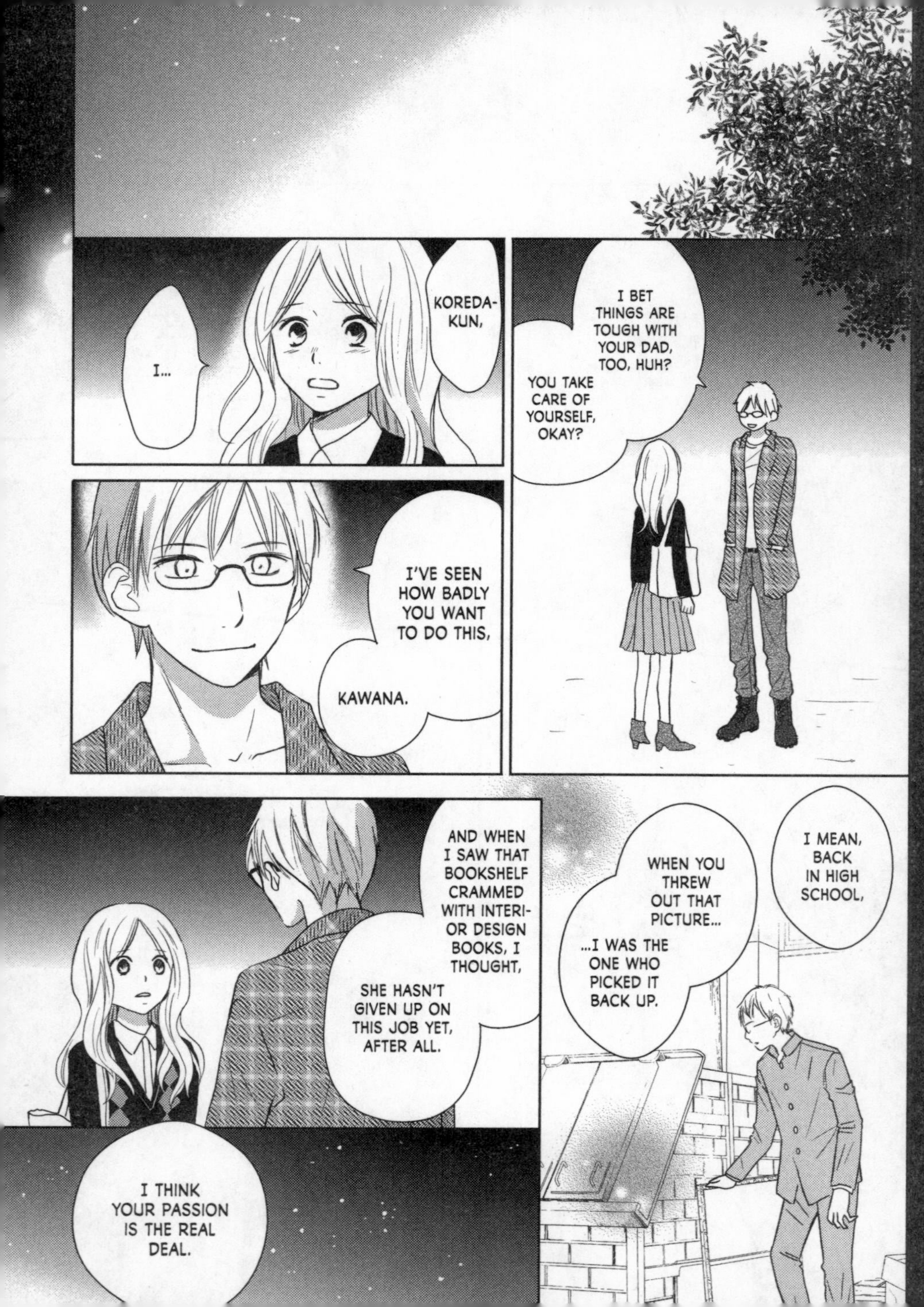
I BET THINGS ARE TOUGH WITH YOUR DAD, TOO, HUH?
YOU TAKE CARE OF YOURSELF, OKAY?
KOREDA-KUN,
I...
I'VE SEEN HOW BADLY YOU WANT TO DO THIS,
KAWANA.
I MEAN, BACK IN HIGH SCHOOL,
WHEN YOU THREW OUT THAT PICTURE...
...I WAS THE ONE WHO PICKED IT BACK UP.
AND WHEN I SAW THAT BOOKSHELF CRAMMED WITH INTERI-OR DESIGN BOOKS, I THOUGHT,
SHE HASN'T GIVEN UP ON THIS JOB YET, AFTER ALL.
I THINK YOUR PASSION IS THE REAL DEAL.

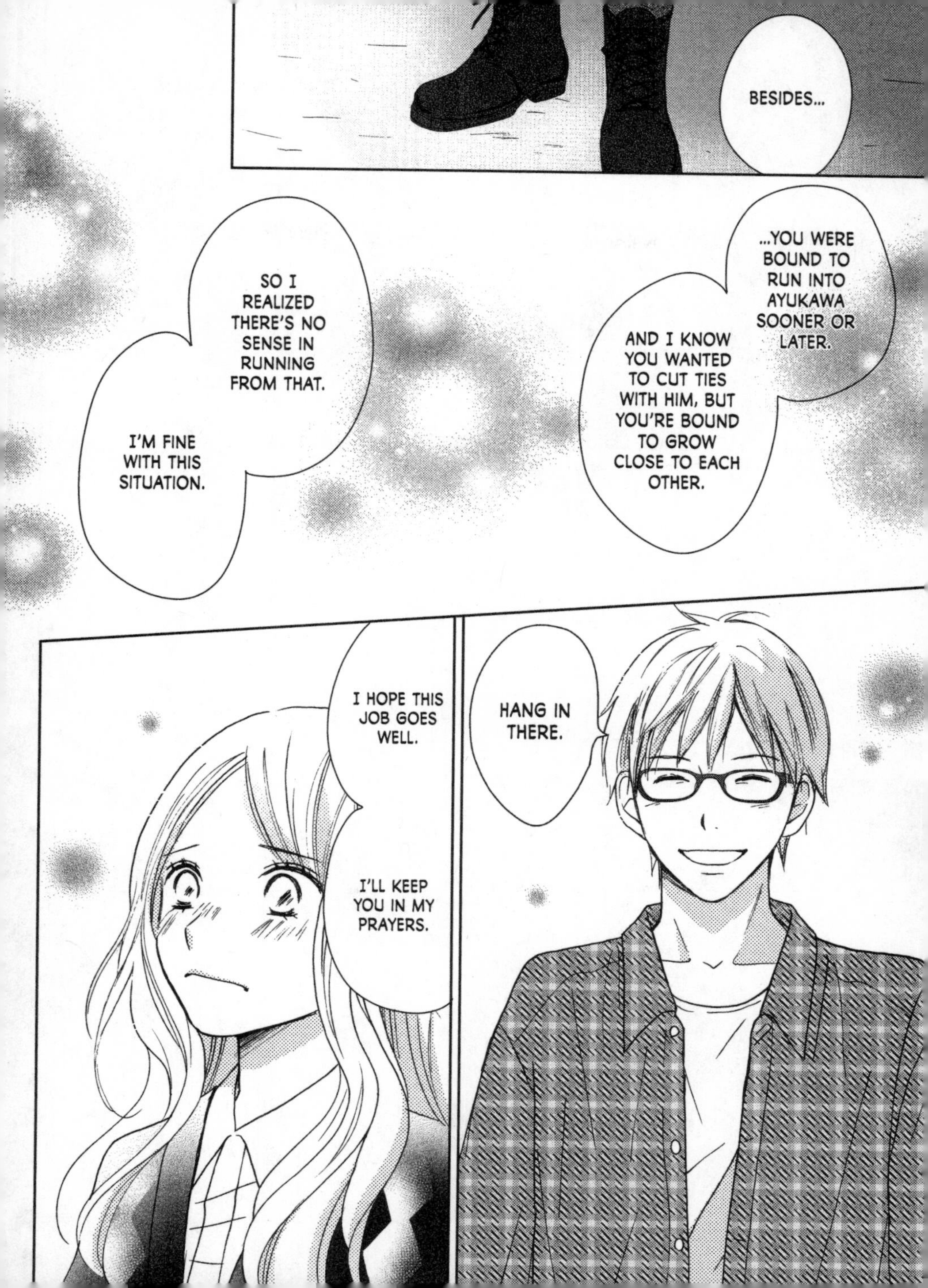
BESIDES...
...YOU WERE BOUND TO RUN INTO AYUKAWA SOONER OR LATER.
AND I KNOW YOU WANTED TO CUT TIES WITH HIM, BUT YOU'RE BOUND TO GROW CLOSE TO EACH OTHER.
SO I REALIZED THERE'S NO SENSE IN RUNNING FROM THAT.
I'M FINE WITH THIS SITUATION.
HANG IN THERE.
I HOPE THIS JOB GOES WELL.
I'LL KEEP YOU IN MY PRAYERS.

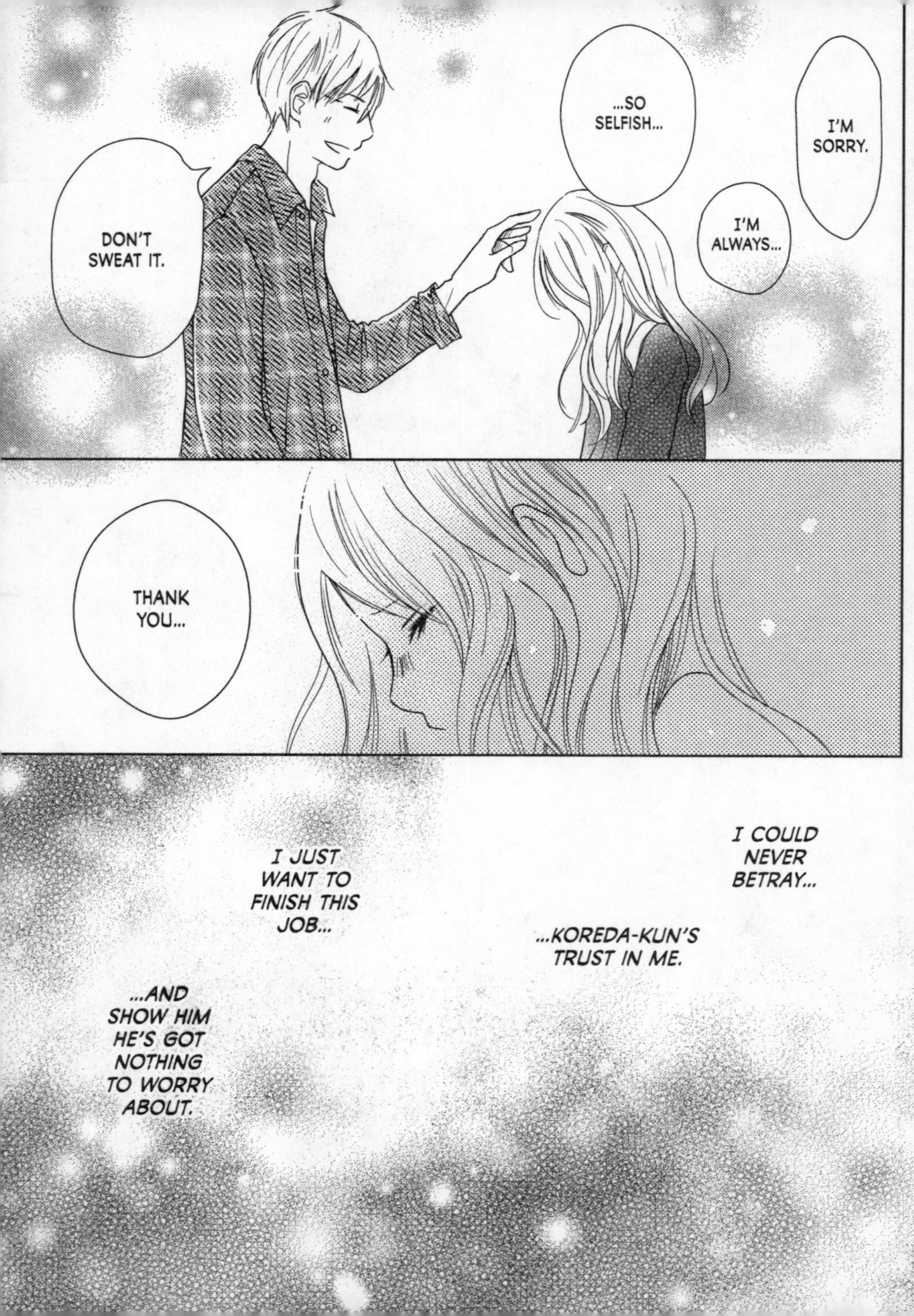
I'M SORRY.
I'M ALWAYS...
...SO SELFISH...
DON'T SWEAT IT.
THANK YOU...
I COULD NEVER BETRAY...
...KOREDA-KUN'S TRUST IN ME.
I JUST WANT TO FINISH THIS JOB...
...AND SHOW HIM HE'S GOT NOTHING TO WORRY ABOUT.

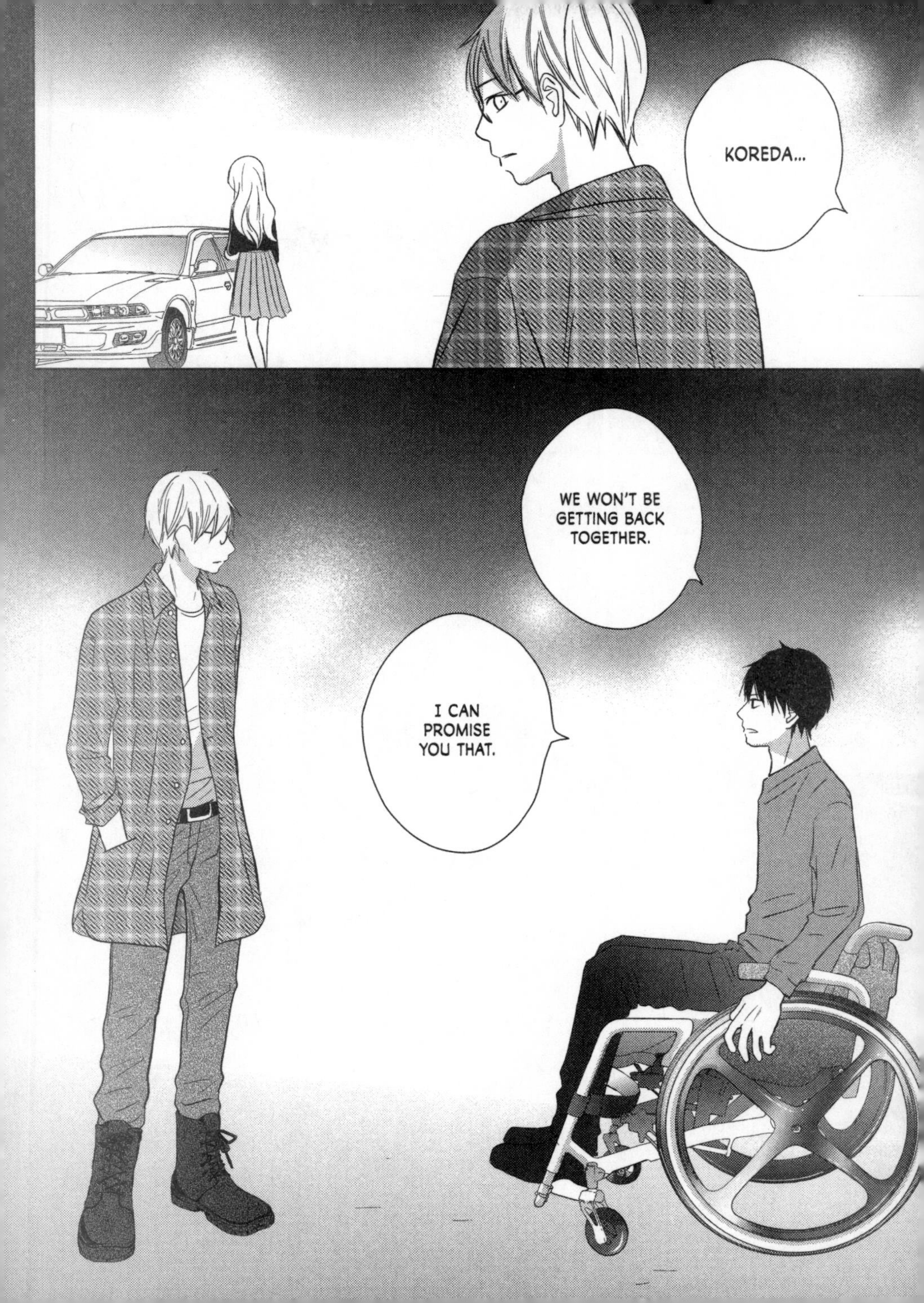
KOREDA...
WE WON'T BE GETTING BACK TOGETHER.
I CAN PROMISE YOU THAT.

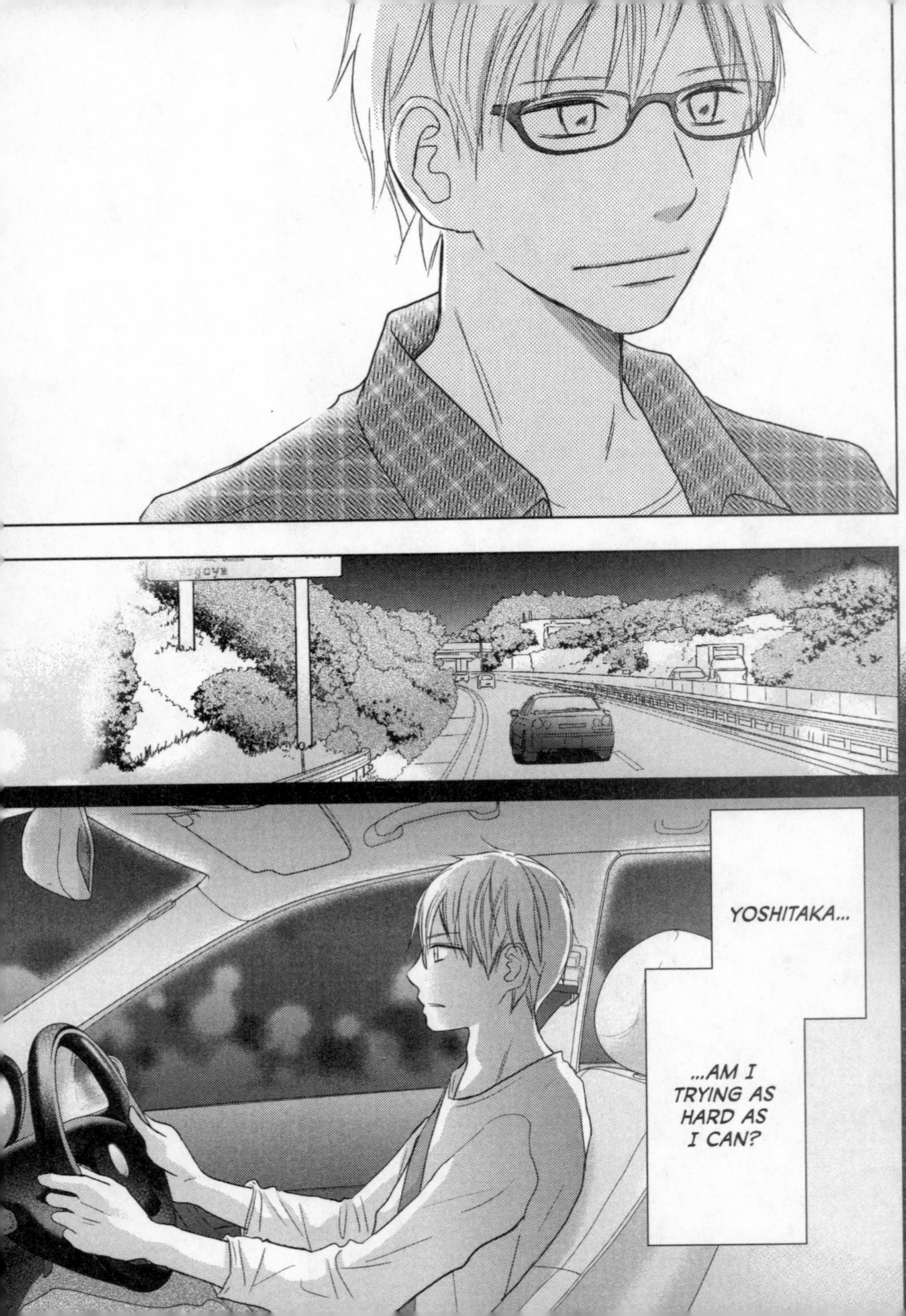
YOSHITAKA...
...AM I TRYING AS HARD AS I CAN?

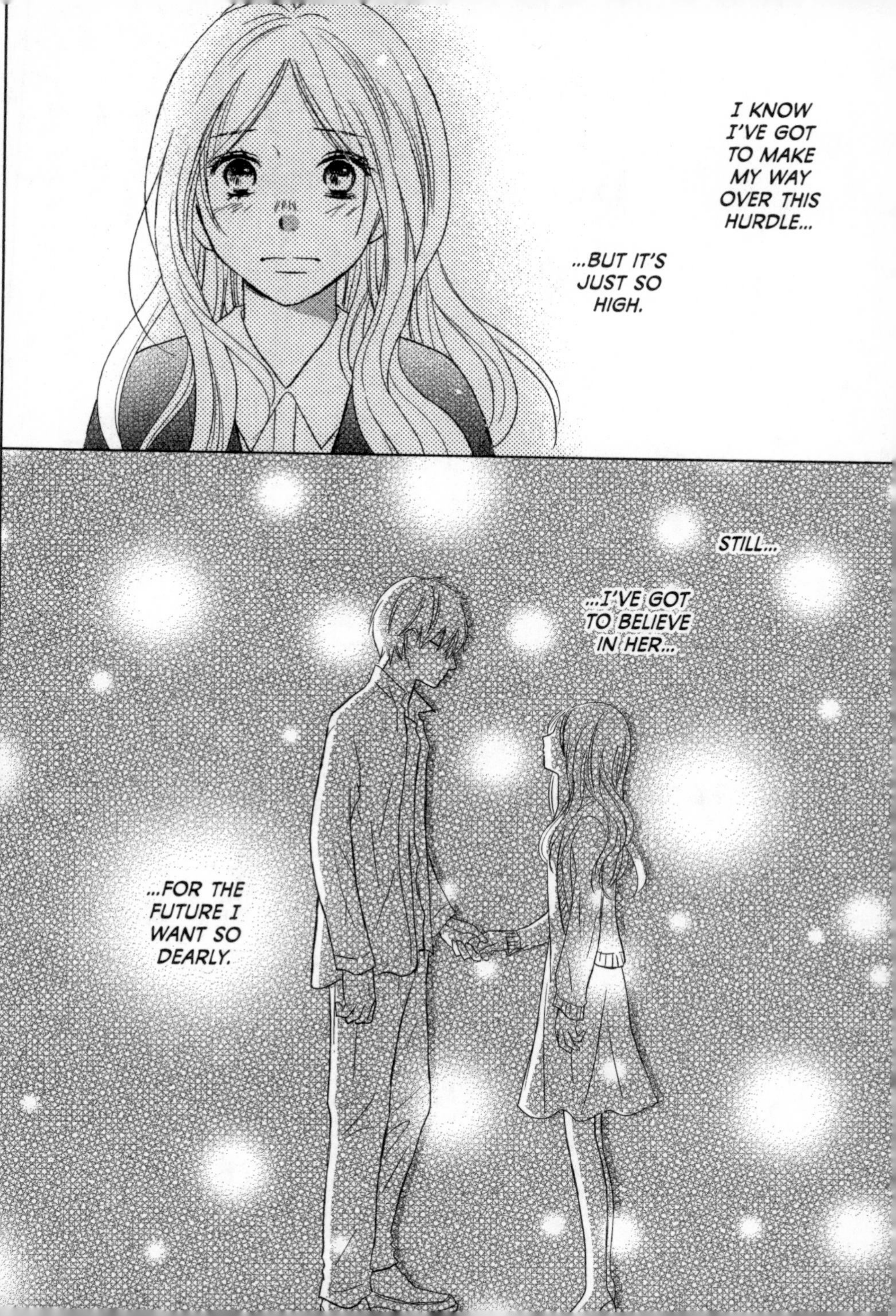
I KNOW I'VE GOT TO MAKE MY WAY OVER THIS HURDLE...
...BUT IT'S JUST SO HIGH.
STILL...
...I'VE GOT TO BELIEVE IN HER...
...FOR THE FUTURE I WANT SO DEARLY.

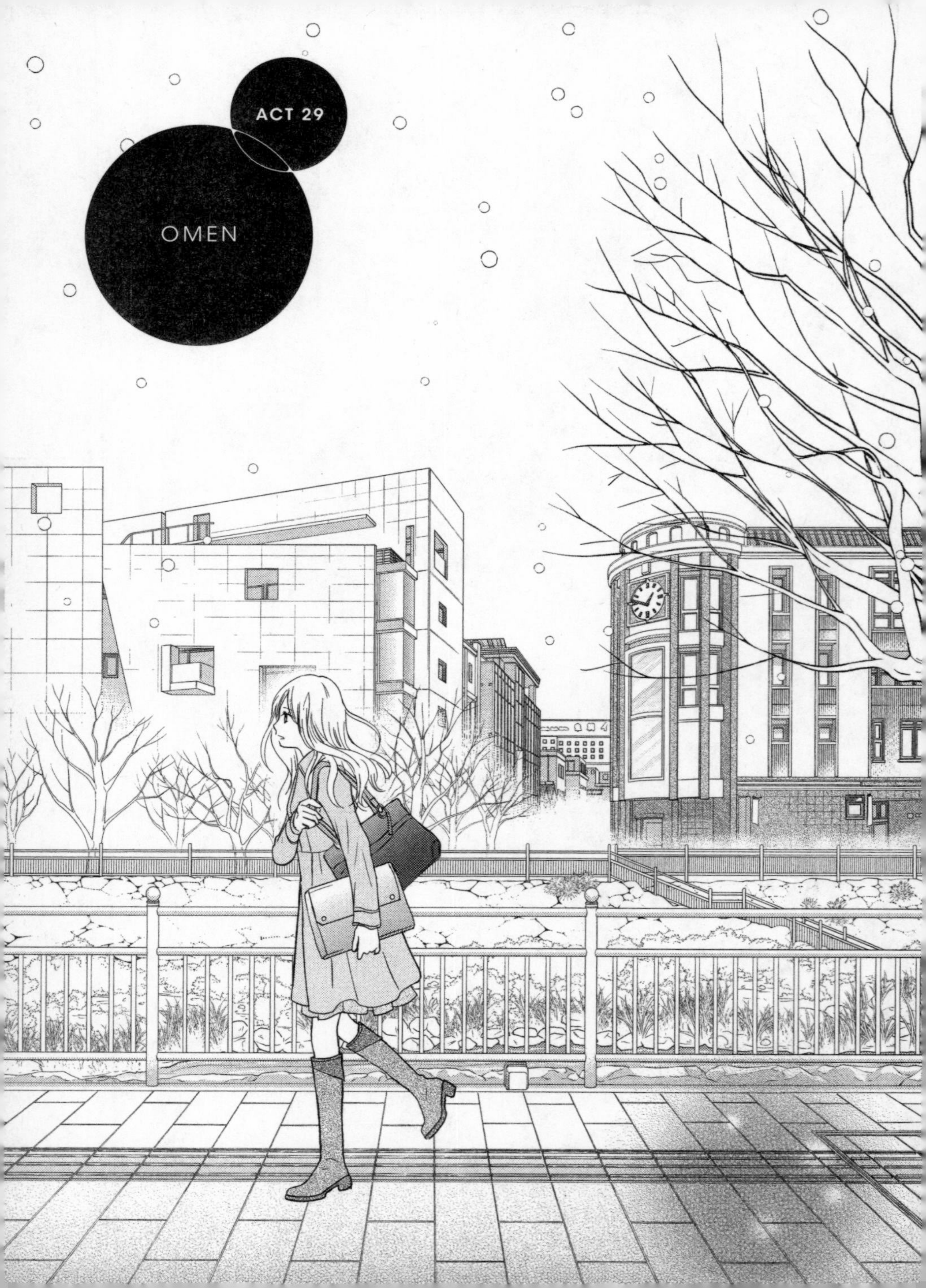
ACT 29
OMEN

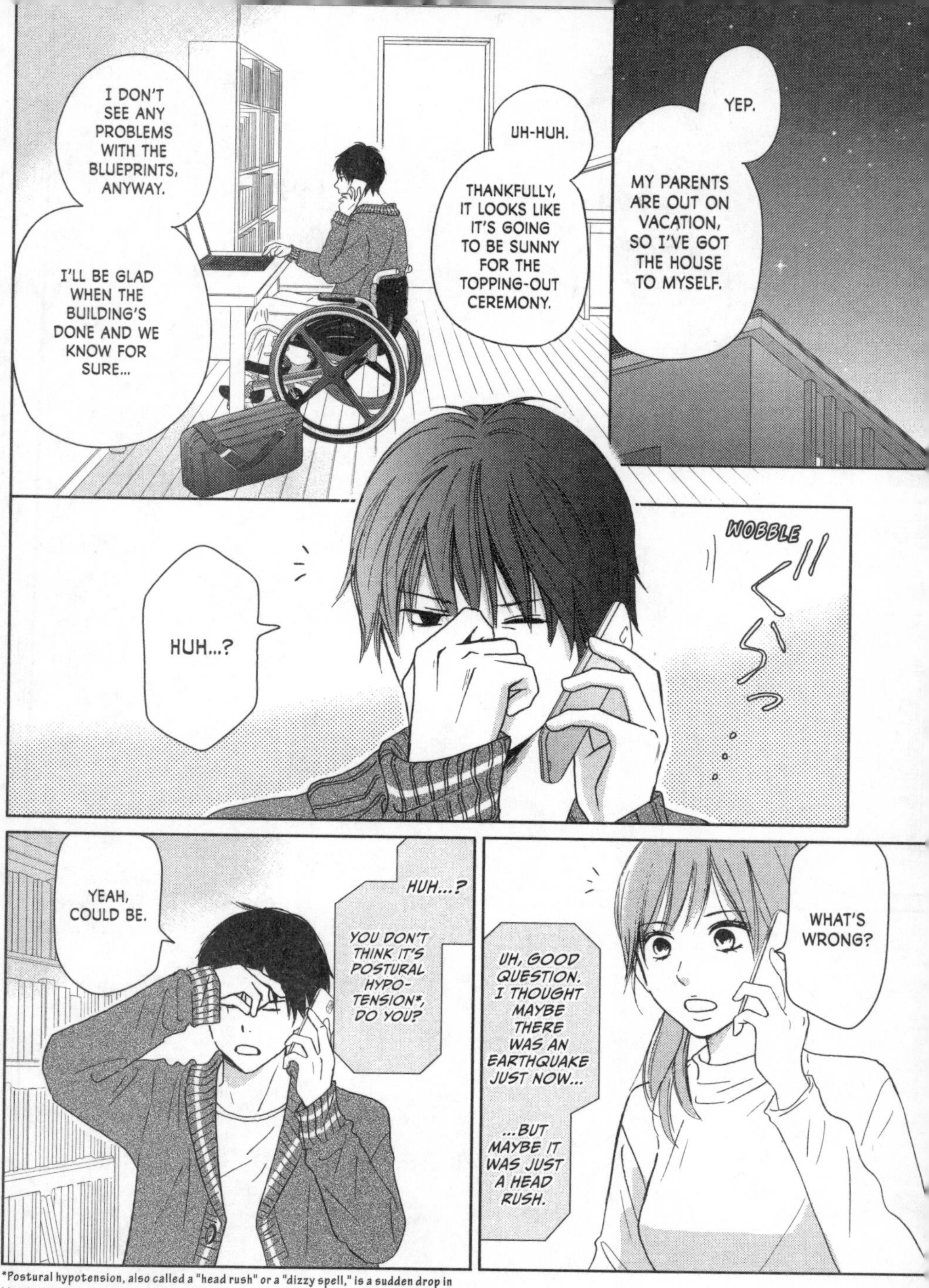
YEP.
MY PARENTS ARE OUT ON VACATION, SO I'VE GOT THE HOUSE TO MYSELF.
UH-HUH.
THANKFULLY, IT LOOKS LIKE IT'S GOING TO BE SUNNY FOR THE TOPPING-OUT CEREMONY.
I DON'T SEE ANY PROBLEMS WITH THE BLUEPRINTS, ANYWAY.
I'LL BE GLAD WHEN THE BUILDING'S DONE AND WE KNOW FOR SURE...
WOBBLE
HUH...?
WHAT'S WRONG?
UH, GOOD QUESTION. I THOUGHT MAYBE THERE WAS AN EARTHQUAKE JUST NOW...
...BUT MAYBE IT WAS JUST A HEAD RUSH.
HUH...?
YOU DON'T THINK IT'S POSTURAL HYPO-TENSION*, DO YOU?
YEAH, COULD BE.

*Postural hypotension, also called a "head rush" or a "dizzy spell," is a sudden drop in blood pressure that usually occurs when a person stands up. People with SCI face risk of postural hypotension when they sit for extended periods of time.

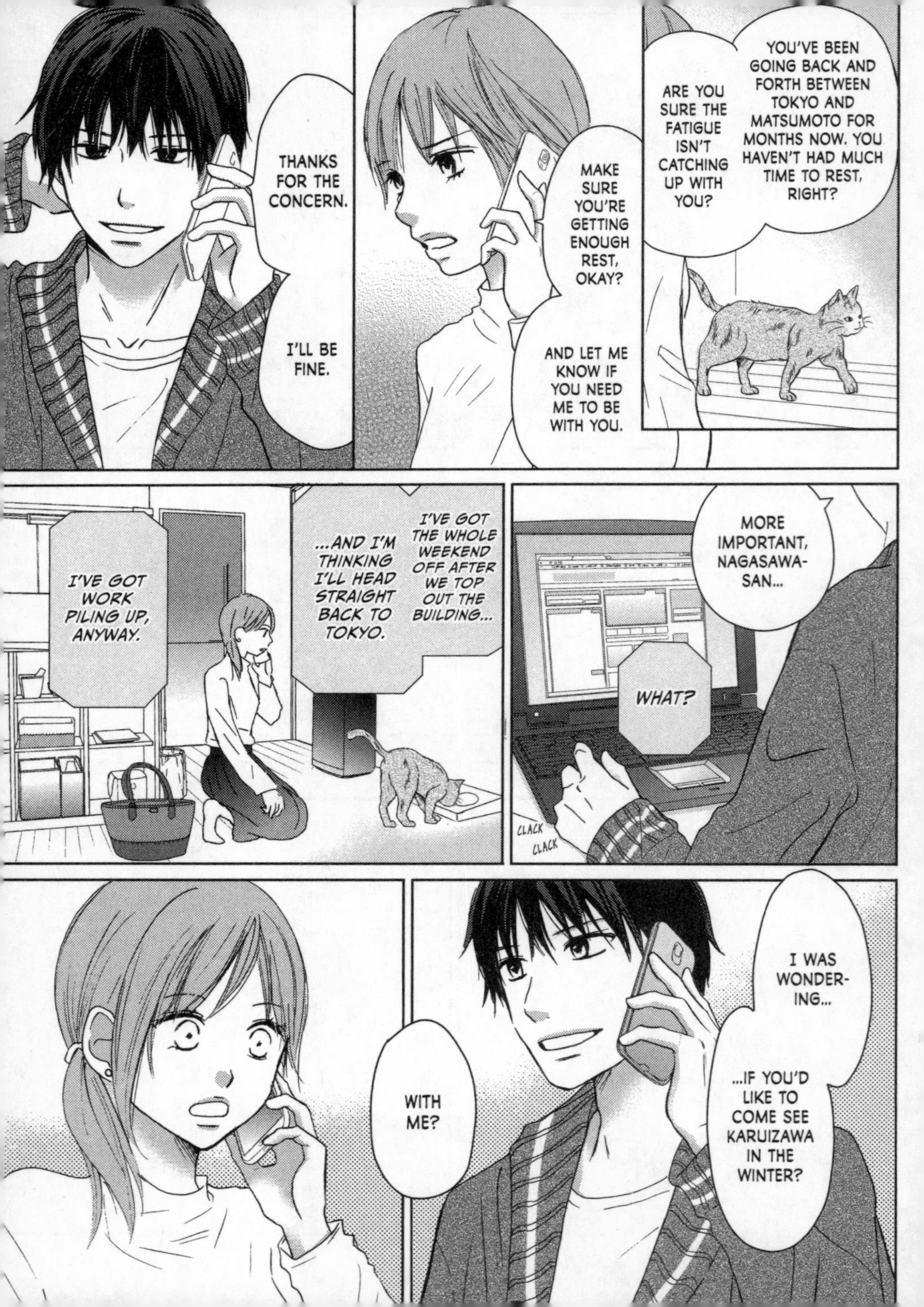
YOU'VE BEEN GOING BACK AND FORTH BETWEEN TOKYO AND MATSUMOTO FOR MONTHS NOW. YOU HAVEN'T HAD MUCH TIME TO REST, RIGHT?
ARE YOU SURE THE FATIGUE ISN'T CATCHING UP WITH YOU?
MAKE SURE YOU'RE GETTING ENOUGH REST, OKAY?
AND LET ME KNOW IF YOU NEED ME TO BE WITH YOU.
THANKS FOR THE CONCERN.
I'LL BE FINE.
MORE IMPORTANT, NAGASAWA-SAN...
WHAT?
CLACK
CLACK
I'VE GOT THE WHOLE WEEKEND OFF AFTER WE TOP OUT THE BUILDING...
...AND I'M THINKING I'LL HEAD STRAIGHT BACK TO TOKYO.
I'VE GOT WORK PILING UP, ANYWAY.
I WAS WONDER-ING...
...IF YOU'D LIKE TO COME SEE KARUIZAWA IN THE WINTER?
WITH ME?

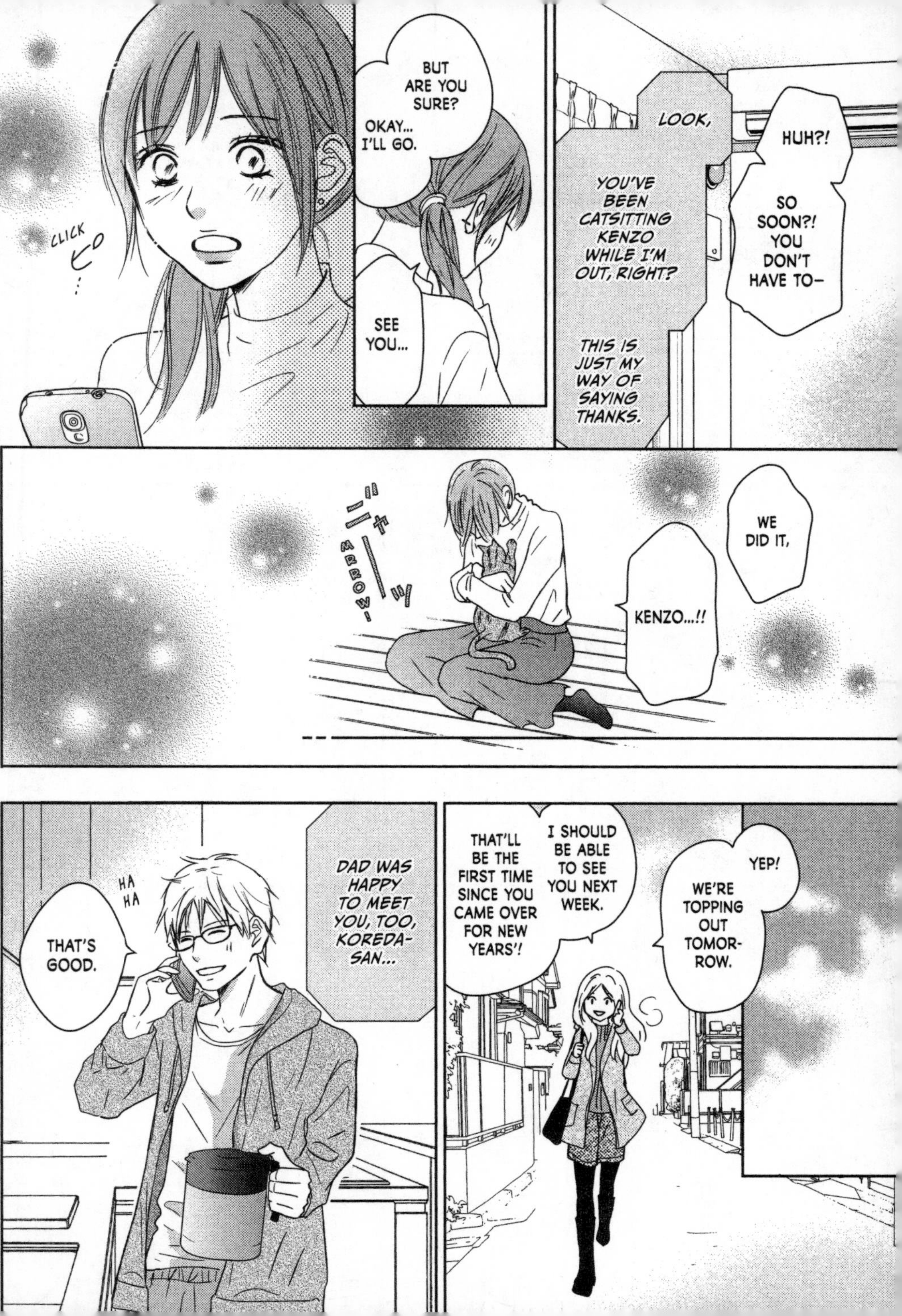
HUH?!
SO SOON?! YOU DON'T HAVE TO—
LOOK,
YOU'VE BEEN CATSITTING KENZO WHILE I'M OUT, RIGHT?
THIS IS JUST MY WAY OF SAYING THANKS.
BUT ARE YOU SURE?
OKAY... I'LL GO.
SEE YOU...
CLICK
WE DID IT,
KENZO...!!
MRROW!
YEP!
WE'RE TOPPING OUT TOMORROW.
I SHOULD BE ABLE TO SEE YOU NEXT WEEK.
THAT'LL BE THE FIRST TIME SINCE YOU CAME OVER FOR NEW YEARS'!
DAD WAS HAPPY TO MEET YOU, TOO, KOREDA-SAN...
HA HA
THAT'S GOOD.

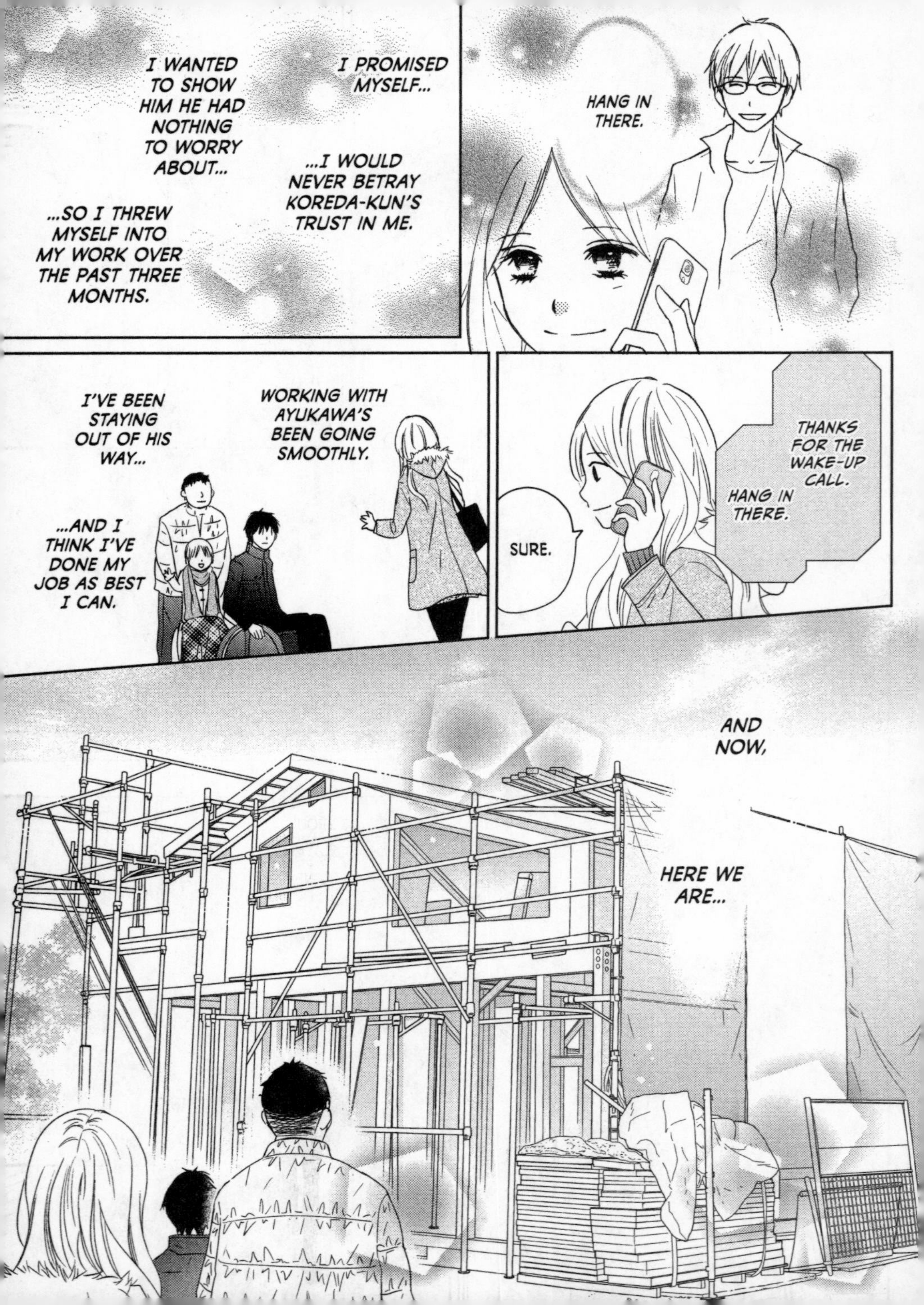
HANG IN THERE.
I PROMISED MYSELF...
...I WOULD NEVER BETRAY KOREDA-KUN'S TRUST IN ME.
I WANTED TO SHOW HIM HE HAD NOTHING TO WORRY ABOUT...
...SO I THREW MYSELF INTO MY WORK OVER THE PAST THREE MONTHS.
THANKS FOR THE WAKE-UP CALL.
HANG IN THERE.
SURE.
WORKING WITH AYUKAWA'S BEEN GOING SMOOTHLY.
I'VE BEEN STAYING OUT OF HIS WAY...
...AND I THINK I'VE DONE MY JOB AS BEST I CAN.
AND NOW,
HERE WE ARE...

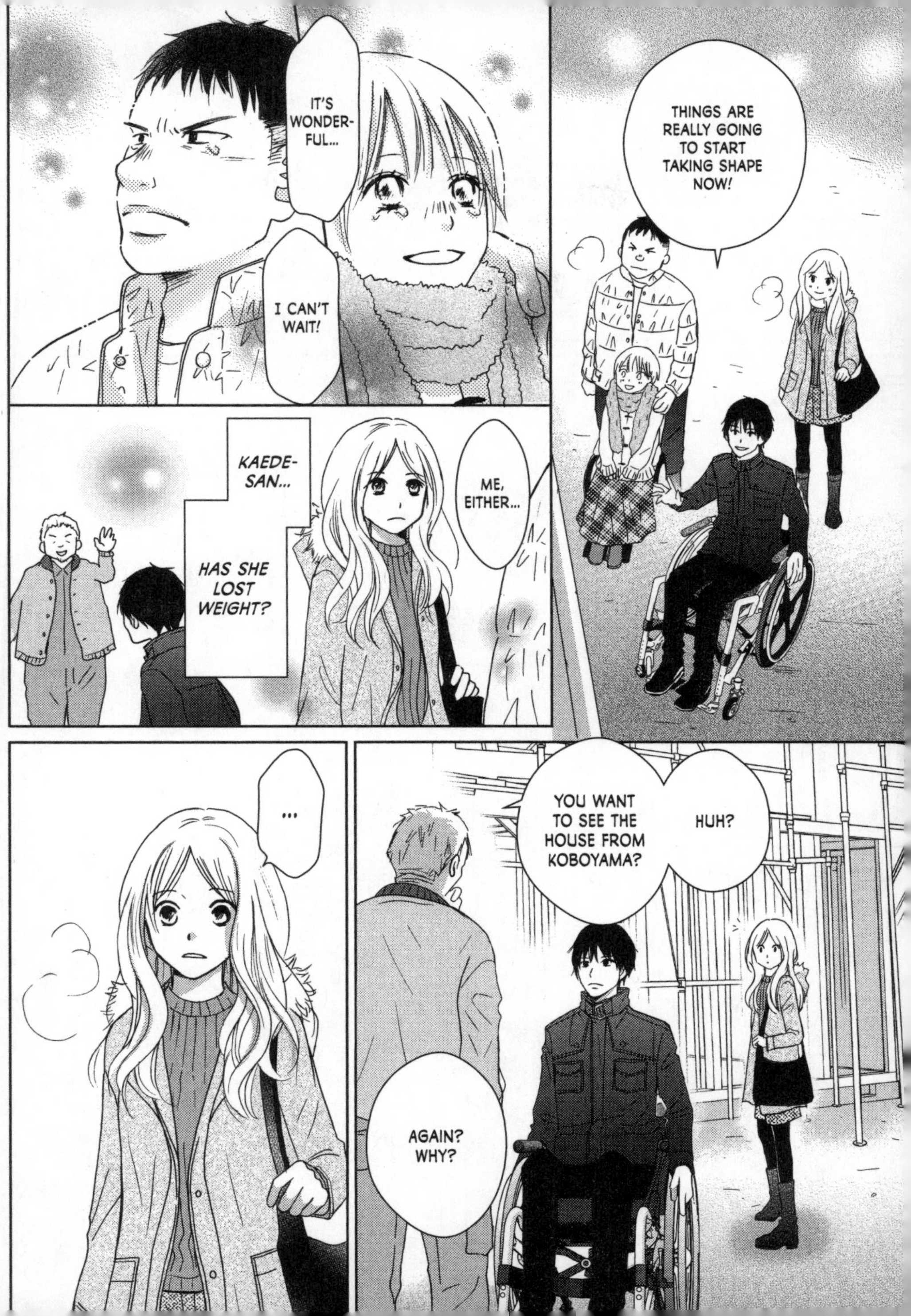
THINGS ARE REALLY GOING TO START TAKING SHAPE NOW!
IT'S WONDERFUL...
I CAN'T WAIT!
ME, EITHER...
KAEDE-SAN...
HAS SHE LOST WEIGHT?
HUH?
YOU WANT TO SEE THE HOUSE FROM KOBOYAMA?
AGAIN? WHY?
...

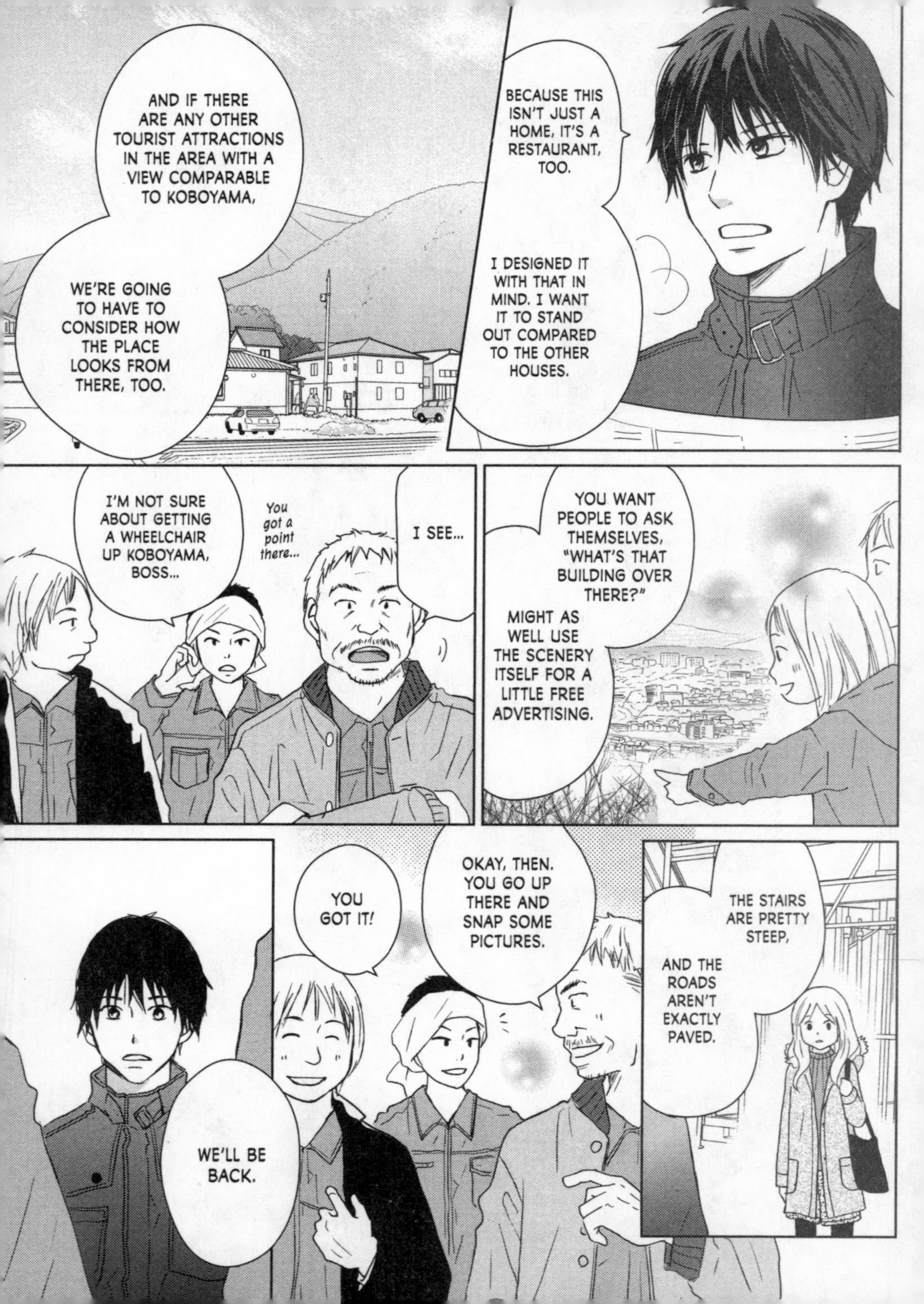
BECAUSE THIS ISN'T JUST A HOME, IT'S A RESTAURANT, TOO.
I DESIGNED IT WITH THAT IN MIND. I WANT IT TO STAND OUT COMPARED TO THE OTHER HOUSES.
AND IF THERE ARE ANY OTHER TOURIST ATTRACTIONS IN THE AREA WITH A VIEW COMPARABLE TO KOBOYAMA,
WE'RE GOING TO HAVE TO CONSIDER HOW THE PLACE LOOKS FROM THERE, TOO.
YOU WANT PEOPLE TO ASK THEMSELVES, "WHAT'S THAT BUILDING OVER THERE?"
MIGHT AS WELL USE THE SCENERY ITSELF FOR A LITTLE FREE ADVERTISING.
I SEE...
You got a point there...
I'M NOT SURE ABOUT GETTING A WHEELCHAIR UP KOBOYAMA, BOSS...
THE STAIRS ARE PRETTY STEEP,
AND THE ROADS AREN'T EXACTLY PAVED.
OKAY, THEN. YOU GO UP THERE AND SNAP SOME PICTURES.
YOU GOT IT!
WE'LL BE BACK.

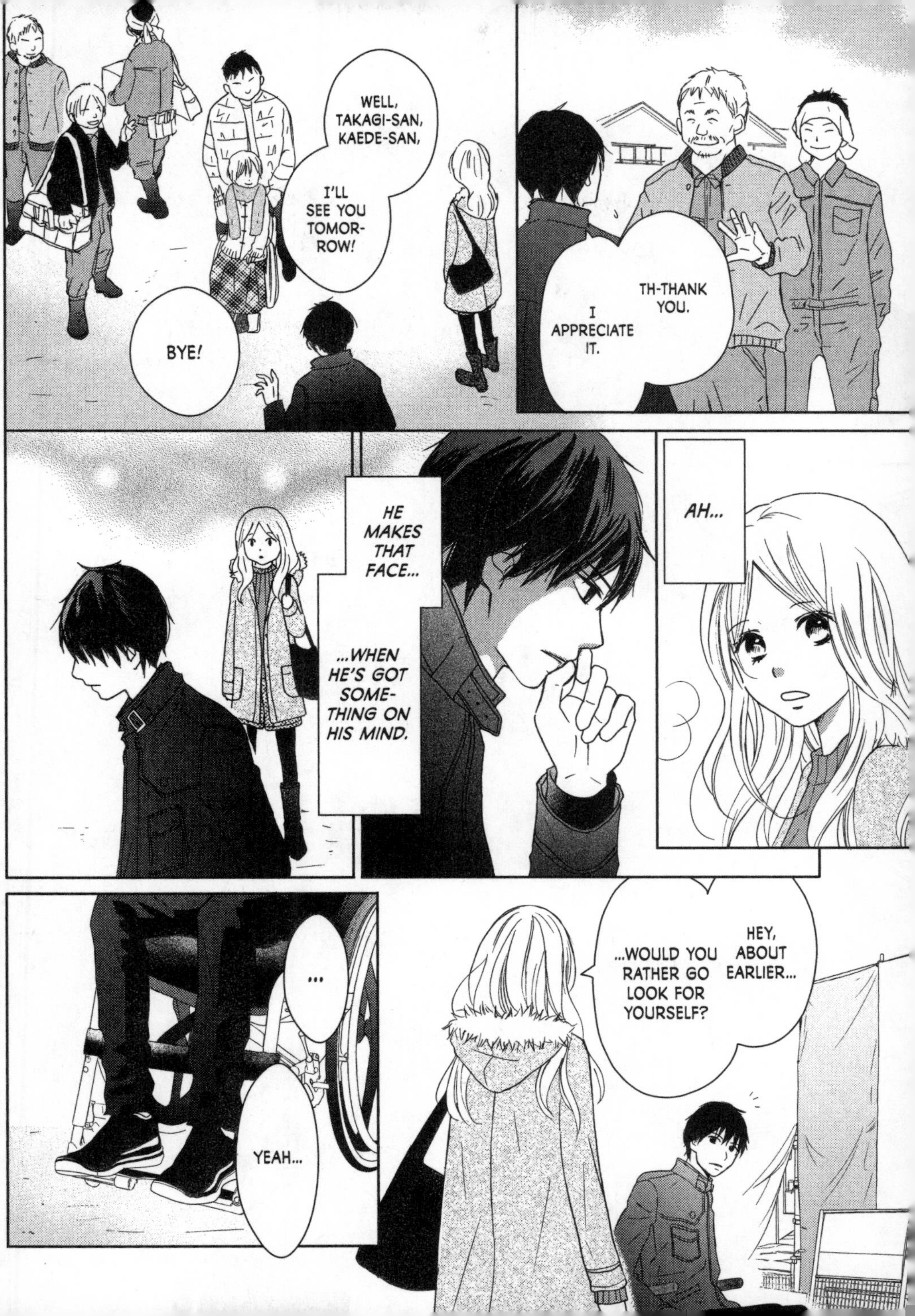
TH-THANK YOU.
I APPRECIATE IT.
WELL, TAKAGI-SAN, KAEDE-SAN,
I'LL SEE YOU TOMORROW!
BYE!
AH...
HE MAKES THAT FACE...
...WHEN HE'S GOT SOMETHING ON HIS MIND.
HEY, ABOUT EARLIER...
...WOULD YOU RATHER GO LOOK FOR YOURSELF?
...
YEAH...

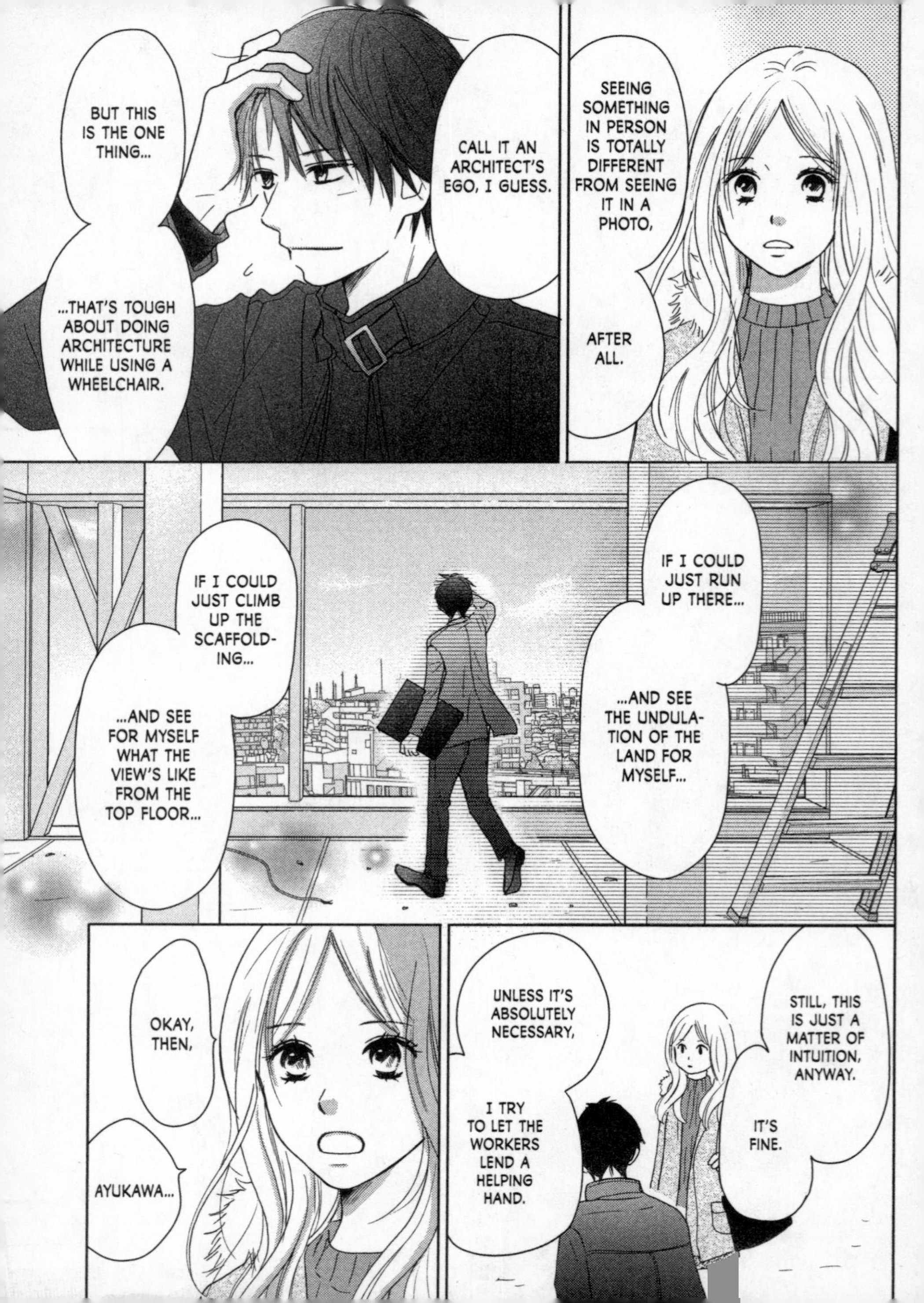
SEEING SOMETHING IN PERSON IS TOTALLY DIFFERENT FROM SEEING IT IN A PHOTO,
AFTER ALL.
CALL IT AN ARCHITECT'S EGO, I GUESS.
BUT THIS IS THE ONE THING...
...THAT'S TOUGH ABOUT DOING ARCHITECTURE WHILE USING A WHEELCHAIR.
IF I COULD JUST RUN UP THERE...
...AND SEE THE UNDULATION OF THE LAND FOR MYSELF...
IF I COULD JUST CLIMB UP THE SCAFFOLDING...
...AND SEE FOR MYSELF WHAT THE VIEW'S LIKE FROM THE TOP FLOOR...
STILL, THIS IS JUST A MATTER OF INTUITION, ANYWAY.
IT'S FINE.
UNLESS IT'S ABSOLUTELY NECESSARY,
I TRY TO LET THE WORKERS LEND A HELPING HAND.
OKAY, THEN,
AYUKAWA...

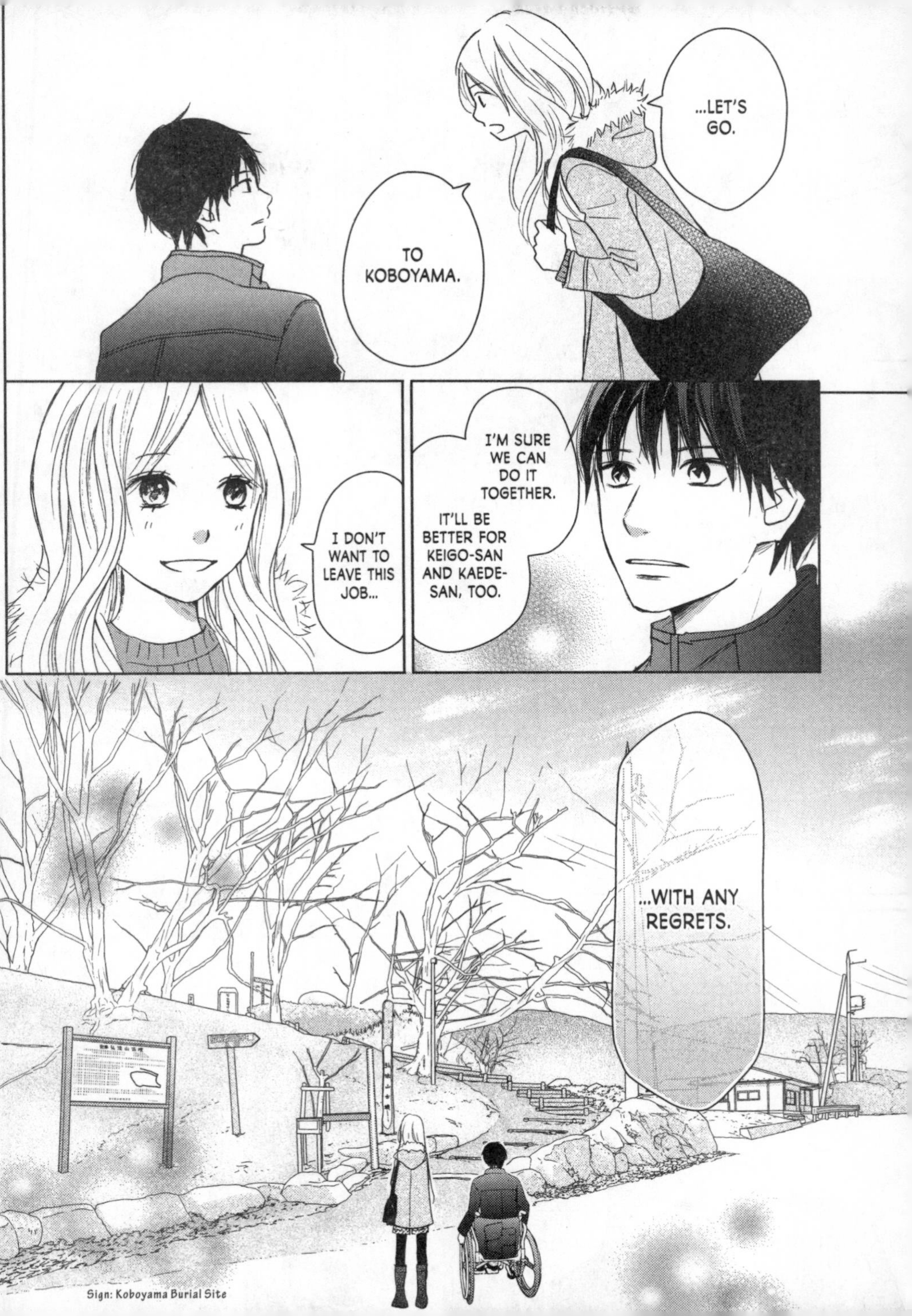
...LET'S GO.
TO KOBOYAMA.
I'M SURE WE CAN DO IT TOGETHER.
IT'LL BE BETTER FOR KEIGO-SAN AND KAEDE-SAN, TOO.
I DON'T WANT TO LEAVE THIS JOB...
...WITH ANY REGRETS.
Sign: Koboyama Burial Site

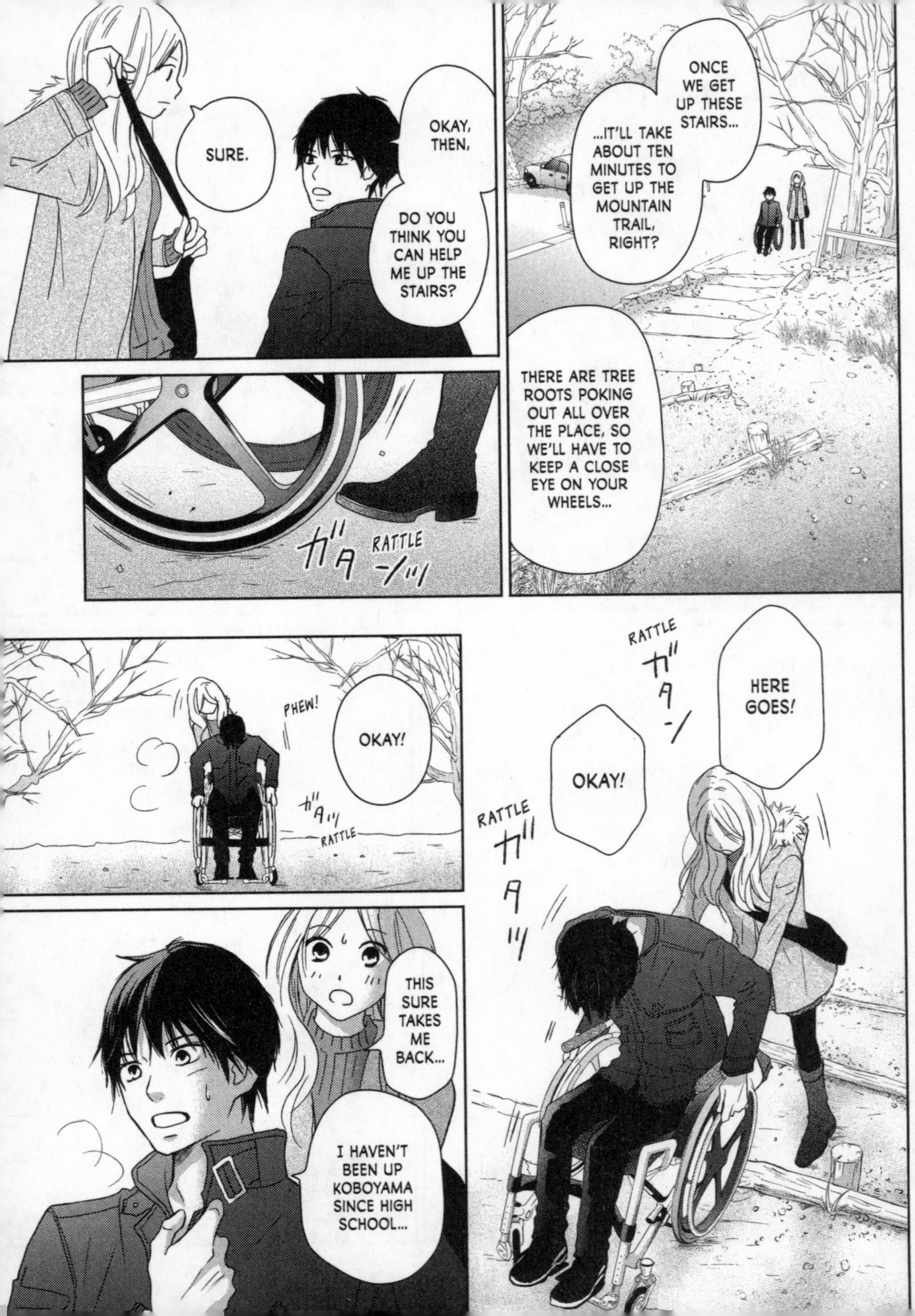
ONCE WE GET UP THESE STAIRS...
...IT'LL TAKE ABOUT TEN MINUTES TO GET UP THE MOUNTAIN TRAIL, RIGHT?
THERE ARE TREE ROOTS POKING OUT ALL OVER THE PLACE, SO WE'LL HAVE TO KEEP A CLOSE EYE ON YOUR WHEELS...
OKAY, THEN,
DO YOU THINK YOU CAN HELP ME UP THE STAIRS?
SURE.
RATTLE
RATTLE
HERE GOES!
OKAY!
RATTLE
OKAY!
PHEW!
RATTLE
THIS SURE TAKES ME BACK...
I HAVEN'T BEEN UP KOBOYAMA SINCE HIGH SCHOOL...

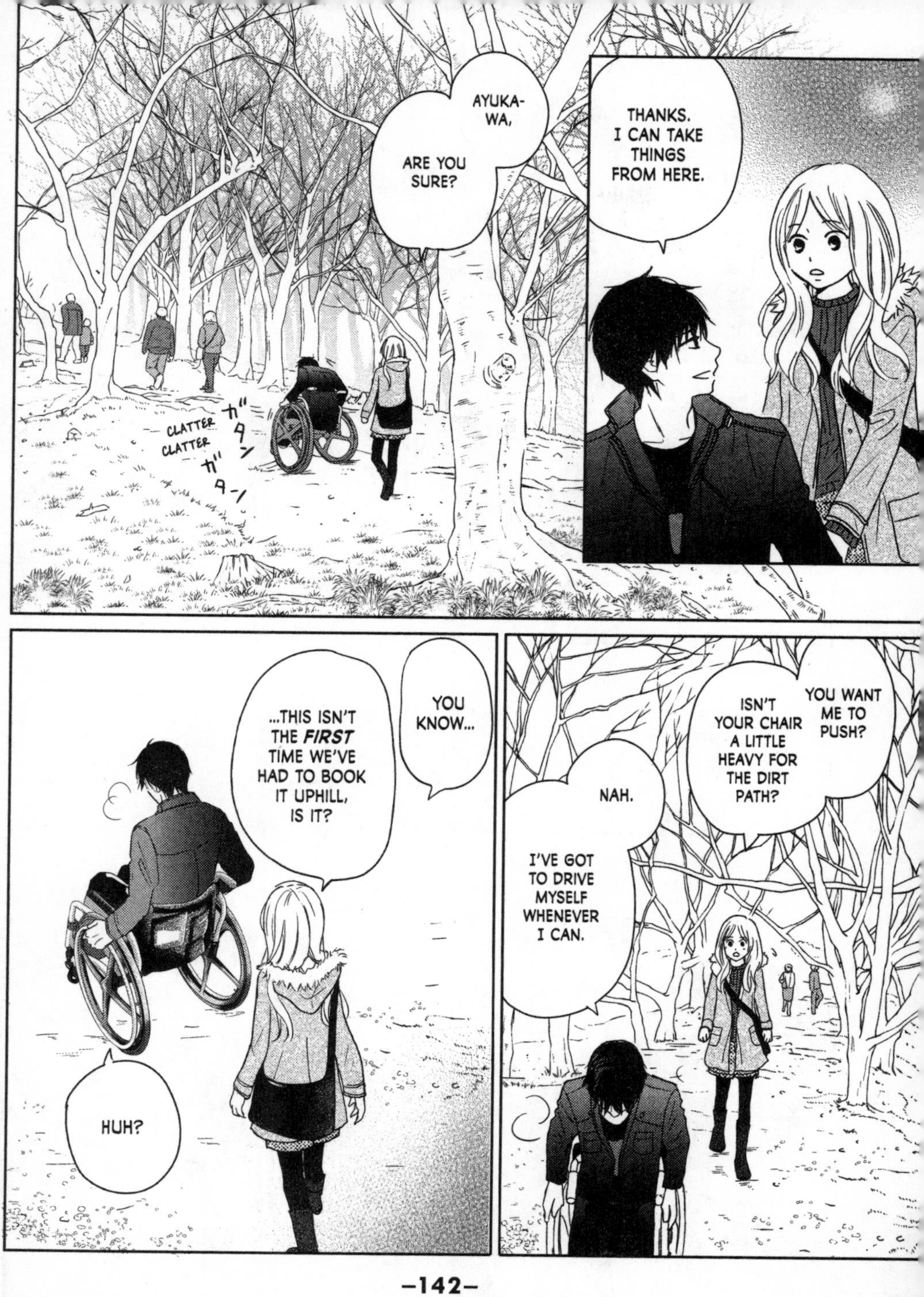
THANKS. I CAN TAKE THINGS FROM HERE.
AYUKA-WA,
ARE YOU SURE?
CLATTER
CLATTER
YOU WANT ME TO PUSH?
ISN'T YOUR CHAIR A LITTLE HEAVY FOR THE DIRT PATH?
NAH.
I'VE GOT TO DRIVE MYSELF WHENEVER I CAN.
YOU KNOW...
...THIS ISN'T THE *FIRST* TIME WE'VE HAD TO BOOK IT UPHILL, IS IT?
HUH?

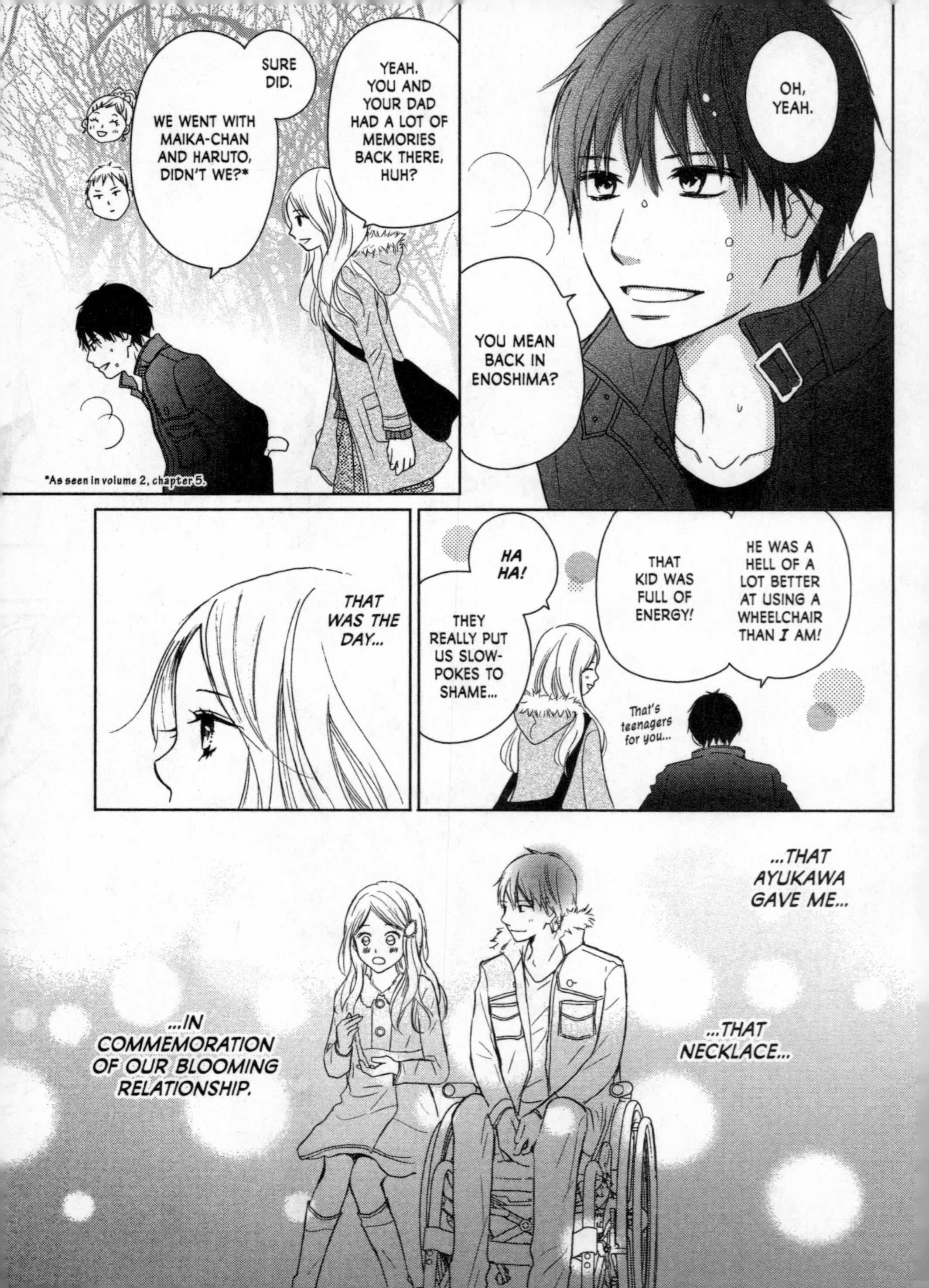
OH, YEAH.
YOU MEAN BACK IN ENOSHIMA?
YEAH. YOU AND YOUR DAD HAD A LOT OF MEMORIES BACK THERE, HUH?
SURE DID.
WE WENT WITH MAIKA-CHAN AND HARUTO, DIDN'T WE?*
*As seen in volume 2, chapter 5.
HE WAS A HELL OF A LOT BETTER AT USING A WHEELCHAIR THAN *I* AM!
THAT KID WAS FULL OF ENERGY!
HA HA!
THEY REALLY PUT US SLOW-POKES TO SHAME...
That's teenagers for you...
THAT WAS THE DAY...
...THAT AYUKAWA GAVE ME...
...THAT NECKLACE...
...IN COMMEMORATION OF OUR BLOOMING RELATIONSHIP.

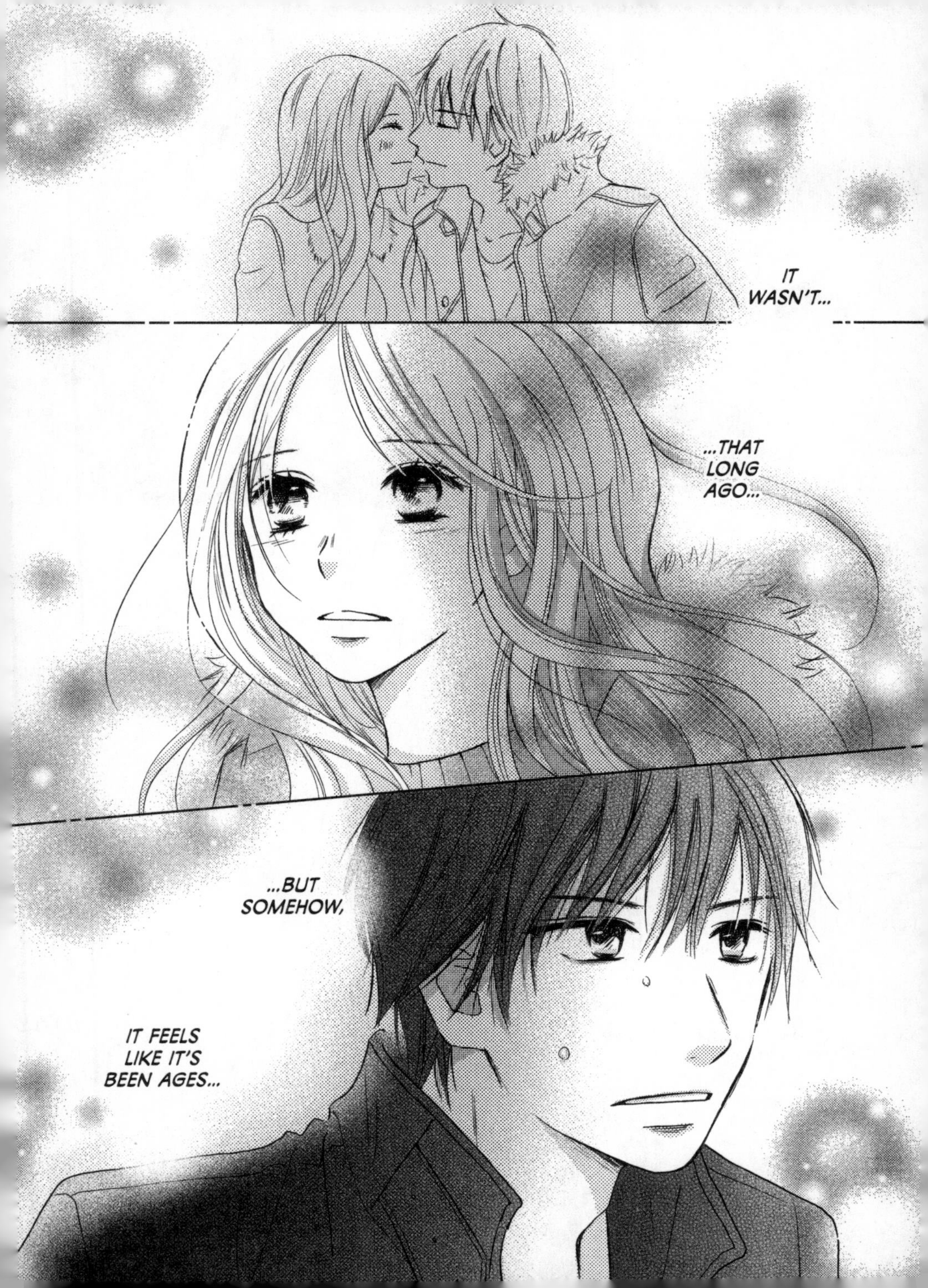
IT WASN'T...
...THAT LONG AGO...
...BUT SOMEHOW,
IT FEELS LIKE IT'S BEEN AGES...

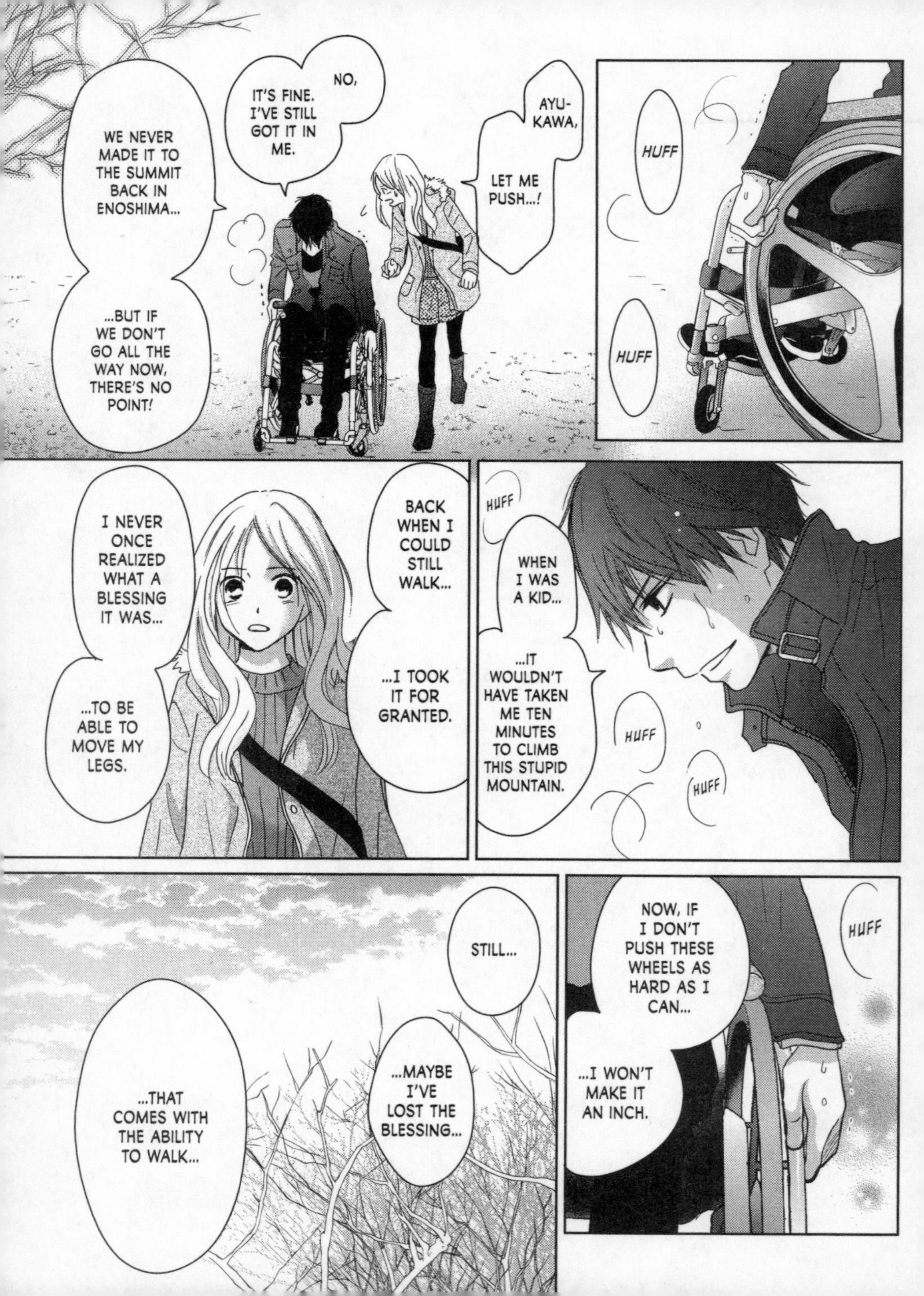
HUFF
HUFF
AYU-KAWA,
LET ME PUSH...!
NO,
IT'S FINE. I'VE STILL GOT IT IN ME.
WE NEVER MADE IT TO THE SUMMIT BACK IN ENOSHIMA...
...BUT IF WE DON'T GO ALL THE WAY NOW, THERE'S NO POINT!
HUFF
WHEN I WAS A KID...
...IT WOULDN'T HAVE TAKEN ME TEN MINUTES TO CLIMB THIS STUPID MOUNTAIN.
HUFF
HUFF
BACK WHEN I COULD STILL WALK...
...I TOOK IT FOR GRANTED.
I NEVER ONCE REALIZED WHAT A BLESSING IT WAS...
...TO BE ABLE TO MOVE MY LEGS.
HUFF
NOW, IF I DON'T PUSH THESE WHEELS AS HARD AS I CAN...
...I WON'T MAKE IT AN INCH.
STILL...
...MAYBE I'VE LOST THE BLESSING...
...THAT COMES WITH THE ABILITY TO WALK...

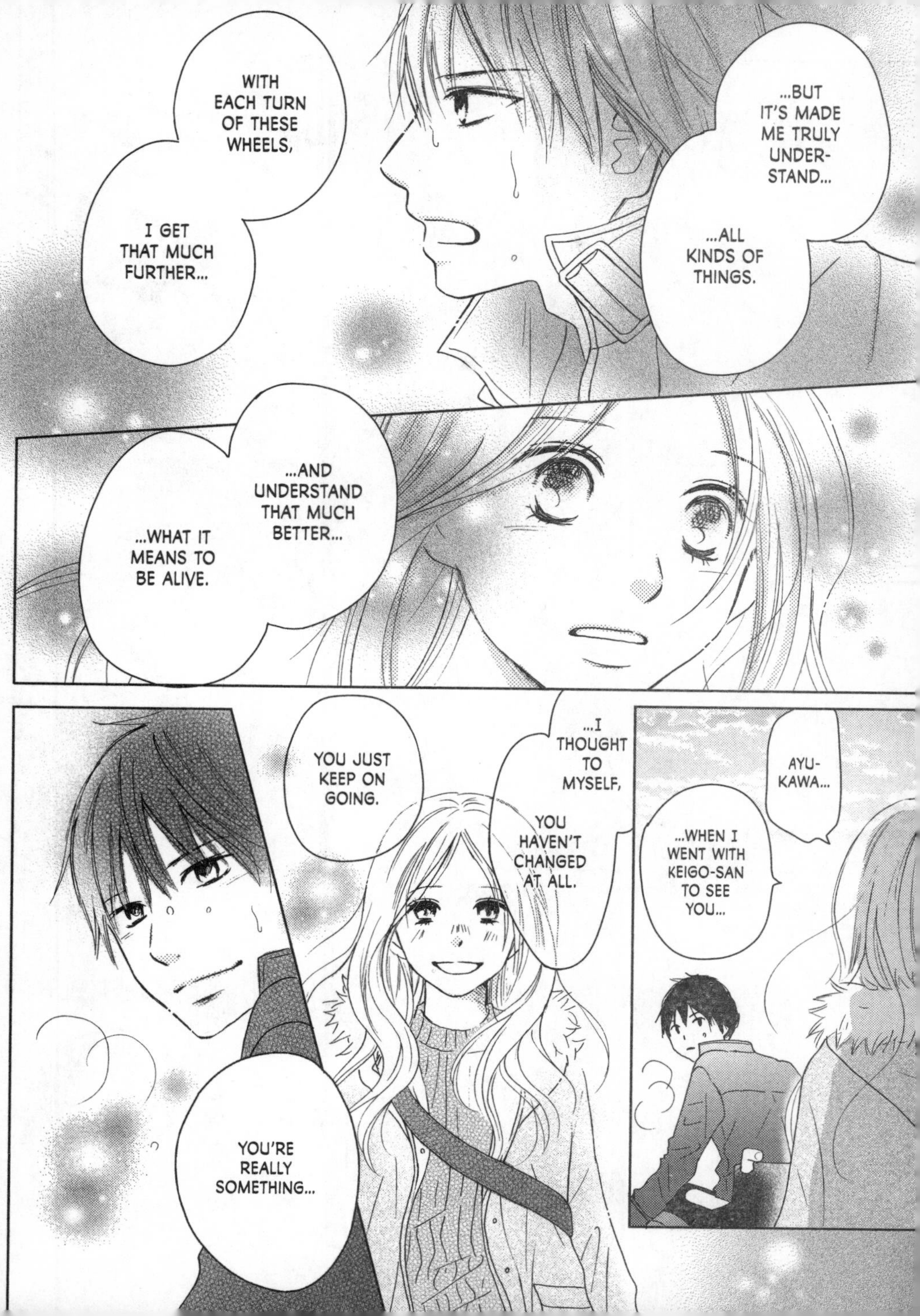
...BUT IT'S MADE ME TRULY UNDER-STAND...
...ALL KINDS OF THINGS.
WITH EACH TURN OF THESE WHEELS,
I GET THAT MUCH FURTHER...
...AND UNDERSTAND THAT MUCH BETTER...
...WHAT IT MEANS TO BE ALIVE.
AYU-KAWA...
...WHEN I WENT WITH KEIGO-SAN TO SEE YOU...
...I THOUGHT TO MYSELF,
YOU HAVEN'T CHANGED AT ALL.
YOU JUST KEEP ON GOING.
YOU'RE REALLY SOMETHING...

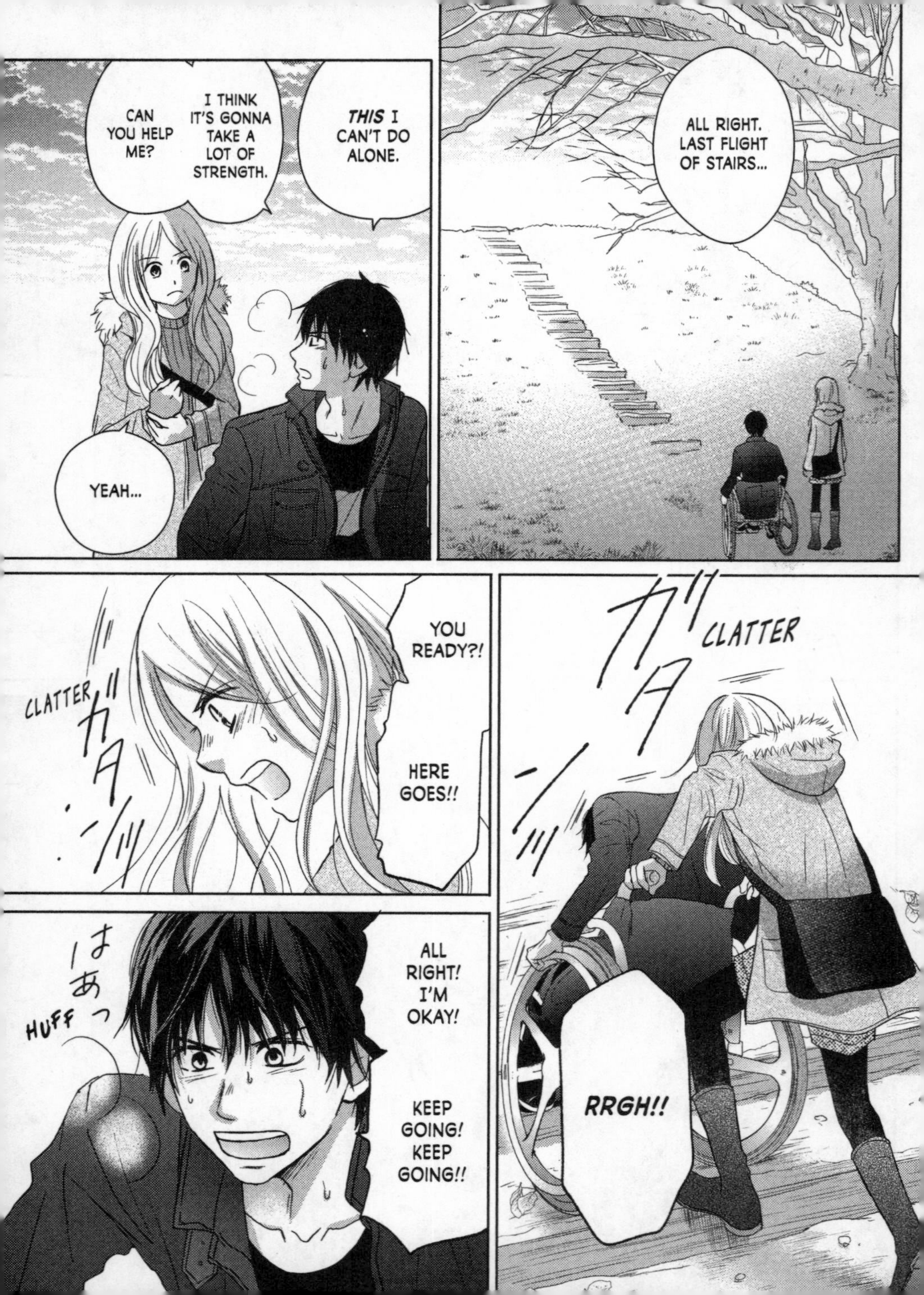
ALL RIGHT. LAST FLIGHT OF STAIRS...
THIS I CAN'T DO ALONE.
I THINK IT'S GONNA TAKE A LOT OF STRENGTH.
CAN YOU HELP ME?
YEAH...
ガタン
CLATTER
RRGH!!
YOU READY?!
HERE GOES!!
ガタン
CLATTER
ALL RIGHT! I'M OKAY!
KEEP GOING! KEEP GOING!!
はあっ
HUFF

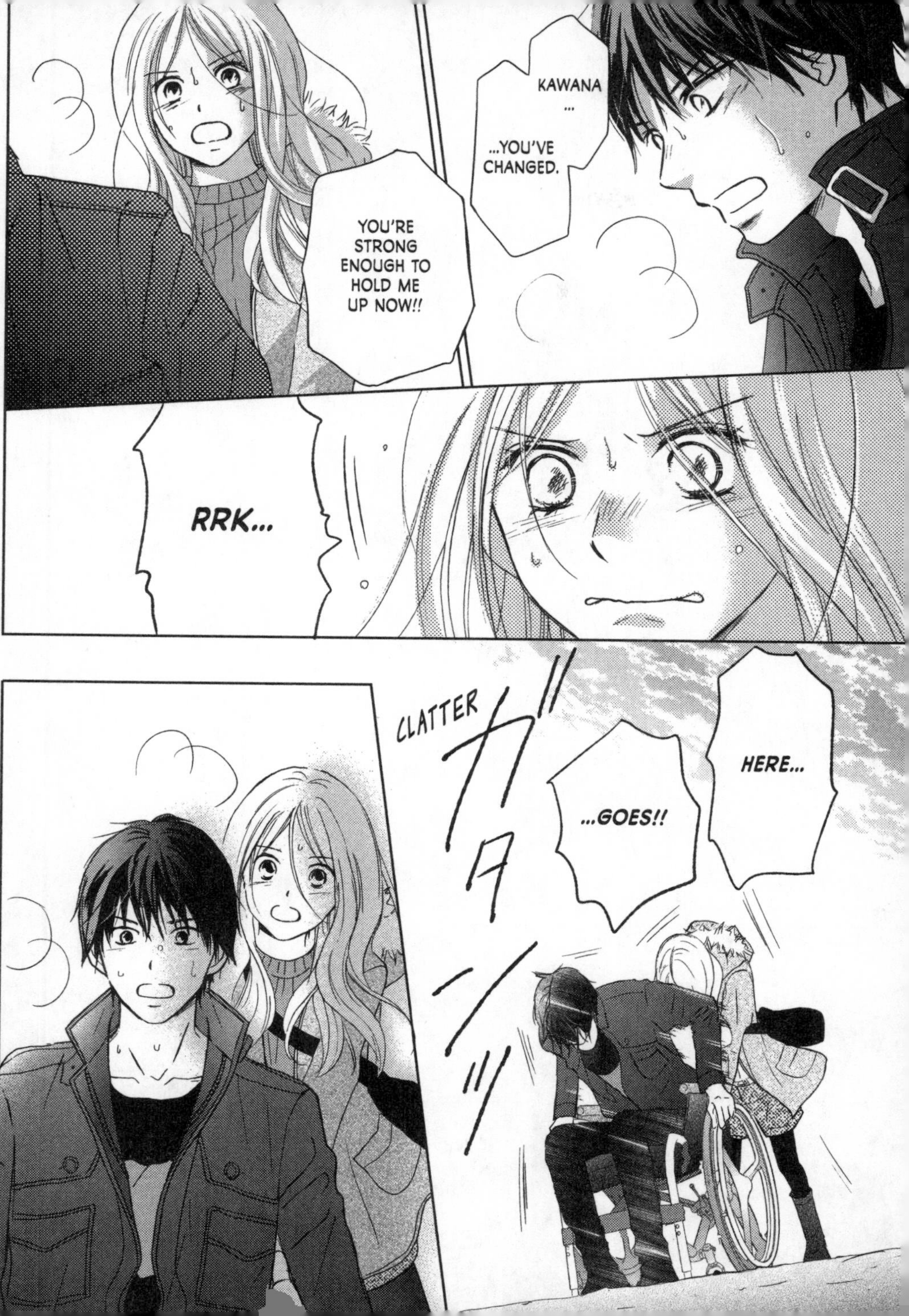
KAWANA ...
...YOU'VE CHANGED.
YOU'RE STRONG ENOUGH TO HOLD ME UP NOW!!
RRK...
HERE...
...GOES!!
CLATTER

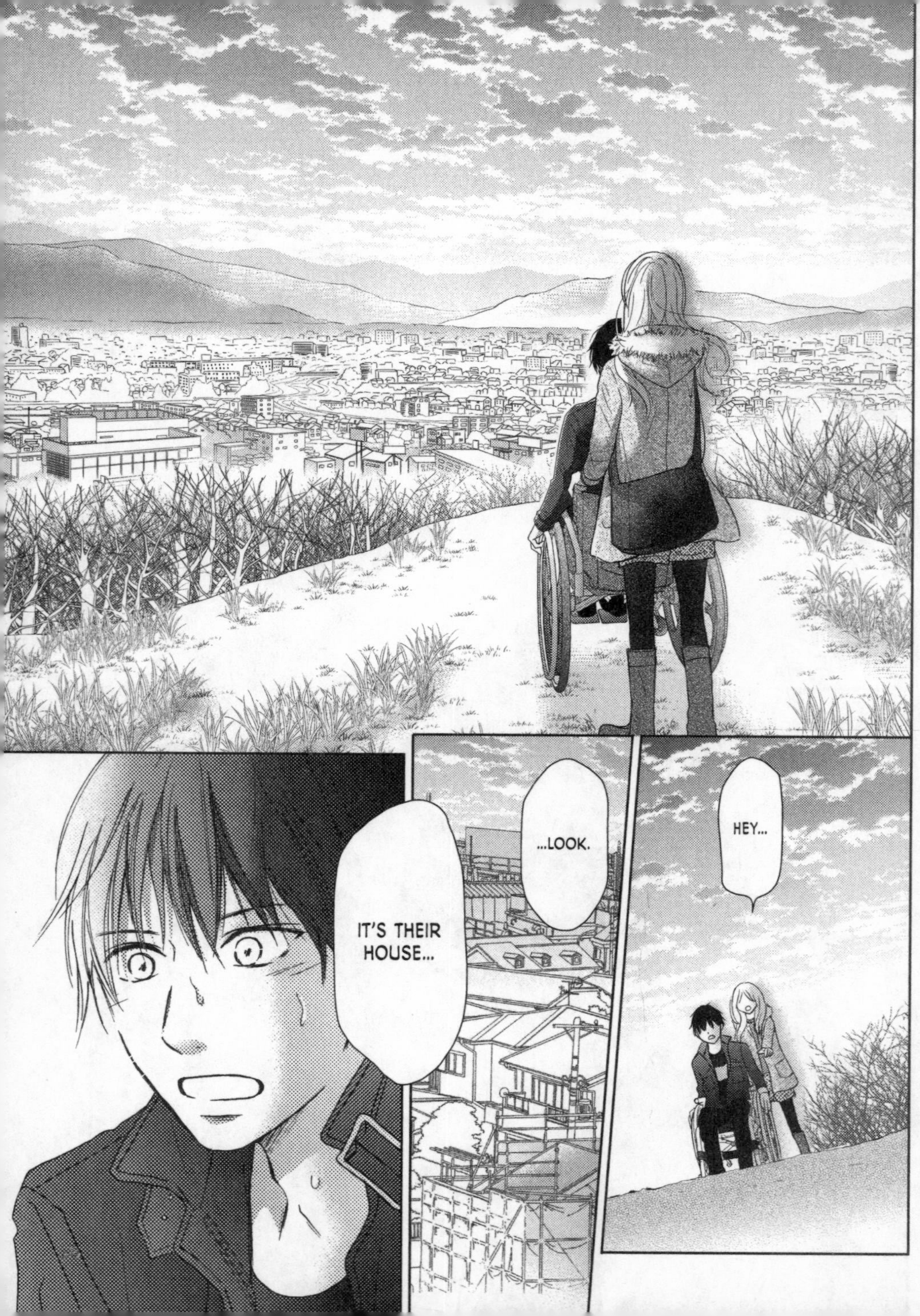
HEY...
...LOOK.
IT'S THEIR HOUSE...

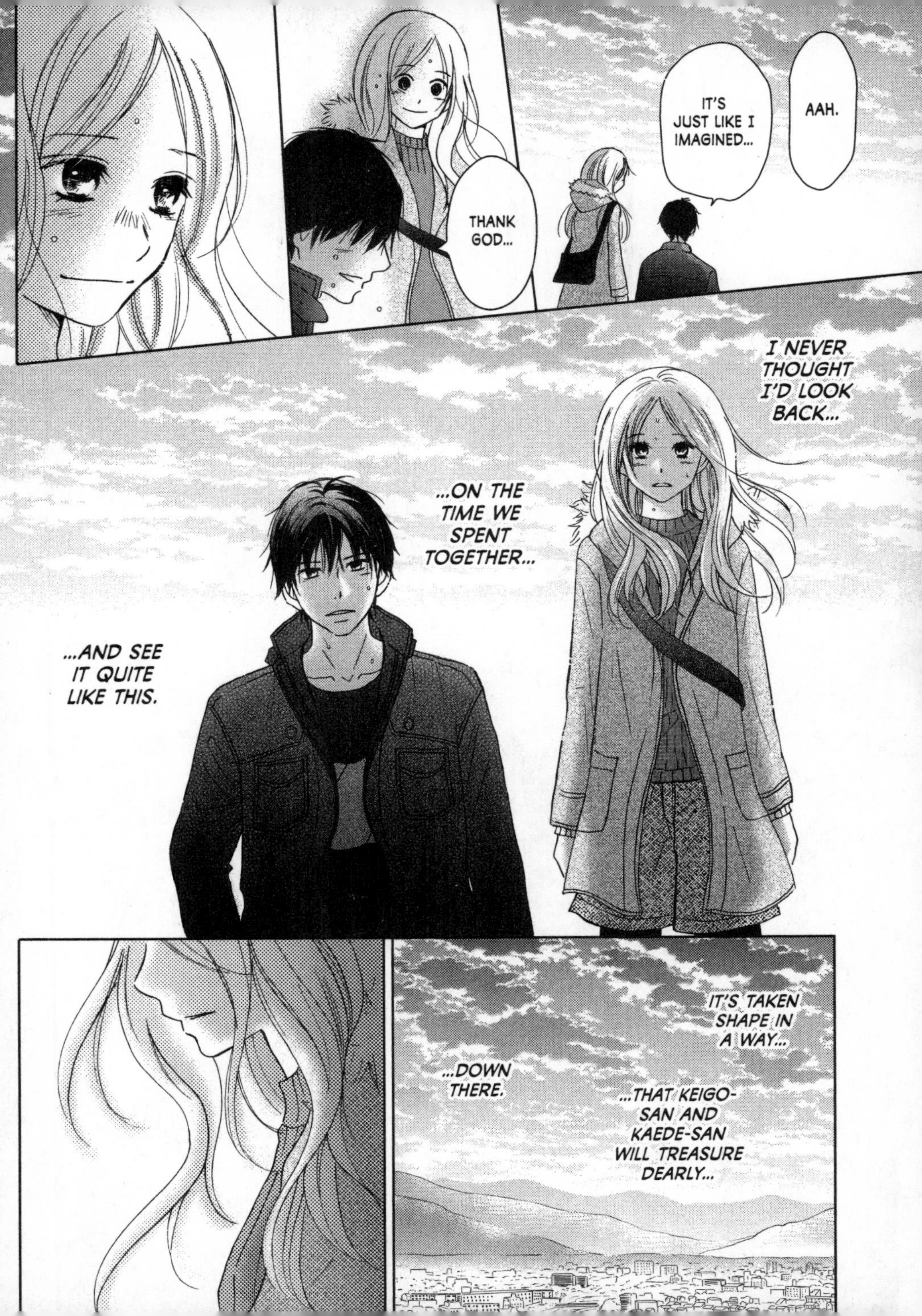
AAH.
IT'S JUST LIKE I IMAGINED...
THANK GOD...
I NEVER THOUGHT I'D LOOK BACK...
...ON THE TIME WE SPENT TOGETHER...
...AND SEE IT QUITE LIKE THIS.
IT'S TAKEN SHAPE IN A WAY...
...THAT KEIGO-SAN AND KAEDE-SAN WILL TREASURE DEARLY...
...DOWN THERE.

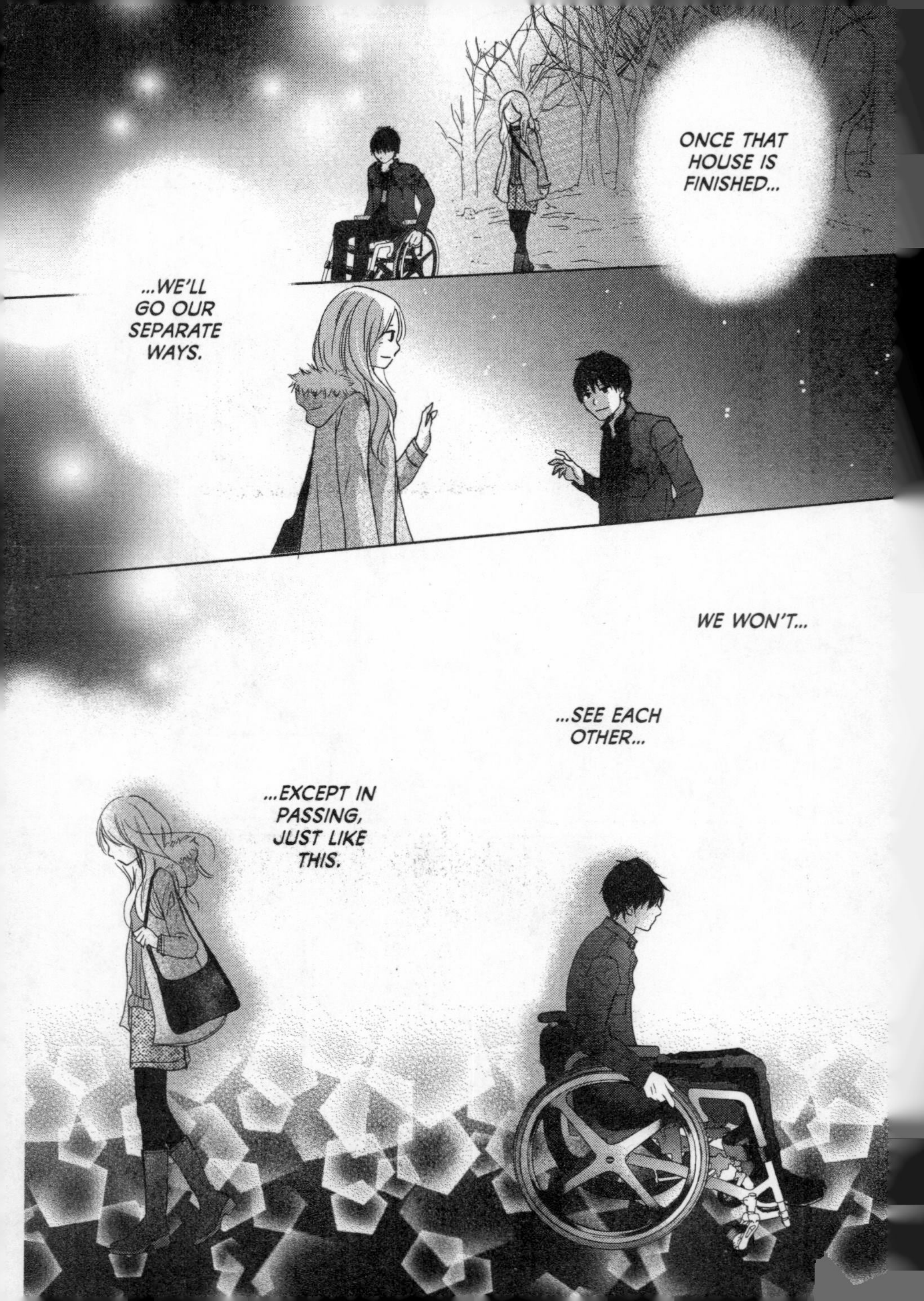
ONCE THAT HOUSE IS FINISHED...
...WE'LL GO OUR SEPARATE WAYS.
WE WON'T...
...SEE EACH OTHER...
...EXCEPT IN PASSING, JUST LIKE THIS.

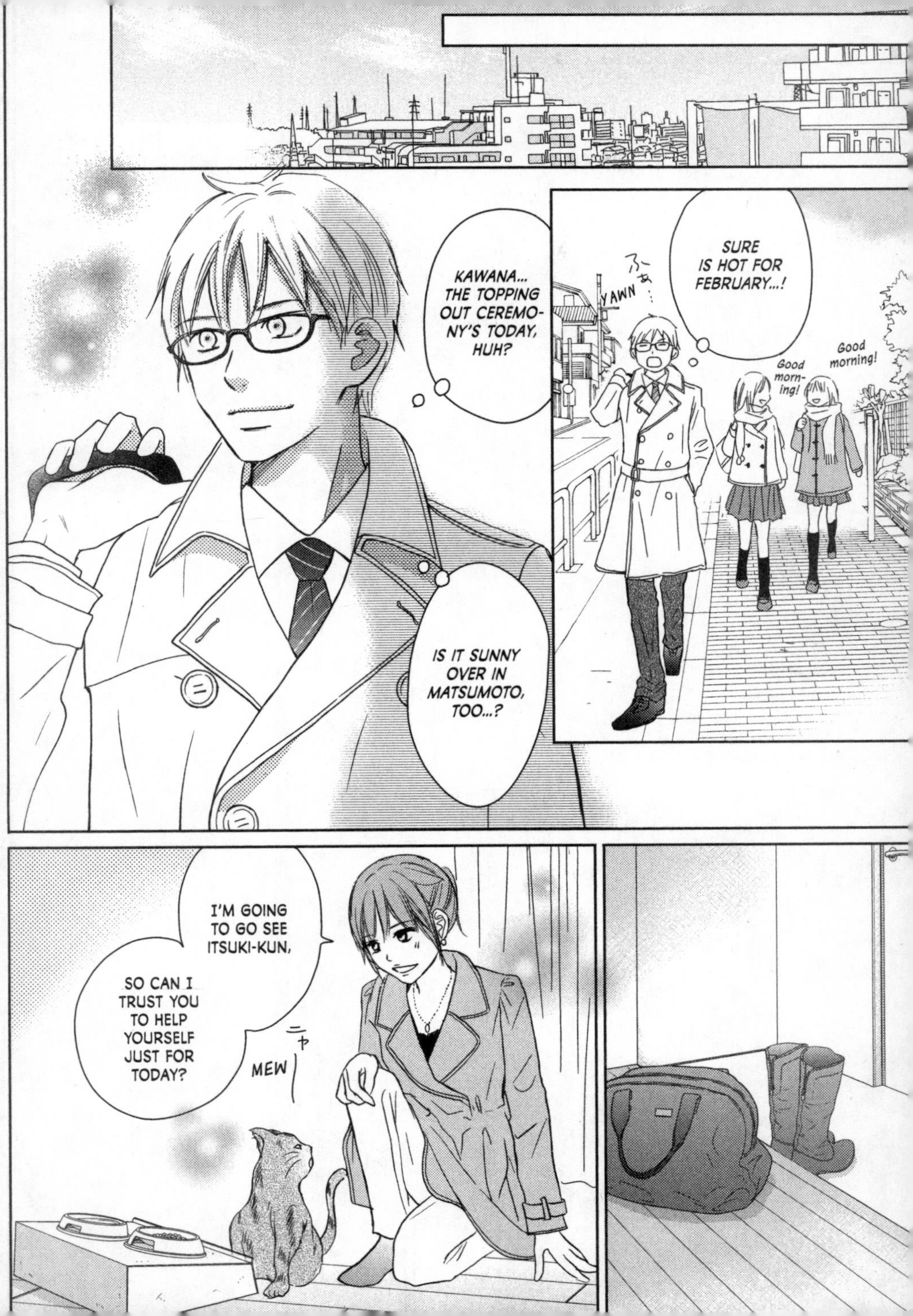
SURE IS HOT FOR FEBRUARY...!
ふぁ...
YAWN
Good morning!
Good morn-ing!
KAWANA... THE TOPPING OUT CEREMO-NY'S TODAY, HUH?
IS IT SUNNY OVER IN MATSUMOTO, TOO...?
I'M GOING TO GO SEE ITSUKI-KUN,
SO CAN I TRUST YOU TO HELP YOURSELF JUST FOR TODAY?
ニャ
MEW

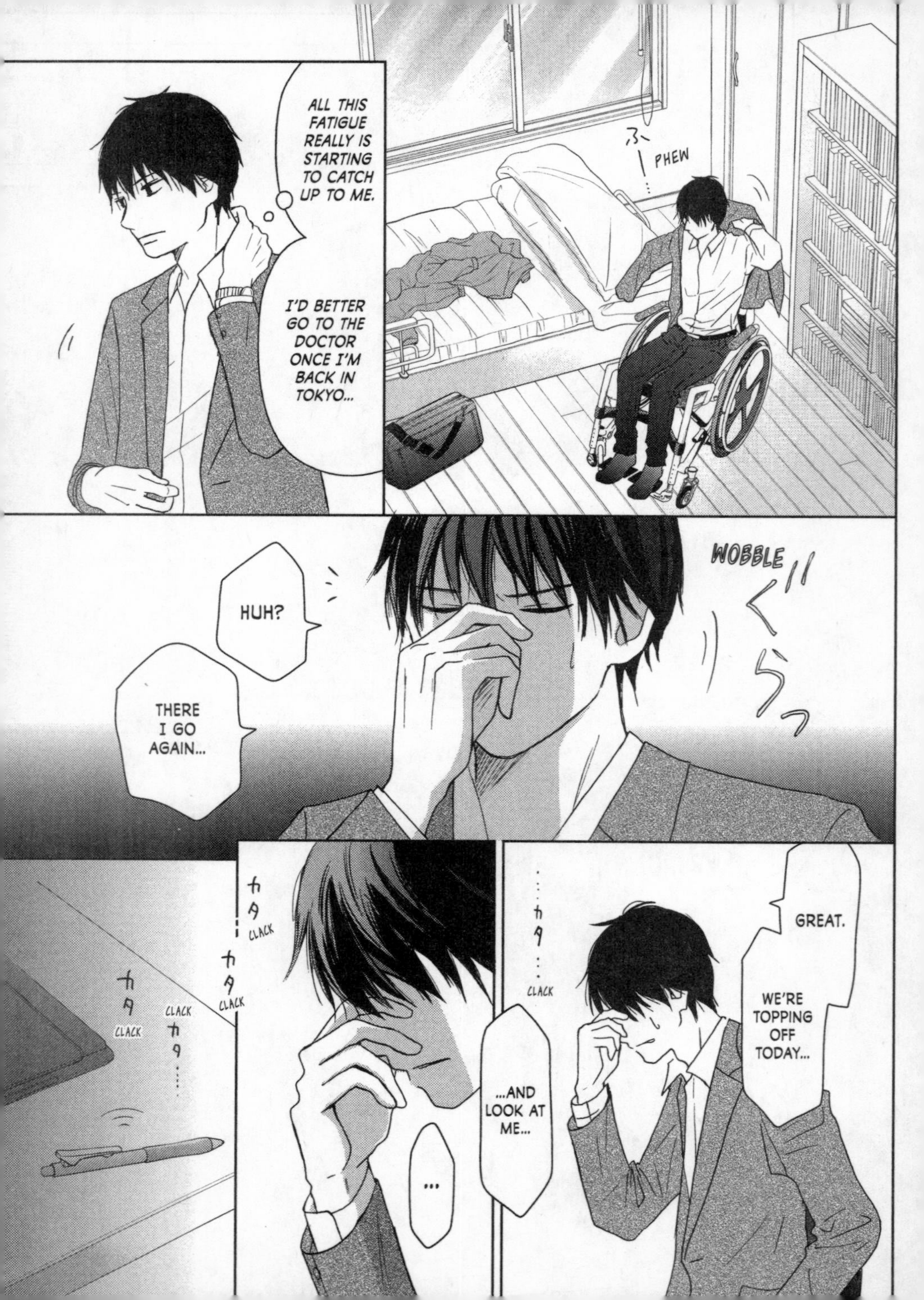
ふー
PHEW
…
ALL THIS FATIGUE REALLY IS STARTING TO CATCH UP TO ME.
I'D BETTER GO TO THE DOCTOR ONCE I'M BACK IN TOKYO...
WOBBLE
ぐらっ
HUH?
THERE I GO AGAIN...
…カタ…
CLACK
GREAT.
WE'RE TOPPING OFF TODAY...
...AND LOOK AT ME...
...
カタ
CLACK
カタ
CLACK
CLACK
カタ....
カタ
CLACK

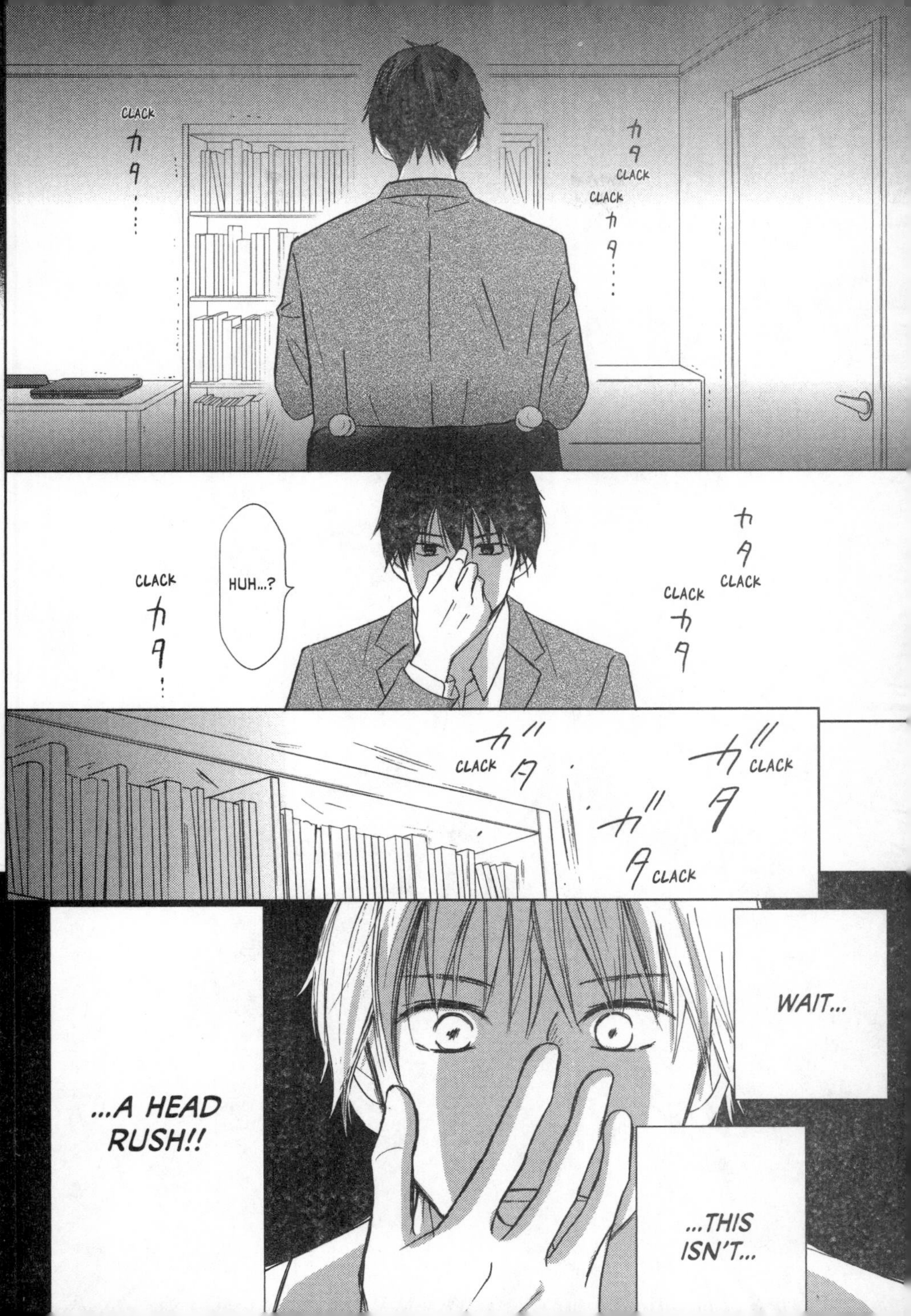
カタ CLACK
CLACK カタ…
CLACK カタ…
カタ CLACK
CLACK カタ
HUH...?
CLACK カタ…
ガタ CLACK
ガタ CLACK
CLACK ガタ
WAIT...
...THIS ISN'T...
...A HEAD RUSH!!

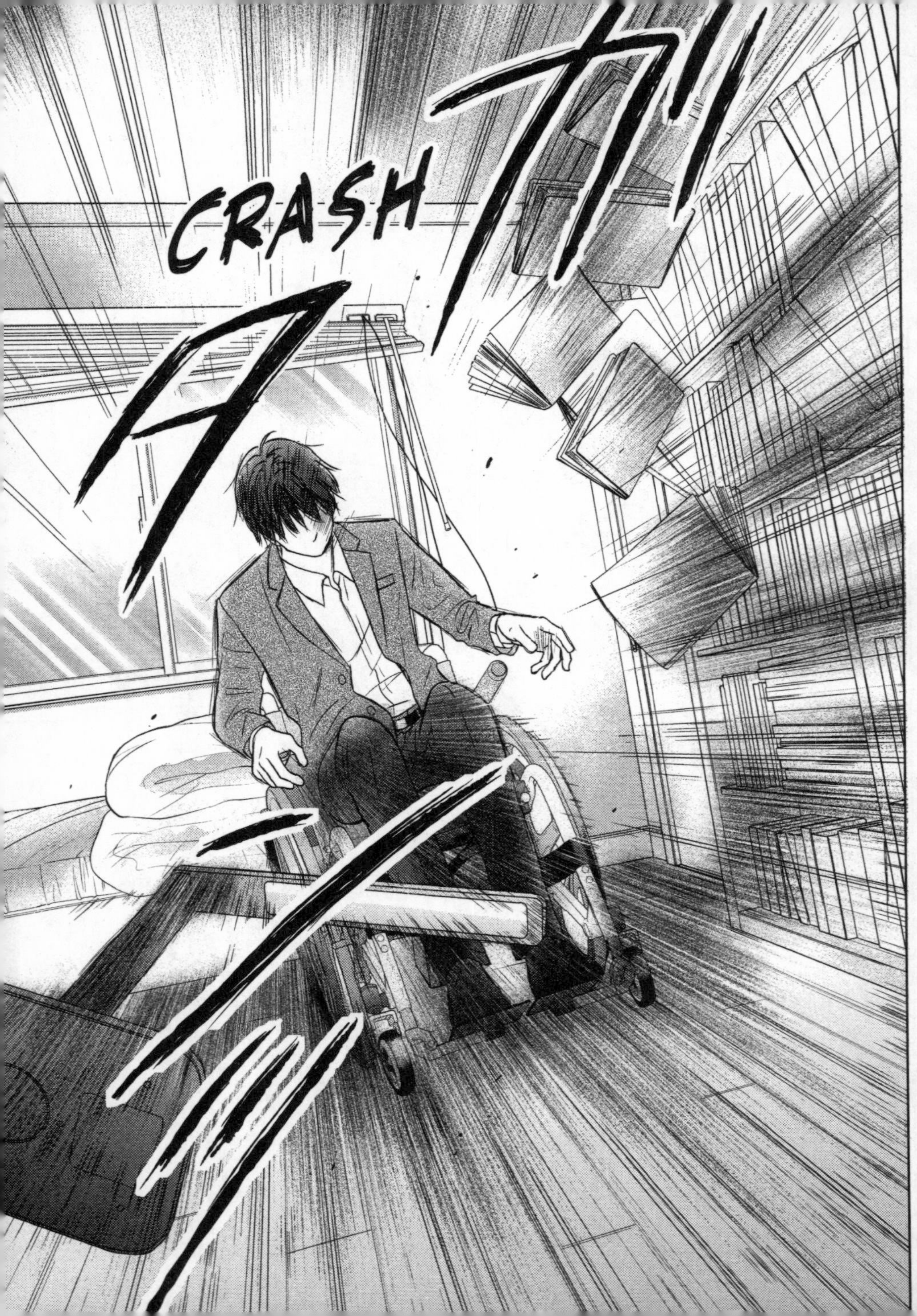
CRASH

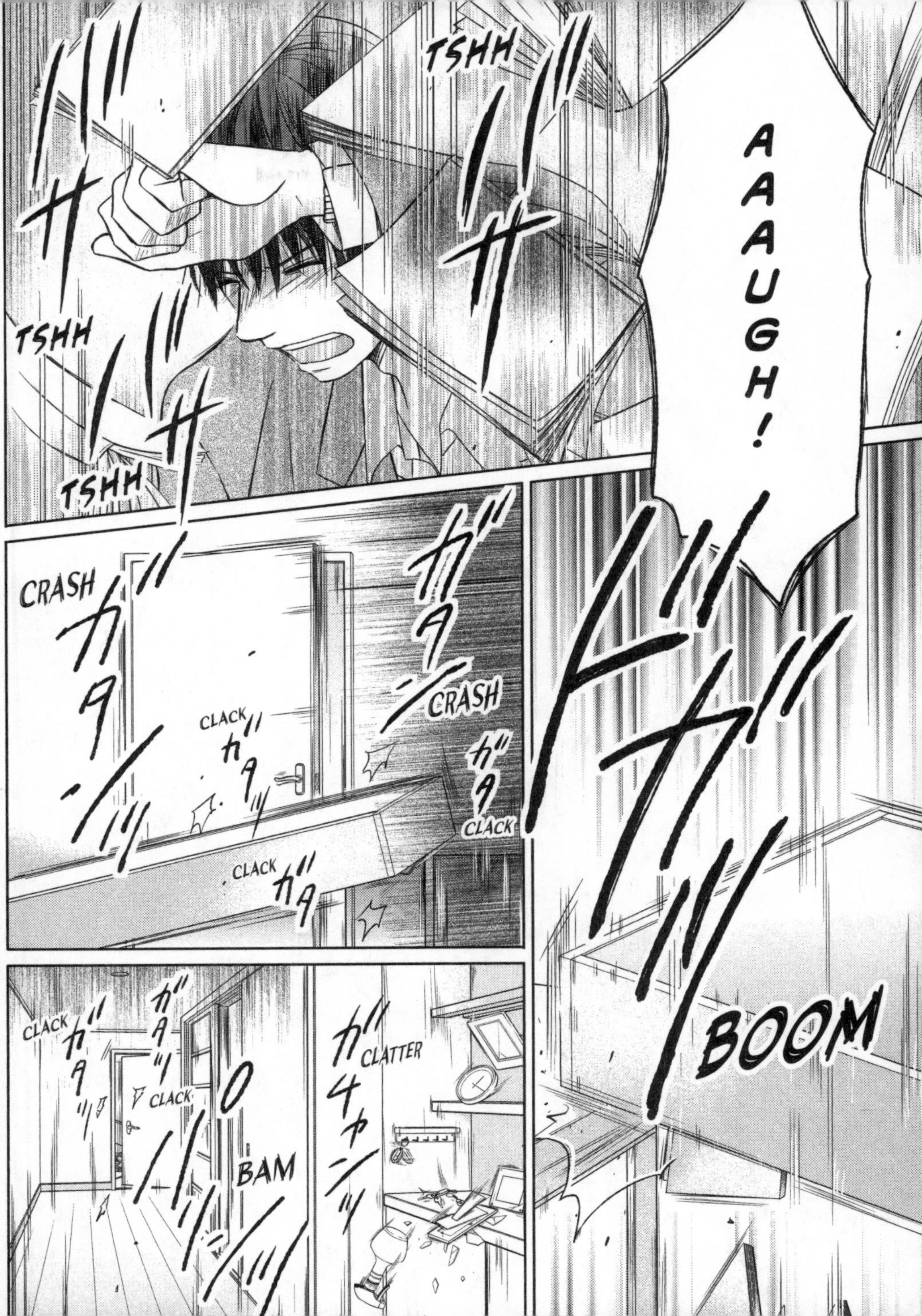
AAAUGH!
TSHH
TSHH
TSHH
BOOM
CRASH
CLACK
CLACK
CLACK
CRASH
CLATTER
BAM
CLACK
CLACK

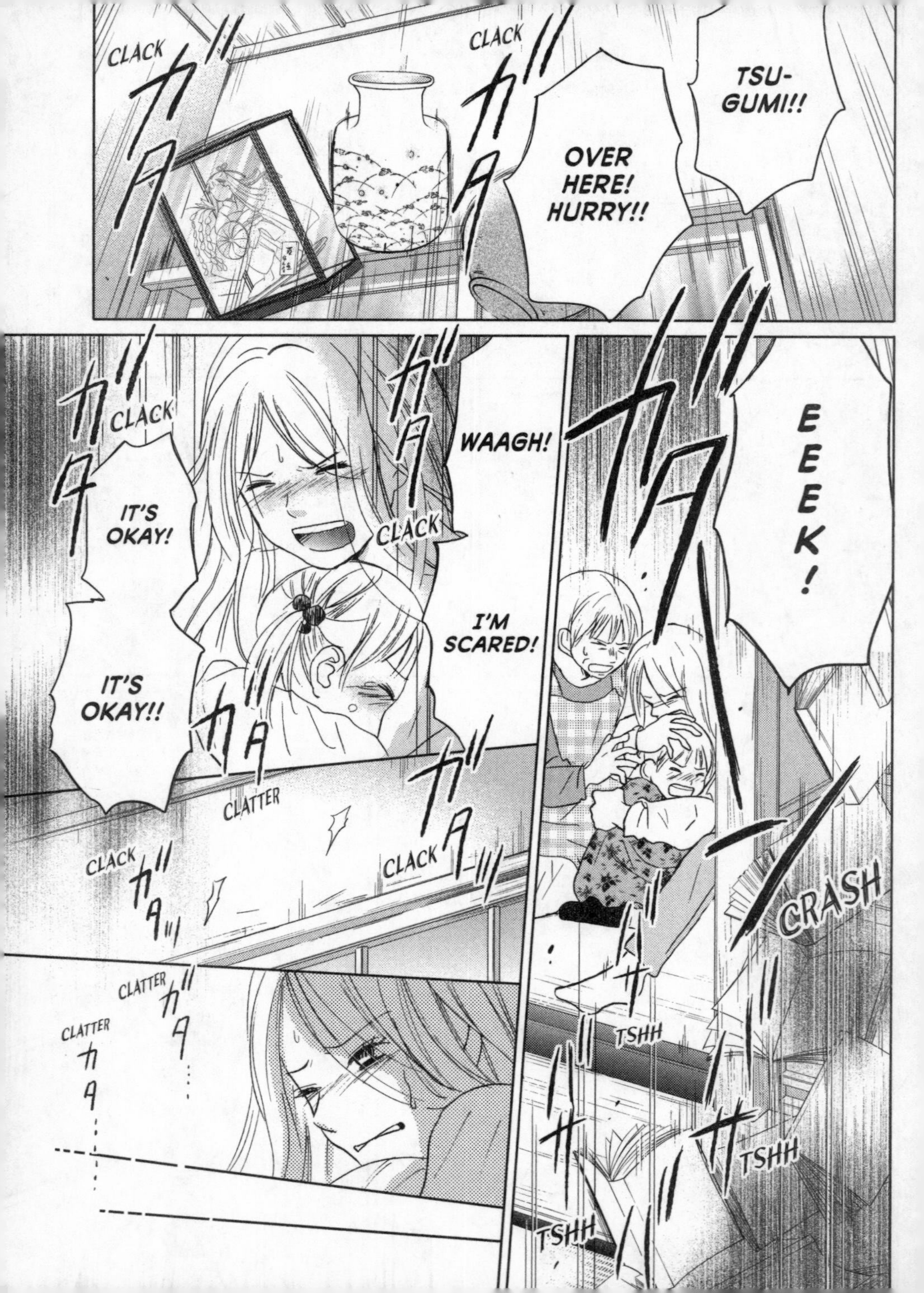
TSU-GUMI!!
OVER HERE! HURRY!!
CLACK
CLACK
EEEK!
CRASH
TSHH
TSHH
TSHH
WAAGH!
I'M SCARED!
CLACK
CLACK
IT'S OKAY!
IT'S OKAY!!
CLATTER
CLACK
CLACK
CLATTER
CLATTER

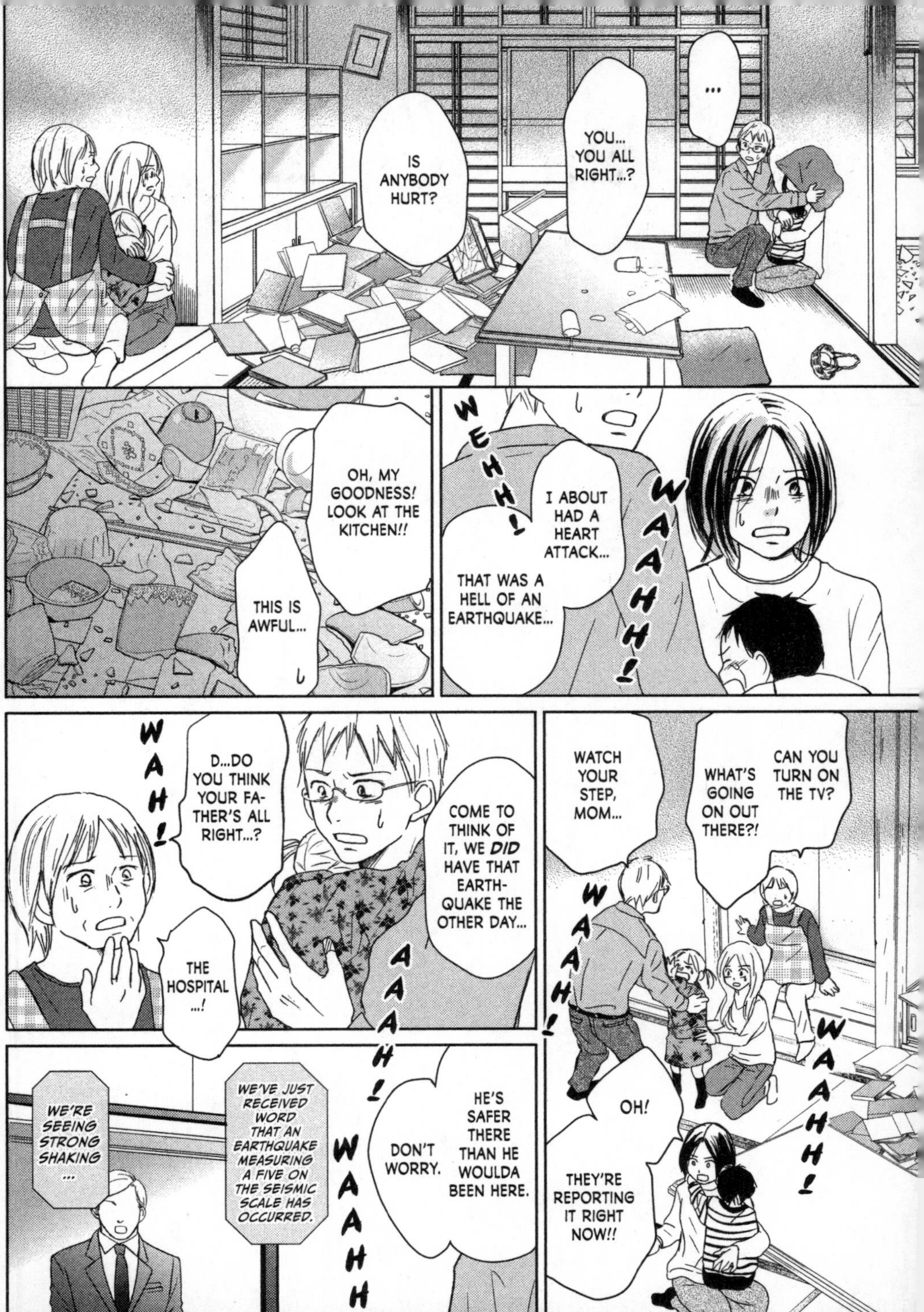
...
YOU... YOU ALL RIGHT...?
IS ANYBODY HURT?
WAAAHHH!
I ABOUT HAD A HEART ATTACK...
WEHHH!
THAT WAS A HELL OF AN EARTHQUAKE...
OH, MY GOODNESS! LOOK AT THE KITCHEN!!
THIS IS AWFUL...
CAN YOU TURN ON THE TV?
WHAT'S GOING ON OUT THERE?!
WATCH YOUR STEP, MOM...
WAAAH!
WAAAHH!
OH!
THEY'RE REPORTING IT RIGHT NOW!!
COME TO THINK OF IT, WE *DID* HAVE THAT EARTH-QUAKE THE OTHER DAY...
D...DO YOU THINK YOUR FA-THER'S ALL RIGHT...?
WAH!
THE HOSPITAL ...!
AAAAH!
HE'S SAFER THERE THAN HE WOULDA BEEN HERE.
DON'T WORRY.
WAAHH!
WE'VE JUST RECEIVED WORD THAT AN EARTHQUAKE MEASURING A FIVE ON THE SEISMIC SCALE HAS OCCURRED.
WE'RE SEEING STRONG SHAKING ...

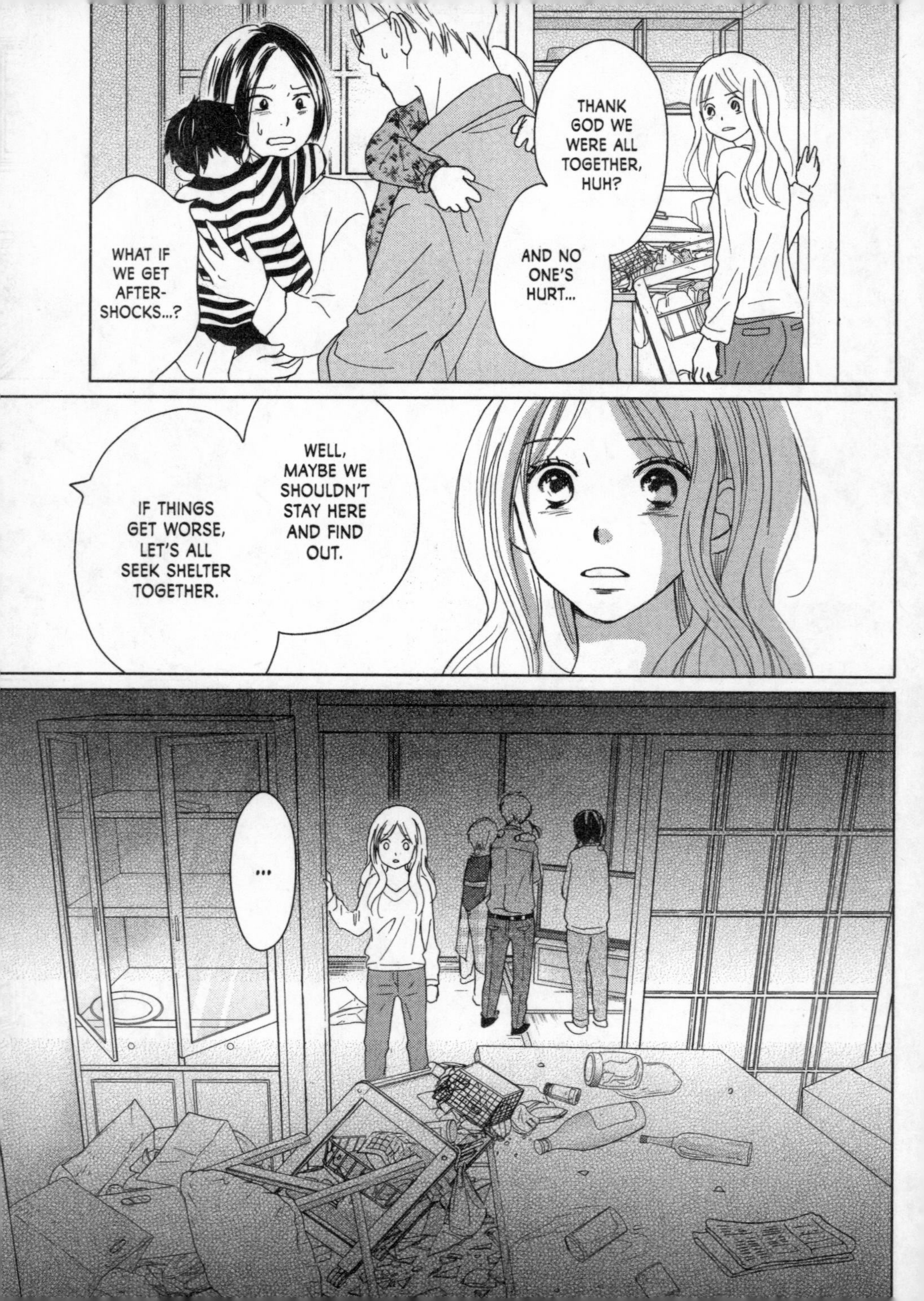
THANK GOD WE WERE ALL TOGETHER, HUH?
AND NO ONE'S HURT...
WHAT IF WE GET AFTER-SHOCKS...?
WELL, MAYBE WE SHOULDN'T STAY HERE AND FIND OUT.
IF THINGS GET WORSE, LET'S ALL SEEK SHELTER TOGETHER.
...

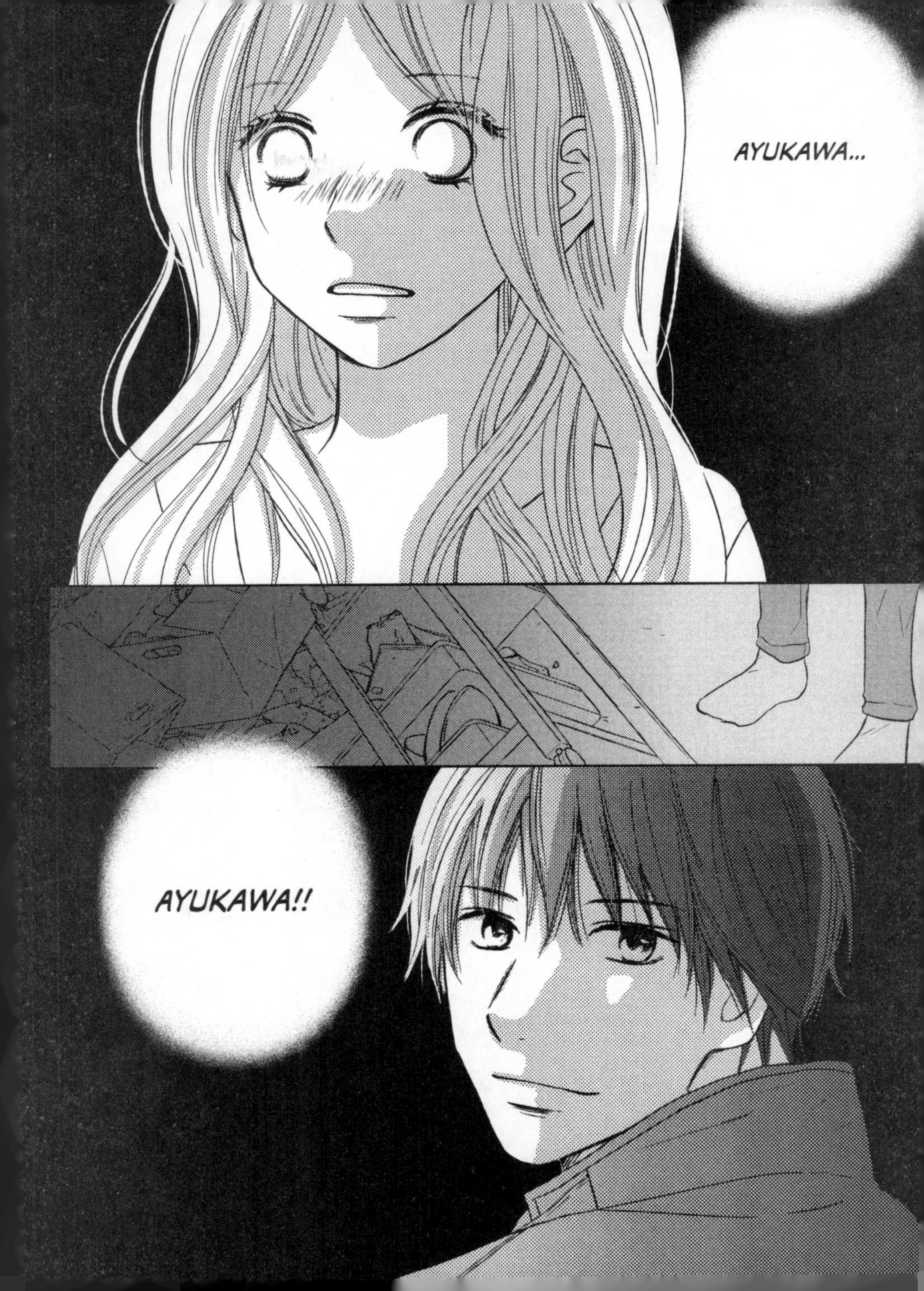
AYUKAWA...
AYUKAWA!!

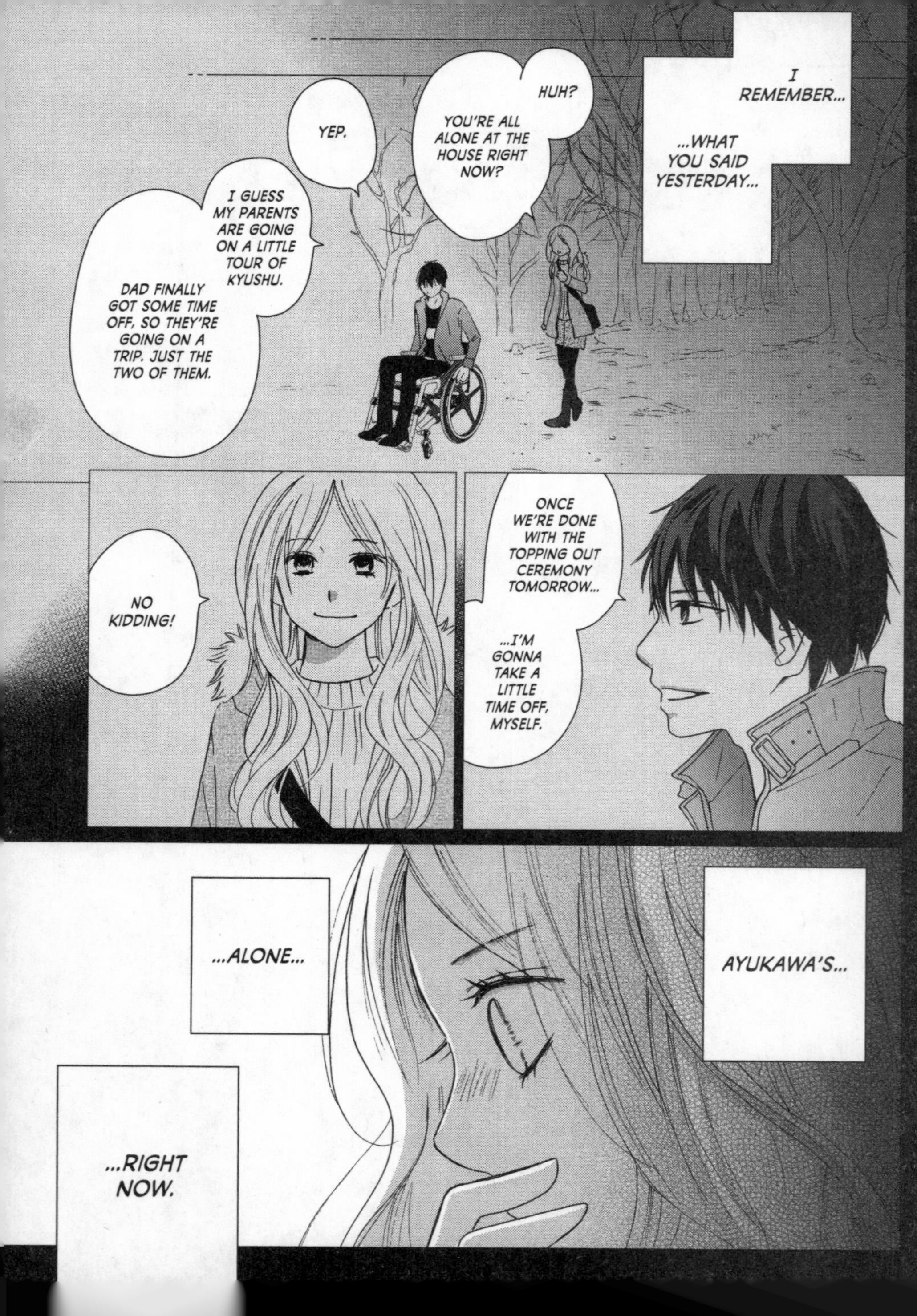
I REMEMBER...
...WHAT YOU SAID YESTERDAY...
HUH?
YOU'RE ALL ALONE AT THE HOUSE RIGHT NOW?
YEP.
I GUESS MY PARENTS ARE GOING ON A LITTLE TOUR OF KYUSHU.
DAD FINALLY GOT SOME TIME OFF, SO THEY'RE GOING ON A TRIP. JUST THE TWO OF THEM.
ONCE WE'RE DONE WITH THE TOPPING OUT CEREMONY TOMORROW...
...I'M GONNA TAKE A LITTLE TIME OFF, MYSELF.
NO KIDDING!
AYUKAWA'S...
...ALONE...
...RIGHT NOW.

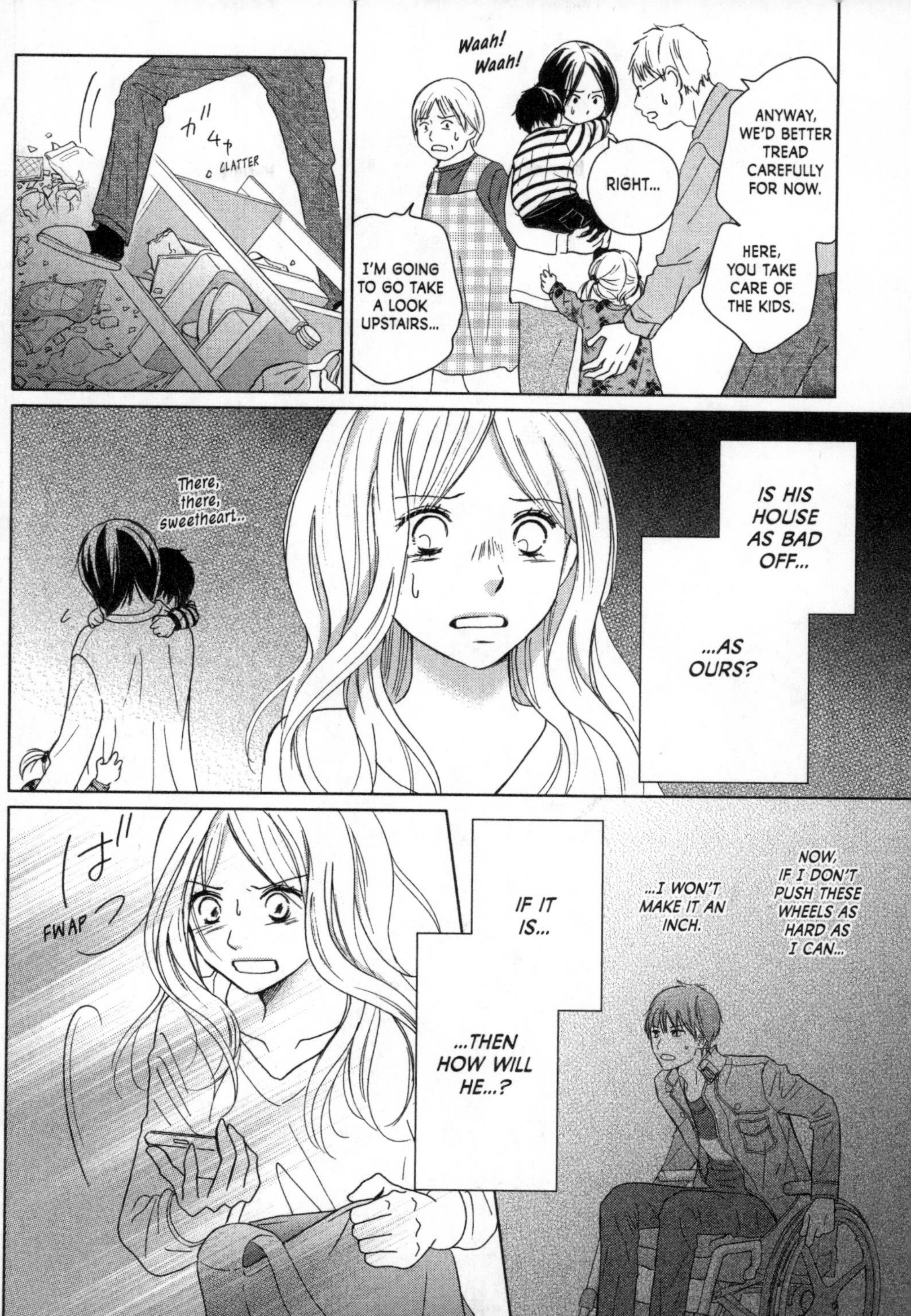
Waah! Waah!
ANYWAY, WE'D BETTER TREAD CAREFULLY FOR NOW.
RIGHT...
HERE, YOU TAKE CARE OF THE KIDS.
I'M GOING TO GO TAKE A LOOK UPSTAIRS...
ガムッ
CLATTER
IS HIS HOUSE AS BAD OFF...
...AS OURS?
There, there, sweetheart..
NOW, IF I DON'T PUSH THESE WHEELS AS HARD AS I CAN...
...I WON'T MAKE IT AN INCH.
IF IT IS...
...THEN HOW WILL HE...?
ばっ
FWAP

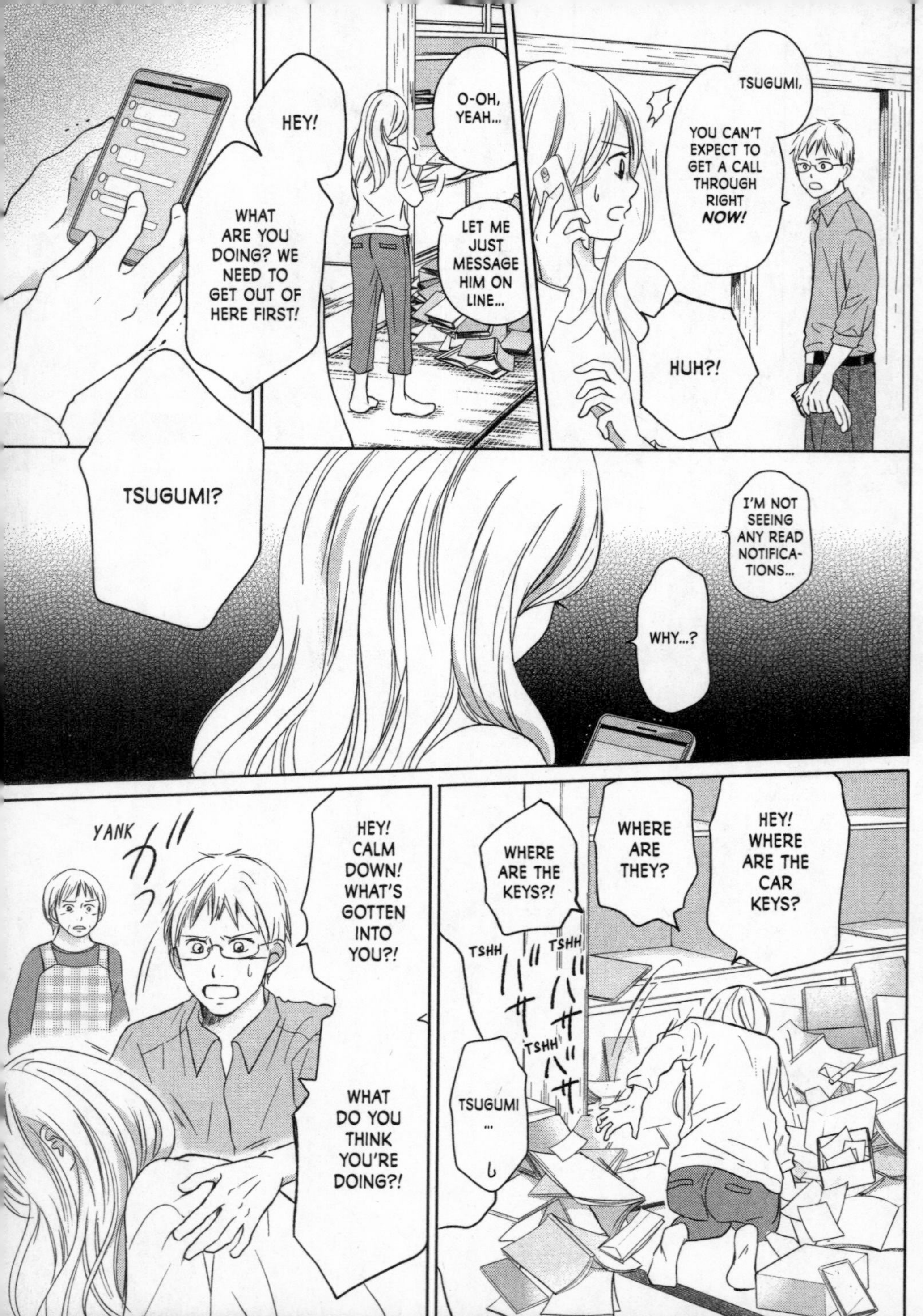

TSUGUMI, YOU CAN'T EXPECT TO GET A CALL THROUGH RIGHT *NOW!*
HUH?!
O-OH, YEAH...
LET ME JUST MESSAGE HIM ON LINE...
HEY!
WHAT ARE YOU DOING? WE NEED TO GET OUT OF HERE FIRST!
TSUGUMI?
I'M NOT SEEING ANY READ NOTIFICA-TIONS...
WHY...?
HEY! WHERE ARE THE CAR KEYS?
WHERE ARE THEY?
WHERE ARE THE KEYS?!
TSHH
TSHH
TSHH
TSUGUMI ...
YANK
HEY! CALM DOWN! WHAT'S GOTTEN INTO YOU?!
WHAT DO YOU THINK YOU'RE DOING?!

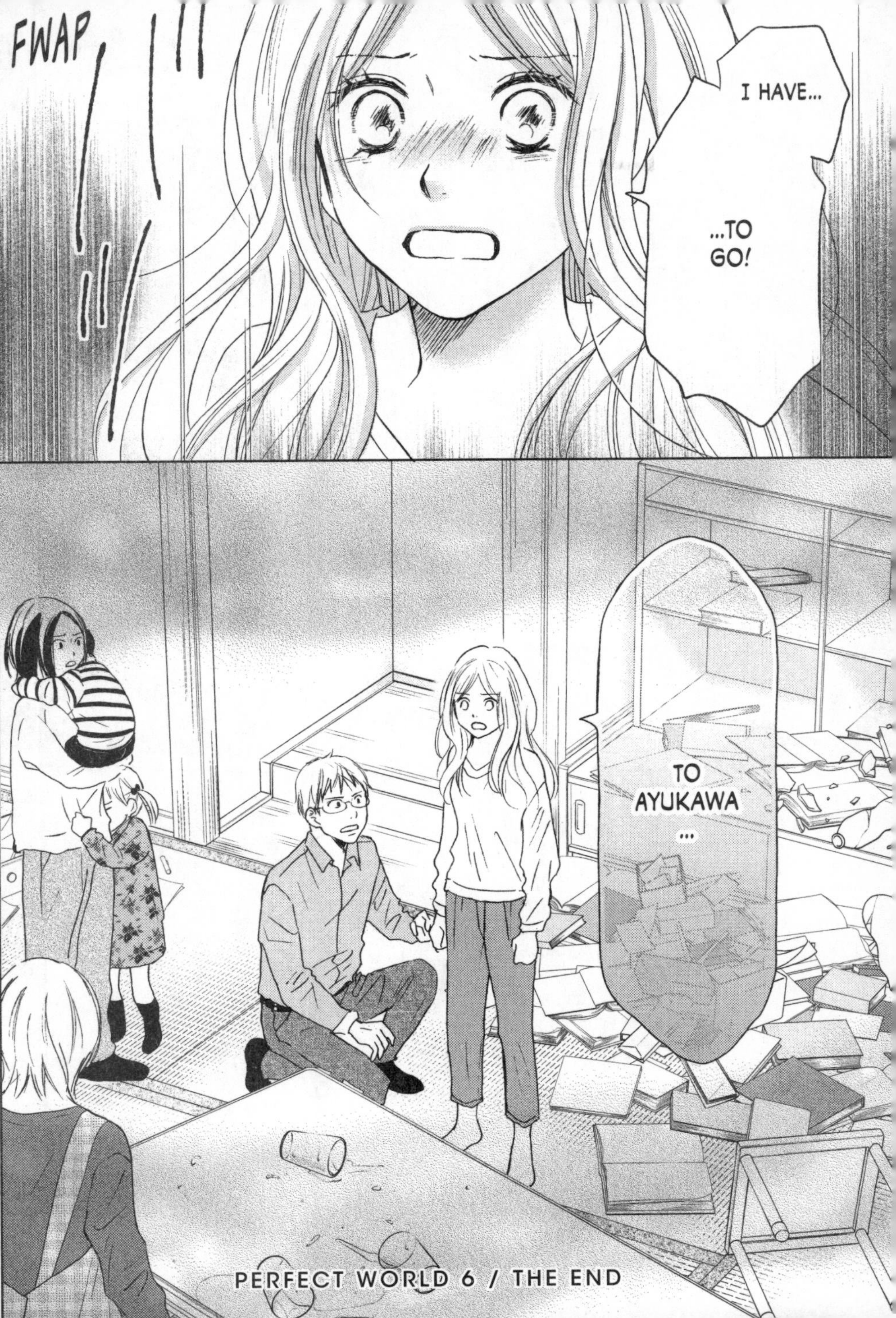
I HAVE...
...TO GO!
FWAP
TO AYUKAWA ...
PERFECT WORLD 6 / THE END

— From the bottom of my heart, thank you to all of those who helped me. —

* Kazuo Abe-sama from Abe Kensetsu Inc.
* Ouchi-sama * Yamada-sama * Kamata-sama * Yaguchi-sama

* Those at OX Kanto Vivit
* Those at AJU Independent Housing Social Services
* Those at Fureai Social Services in Nagoya

* My editor, Ito-sama   * Everyone from editorial at *Kiss*
* The designer, Kusume-sama and Agata-sama
* My assistants, T-sama, K-sama, and TN-sama

* Those who I met on Twitter who are in the medical/nursing field
* Everyone involved in getting this sold
* My family, friends, and also my readers

Now, then, I've got three pages for the afterword this time around, so I've been wondering what to write here (I'm not the best at these things, to be honest)...

We're over half-way done with the serialized release now, so I figure now's as good a time as any to talk a little bit about the work and about myself.

First things first, when I was sketching things out for the one-shot, well before *Perfect World* got picked up for serialization, Itsuki and Tsugumi were both completely different characters. First, you had our female lead, who was shocked by her partner's disability at first... but she came to terms with it right after that. That's the sort of character she was.

Tsumugi during the initial planning phase.

Her hair was black. Good thing I changed my mind on that!
← All that inking's a lot of work!

Next up, there are people in the world whose devotion to their loved ones never falters, no matter what becomes of them. Keigo, who we first met in volume five, is that sort of person... and he's actually based on a man I've met in real life.

But that first main character I had in mind may have just been a bit too shallow. They rejected the first draft outright, and I couldn't really get behind her as a protagonist, either. That might be because I know all too well what it's like not to be able to comprehend the scope of a chronic illness.

It's nothing like spinal cord injury, or Itsuki and Tsumugi's story, but I've been around chronic illness and involved in caregiving for quite a while now.

During serialization of *Perfect World*, a little over a year ago now, my mother passed away.

She developed a degenerative brain disease at a very young age. In other words, chronic illness has been a part of my life for a long time. My siblings and I were quite young when she first fell ill, so it wasn't easy for us to accept the reality of her situation. We lost friends over her chronic illness, too. We were never sure what the future might hold, and as dear and beloved as our mother was to us, there were times we didn't have a very good relationship with her. I did plenty of things I now regret, and there were times I let her down.

But on the bright side, we were blessed to meet many kind people along the way. For as many relationships as we lost, we had a lot of people around us to help. With their support, my mother managed to hang in there for a long time before we finally said goodbye.

Tsugumi, who ended up becoming the protagonist of the *Perfect World* you know today, has had her fair share of doubts, hasn't always managed to stick to her guns, and has regrets she'll carry with her for a long time. I can't say she's always handled things well, but she's still doing her best to keep her eyes forward and work toward the future.

She might make mistakes, but I hope you'll be by her side to support her from here on out.

...Which makes this sound like the last volume, but we're not quite there yet...

Thank you so much!
I look forward to seeing you again in volume seven!

Rie Aruga

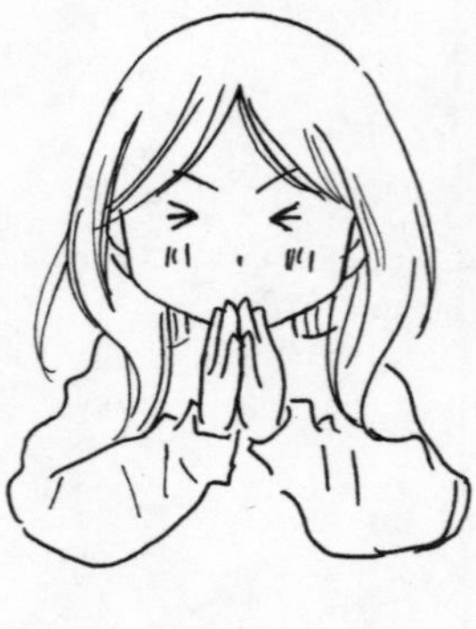

Knight of the Ice ©Yayoi Ogawa/Kodansha Ltd.

Yayoi Ogawa

SKATING THRILLS AND ICY CHILLS WITH THIS NEW TINGLY ROMANCE SERIES!

A rom-com on ice, perfect for fans of *Princess Jellyfish* and *Wotakoi*. Kokoro is the talk of the figure-skating world, winning trophies and hearts. But little do they know... he's actually a huge nerd! From the beloved creator of *You're My Pet* (*Tramps Like Us*).

Chitose is a serious young woman, working for the health magazine *SASSO*. Or at least, she would be, if she wasn't constantly getting distracted by her childhood friend, international figure skating star Kokoro Kijinami! In the public eye and on the ice, Kokoro is a gallant, flawless knight, but behind his glittery costumes and breathtaking spins lies a secret: He's actually a hopelessly romantic otaku, who can only land his quad jumps when Chitose is on hand to recite a spell from his favorite magical girl anime!

A SMART, NEW ROMANTIC COMEDY FOR FANS OF *SHORTCAKE CAKE* AND *TERRACE HOUSE*!

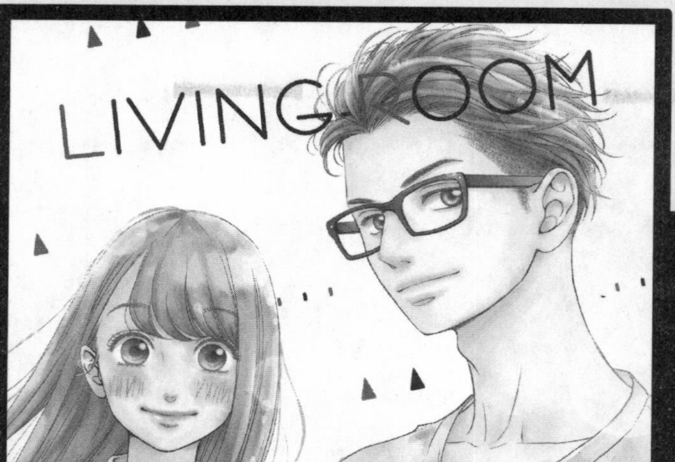
LIVING-ROOM
1
Keiko Iwashita
MATSUNAGA-SAN

A romance manga starring high school girl Meeko, who learns to live on her own in a boarding house whose living room is home to the odd (but handsome) Matsunaga-san. She begins to adjust to her new life away from her parents, but Meeko soon learns that no matter how far away from home she is, she's still a young girl at heart — especially when she finds herself falling for Matsunaga-san.

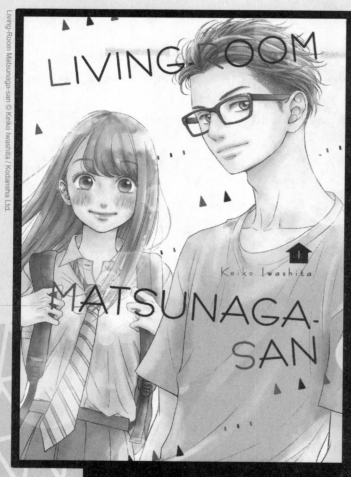

KC KODANSHA COMICS

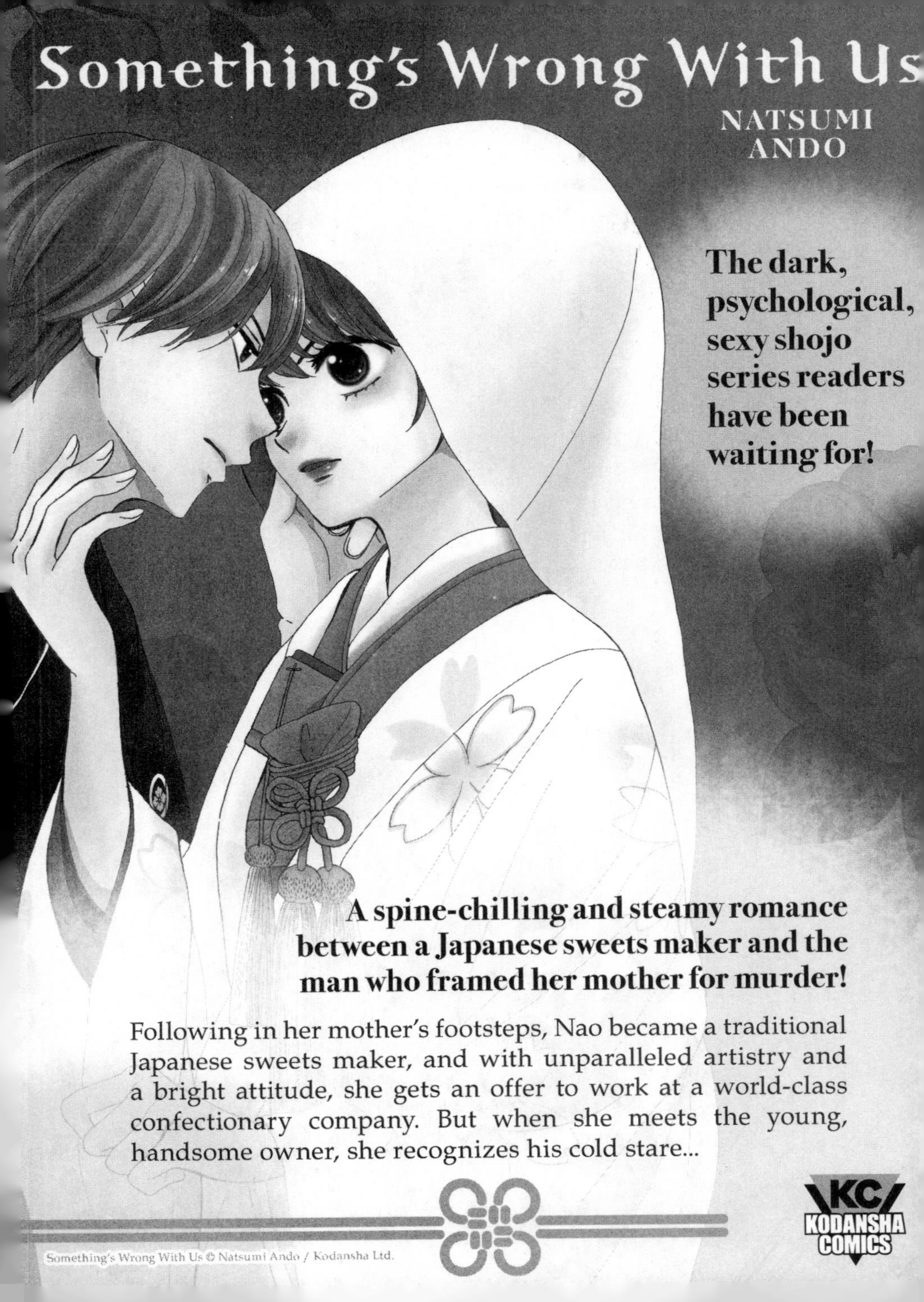
Something's Wrong With Us
NATSUMI ANDO
The dark, psychological, sexy shojo series readers have been waiting for!
A spine-chilling and steamy romance between a Japanese sweets maker and the man who framed her mother for murder!
Following in her mother's footsteps, Nao became a traditional Japanese sweets maker, and with unparalleled artistry and a bright attitude, she gets an offer to work at a world-class confectionary company. But when she meets the young, handsome owner, she recognizes his cold stare...
KC KODANSHA COMICS
Something's Wrong With Us © Natsumi Ando / Kodansha Ltd.